CONCEIVING THE GODDESS

An old woman drawing a picture of Durga-Mahishasuramardini on a village wall, Gujrat State, India. Photo courtesy Jyoti Bhatt, Vadodara, India.

CONCEIVING THE GODDESS

TRANSFORMATION AND APPROPRIATION IN INDIC RELIGIONS

Edited by
Jayant Bhalchandra Bapat and Ian Mabbett

MONASH University
Publishing

Monash University Publishing
Matheson Library and Information Services Building, 40 Exhibition Walk
Monash University
Clayton, Victoria 3800, Australia
www.publishing.monash.edu

www.publishing.monash.edu/books/cg-9781925377309.html

Design: Les Thomas.

Cover image: The Goddess Sonjai at Wai, Maharashtra State, India. Photograph: Jayant Bhalchandra Bapat.

The Monash Asia Series

Conceiving the Goddess: Transformation and Appropriation in Indic Religions is published as part of the Monash Asia Series.

The Monash Asia Series comprises works that make a significant contribution to our understanding of one or more Asian nations or regions. The individual works that make up this multi-disciplinary series are selected on the basis of their contemporary relevance.

The Monash Asia Series of the Monash Asia Institute replaces Monash University's MAI Press imprint, which, from the early 1970s, has demonstrated this University's strong interest and expertise in Asian studies.

National Library of Australia Cataloguing-in-Publication entry:

Title:	Conceiving the Goddess : transformation and appropriation in Indic religions / Jayant Bhalchandra Bapat; Ian Mabbett.
ISBN:	9781925377309 (paperback)
Subjects:	Goddesses, Indic--South Asia. Women and religion--South Asia. South Asia--Religion.
Other Creators/Contributors:	Bapat, Jayant Bhalchandra, 1938- editor. Mabbett, I. W. (Ian William), 1939- editor.
Dewey Number:	294.5211

Printed in Australia by Griffin Press an Accredited ISO AS/NZS 14001:2004 Environmental Management System printer.

MIX
Paper from responsible sources
FSC www.fsc.org FSC® C009448

The paper this book is printed on is certified against the Forest Stewardship Council ® Standards. Griffin Press holds FSC chain of custody certification SGS-COC-005088. FSC promotes environmentally responsible, socially beneficial and economically viable management of the world's forests.

Contents

Dedication vii
Acknowledgments viii
Preface ix
A Note on Style and Diacritics xi

Chapter 1 1
On Appropriation and Transformation
Ian Mabbett and Jayant Bhalchandra Bapat

Chapter 2 25
Crowns, Horns and Goddesses: Appropriation of Symbols in Gandhāra and Beyond
Angelo Andrea Di Castro

Chapter 3 56
The Appropriation of the Goddess into the Purāṇic Narrative: Integration/Appropriation in the *Vāmanapurāṇa*
Greg Bailey

Chapter 4 78
The Yakṣiṇī Devī of Mangaon: Appropriation of a Jain Goddess by Brāhminic Hinduism
Jayant Bhalchandra Bapat

Chapter 5 102
Appropriating the Inappropriate
John R. Dupuche

Chapter 6 126
Ravidās and the Gaṅgā: Appropriation or Contestation?
Peter Friedlander

Chapter 7 142
The Goddess Chinnamastā's Severed Head as a Re-Appropriation of the Cosmic Sacrifice
Ian Mabbett

Chapter 8 160
The Appropriation of Durgā
Pratish Bandopadhayay

Chapter 9 179
From a *Śaktipīṭha* to *Kuladaivata*: The Appropriation of Goddess Jogāī of Ambe
Madhavi Narsalay

Chapter 10 211
The Female Protector of Yolmo's Hidden Land
David Templeman

Chapter 11 225
Ekveera Devi and the Son Kolis of Mumbai: Have the Kolis Appropriated the Karle Buddhist *Chaitya*?
Marika Vicziany, Jayant Bhalchandra Bapat and Sanjay Ranade

Chapter 12 257
Modern Appropriations of Devī
Martin Hříbek

About the Editors and Contributors 278
Index 281

Dedication

Dr. R. C. Dhere (21/7/1930 – 1/7/2016)
Photo courtesy of the Dhere family.

The scholars who have contributed to this volume are committed to bridging the knowledge gap that exists because outstanding scholarship in Indian languages is not readily accessible to English-speaking audiences. For this reason we dedicate this volume to the late Dr Ramchandra Chintaman Dhere, a prolific writer on many aspects of folk culture and religion in India. Dhere's extraordinary research publications, comprising over a hundred books and several hundred articles, are written mainly in Marathi. Only a small proportion of his work has been translated. His unique insights into the complexities of Indian history and culture deserve widespread international recognition. Known fondly as Aṇṇā, Dhere was actively pursuing his research and writing until his sad demise on July 1st 2016. He knew that we had decided to dedicate this work to him in recognition of his contributions to research. Those of us who knew him personally have felt a great loss, but all of us will miss his imaginative insights into Indian life. Our appreciation of the extraordinary efforts he made to record aspects of Maharashtrian history and culture (not easily accessible even to scholars) is the basis for this dedication.

Jayant Bhalchandra Bapat and Ian Mabbett

Acknowledgments

This book is a sequel to the earlier publication, *The Iconic Female: Goddesses of India, Nepal and Tibet*, edited by us and published by the Monash Asia Institute in 2008. The present volume brings together outstanding research by twelve authors, many of whom contributed to the previous volume. However, in addition, it contains contributions from researchers in two other continents.

The co-ordination of twelve major contributions and integrating them into a thematically unified and cohesive whole with a central theme has been a long, complex, time-consuming and, at times, frustrating task. As editors, we are very pleased to see the successful conclusion of our labours. We are grateful to the contributors for the enthusiasm, responsiveness and patience with which they have adapted the perspectives of their individual pieces of research to fit into a collection that to us is a lot more than the sum of its parts.

A work of such complexity requires major effort and contributions from a number of people. We thank them all. However, we must particularly mention the continuing inspiration and the constant practical involvement of Professor Marika Vicziany, whose energy and encouragement have contributed as much as anything else to make the publication of this book possible. We thank members of the Monash Publications Committee for their useful feedback and encouragement. We are grateful to the team at Monash University Publishing, especially Nathan Hollier, Joanne Mullins, Les Thomas, Laura McNicol Smith and others, for their meticulous work and infectious enthusiasm in producing this volume with the utmost care and attention to detail. Our friend and mentor, Dr Rashmi Desai, has also been a constant source of help in spite of his health problems. We also thank him for alerting us to the photograph on the frontispiece of this book. We are deeply indebted to Mr Jyoti Bhatt who took the photograph and has kindly allowed us to use it. We thank Alfonso Martínez Arranz for painstakingly preparing the index for this book. Finally, we thank John Harris, who has provided the superb line drawings for many of the chapters in this book.

Having long been retired, we are both at an age where family, children, grandchildren and social interaction need to take a higher priority than academic pursuits such as this book. We are grateful to our respective spouses, Sunanda and Jaccy, for allowing us to pursue our interests, often at the expense of our families.

Jayant Bhalchandra Bapat and Ian Mabbett

Preface

Australian scholarship about India has grown enormously during the last ten years, but mainly in the field of business and economics. Interest in Indology, broadly defined as the study of India's culture, history, literature, philosophy, languages and social life, has continued to decline with few young scholars replacing the rapidly ageing population of the 'old hands'. This is a problem that worries us and is being addressed by the South Asian Studies Association of Australia.

One way of responding to the problem of how to increase interest in Indology is for the 'old hands' to demonstrate how relevant and exciting their research is, in the hope that this will stimulate younger scholars to join us. For this reason, the present collection of essays about Indian goddesses is more than just an intellectual exercise.

As an intellectual exercise this volume fulfils a promise that we made in 2008, when we published *The Iconic Female: Goddesses of India, Nepal and Tibet.* At that time we foreshadowed a second volume about South Asian goddesses because we had identified a small group of Australian scholars who were deeply engaged in ongoing research in this field. This is the second volume that we imagined.

The twelve scholars who contributed to the present collection agreed prior to writing their chapters that we should focus on a single theme. We wanted to go beyond reflecting on the variety and complexity of South Asian religious worship captured in the previous volume published in 2008. We compared our textual research and fieldwork to see whether there was any large, overarching theme that reflected our shared interests. Many cross-cutting issues emerged, but of these we agreed that the problem of how particular communities 'appropriated' religious beliefs and customs was the most challenging. 'Appropriation' was therefore selected as our common theme. As the first chapter explains, this is a strong word going well beyond notions of cultural borrowing, imitation, emulation or syncretic processes. It is a word that imagines active protagonists reaching out and determining a conscious process of cultural elaboration.

This is the second volume to be published by Monash University on the subject of the South Asian goddesses in the hope of Australian scholarship contributing to a deeper understanding of the history and present religious culture of South Asia. These cultural underpinnings are increasingly recognised as playing a critical role in coming to terms with the momentous social and political transformation of that region.

Marika Vicziany

Director, National Centre for South Asian Studies
Faculty of Arts,
Monash University,
Melbourne, Australia

A Note on Style and Diacritics

There is no conventionally agreed single standard for the spelling and use of diacritics in words belonging to, or derived from, Indian languages. Any attempt to impose a uniform standard here would be difficult because the contributions below concern a variety of different regions and historical periods, and belong to a variety of scholarly disciplines.

We accordingly distinguish between two broad categories of scholarship. The first is indological. Where the author's sources are texts in Sanskrit or related ancient languages, it is appropriate to apply the standard diacritics convention for Sanskrit and the spellings that go with them (e.g. Gaṅgā, not Ganges; Kṛṣṇa, not Krishna). This usage affects quotations from texts, Sanskrit words used as technical terms (e.g. *varṇa, darśana*), titles of texts (e.g. *Vāmana Purāṇa*), classes of texts (e.g. 'the *upaniṣads*'), and even proper names generally, where these are names figuring in texts studied.

Many of the same words might, however, be familiar in other spellings and without diacritics in non-indological contexts. Further, many Sanskrit words are more familiar in light disguise as they appear in modern Indian languages or anglicised usage in modern times (e.g. Ekveera, *pujari*, Shankaracharya). We therefore identify a second category which contains studies of topics belonging to modern times, using modern Indian languages, or based upon fieldwork or contemporary sources; in such contexts we prefer to use the more familiar forms, including names such as may be found written in gazetteers or English-language telephone directories, rather than attempt Sanskritic purification. We hope that, knowing this, the reader may not be unduly confused.

Here are some examples in two columns showing Sanskritic and modern or anglicised forms.

Sanskritic	**Modern/Anglicised**
Śiva	Shiva
Kṛṣṇa	Krishna
Durgā	Durga
Gaṅgā	Ganga/Ganges
Viṣṇu	Vishnu
Śankarācārya	Shankaracharya

Ācārya	Acharya
Paṇḍita	Pundit
Liṅga	Linga(m)
Īśvara	Ishwara
Pūjā	Puja
Yakṣiṇī	Yakshini
Devī	Devi
Ekvīrā	Ekveera
Ambādevī	Ambadevi
Candraprabhā	Chandraprabha

In some cases (such as in Chapter 4), the authors have chosen to quote the currently used spelling for the name, with a footnote which explains how the word is pronounced either in the local Indian language or in Sanskrit. Diacritics have been used for this purpose (for example, for the word *Pashan*, the correct pronunciation is *Pāṣāṇa*). A macron (as in 'ā') denotes a long vowel; a subscript dot (as in 'ṇ') denotes a lingual or retroflex consonant (with the tongue curled upward); 'n' with a superscript dot ('ṅ') denotes the guttural 'ng' sound.

Chapter 1

On Appropriation and Transformation

Ian Mabbett and Jayant Bhalchandra Bapat

When we edited our first volume on the Goddesses of the Indian subcontinent (Bapat and Mabbett 2008), we were well aware that the volume was a sample of larger works in progress about the many forms taken by goddess cults of South Asia. During the last six years, further significant research findings have been made and so it is with great pleasure that we bring out this second volume as an example of the new work undertaken by Australian scholars. Except for two newcomers, contributors from the Czech Republic and from India, all of the authors contributed to the previous volume.

In preparing the present volume we had many discussions about the kinds of themes that might draw together the ideas and interests of the contributors and give unity to this book. Finally, we all decided that the idea of 'appropriation', a conceptual tool widely used in humanities research, provided the right framework.

Appropriation is a complex idea and can be understood in many contrasting ways. Frequently it is deployed in the service of theories that open up broad issues and call into question fundamental principles of interpretation. In the scope of the present short essay, we cannot hope to solve any major problems. What is in view here is essentially a survey of different types of appropriation in the history of Indian religion, with special, but by no means exclusive, reference to the cults of goddesses. This should provide a useful context for the studies that follow.

There is, however, a lesson suggested by this survey. We wish to suggest that the variety of types of appropriation to be reviewed has implications for theories about the relationships between religion and society in India. We argue that, in conceptualising the religious cultures we study, we should indeed give proper heed to the importance of the vertical dimension (of dominance and subordination) in social organisation, but not be mesmerised by it. We should resist any temptation to interpret all cases of conflict as issues of oppression or subversion within the vertical scale of claimed authority. We need to be ready to explore the rich variety of other cultural mechanisms of appropriation that may be at play, requiring conceptualisation of horizontal or oblique dimensions.

It will be useful to begin by making quite explicit the underlying plan of the discussion that follows. We wish to start with a particular concept – the vertical dimension of hierarchy and authority – as a central idea common to many or most discussions about appropriation in the history of Indian religions, and then to subject this concept to a series of qualifications by looking at a number of other ways in which appropriation of religious motifs may work. In general, the successive variations in the series depart increasingly from the original vertical dimension; this means not that there is anything wrong with the concept of a vertical dimension but only that it needs to be appropriately supplemented. Both the vertical dimension and the departures from it have hermeneutical value in appropriate contexts; several different perspectives are needed to comprehend the complex patterns of cultural flow that define the relations between social groups.[1]

The first task is to set out the initial concept of the Indian social scale as an arrangement of elements in a vertical dimension, and then to list in summary form some variations. The assumption behind the initial concept is that the agents of religious history are social groups that rank themselves upon a scale of social status. Elements of religious practice and belief have different degrees of value within the culture shared by different social groups, and appropriation takes place when one group adopts an element of practice or belief that was not previously its own in order to protect or enhance its status upon the ladder of degree.

Let us explain this by looking at some possible variations. Although we list seven of them below, there is no doubt in our minds that the number could be larger.

1 The black and white photograph on the frontispiece of this volume is a telling example of what we mean. The mother goddess, who was probably worshipped by early Indians in her form as an autochthonous stone, became Durgā in Brāhminic religion and assumed an elaborate iconographic form. The village woman in this photograph is now using her, probably, for some village ritual, a classic case of appropriation and re-appropriation.

1. **Rigid *varṇa* theory.** At a theoretical extreme is the claim that Indian society, at least (with approximations in other parts of South Asia to the extent that they have historically had something like the Indian caste system), has traditionally been governed by the *varṇa* hierarchy, and that this hierarchy fixes a scale of purity upon which religious usage is mapped, with the Brāhmin groups as the purest and the 'untouchables' as the most polluted or polluting. Adoption by a caste in one *varṇa* of any religious practice followed by a caste in another is likely to be seen as a violation of the scheme. This kind of claim represents a rigid and literal version of the sort of doctrine advanced in Brāhminical texts such as, most notably, the *Manusmṛti*, but it is really a straw man as far as modern scholarship is concerned. Louis Dumont's interpretation of caste and religion in India certainly emphasised hierarchy as a fundamental principle (Dumont 1980), but he fully recognised the considerable fluidity of relationships between social groups at all points between the top and bottom of the scale. Nevertheless, the *Manusmṛti's* doctrine of hierarchical ritual status eloquently expresses a coherent and powerful cosmological theory likely to have been persuasive to many, much the same as the one vividly embodied in the 'ladder of degree' speech in *Troilus and Cressida*. 'Take but degree away, untune that string / And hark what discord follows!'

2. **Internal top-down appropriation.** Admitting then that there is much fluidity in practice, we can certainly identify many cases in which groups with higher status 'appropriated', or in some way took control of, the usages of lower groups. Rulers could promote throughout their kingdoms the institutions of the court priesthood they patronised, much as this same principle, tagged '*Cuius regio eius religio'*, was asserted at the Diet of Augsburg in 1555 to describe the religious map of the Reformation in Europe. The process of 'Sanskritisation' (discussed below), by which Brāhminical religion came to pervade the culture of many or most social groups, is often seen as an initiative by the Brāhmins themselves – a refashioning of the religious landscape in the interests of the Brāhminical worldview, giving local cults a subordinate status within a unifying scheme and re-interpreting popular cults as local embodiments of the worship of Brāhminical

pan-Indian deities prominent in the Sanskrit scriptural corpus. The Purāṇa texts are often thought to exhibit the results of this process, with many goddesses not mentioned in earlier literary sources (and, therefore, likely to have originated from popular oral tradition) being worked into the Brāhminical pantheon. The appropriation in question is not of the popular practices as such but of their believed spiritual essence. Brāhmins do not become worshippers of local goddesses; local goddesses become Durgā or Gaṅgā. However, as Greg Bailey warns in Chapter 3 of this volume, we are not entitled to treat this as more than a surmise in the absence of solid evidence of the transition.

3. **External top-down appropriation.** All the same things can be said of the cultural domination exercised, not by the Brāhmins, but by an incoming non-Brāhminical imperial power not initially bred in a culture professing Brāhminical religious practices, whether Hellenic, Muslim or European. This sort of claim has become prominent in recent scholarship on contemporary South Asia, where the imperial power is not even a foreign government as such but rather the non-Indian culture now implanted as a result of former colonisation and more recent globalisation; international secular culture is said to have appropriated the very language of debate about culture in general, so that Indians are subtly led to look at their own traditions through the eyes of aliens. This sort of appropriation is a special case receiving more attention below.

4. **Bottom-up appropriation or social climbing.** 'Bottom-up' interpretations belong typically to closely focused social or historical studies of particular localities and communities, showing how members of relatively low-status groups seek to acquire the religious practices and beliefs characteristic of relatively high-status groups – the services of Brāhmin priests, Sanskrit liturgy, identification with major deities such as Durgā, forms of dress, eating and ritual deemed spiritually purer, and so forth. This is 'Sanskritisation', the perhaps rather unhappily named process whereby, through the course of many centuries, local cults of gods or goddesses have come to acquire the trappings of higher status.

5. **Subversive contestation.** In the course of time, assertions of higher status by previously less-privileged groups may come to be generally accepted, though the ritual status of many castes has been, or is, subject to conflicting valuations. We may usefully distinguish as a separate category the sorts of cases that arise when the aspiring religious group does not so much seek to elevate itself upon a commonly recognised scale, but rather denies the right of Brāhmins (or other authorities) to decide upon the validity of its practices. Such a case, concerning the followers of Ravidās, is discussed by Peter Friedlander in Chapter 6 of this book. He emphasizes that the assertion by an underprivileged group of its right to frequent particular sacred sites and claim a close relationship with particular deities is not appropriation if the sites and the cult previously belonged to the population at large; it is the Brāhmins who are 'appropriating' when they seek to deny to others access to the sites and cult. This sort of contestation may implicitly call into question the foundations of the authority of Brāhmins in the vertical scale of social status. In more extreme cases, many of the poorest groups in society have seen the advantage in denying the validity of the entire religious worldview of the Brāhmins and stepped sideways to something else which promised a better life, such as Islam in the period of extension of Muslim power (particularly in Bengal) or Buddhism in the period following Independence.

6. **Simultaneous upward and downward appropriation.** It should now be apparent that several of these claimed processes can in fact happen at the same time. In particular, in the course of the sort of evolution likely to qualify as 'Sanskritisation', members of a local religious cult may recognise benefits for their own interest in identifying their traditional deity with a pan-Indian deity celebrated in Brāhminical scriptures (bottom-up appropriation), while at the same time Brāhmins choose to recognise the same identification in pursuit of their vision of a world standardised and regulated within a Brāhminical scheme (top-down). It may be difficult to decide whether it is chiefly bottom-up or top-down integration that is going on. It may even not matter very much. It may be something else involving a variety of motivations on the part of the groups involved. It is scarcely relevant to speak either

of oppression or of subversion. The case of Vindhyavāsinī is an interesting example, noticed further below.

7. **Metropolitan–provincial appropriation.** Sometimes groups may appropriate texts, rituals or iconography from a distant metropolitan centre without having any disposition whatsoever to doubt that what is appropriated is and always has been their own religious possession, differing only in acquiring an improved form of expression. Provincials visiting the metropolis may defer to its cultural sophistication without feeling that they are inferior to its inhabitants; they may display their own status by donating funds to metropolitan monuments and endowing pilgrimage centres for pilgrims from their own localities. The work of Paul Mus (2011) on cultural relations between India and the Hindu-Buddhist kingdoms of South-East Asia richly illustrates this sort of process.

These categories represent a variety of culturally derived motivations, not all of which can be simply described by reference to the vertical scale of social status in general, or the 'top-down' form of appropriation within it in particular, and our ideas of power and domination as hermeneutical principles need to be supplemented by other relationships, such as that between metropolis and province, which deserve more consideration than they sometimes receive.

In what follows, the procedure will not be to attend turn by turn to all these listed categories; we prefer to concentrate on two prominent topics – the argument that international commercial culture has appropriated the terms of discussion about Indian religious culture, stifling its authenticity (external top-down appropriation), and the concept of Sanskritisation (which can be many things, including both top-down and bottom-up appropriation and other things). Reference to the list above, we hope, will make the argument clearer at certain points.

The concept of 'appropriation'

For the particular purposes of this discussion, appropriation is a cultural phenomenon that has been frequent in the history of Indian religious communities. It takes place when a group adopts an element of practice or belief that was not previously its own in order to protect or enhance its status, or to enrich the experience of its members. In particular cases, many different motivations may be at work, and the consequences of appropriation may be understood from many different perspectives. The contributors to this volume, who work within various disciplines, have applied the concept of appropriation in different ways, but the working definition suggested above is a common denominator, and it supplies a convenient conceptual tool for the development of the view developed in the following paragraphs here. However, we should not proceed without acknowledging the connotations that the term has acquired, and the mosaic of ideas clustering around its use in scholarship.

'Appropriation' has many nuances. Ordinarily, its connotations are pejorative, but this need not always be so. For instance, artists such as Andy Warhol have called some of their work 'appropriation art' by borrowing an object or a well-known work of art and modifying it to bring about a new resonance. By doing so, they hope that the viewer will recontextualise the original meaning or purpose of the image.

Again, appropriation may be thought of as something very close to plagiarism. When Brāhmins appropriated local cults of goddesses, they represented them as having an essential nature identical with the great goddess(es) of the higher tradition, thereby claiming ownership.

Traditionally, appropriation can simply mean distributing, sharing, assigning, carving-up, dividing or designating. It can also mean taking, annexing, confiscating or usurping. At one extreme end of the scale, it can mean robbing, stealing, thieving and forcibly acquiring for one's own purpose. Appropriation can be of culture, ideas, objects, symbols, artefacts, images, styles and so on. Many of these different meanings appear in the chapters in this volume. Cultural appropriation of any sort might be seen in various ways – as an act of cultural domination, as a sort of false consciousness inculcated by domination by others, as an insistence upon an assumed right to a monopoly of something, as an act of homage to an exotic sort of culture, as an assertion of entitlement to adopt any sort of custom one likes, or as a piece of harmless whimsy. An observer's characterisation of an act of appropriation may say as much about the observer's sensitivities as about the behaviour observed. An example from within this volume can make the point: some people complained to a Muzaffarpur court about the appropriation of Durgā implicit in the publication of photographs showing Sonia Gandhi as the goddess (Bandopadhayay, Chapter 8); this shows much about the sensitivities of the plaintiffs.

Many uses of 'appropriation' imply some theoretical assumption about the vertical scale of society already discussed, with a group's relative position on this scale being variously asserted, denied or brought into question. At its simplest, the mechanism in question is illustrated by any assertion of privilege by an elite, such as the denial by the 'twice-born' classes to the *shudras* of the right to hear or study the Vedas, or by the monopoly of the priestly function by the Brāhmins.

Religion and political power

According to many historians of pre-colonial India, appropriation of religion, either orthodox Brāhminism or any of the various heterodoxies, was a normal device employed by rulers to strengthen their own grip on power. For example, D.N. Jha (1998, 108) has written that the cult of Viṣṇu acted as an effective instrument for reconciling the masses to their lot and maintaining the social division based on *varṇa*. Jha here credits kings with the initiative in appropriating religion as a political resource; Romila Thapar, in the 1966 version of her history of pre-Muslim India, gives more weight to the Brāhmins in exploiting religion for power:

> The priests were not slow to realize the significance of such a division of society and the supreme authority which could be invested in the highest caste. They not only managed to usurp the first position by claiming that they alone could bestow divinity on the king (which was by now essential to kingship) but they also gave religious sanction to caste divisions (Thapar 1966, 39).

Whether the leading role is accorded to the king or to the priests, such views agree in seeing religion as a tool appropriated by the social or political elite in pursuit of power, giving legitimacy to their authority.

'Power' here may not necessarily be political, legal or economic; rather it may be the ability of a dominant cultural group to shape the goals, assumptions and understandings of a whole population, so that it is only on terms controlled by this elite that groups within the population can perceive the relations among them. Those who think in this way about knowledge, power and culture detect subtle currents of social control at work in the influences that induce people to make seemingly innocent cultural choices, adopting this or that ritual, this or that form of dress or ornament.

We will come in a moment to some more examples displaying the interpretations just described, but first a note of caution is in order. We can agree that this way of thinking about a political role for religious institutions – the imposition of religion upon a population by an elite – probably occurred to rulers and senior priests often enough, but it is worth pointing out that, as a way of actually accounting for popular acceptance of the legitimacy of political or sacerdotal elites, the argument begs the question. As Ian Copland *et al.* (2012, 21) remarked:

> To whatever extent a people can be said to have accepted a particular power structure through having a belief system imposed upon them, they must have been ready to accept the authority of those who imposed it upon them before the imposition took place. The belief systems as such cannot be used to explain the preconditions of their own arising.

We should be cautious in our attitude to any theory that religious institutions functioned essentially as a device, manipulated from above, to give the populace an adequate reason to defer meekly to the authority of their supposed betters. A searching analysis of the weaknesses of such theories has been offered by Sheldon Pollock (1996, 236ff.).

This qualification represents what is intended as the chief recurring *motif* in this essay: explanations of religious history that emphasise the ladder of degree, and the exercise of power and domination by those at the top of it, should not be pressed too far. We accept that top-down appropriation (the second of the categories proposed above) has very often taken place; it cannot, however, be used as an explanation of everything.

Top-down appropriation and the impact of globalisation

To be sure, there can be no doubt that many Indian rulers had an instrumental attitude towards the religious institutions in their kingdoms. Such an attitude makes itself stridently manifest throughout the *Arthaśāstra* attributed to Kauṭilya (Mabbett 2010), an authoritative ancient Sanskrit manual of kingship. It is not surprising, then, that varieties of top-down appropriation should often figure in scholars' analyses of the exercise of power in Indian religious history. In this section we wish to give special attention to a class of scholarly interpretations that make most thoroughgoing use of the concept of top-down appropriation in broad-brush studies of cultural influence in the modern world.

The class of interpretations in question steps beyond the appropriations made by priests and rulers in traditional society, even beyond the cultural manipulations of colonial rulers, and identifies insidious forms of cultural control over Indian culture exercised in modern times by international civilisation.

Obviously pertinent as a key to the theory of global appropriation under consideration would be the work of Edward Said. To be sure, his best-known work, *Orientalism* (Said 1977), was about the Arab Middle East, not India at all, in spite of the way many of its readers have applied its lessons to all other parts of Asia; but it is clear enough that what he wrote about the Middle East was intended to apply more generally to the West's attitudes to the East (see Said 1993). In Said's view, knowledge is power, so control of the organs of cultural expression – education, the press, literature in the language of the metropolis – gives control over the way people think about the world and, therefore, leads even unconsciously to the acceptance of a worldview that systematically privileges the dominant power. This process has led to the entrenchment of Western values even after decolonisation. Many scholars, influenced by this trend of thought, have made a pessimistic assessment of the ability of Eastern civilisations to contribute an authentic and uncontaminated version of their own cultures to any East–West dialogue. According to William Halbfass (1988, 339-40), 'In the modern planetary system, Eastern and Western cultures can no longer meet one another as equal partners. They meet *in* a Westernized world, under conditions shaped by Western ways of thinking'. For others, the dominant power is no longer specifically the West but an internationalised capitalist oecumene which is permeating and subverting everything; while its victory is not complete, its rivals can only be fragmented and localised particularistic cultures. Thus, Benjamin Barber can see in modern times a powerful trend to combine the worst of both worlds: on the one hand, 'a threatened balkanization of nation-states' constantly locked in violent cultural and military conflict and, on the other, 'one McWorld tied together by communications, information, entertainment and commerce'. In this vision the planet is 'caught between Babel and Disneyland' (Barber 1992, 4).

This sort of judgment upon the prospects for the evolution of an autonomous and authentic Indian religious culture in the modern world is profoundly pessimistic. It makes an interesting contrast with the findings of many anthropologists studying local cults. Such people have frequently found that cultural changes spring from local initiatives. Village religion is to be understood, according to their research, not by looking at influences from above (whether those of Brāhmins, governments, or even international capitalism), but by exploring the devolved institutions of pilgrimage and festival, annual ritual and popular legend.

Let us anticipate for a moment and take a case that will be noticed again below – the cult of Vindhyavāsinī, which in various ways can be seen as a good example of Sankritisation, but with much of the dynamism coming from 'bottom-up' appropriation. A valuable source is Cynthia Ann Humes' (1996) study of the shrine and its role as a pilgrimage centre increasingly popular in modern times. What is important to note about it here is that the evolution of the goddess into a 'Great Goddess' identified with the universal female divinity of the *Devīmāhātmya* has been driven by popular demand, as it were; increasing numbers of pilgrims from far afield have made the shrine more cosmopolitan, and it comes naturally to identify the goddess with the sort of pan-Indian deity likely to be familiar to the many urbanised visitors.

Perhaps the differing perspectives offered by the pessimistic globalisation theorist and the anthropologist of the locality who emphasises local initiative simply reflect different points of view. But it is interesting to reflect that perhaps the materials are available for a 'globalisation' theorist to argue that Vindhyavāsinī, in her modern exalted form as the Great Goddess of the *Devīmāhātmya,* is not really an authentic product either of the ancient local tradition that gave birth to her shrine or of Brāhminical appropriation, but instead is the creation of a monotone global culture. It could be claimed, after all, that the increasing numbers of pilgrims whose homage at her shrine gives prominence to her cult come from all over the world as well as from all over India; they travel thither in trains and cars that may be designed in Germany or Japan; they may speak to local *pujaris* in English; they may come to know about the goddess from watching television programmes; and they may enhance their knowledge of her by reading scholarly books about Indian goddesses. Some of them may have been (as Benjamin Barber would point to as significant) to Disneyland. The image (which in a sense is the reality) of Vindhyavāsinī (somebody might thus argue) inhabits a constructed space designed by modern commerce, anthropology, history and geography as much as by any ancient and indigenous numinous sensibility.

This thesis, which we can imagine being propounded by a theorist of globalisation about Vindhyavāsinī, is rather extreme; ancient numinous sensibilities are not dead in India. But centuries of intimate contact with the modern world have necessarily affected the self-awareness even of acknowledged spiritual masters, *siddhas* and *sādhus*.

The 'Hinduism' that the Western student meets in India may turn out to have been Vedanticised by Indian tastes in Western writings. Ever since Vivekananda went to Chicago, if not well before, the Western vogue for certain types of Indian mysticism has been quietly influential among English-educated Indians, and globalisation has obviously favoured a disposition for Indian teachers to think and write in ways that are responsive to the knowledge and vocabulary of a Western audience. Take *tantra*, which teems with goddesses and is intimately germane to the concerns of this volume: Hugh Urban concludes his study of *tantra* on a pessimistic note, aspiring to discover in modern Tantric traditions some authentically Indian and uncorrupted contribution to the store of human culture, yet uncertain about the prospects for such a quest in a world where the grammar and vocabulary of intercultural dialogue have been (in his view) appropriated by the denaturing forces of global commerce:

> With Sahlins, I would like to highlight, even celebrate, the power of non-Western cultures to appropriate and transform the forces of global capitalism, to adapt them on their own terms, according to their own cultural logic. Yet it seems to me that the rules of the game are still largely conditioned and structured by the logic of the global capitalist market. Thus, any resistance tends to become resistance to the market, a deformation of capitalism, and yet still largely ruled by the laws of the market … And if 'resistance' means nothing more than adding an Indian 'curry' flavor of Chicken McNuggets to the McDonald's menu, it seems a fairly pathetic form of resistance (Urban 2003, 279).

Such views as these represent a current in modern scholarship that clearly favours a strong 'top-down' sort of appropriation exercising a corrosive influence upon the autonomy of Indian worldview and religious culture. They cannot be ignored; it is always salutary to recognise that what we study can all too often be affected (like Schrödinger's cat) by our (or our predecessors') observation of it, and that the phenomena of Indian religious cults cannot be expected in all respects to present to us an easily isolated 'authentic' content.

Nevertheless, for our part, the privileging of power and oppression as hermeneutic principles seems to us to marginalise other processes that are less adversarial. As Copland *et al.* (2012, 22) point out:

> History shows that bad times are not permanent and inevitable. The mechanism of naked personal power-hunger is complemented by an alternative one that often acts to maintain a degree of political stability; most people ... prefer to live within ordered and orderly systems (or, if you like, moral economies).

Sanskritisation

The concept of Sanskritisation was given currency originally by M.N. Srinivas, whose anthropological research made manifest to him the pervasiveness throughout Indian social history of a process by which caste groups of lower ritual status would take on the attributes of higher status (Srinivas 1952). This sort of adoption of religiously significant customs, rituals and other practices obviously exhibits mechanisms of appropriation.

The term 'Sanskritisation' was not immediately accepted, though the ideas behind it occasioned ongoing debate (see Staal 1963). To many, the term did not seem to identify what is really at stake in the process identified. After all, the taking on of attributes signifying greater ritual purity did not always involve an increase in the Sanskrit content of liturgy. Again, it might seem to some that the term implies a not very useful division of Indian society into Sanskritic and non-Sanskritic portions. Most people disliked it, but everybody recognised the reality of the process it designates in some sense, and it has stuck.

The action of a lower caste in adopting the usages of Brāhmins or other ritually superior groups is a fairly clear example of bottom-up appropriation (category 4 in the list), but as we have already seen here it was not as simple as this; much the same process could be seen as resulting from the initiative of Brāhmins when they co-opted local cults into their orthodox cosmography, identifying village or regional deities as manifestations of more widely worshipped divinities figuring already in Sanskrit texts. This can be seen as top-down appropriation.

Here we shall look very briefly at some examples of appropriation that certainly demand to be identified as 'Sanskritisation'; one or two of them may be unambiguously 'top-down' or 'bottom-up', but what is interesting to notice is the frequent ambiguity. Many such processes may appear, from a broad perspective or long after the event, to be classic cases of Brāhminical aggrandisement, colonising popular cults in the interests of a Sanskritising worldview; yet, seen close to by their own contemporaries, they may appear to be better described as adaptations by local devotees re-interpreting their own cultural possessions as their horizons widen.

A fairly clear case of ('top-down') Brāhminical initiative seems to be offered by the cult described by Bapat in Chapter 4 of this volume. The appropriation process appears to be two-fold: first a *yakṣa* cult which may have been local was absorbed by the spread of Jainism in the area and came to be worshipped in a Jain temple; later, as Jainism receded, the temple was substantially reconfigured according to Brāhminic standards, with the image of a Jain Tīrthaṃkar shifted to a corner and the existing Jain goddess renamed as Durgā.

A little less clear-cut is the case of the local river goddess Pampā. Her embodiment was the river Tungabhadra in Karnataka. By the end of the twelfth century, she was identified as the consort of the god Virupaksha, and their temple became an important cult centre as the state of Vijayanagara grew. In the fourteenth century, it was a major regional power in which the cult of Pampa was strong. Virupaksha came to be recognised as a form of Śiva, and Pampa was recognised as the great goddess Devī. This has been called a 'classic instance of Sanskritization' by Richard Eaton (2005, 82). Such promotions of local goddesses to be recognised as forms of great Brāhminical deities (especially Devī or Durgā) are really commonplace in the historical record, particularly in places where urbanisation during a particular period of history generated a relatively cosmopolitan culture and people's horizons widened. In principle, such changes might follow from the initiatives either of 'sanskritising' Brāhmins or of the communities whose deities are ennobled.

Let us now look a little more closely at Vindhyavāsinī, whose shrine at Vindhyachal was mentioned above as a significant pilgrimage centre. The widening of horizons seems to be a particularly relevant factor here in the way that the local goddess has come to be identified with universal Great Goddess Devī as celebrated in the *Devīmāhātmya*. Cynthia Ann Humes (1996) made a study of the shrine and of both the *Devīmāhātmya* (the scripture glorifying the universal Great Goddess) and of the corresponding scripture of the regional goddess (now much less used), the *Vindhyamāhātmya* dating from the early nineteenth century. The cult had by that time already acquired a long history, in the course of which a considerable degree of 'Sanskritisation', in various ways, had taken place.

Vindhyavāsinī had an elaborate mythology, identifying her especially as a mountain goddess, which acquired a wide regional presence, and was associated already with certain Brāhminical deities – Viṣṇu, Indra and Kṛṣṇa. Thus, her considerable prestige and rich mythology qualified her well enough to attract devotees from far afield. However, it was in more recent times, particularly in the twentieth century with the major improvement in communications, that her career blossomed. As Humes writes,

> In part, this shift reflects the concern of the guides and pandits to universalize her appeal: by downplaying her specificities and appropriating a more universalistic glorification that also allows for a variety of interpretations, they hope to increase the number of her potential adherents – their potential customers. I believe that financial considerations are a major reason why most of the *Vindhya Māhātmya* is ignored, whereas the *Devī Māhātmya* is inscribed in temple walls, recited by pandits, and quoted by guides (Humes 1996, 60).

The result of this shift was to change radically the image of the goddess presented to pilgrims by the local temple 'pandits'. Visitors from nearby could still find out about various attributes of the divinity derived from the *Vindhyamāhātmya*, but this text had by now been sidelined, its frankly Tantric parts now forgotten, and all the emphasis was upon the universal Devī. Humes comments:

> Thus, we see that a once complex understanding of the goddess and her relations to deities of the Hindu pantheon, which was preserved in local traditions glorifying her, has become radically simplified by efforts to universalize the Goddess, uprooting her from a proximate, immediate, and localized immanence and supplying her with a more lofty and dislocated transcendence (Humes 1996, 71).
>
> Perhaps priests have discovered that the world of many of their pilgrim clients is larger than the Vindhya range nowadays, and that these clients bring with them a broader range of issues and identities that they seek to integrate into themselves as they worship. To furnish them with a means to make sense of their world, priests have constructed a correspondingly extended framework to describe the goddess at Vindhyachal. This more universal goddess can assure pilgrims that they are worshiping the goddess of the dominant group, not a backward superstition left over from an unenlightened past (Humes 1996, 74).

This sort of process clearly owed little to the colonising efforts of Brāhmins with pan-Indian perspectives; indeed the main thrust of 'top-down' Brāhminisation of local cults, which may perhaps be associated pre-eminently with the period of the classical Purāṇas, was long past.

Sometimes though, the operation of bottom-up appropriation can be detected even in events that occurred long ago. An example of the appropriation of a temple site by a relatively low-tribal regional group, in circumstances which cannot be precisely dated, is considered on later pages by Vicziany, Bapat and Ranade (Chapter 11), where the act of appropriation may be seen as a historically justified assertion of entitlement:

> at some time between the construction of the Karle Buddhist *chaitya* in the second century BCE and the Indian government notification of 1909, the Son Kolis of Mumbai appropriated the part of the Karle sacred hill that we today describe as the Ekveera Devi temple. They probably did so with a sense of entitlement, as the worship of Koli mother goddesses long predates the evolution of Buddhism in India.

It is necessary to recognise that very frequently the initiative of the 'Sanskritised' group in evolving its own view of itself is frequently the driving force, and those who are 'Sanskritised' perceive the adopted 'Sanskritic' teachings, rituals or icons not as alien imports but as improved restatements of what has always been their own possession. Very early in the historiography of 'Sanskritisation', Dumont and Pocock interpreted Sanskritisation 'not as the imposition of a different system upon an old one,' but as 'the acceptance of a more distinguished or prestigious way of saying the same things' (Dumont and Pocock 1959, 45). There is no need here to assess the many criticisms since advanced against their theoretical approach (sometimes called 'ahistorical') to Indian society; however valid many of these criticisms may be, it is enough to recognise that these authors were alive to the dynamism of the constant traffic in religious beliefs and practices between different elements in Indian society.

At this point it is easy to see that 'Sanskritisation' may operate in a way that does not lend itself well to conceptualisations of superior and subordinate, top and bottom. We have noticed in the preceding pages how the process of appropriation can reach upwards, downwards or sideways upon the vertical scale of higher and lower status, but none of these directions seems perfectly apt to match the sort of appropriation involved when a religious community reaches out for 'a more distinguished or prestigious way of saying the same things.' We should never forget that 'The real structure of tradition, in any civilization or part thereof, is an immensely intricate system of relationships between the levels or components of tradition, which we enormously oversimplify by referring to as "high" and "low" or as "great" and "little"' (Staal 1963, 263). The vertical scale is itself a construct, which can capture only some aspects of social reality.

Here we would like to introduce a different polarity which is likely to be misunderstood if we insist upon fitting the observed cultural processes into a mould of hierarchy, oppression and subversion, important though these things often are. The additional polarity we should recognise is that between metropolitan centres and provinces within a civilisation; the 'provincials' recognise that the urban culture is the home of sophisticated culture and advanced intellectual discussion, but after a generation or so of familiarity with the sophisticated trappings of urban religion do not feel inferior or oppressed by them – they thoroughly internalise them. (The onus of proof is then upon whoever would claim that this is merely 'false consciousness'.) Provincial and metropolitan forms of religious belief and practice are felt to be equivalent as expressions of a single experience.

This relationship is clear when we look at cases where the original geographical and social gap between the appropriator and the appropriated is at its widest. That is why it is useful to take as an example the relationship between the urban centres of religious culture in India and the previously unlettered cultures of South-East Asia which adopted Brāhminism and Buddhism. Even here, we find that the recipients of Sanskritic traditions were not submitting to the imposition of something alien, but rather, even as they absorbed, adapted and transformed the Indian imports to suit their own genius, re-articulating, in a more sophisticated form, their own immemorial traditions. This, at least, is the conclusion of Paul Mus, whose insights into the ancient civilisation of the Chams, first published in the 1930s, have retained their cogency and relevance ever since:

> The Brahmanical formulation assured a theoretical predominance to the Indo-European element. But beneath it persisted the religion of the soil, malleable and tenacious. Thus it came about that when Hinduism, with its Sanskrit literature, reached the Far East, what we witness is above all a diffusion of the old Asiatic ideas: ideas that were instantly recognized, understood and endorsed by peoples who perhaps were not always aware of

wholly changing their religion in adopting those of India (Mus 2011, 51-52).

We conclude, then, by suggesting that the processes of gradual and cumulative adaptation and change that pervade religious life, which we may call the crystallisation of latent possibilities, occupy a different sort of space from that of the hierarchical distribution of *varṇas* and *jātis* in Indian society. We cannot know what contests between all sorts of local groups, some attempting to achieve social mobility and some attempting to deny it to others, are now lost to history. It is likely that developments in the distant past that we can now know only as examples of 'Sanskritisation' in fact involved all kinds of local motivations, probably many more than are captured in the sketch of seven categories with which we began here.

It is therefore useful to distinguish between two major contrasting approaches to the phenomena of appropriation in religious history: on the one hand, an approach which emphasises the vertical dimension of societal relationships and top-down actions by elites, and, on the other, an approach which emphasises reciprocal influences affecting groups in all kinds of ritual, geographical and economic relationships with each other and the mosaic of local traditions which is likely to prompt responses to change at the level of the face-to-face group. The first is likely to be favoured by social theory and broad-brush portrayals of large-scale cultural movements, the second by studies of particular communities or literary sources. Both can yield good insights if appropriately deployed. Total understanding of religious history, if such were possible, would ideally combine both.

A foreshadowing of the contributions

So we should expect to find, in the historical record of religious appropriations and adaptations, that the most prominent features may be the frequent documented episodes of contestation, but these mark moments of crisis that punctuated the underlying processes of gradual evolution and exploration of possibilities by religious teachers. The chapters in this collection reflect this chequered narrative.

Di Castro presents a richly detailed survey of the iconography of goddess images as they travelled through the cultures of India and Central Asia in ancient times. He emphasises that any given set of properties possessed by an image should not be regarded as an indissoluble whole with a single coherent meaning, but instead needs to be analysed as a changing assemblage in which symbolic meanings are appropriated from different environments. He explores, for example, the symbolism of the mural crown worn by some goddesses, which changed from culture to culture. Other symbols examined include the cornucopia and the goddess associated with a lion. These are traced through Sumer, the Achaemenid Empire, Gandhara, Scythian kingdoms, and the Indian realms up to the time of the Guptas, with special attention to the goddesses Ardoksho, Tyche, and Nanā and the other goddesses they influenced. Di Castro detects a gradual shift in the symbolism from an earlier focus upon the embodiment of political power to more social and even personal religious values. The lesson is that images do not have immutable symbolism; they appropriate different meanings from the repertoires of different cultures through which they pass.

Bapat's chapter tells the story of the blatant and forceful appropriation of a Jain goddess by the *Kokaṇastha* Brāhmins in the area. It is so blatant that the large image of the Jain Tīrthaṃkar that originally occupied the sanctum sanctorum, when Jainism held its sway in Maharashtra, still sits in one corner of the sanctum. No attempt has been made to hide this act of blatant usurpation. The Jain goddess Yakṣiṇī that replaced the Tīrthaṃkar, on the other hand, has been forcefully converted to Durgā, the well-known Hindu deity, the slayer of demons. In another act of total disregard for the vanquished, even the Jain name of the goddess has not been changed. She thus remains the Yakṣiṇī Devī, alias Durgā. The temple is now a Brāhminic shrine where daily prayers are offered to the goddess Durgā.

Narsalay's chapter tells a similar story. Here the politically astute Peshwas, the ministers of the Maratha kingdom in Maharashtra in the eighteenth century, converted a distant local goddess *Ambejogāī,* a *grāmadevatā*, into the clan goddess of the Peshwas. This clever act had many fruitful consequences for the Peshwas. Firstly, they were now able to pacify the Hindu population in the region, which had suffered under Muslim rule not long before. Secondly, they now legitimised the migration of the *Kokaṇastha* Brāhmins from the poorer Konkan region to a place 400 kilometres away. Thirdly, by bringing a local goddess into the royal fold, the Peshwas were able to control and dominate the religious environment in the region. In support of her argument, Narsalay shows how the regime of worship at Ambejogai incorporated into it a number of rituals that remain specific to the *Kokaṇastha* Brāhmin sub-caste of Marathi Brāhmins. The Peshwas belonged to this sub-caste.

Vicziany, Bapat and Ranade dwell on the economically and to some extent politically motivated appropriation of the site of the Buddhist rock-cut caves at Karle by the Son Koli fisher folk of Mumbai. The Son Kolis, the most influential and well-to-do Kolis in Maharashtra, were able to do this with the help of the Shiv Sena, the Hindu fundamentalist political party. In doing so, the Son Kolis shifted their primary sacred site to an area located well outside Mumbai, some 150 kilometres from the metropolis. The authors argue that by doing so, the Son Kolis not only appropriated the sacred area of the Karle hill from the Buddhists, but also appropriated the goddess Ekveera from the Mahadev Kolis, who were probably the original inhabitants of this hilly area. The process of appropriation created a new pilgrimage site for the Son Kolis, who were already deeply involved in the pilgrimage practices of the *bhakti* devotional movement. The authors comment that since Indian independence in 1947, the Son Kolis have gone from cultural appropriation into appropriating the benefits of the reservation policies from which they had previously been excluded because they had not been listed by the government as a Scheduled Tribe. That process of appropriation has required the Son Kolis to merge their tribal identity with the Mahadev Kolis of western India.

Bailey's paper involves an in-depth study of some of the myths associated with women in the *Vāmanapurāṇa*. As is generally known, the Purāṇas borrowed extensively from Vedic and Vedantic literature and the epics. Bailey asks the question whether the process of appropriation fully describes what happened or whether they contained any original material. He suggests that the latter is most likely. More so than the male gods, goddesses play an extensive role in the mythic narratives of the Purāṇas. He cites examples of the myths associated with three women in this Purāṇa: Pārvatī, a Brāhminic goddess and the wife of Śiva; and two other semi-divine women, Arajā and Citrāṅgadā. Having studied their behaviour towards suitors and the results of these interactions, Bailey concludes that tribal women were absorbed/integrated into the Brāhminic fold by their alliances with kings who did not necessarily observe Brāhminic norms. He suggests that such acts are perhaps better seen as a way of integrating different traditions rather than as appropriations.

Like Bailey, Friedlander explores another aspect of appropriation in regard to Ravidās, a mediaeval poet-saint from the untouchable Chamar (*Camār*; shoesmith) community. Hindus consider the river Ganges (Gaṅgā) a goddess and a mother; she plays an important role in their daily and spiritual life, including the lives of the Chamars. Ravidās was a poet-saint of the *bhakti* tradition who lived around 1500 CE and had a special relationship with the Goddess Gaṅgā. Amongst the Chamars, there are many stories about Gaṅgā performing miracles for the sake of her favourite Bhakta, Ravidās. These involved his confrontations with the Brāhmin community of the time who resisted Ravidās' audacity in challenging their hierarchical superiority; after all, Ravidās was a dalit. While it may be tempting to view this as appropriation on the part of Ravidās, Friedlander argues (as was noted above) that we should call this process of interaction a 'contestation' rather than an 'appropriation'. Friedlander further argues that these stories show us how the Chamar communities' veneration of the goddess Gaṅgā formed part of a narrative of interaction between the Chamar castes and the Brāhminical communities. Since the sixteenth century, this interaction has involved contests about the right to access and inhabit the public and sacred places of India. In his essay, Friedlander coins a new definition of appropriation which he says is nothing but a 'rhetorical flourish used by higher caste communities to criticise the use of symbols by lower caste communities contesting their status in the hierarchy'.

In his essay on the worship of goddess Durgā in Bengal, Bandopadhayay sets out a detailed history of the annual Durgā Pūjā ritual in Bengal. He convincingly shows how a household worship ritual became increasingly a public event from 1790 onwards and how even the British manipulated the ritual for their own political ends. The independence fighters used Durgā as a synonym for mother India and the annual *pūjā* became a front for their meetings and the training of freedom fighters. Since independence, other themes have been added to the repertoire of the Durgā Pūjā festival plays: climate change and global warming; the need to preserve the forests; the tragedy of the terrorist attack in Mumbai in 2008; rampant corruption and nepotism; and lawlessness and crime. Quite recently, politicians such as Mamata Banerjee have used the occasion of Durgā Pūjā to project a positive image of herself to Indian industry leaders. And at least on one occasion, the Indian National Congress president, Sonia Gandhi, has been portrayed as goddess Durgā. Durgā Pūjā has also become an occasion for spectacular extravaganza, glamour and pomp with elaborate stylised displays carefully executed by trained artists, which cost a fortune. As Bandopadhayay says, '*Durgā Pūjā* cannot be adequately encompassed by a single narrative of appropriation, or anything else – it is a constantly changing kaleidoscope.'

John Dupuche, who has worked on Kashmir Śaivism for many years, provides yet another vignette in the complex area of the Trika system.[2] He looks at appropriation in a totally novel way. In *tantra* studies, appropriation does not mean domination, elimination, despising or fearing. Rather, appropriation means that one truth is found in the other, one is preparation for the other. (We might describe this process as a crystallisation of latent possibilities.) Thus in the Kula ritual, while the goddess appropriates the disciple, the disciple appropriates the goddess. They are assimilated into each other. As Dupuche points out, in the practice of the Kaula *tantra*, the *tāntrika* may seem to be the principal actor – along with his female consort, the *dūtī*. It is in fact the Devī who, from the moment of initiation until the final outcome of the ritual, exercises her freedom. She sweeps away all human fears and prejudices and communicates her utter freedom. She appropriates all because she is all.

Mabbett offers a reflection on the familiar problem of the oddly disturbing and even violent imagery characterising the iconography of so many goddesses. He takes as a special case the goddess Chinnamastā (along with her Buddhist equivalent Chinnamuṇḍā), who has cut off her own head and from whose neck pour forth three spouts of blood. He considers the various explanations given for this in the available literature, with special attention to the severed head as a symbol of cosmic sacrifice. He favours a broad perspective in which we discern a long continuity running through Hindu and Buddhist ideas and images; in this perspective the head has special significance as a cosmic principle representing the seat of a transcendent source of creation, both of the self and of the world. This theme was implicit in the network of motifs passed down through the ages, re-appropriated in new forms in each generation and each sect.

Templeman's chapter is distinctive in dealing with very different terrain – the semi-mythical geography of Himalayan Buddhism, which absorbed and very lightly disguised the cults of various local deities, often of violent aspect, which were domesticated during the rise of Buddhist culture. He deals with the phenomenon of 'hidden lands', places supposed to be under the protection of goddesses who variously showed themselves in fierce and demonic or in feminine alluring forms. He suggests that such 'hidden

2 In Kashmir Shaivism, Trika means the trinity of an individual (*nara*), Shakti, the universal energy, and Shiva, the transcendental being, the God-head. Thus, a soul recognises himself as Shiva by means of the realisation of his Shaktis – the powers of God-head. The Trika system advocates a practical path towards complete self-realisation.

lands', with their teasingly ambiguous guardians, may be closely related historically with the Iranian cultic witch figures of ancient times (*pairikas*) and represent a phenomenon more widespread than is generally recognised. He focuses upon one particular such hidden land, that of Yolmo Gangra, corresponding to an actual place north of Kathmandu which is, however, supposed to have an occult history referred to in mythological texts. Using a recently discovered manuscript from the seventeenth or eighteenth century, Templeman discusses what the texts contained in it suggest about attitudes to the alternately demonic and seductive goddess Jomo Yangri Chugmo. Such images suggest that the earthy, robust and even violent imagery of these female divinities may tempt us to regard them as more ancient, pre-Buddhist elements, but Templeman reminds us that at present this is not seriously warranted by the evidence; perhaps the ambiguity is intrinsic to their characters.

In his thought-provoking essay, Martin Hříbek investigates some comparatively modern Indian appropriations of the Devī. Taking three examples, he shows how the image of the goddess was refashioned by Bengali and Tamil nationalists and most recently by social activists to achieve their specific ends. During British times, the famous Bengali author and poet Bankimchandra successfully created Mother India (Bhāratmātā) to disseminate nationalistic ideas. Bankimchandra also wrote the well-known poem, *Vande Mātaram*, which has the same status as the current Indian national anthem, and created the same ethos amongst the nationalists.

Similarly, in the state of Tamilnadu, the Devī was appropriated to create the Tamiḻttāya or mother Tamil to personify the Tamil language and polity. Madhu Kishwar, an academic and a social worker, invoked a cause-specific *avatāra* of Devī, the Svaccha Nārāyaṇī, who was the goddess of cleanliness, self-discipline, good governance and secularity. The broom became the symbol of this goddess and its worship became a regular ritual for Kishwar's followers. To Kishwar, goddess Svaccha Nārāyaṇī represents a creative amalgam of the traditional female trinity – Durgā, Lakṣmī and Saraswatī – with many new attributes and powers required to meet contemporary challenges. Hříbek points out that the appropriations he discusses are part of a larger complex of ideas and practices whereby Indian modernity is in the making.

Bibliography

Bapat, Jayant Bhalchandra, and Ian Mabbett. 2008. *The Iconic Female: Goddesses of India, Nepal and Tibet*. Clayton: Monash Asia Institute.
Barber, Benjamin. 1992. *Jihad vs. McWorld: How Globalism and Tribalism are Reshaping the World.* New York: Ballantine Books.
Bourdieu, Pierre. 1992. *The Logic of Practice.* Stanford: Stanford University Press.
Copland, Ian, *et al.* 2012. *A History of State and Religion in India.* Abingdon: Routledge.
Dumont, Louis. 1980. *Homo Hierarchicus. The Caste System and its Implications.* Chicago/London: Chicago University Press.
Dumont, Louis, and D.F. Pocock. 1959. 'On the different aspects or levels in Hinduism'. *Contributions to Indian Sociology* 3: 40-45.
Eaton, Richard M. 2005. *The New Cambridge History of India. A Social History of the Deccan, 1300-1761. Eight Indian Lives.* Cambridge: Cambridge University Press
Halbfass, William. 1988. *India and Europe: An Essay in Understanding.* Albany: SUNY.
Humes, Cynthia Ann. 1996. 'Vindhyavāsinī: local goddess yet great goddess'. In *Devī Goddesses of India*, edited by J.S. Hawley and D.M. Wulff, 49-76. Berkeley: University of California Press.
Jha, D.N. 1998. *Ancient India in Historical Outline.* Revised ed. New Delhi: Manohar.
Mabbett, I.W. 2010. 'The *Kauṭilīya Arthaśāstra* and the concept of secularism'. *South Asia*, new series 33 (1): 13-32.
Mus, Paul. 2011. *India Seen from the East: Indian and Indigenous Cults in Champa.* Revised Edition. Translated by Ian Mabbett; edited by Ian Mabbett and David Chandler. Caulfield: Monash University Press.
Pollock, Sheldon. 1996. 'The Sanskrit cosmopolis 300-1300 CE: transculturation, vernacularization, and the question of ideology'. In *Ideology and Status of Sanskrit,* edited by J.E.M. Houben, 197-248. Leiden: Brill.
Said, Edward W. 1977. *Orientalism.* New York: Pantheon.
Said, Edward W. 1993. *Culture and Imperialism.* New York: Vintage.
Staal, J.F. 1963. 'Sanskrit and Sanskritization'. *Journal of Asian Studies* 22 (3): 261-275.
Srinivas, M.N. 1952. *Religion and Society among the Coorgs of South India.* Oxford: Clarendon.
Thapar, Romila. 1966. *A History of India.* Vol.1. Harmondsworth: Penguin.
Urban, Hugh B. 2003. *Tantra: Sex, Secrecy, Politics, and Power in the Study of Religion.* Berkeley: University of California Press.

Chapter 2

Crowns, Horns and Goddesses

Appropriation of Symbols in Gandhāra and Beyond

Angelo Andrea Di Castro

The appropriation of particular symbols of Indian and Central Asian goddesses, characteristic of the Indo-Iranian borderland, will be examined in this chapter by looking at how such symbols entered and influenced different cultures over time. Iconography can be one of the ways of studying the sacred across cultures, which should not be limited to a simple synchronic analysis of an exclusive aspect of religious phenomena; rather, it should be an investigation that takes into account the multilinear, disordered, overlapping attributes that characterise divinities.[1]

In what follows, selected iconographic examples of Indian, Hellenistic, Kuṣāṇa and Gupta goddesses from around the second century BCE to the sixth century CE will be considered, together with their antecedents and their relationships with Central and Western Asian cultural contexts. The convergence of factors such as migrations, conquests, and trade contacts contributed to the transmission of symbols and the consequential appropriation and transformation in religious imagery. Material excavated from the royal graves at Tillia Tepe in Afghanistan (Sarianidi 1980) exemplifies this. It demonstrates how different cultural traditions from the Mediterranean to the Eastern Asian regions became re-elaborated into a new syncretic artistic language, which ultimately became characteristic of the Kuṣāṇa Empire (first–third century CE), stretching from the Fergana Valley (Uzbekistan, Kyrgyzstan and Tajikistan), encompassing

1 In this instance I mean a polythetic classification (Needham 1975); see Di Castro (2012a) for further references.

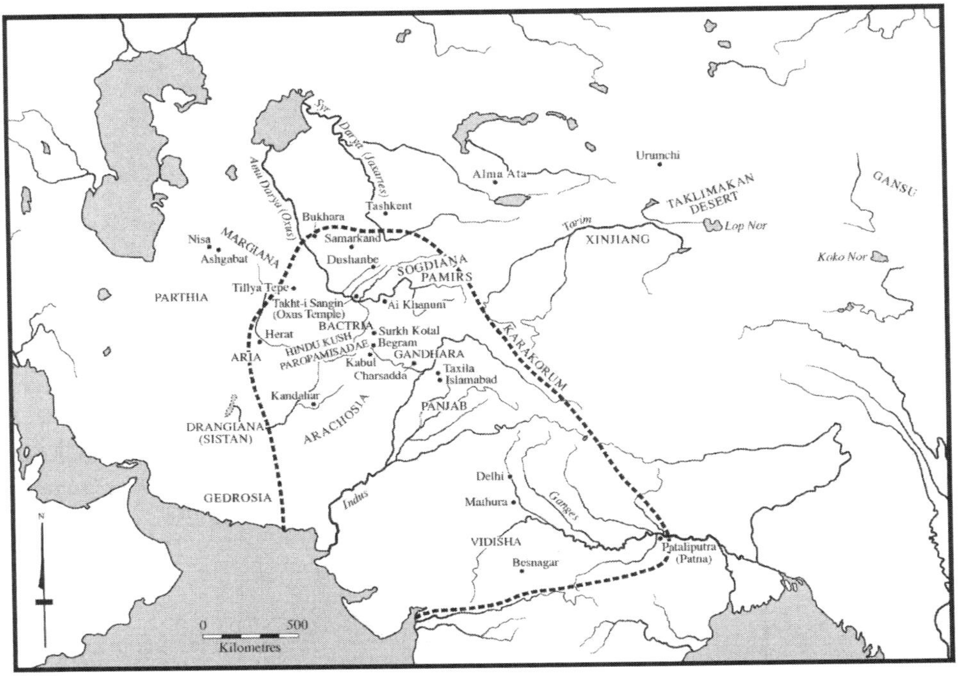

Figure 2.1: Map showing the extent of the Kuṣāṇa Empire.

Bactria, and Gandhāra (Afghanistan and Pakistan), down to the lower Ganges Valley (India).

The origin and the symbolic nature of the mural crown (crowns with towers, battlements, or crenellations) will be investigated together with other symbols carried by some goddesses that we find depicted on Greco-Bactrian, Indo-Greek, Śaka and Kuṣāṇa coins, as well as on other artefacts. For example, images with mural crown are often, but not necessarily, represented as carrying a cornucopia (horn of plenty). In addition other images can be associated with different symbols such as a palm, a staff, or a wreath, or the goddess can be accompanied by a lion. Such symbolic attributes can be represented either collectively or individually when connected with a goddess, as in the representation of Śrī-Lakṣmī with a cornucopia flanked by the lustrating elephants (Srinivasan 2010; Di Castro 2012b). Generally, it can be assumed that the mural crown points to values related to kingship and power/protection over a city or a country, whereas the cornucopia refers to the promised prosperity of the people ruled by the king/queen; however, when one considers the Tyche/Fortune of the individual, in private life, the mural crown may allude to specific personification of a city goddess.

The Gandhāran context

Mural crowned figures are not uncommon in Gandhāran art. In fact they are often represented in Buddhist narrative friezes depicting the *Abhiniṣkramaṇa*, the Great Departure of the Buddha from his paternal palace at Kapilavastu. In the early twentieth century the French scholar Alfred Foucher (1905, 360-361) had already recognised how the mural crown was adapted into Buddhist art in Gandhāra in order to characterise the personification of the Buddha's hometown, the *nagaradevatā*, city protecting goddess, of Kapilavastu.

At first it appears that the Gandhāran artists adopted the classical style of the poliadic goddess Tyche from the Greco-Bactrian and Indo-Greek coinage. In fact the city goddesses depicted on coins allude to values of land protection and fertility, and to the good fortune of the ruler, and this likely determined the choice of the adoption of such a model. In some Gandhāran reliefs the goddess of Kapilavastu can be seen wearing cylindrical headgear, a *polos*, carrying a cornucopia, or depicted in a pensive attitude, or in a gesture displaying homage (*añjali mudrā*) to the Buddha.[2] A goddess with *polos* and cornucopia is generally represented sitting on an isolated throne, or next to a god, which formed a tutelary couple.[3]

The mural crown that appears mainly in association with scenes of the Great Departure was also adopted in the Kuṣāṇa period in non-narrative scenes and in religious contexts and is apparently not explicitly Buddhist.[4] The religious imagery varies noticeably: for example, in a *parinirvāṇa* scene a goddess with a turreted crown is possibly representing a city goddess, the *nagaradevatā* of Kuśīnagara, paying homage, with other divinities, to the dying Buddha in the vicinity of Kuśīnagara.[5] Other examples

2 For images of the goddess of Kapilavastu, see, for instance, Kurita (2003a, figs. 27, 125, P2–II, 144, 147, 151–153, 156, 613, 614). For an extensive bibliographic list of references for this Buddhist narrative scene (*Abhiniṣkramaṇa*), see the descriptive catalogue of the sculptures excavated at Buktara, in the Swat Valley (Taddei 1962, 29). A more recent list can also be found in Santoro (2002).

3 Kurita (2003b, figs. 417, 420, 421, 479-481, 485, 484). Kurita (2003b, 165) defined this divinity as Fecundity Goddess.

4 The only coins published by Göbl (1984, nos. 1028-1029) referring to a mural crown are those of the Kuṣāṇo-Sasanian Ardashir I, respectively showing the goddess Anāhitā in throne under an aedicule and a scene of investiture. Santoro's claim (2002, 226) that the mural crown is conspicuously absent from the Kuṣāṇa coinage, with the only exception of one Huviṣka's coin type, follows the interpretation of Czuma's catalogue (1985, 141, pl. 62 G) but ignores the massive evidence of Göbl (1984).

5 Kurita (2003a, 233, fig. P4-I); see also Santoro (2002, 225 and fig. 6). Although partly speculative, this suggestive interpretation deserves more attention.

vary from a goddess with mural crown associated with other gods on an architectural fragment excavated in the Swat Valley (Taddei 1964, 107, pl. CCCXXXVI) to a sculpture of the goddess Hārītī with mural crown surrounded by children (Kurita 2003b, fig. 493). Additionally we find personal ornaments and jewellery like an elegant gold medallion decorated with a turreted female head (Bopearachchi *et al.* 2003, 191, fig. 181) and a bronze pendant depicting a miniature goddess with cornucopia, mural crown and towers on her shoulders (Pal 1986, 157-58, cat. S33). Two intriguing stone palettes, or toilet trays, also show mural crowns: one depicts a scene from the Trojan cycle with Achilles and Penthesilea (Di Castro 2012c, 7-12), the other a sacrifice (Siudmak 2013, 57-59, pl. 16).

Figure 2.2: Tutelary Couple (Guimet Museum, Paris).[6]

While analysing images of goddesses with mural crowns, Santoro (2002) points to the originality of Gandhāran iconography in the Kuṣāṇa period with its innovative representations in which the divinity is also shown with shoulder towers. Santoro identifies this divinity with the Kuṣāṇa goddess Ardoksho (ArdokÞo). Despite Santoro's suggestive observations and relevant documentation, her hypothesis is not exhaustive because of the aprioristic attempt to identity the goddess of Kapilavastu with Ardoksho.

6 Please note that all figures in chapter 2 are not to scale.

Figure 2.3: Kuṣāṇa coin of Kaniṣka with the goddess Ardoksho holding a cornucopia.

Her identification is based on an assumption that a goddess, connected to the cult of the Kuṣāṇa god Pharro,[7] must take the symbolic use of shoulder attributes associated with this divinity. Santoro (2002, 227) talks of pleonastic symbolism, where the repetition of the symbols is used to reinforce the notion they are implying. She explains this iconographic innovation by looking at the flaming shoulders of the god Pharro and the Kuṣāṇa kings depicted on various coins.[8]

Figure 2.4: Kuṣāṇa coin of Huviṣka displaying the god Pharro with flames on the shoulders and holding a receptacle with flames.

7 The Kuṣāṇa divinities Pharro and Ardoksho appear to be associated in a number of representations of tutelary couples, often labelled as 'Pharro and Ardoksho' or 'Pañcika and Hārītī'. On the tutelary couple, see Bachhofer (1937) and Bussagli (1951, 141-154; 1984).

8 See Gnoli (1996 and 1999) on Pharro symbolising the Royal Glory or Fortune of the Kuṣāṇas (*Khvareno*, *xvarənō*, '*Xvarənah*). Pharro, as the *Khvareno*, the Royal Glory that embodies and legitimates the mystical power of the Iranian kings, is represented on some Kuṣāṇa coins of Huviṣka (Göbl 1984, nos. 1, 10-16, 18, 25, 31, 34, 69-74, 201-205, 253-254). See also Rosenfield (1967, 92, 96, 128, 197-199, 201, pls. IX.177-179, XIV.273), who pointed to this symbolical and iconographic similarity. For the iconographic similarities between Pharro and a goddess holding a receptacle with flames represented on the Indo-Scythian coins, see Di Castro (2012c, 1-6).

Here the peculiar iconography of turreted shoulders is exclusively equated with the flames on the shoulders of the god Pharro. Misguidedly, Santoro does not consider the same phenomenological aspects that can be seen in several sculptures in which the goddess Hārītī is characterised by the presence of a child on each shoulder.[9]

As a result, Santoro's semantic reductionist analysis appears limited, owing to her exclusive focus on a singular feature (Pharro's flames) which fails to take into account the inherent symbolic value of the children on Hārītī's shoulders, even though the goddess is depicted wearing a mural crown.[10] Rather than being preoccupied with making a definitive attribution – labels supported by the literary evidence – it is more relevant to consider the variability of these images, their polysemy, and the process by which the appropriation of symbolic elements was determined.

Figure 2.5: Hārītī with children on the shoulder and wearing a mural crown (Private collection).

9 See, for instance, Kurita (2003b, figs. 491, 493, 494, and 497) with only one child.

10 Curiously Santoro (2002, 224) referred to this image in her paper, yet she did not consider this meaningful evidence was worth additional attention.

Tyche and the mural crown

When we consider the mural crown, it is useful to look at its origins and its association with the Greek goddess Tyche, a goddess who embodies and protects a town by bestowing royal power and fertility. The mural crown symbol was introduced to Bactria and Gandhāra during the Greek domination of the region (third–first century BCE). According to Pausanias (*Description of Greece* IV. 30. 3, 6), in the mid sixth century BCE, Boupalos of Chios made a statue of Tyche wearing a *polos* and holding the horn of Amalthea for the temple of Smyrna. The association of a mural crown and cornucopia with Tyche, the goddess of Fortune, was likely made by Eutychides in the fourth century BCE. Pausanias (VI. 2. 7) states that Eutychides produced a highly valued image of Fortune for the Syrians on the Orontes.

Figure 2.6: Tyche of Antiochia by Eutychides (Vatican Museums).

When he sculpted this famous Tyche for the city of Antioch, he was possibly looking at Boupalos' statue. By placing a mural crown on her head as a city goddess marker, Eutychides was showing he was aware of the poliadic value of other Greek, Anatolian and Near Eastern goddesses, like Artemis, Cybele and Astarte.[11] The mural crown was

11 For the archaic notion of the Greek poliadic Tyche (*pherepolis*, 'who holds up the city', or 'city-bearing'), see Matheson (1994a, 21) and Metzler (1994, 82).

therefore used mainly to represent personifications of cities or regions, or to connect religious images to particular towns or countries in the classical world.[12]

In a Near Eastern context, the symbolic iconographic value of a mural crown has a long history that can be traced back to late Bronze Age Syrian and Anatolian goddesses. Near Eastern queens were also represented by this symbol (Metzler 1994, 77), implying that there was a close symbolic connection between the values of kingship and the kingdom itself, along with the possession and protection of cities. This is exemplified by a fourteenth century BCE gold 'mural crown' that was recorded as having being in the inventory of Queen Ahatmilku's treasure at Ugarit, in northern Syria (Nougayrol 1955, 182-83). Hoffner (1969) demonstrated by combining philological and epigraphic evidence that this artefact can be regarded as a mural crown rather than a city model. Hoffner also refers to a renowned rock relief at Yazılıkaya near Hattusha/Boğazköy where the carved Hittite goddess Hepat is wearing a mural crown standing on a lion.

Figure 2.7: Detail from Yazılıkaya relief displaying the Hittite goddess Hepat with mural crown standing on a lion.

The relationship between mural crowns and queenship is further supported by other Near Eastern examples. Neo-Assyrian queens are represented with mural crowns in a number of sculptures (Metzler 1994, fig. 49; Ornan 2002, figs. 1-4). A famous seventh century BCE relief from

12 For early numismatic examples in the Mediterranean world, see Broucke (1994).

Nineveh depicting the banquet of King Ashurbanipal and his queen, Ashursharrat, celebrating victory over the king of Elam, shows the queen wearing a crown decorated with small towers. Ornan (2002, 475-476) believes that the abovementioned crown of Ahatmilku's treasure sets a precedent for a mural crown worn by the queen herself. It appears certain though that Hittite and Neo-Hittite traditions played an important role in shaping attributes of Phrygian mother goddesses, and these influences can be recognised in the iconography of the Greco-Roman goddess Cybele.[13]

Migrating goddesses

The Sumerian goddess Nanā is one of the ancient divinities that influenced the development of numerous northern Indian, Gandhāran and Bactrian goddess images during the Kuṣāṇa and Gupta periods (c. first–fifth century CE), and beyond. This Mesopotamian divinity became particularly popular in late Hellenistic Bactria.

Figure 2.8: Detail of the Mesopotamian *kudurru* of Melishipak with the Sumerian goddess Nanā (Louvre Museum, Paris).

Some of Nanā's Mesopotamian symbolic attributes travelled in time to the Kuṣāṇa period, like values such as those connected to kingship, political power as well as the protection of the individual in the private domestic sphere. The complex processes of transformation mediated by a number of factors including different historical, cultural and ethnic contexts need to be taken into account, particularly when considering connective lines between this ancient Mesopotamian divinity

13 For the relations between the Hittite goddesses, the poliadic goddess Kubaba the 'Queen of Karkamiš', Kybebe/Kubele and the Phrygian mother goddesses, see Roller (1999, 41-115).

with the goddesses worshipped in pilgrimage places in Baluchistan and Afghanistan (see below).

As Burkert (2000, 3) states we should always be aware that

> [w]hen we speak of "migration", "expansion", "transfer" and "influence", we should not presume that the contents transferred and accepted were left unchanged in the process. New functions, perspectives and interpretations will always arise. In consequence, new cults and new gods may come into existence, syncretising elements of different origins in a new arrangement.

From the second millennium BCE the popularity of Nanā, the lunar goddess of Uruk, increased beyond Mesopotamia; she was worshipped in Susa for a long period before her cult images were returned to Uruk by the Assyrian king Esarhaddon in the seventh century BCE (Potts 2001, 28-30). Clearly the images of Nanā were 'taken' to Susa during some of the numerous incursions by the kings of Elam. What is relevant here is the possibility that the goddess could have already reached Bactria via Elam in the second millennium BCE (Potts 2001, 30), sharing, or likely appropriating features of the Babylonian goddess Ishtar/Inanna. While maintaining a distinct identity from Ishtar, she displays a warrior-like character and stands on a lion. Without resorting necessarily to Sarianidi's idea of a great goddess of Bactria, a goddess in the presence of lions found on some Bronze Age Bactrian seals can be explained as a process of acculturation and appropriation from Near Eastern/Western Asian cultures via ancient Elam.[14]

The lapis lazuli trade may have played an important role in facilitating a number of exchanges beyond the purely economic sphere. However, one may wonder whether another process of religious appropriation was underway during the Achaemenid period (sixth–fourth century BCE), parallel to the socio-political and economic impact the Achaemenid power exerted on its peripheral provinces of Sogdiana, Bactria, and Gandhāra. The symbolism and iconography of Achaemenid kingship were largely inspired by Assyrian and Babylonian royal imagery. The

14 Sarianidi (1980, 131) refers to the continuity of Bronze Age Bactrian culture down to the Hellenistic period through iconographic similarities and points to the possibility of investigating 'the millenary tradition in the evolution of the image of the mistress of animals in Bactria'. On the Mesopotamian origins of Nanā, see Potts (2001). For the relation of the Mesopotamian goddess with the context of the Kuṣāṇa and Sogdian goddesses, see Grenet and Marshak (1998) and Ambos (2003).

mural crown with stylised stepped pyramid-like miniature battlements is one of these Near Eastern elements used as a royal attribute by Achaemenid artists in various iconographic representations of kingship. For instance, on the famous rock relief at Bisutun (Behistun), the great Persian king Darius is shown wearing such a crown.[15] This type of crown with small stepped battlements was adopted throughout the Achaemenid and into the Sasanian period to represent queens and the goddess Anāhitā.[16]

By the end of the fifth century BCE Artaxerxes II had established royal patronage and the official cult of Anāhitā in the principal towns of the Persian Empire. We have the testimony of Berossus, referred to by Clemens of Alexandria (*Protreptikos* V, 3), that Artaxerxes II was the first to set up statues and worship the goddess – called in Greek Aphrodite Anaitis – in several major regional temples, including one in Bactria. The hymn to Anāhitā (in the *Yašt* 5 of the *Avesta*) presents a series of verses that vividly describes the image of the goddess. Boyce (1982/2011) asserts that the person who composed the verses was probably inspired by actually looking at icons of the goddess. These verses and other elements shift the final rendition of this hymn to the Sasanian period (third-seventh century CE). Anāhitā was a river goddess – perhaps originally a local goddess from Arachosia (the region around Kandahar). She was expected to grant fertility to the land and appears to have assimilated elements from Aši, the Iranian goddess of Fortune. Both are described as beautiful goddesses who ride chariots (Boyce 1982/2011). The chariot is an important symbolic element that Anāhitā and Aši have in common with other Near Eastern goddesses whose warrior nature is linked to Assyrian, Babylonian, and Persian ideas of kingship. However, there are differing opinions regarding the possibility that the cults of Nanā and Ishtar were each conflated with the cult of Anāhitā.[17] In describing Anāhitā's diadem as having one hundred stars (*Yašt* 5, 128), Panaino (2000, 38) notes that the goddess' crown is adorned with eight towers or palaces rather than eight

15 For an actual example of this kind of crown worn by Darius in the Bisutun relief, see Metzler (1994, fig. 51).

16 See, for instance, two gems from the Oxus treasure with Anāhitā (royal women?) holding a flower and a bird (Shepherd 1980, figs. 6 a-b). For other royal depictions with such an attribute, see, for instance, Spycket (1980, 43-44, figs. 1, 6, 7).

17 See, for instance, Rosenfield (1967, 87-88) and Boyce, Chaumont and Bier (1989/2011); for critical discussions about the Babylonian influence, see Panaino (2000, 36-39) and Ambos (2003, 255-258).

rays of light. Apart from a seal showing a Persian king (possibly Artaxerxes II) worshipping Anāhitā with a radiating halo standing on a lion,[18] there is no general consensus about how to interpret the Achaemenid evidence and identify images of female figures with mural crowns.

Figure 2.9: Achaemenid seal with king (possibly Artaxerxes II) worshipping Anāhitā standing on a lion.

Regardless of whether they represent goddesses or royal women (see Note 15), what is noticeable is the impact these images had on later Indo-Greek, Parthian, Kuṣāṇa, and Sasanian depictions of queens and goddesses with mural crowns in both Bactria and Gandhāra.

Numismatic evidence

The Hellenistic poliadic goddesses of Fortune, Tyche, 'arrived' in Bactria and the North-Western Indian regions after Achaemenid rule. Female divinities with mural crowns are represented on specific Greco-Bactrian and Indo-Greek coins. Through transmutations and appropriations evident on Indo-Scythian, Parthian and Kuṣāṇa coins, such poliadic representations can be part of a syncretic process in the formation of Indo-Iranian goddesses such as Ardoksho, Nanā, Durgā and Śrī-Lakṣmī during the Kuṣāṇa, Gupta, and Sasanian periods (c. second to seventh century CE).[19] Images minted by Andragoras, the satrap of Parthia, with mural crowns representing the embodiment either of cities or the power of the state, began to circulate in Central Asia around the fourth–third century BCE (Ghirshman 1974, pl. X.1; Widemann 2009, 47).

18 It is possible that the lion is of Assyrian inspiration.

19 For the numismatic aspects of the Greco-Bactrian and Indo-Scythians, see Mitchiner (1975-1976), Bopearachchi (1991) and Senior (2001); for the Kuṣāṇas, see Rosenfield (1967) and Göbl (1984).

Figure 2.10: Coin of Andragoras with a goddess wearing a mural crown.

The exact identification of the two satraps named Andragoras, mentioned by Justin (*Epitome* XII, 4. 12 and XLI, 4. 7-8) and respectively contemporaneous with Alexander the Great and Arsaces, remains controversial. It appears that the numismatic model of a turreted Tyche for Andragoras' coins was used around the mid-fourth century BCE by the rulers of Salamis of Cyprus, Evagoras II and his successors Pnytagoras and Nicocreon (Broucke 1994, 36, fig. 17; Matheson 1994a, 25; Matheson 1994b, 111, cat. no. 22).

It is possible that the notion of a 'national goddess' heralded by these coins was evolving in this eastern Mediterranean environment, characterised by a cross-pollination of religious ideas from various areas of influence (e.g. Persian, Syro-Phoenician, Cypriotic, Aegean, etc) related to aspects of war and protection. These notions, typical of the Syro-Anatolian goddesses, were beginning to overlap and merge with those of the classical Tyche. The religious syncretism of the Hellenised eastern regions can easily be illustrated by symbols associated with female images wearing a mural crown on Greco-Bactrian, Indo-Greek and Indo-Scythian coins. The basic symbolism of the city goddess developed into a more complex iconographic phenomenon from around the first half of the second century BCE. The amalgamation and appropriation of Persian, Bactrian, Classical, and Indian cultural aspects had already occurred with the Greek kings Pantaleon and Agathocles in the early second century BCE.[20]

20 The Greco-Bactrian coinage of this period shows a remarkable process of Indianisation with the adoption of diverse numismatic standards, shapes, languages and symbols. For the innovation introduced by Agathocles and Pantaleon, see, for instance, Bopearachchi (1991, 56-59) and Widemann (2009, 109, 116-117, 118); for the inception of a 'barbarised' culture with the introduction of bilingual coins, see also Di Castro (2005, 3, 6).

On coins issued by Greek rulers various goddesses with mural crowns can be seen carrying a palm leaf, a symbol of victory, and a lotus flower, a typical Indian attribute. The coins of Eucratides I show the city goddess of Kapiśa enthroned wearing a mural crown and flanked by the head of an elephant and a conical object; she holds a palm in her left hand, her right hand outstretched towards the elephant.[21] Hippostratos too adopted a victory palm for his Tyche.[22] It was only under the Indo-Greek king Peucolaos, who lived at beginning of the first century BCE, that the poliadic, or city goddess, departed from this model taking a lotus in her hand in addition to the palm (Mitchiner 1975-1976, no. 370; Bopearachchi 1991, 106, pl. 48.R).

Figure 2.11: Goddess with lotus, palm and mural crown on a coin of Peucolaos.

It appears that by adopting the highly symbolic lotus flower Peucolaos was attempting to connect with his Indian subjects. It is also possible that the iconography of the lotus goddess of Peucolaos is connected to images of the goddess of Puṣkalavatī[23] depicted on anonymous gold coins, dated from the second century to the mid-first century BCE.[24] The standing god-

21 As indicated on the legend of Eucratides' coins, this is the *Kavisiye nagara devatā* or 'the city goddess of Kapiśa'; see Mitchiner (1975-1976, no. 194) and Bopearachchi (1991, 216, pl. 22.121-122). For different interpretations, see also Narain (1957, 62-64) and Widemann (2009, 378, fig. 16-8), who considers this as an issue from Eucratides III.

22 See Mitchiner (1975-1976, no. 446) and Bopearachchi (1991, 360, pl. 64.10) (although Bopearachchi does not recognise the mural crown in the example of the Cabinet des Médailles of Paris).

23 The name Peucolaos seems to derive from Peukelaitis (Mukherjee 1969, 74, n. 27).

24 See Mukherjee (1969, 13, 71-74, 122-123, pl. XV.54). Mitchiner (1975-1976, no. 162) believes that it is datable to the period of Agathocles, first quarter of the second century BCE, while Widemann (2009, 172, fig. 8.4) dates it to the second half of the second century BCE. On the other hand, Sachs identifies the goddess as Lakṣmī because of the lotus in her hand, and dates it to the period of the Indo-Scythian king Azes, corresponding to the mid first century BCE (Bopearachchi

dess of Puṣkalavatī wearing classical garments, an unusual three-pronged headgear (only visible on one specimen), and holding a lotus in her right hand was interpreted originally as Ambā-Durgā, owing to a mistaken reconstruction of the legend.

From evidence found on a coin with a better preserved inscription, the name of the goddess can be read as *drupasaya*, which may correspond to the Sanskrit *duṣprasahya*, meaning 'hard to conquer'. Therefore, a possible reading can be 'the invincible deity of Puṣkalavatī' (Senior and Babar 1998, 13; Senior 2001, vol. II, 116).[25] The attribute *drupasaya* or 'unconquerable' could be appropriate both for a warrior goddess and a town; it alludes to the warrior goddess Durgā that may have a direct relationship in the Śaivite milieu (Di Castro 2012c, 15). In the Kuṣāṇa period Durgā is generally represented on a lion and armed with a trident (see Srinivasan 1997, 285-286, pls. 20.1, 20.2, 20.9; Di Castro 2015, 277).

Figure 2.12: Coin of Puṣkalavatī with the bull and the goddess holding a lotus.

A trident standing alone already appears on Demetrios I's coins (Bopearachchi 1991, 167, pl. 5), and also appears on some Kuṣāṇa coins of Wima (Rosenfield 1967, pls. II.28, VIII.157; Göbl 1984, no. 9).[26] On

et al. 2003, 143, no. 126).

25 But see also the perplexities about the name expressed by Fussman (2001, 258).

26 The connections between the iconography of Śiva and Poseidon on pre-Kuṣāṇa coins have been discussed by various scholars, for example, by Cribb and Bopearachchi in Errington, *et al.* (1992, 64, 85, cat. nos. 32-33, 85, 87) and MacDowall (2007, 240, 253, 255, fig. 9.72). On the *triśūla*, see also Giuliano (2004). The trident clearly refers to the natural phenomena that are under Poseidon's control. With this weapon he causes earthquakes and lets waters flow out of the ground. Poseidon embodies primordial natural forces of immeasurable energy; he is, interestingly, also associated with the bull and can, in fact, be called *Taureos*, 'Bull-Poseidon' (Burkert 1985, 138-139). In some later narratives, Śiva is using the trident/*triśūla* to release water from the earth. A medieval Sanskrit source from Kashmir describes how the river Vitastā/Jhelum emerged from underground after Śiva hit the earth with his *triśūla* at Śūlabheda, meaning 'the place where the Śūla of Śiva struck the earth' (Sanderson 2004, 281).

Figure 2.13: Durgā standing on a lion and holding a trident from Mathura (Berlin Museum for Asian Art).

the obverse of the Puṣkalavatī coin there is a bull with Greek and Kharoṣṭhī legends (*tauros – ushabe*), both terms meaning bull. Here the bull most likely indicates a reference to the Indian god Śiva. In the *Lexicon* of Hesychius of Alexandria (fifth century CE), there is a mention of Gandhāra and the cult of the bull: *Gandaros: o taurokrates par Indois* (Γάνδαρος: ὁ ταυροκράτησ παῤ Ἰνδοῖς, 'the Gandhāran god: the Indian lord of the bull'). Tucci (1963, 159, 160) asserts that 'Śiva is called Gandhara'; the name *Gandaros* can mean the 'lord of the bull' that is Śiva's vehicle; consequently *Gandaros* – the god of Gandhāra – can be identified with Śiva. It is reasonable, therefore, to consider a Śaivite connection for the goddess of Puṣkalavatī. Moreover, it is logical to question whether Peucolaos was representing the Tyche of the Greek Peukelaitis, as an *interpretatio graeca* of a local goddess (also called the 'unconquerable', *drupasaya*), or another goddess associated with the lotus, like Lakṣmī, if not a local Yakṣiṇī (dryad or nymph). Whether an Indian goddess was appropriating classical attire or, conversely, a classical tutelary divinity appropriated an Indian name, hence assuming an Indian identity, is still uncertain.

Religious and artistic syncretism, a feature most evident on numismatic emissions, became more prominent with the migrations of the Śaka and Yuezhi/Kuṣāṇa groups into Bactria and Gandhāra around the mid-first century BCE. A different organisation of symbols emerged in Indo-Scythian coinage; the mural crown now became associated with a staff, a palm, a lotus flower, a wreath, a wheel, or a lamp.[27] All these symbols are generally correlated to ideas and values of royal investiture, power, justice and victory. Moreover, actual historical personages could also be depicted wearing the mural crown; Machene, the Greek queen of Taxila and consort of the Indo-Scythian king Maues, is shown wearing a mural crown, a classical Greek garment and sitting on a throne with an outstretched hand and a long staff.[28]

Figure 2.14: Coin of Machene Queen of Taxila.

Despite uncertainty as to whether this image is a city goddess or not (Bopearachchi *et al.* 2003, 140, fig. 115), the obverse Greek legend – *Basilisses Theotropou Machene* – indicates a process of deification of the queen. The title *Theotropou*, meaning 'godlike', had been used some thirty years earlier during the late second century BCE by the Indo-Greek queen Agathocleia, Menander's widow.[29]

The mural crown reappeared on many coins in the Parthian and Sasanian worlds, after it had been appropriated by the Hellenistic Tyche. The Parthian queen Musa, who was originally a Roman slave donated to Phraates IV by Augustus, went from favourite concubine to 'heavenly queen goddess' as indicated on a coin legend issued in association with her royal son, Phraataces (c. 2 BCE – 4 CE).[30] Queen Musa is also depicted

27 See, for instance, Mitchiner (1975-1976, nos. 714, 720, 722, 723, 780, 781-782, 795) and Senior (2001, vol. I, 157-158, 164, vol. II, types 3.1, 4.1, 19.1, 22.1, 23.1, 34.1, 35.1).

28 See, for example, Le Rider (1967, fig. 3), Senior (2001, vol. II, 27-28, type 4.1T (the same type of goddess in throne with mural crown but without the name Machene is on the types 3.1T, 3.2T, 3.1D-3.5D)), and Widemann (2009, 249-251).

29 On a joint emission with her son Strato, see Bopearachchi (1991, 88-90, 251-253, pls. 34.E-I, 35.A-D) and Widemann (2009, 249-252).

30 '*Theas Ouranias Mouses Basilisses*' (Wroth 1903, 139-140, pl. XXIV.1-3). There

wearing the traditional Persian mural crown with crenellations on a marble portrait from Susa.[31] Similarly, a Sasanian princess, perhaps Šāpūr I's queen, was portrayed on a seal wearing a crown with stepped crenellations (Ghirshman 1982, 241, fig. 294 B). Various images of the goddess Anāhitā with a mural crown were made during the Sasanian period, as can be seen on the investiture relief of Narseh (c. 293–302 CE) at Naqš-e Rostam,[32] and on a coin of Hormozd I, representing the king and a goddess with a mural crown before a fire altar (Pope 1938-1939, vol. 4, pl. 254.b; Shayegan 2004/2012). Finally, by the last quarter of the fourth century CE, the goddess Anāhitā sitting on a throne under an arch, with halo, mural crown, wreath and staff, is attested on Bactrian and Gandhāran coins of the Kuṣāṇo-Sasanian ruler Ardašīr II Kušānšāh (Carter 1985, pl. 47.3; Göbl 1985, no. 1028).[33]

The cornucopia

The cornucopia – a large horn full of fruits and sheaves of grain, signifying abundance, wealth and fertility – is mythically connected to Amalthea the goat/nymph and wet-nurse to the baby Zeus.[34] The cornucopia, a typical attribute of the Greek goddesses Demeter and Tyche, can be found on Bactrian Hellenistic artefacts and coins like the elegant double decadrachme of Amyntas (Mitchiner 1975-1976, no. 386; Bopearachchi 1991, 299, pl. 46 C, série 2; Di Castro 2015, 282-285), and can also be associated with other goddesses seen on Indo-Scythian and Indo-Parthian coins like those minted by Azes (Mitchiner 1975-1976, no. 873; Senior 2001, vol. II,

is a noteworthy similarity between some coins of Phraates IV (Phraataces) and the Indo-Scythian Kshatrap Jihoṇika/Zeionises, depicting a Tyche-like goddess with cornucopia and wreath performing the investiture of the king. Interestingly, Phraates IV fled among the Indo-Scythians during the civil war which lasted for several years (c. 31–25 BCE) in Parthia (Senior 2001, vol. I, 119, 147, no. 132; Rosenfield 1967, pl. XV.278-279; Errington *et al.* 1992, 83 cat no. 81). Srinivasan (2010, 83) identifies the goddess on the Parthian coins as Ardoksho.

31 According to Colledge (1977, 84), this can be an image of a classical Fortune or Tyche.

32 Where she is represented with a tall stepped crown; see Boyce, Chaumont and Bier (1989/2011), Ghirshman (1982, figs. 158, 218) and Shepherd (1980, fig. 1).

33 On the Kušānšāh and their chronological sequence, see also Cribb (1990) and Dani and Litvinsky (1996, 104-108).

34 The cornucopia is also connected to the confrontation of Heracles and the river god Achelous in his bull form. For references to classical authors, see Di Castro (2012b, 176 n. 2); for the symbolic implications of the cornucopia with a goat's head termination, see Di Castro (2015).

types 94, 101, 112, 122-123, 132, 139). From monetary evidence it appears that, with the exception of a few coin types, the cornucopia became the main attribute of the Kuṣāṇa goddess Ardoksho.[35] The transmission of symbols used in official numismatic iconography reflects state propaganda and ideology. Although the religiosity evident on the private seals from the Indo-Scythian to the later Kuṣāṇa appears quite different from that on the coinage of the period, the data from the seals' diffusion shows that, by around the first century BCE, the cornucopia had become a popular symbol in the personal domain.[36] As cited above the cornucopia was associated in Gandhāran sculptures as personifying the goddess of Kapilavastu, as a tutelary couple, or it appeared in isolated images like the statuette of Śrī standing next to a cornucopia with a goat head at its narrow tip.[37] In India the symbol of fecundity and prosperity is also expressed by the lotus; hence the cornucopia could be transformed into a flower element, which eventually led to the replacement of the cornucopia by a lotus in later iconography. Around the fourth century CE Ardoksho became the model used on Gupta coins which depicted Lakṣmī with cornucopia, either standing, or sitting on a throne, or a lion. It is with Huviṣka's coins that a number of stylisations of cornucopia are perceived. It is possible that this variability on Kuṣāṇa coins could mean that the transition to a flower-like symbol had

35 For a summary of the interpretations regarding the nature of Ardoksho, see Rosenfield (1967, 74-75). Harmatta (1961, 198-199; Harmatta *et al.* 1994, 325) maintains that Ardoksho is connected to the Avestan goddess Ardvī Sūra Anāhitā who grants boundless royal powers to just kings. Some coins of Huviṣka show a goddess exactly like Ardoksho but with the legend 'Mao' (Mah), which designates the Iranian lunar god (Rosenfield 1967, 100, pl. III. 43; Göbl 1984, nos. 880-883); one may speculate in this case whether a female goddess is appropriating the name and function of the male lunar god. In another coin type of Huviṣka Oanindo, the winged goddess of Victory, has a wreath in her right hand and a cornucopia in her left (Rosenfield 1967, 91, pl. VIII. 151; Göbl 1984, no. 245).

36 See, for instance, Callieri (1997, 270, 272, 274 Table 16, cat. nos. 1.10, 5.2, 6.3, 7.5-7.12, S 13, U 6.1, U 7.11-12, U 7.15-20, U 7.22; 2002, 54-55, 58 (incorrectly referred to as 'Callieri 1999' in Di Castro 2012b, 177, 183)); see also Rahman and Falk (2011, cat. nos. 06.05.01-06.05.30, 07.02.01-07.02.02, 07.04.13, 07.04.17-07.04.20, 07.04.22-07.04.23). The diffusion of the cornucopia around the first century BCE to the first century CE is also confirmed by other material evidence, such as silver bowls, bronze figurines, etc.; see, for instance, Di Castro (2015, 282-283).

37 See, for instance, Kurita (2003b, figs. 417, 420, 421, 479-482, 484-486, 497-505, 916); for the image of Śrī, see Fussman (1988); on the tutelary couple, see Note 6 above. On a stele from Paitava representing the Miracle of Śrāvastī, the small female figure on the left side of the Buddha is carrying a cornucopia while the male counterpart (Vajrapāṇi) is holding an object like a *vajra* or a club (Rosenfield 1967, pl. 106). See also the niche V2 from Hadda in Afghanistan with a similar 'tutelary couple' at the sides of the main Buddha (Tarzi 1976, figs. 9-13).

already started before the Gupta period.[38] A similar development can also be ascertained on two gold repoussé pendants depicting a goddess regarded as Hārītī holding a lotus and stem-like cornucopia, dating from the third–fourth century CE (Czuma 1985, 157-158, no. 75; Errington *et al.* 1992, 143, no. 143). Modifications and substitutions of Lakṣmī's cornucopia with a floral symbol (lotus) are discernible in a number of numismatic and sculptural artefacts of both the Gupta and post-Gupta periods.[39]

Figure 2.15: Gold pendant depicting a goddess and floral cornucopia (Cleveland Museum of Art).

In Pakistan, the Swat cave of Kashmir Smast is the sacred place where a popular miraculous image of the goddess Bhīmādevī, carved in the rock on the mountain above a temple of Maheśvara Śiva, is mentioned by Xuan Zang, the Buddhist monk who visited this area in the seventh century. The goddess attracted many pilgrims and the temple was attended by ascetics

38 For the Huviṣka's types showing a standing Ardoksho, see Göbl (1984, nos. 154, 182-183, 218-223A, 261-262, 284-287, 306-307, 316, 330-331, 362-365A, 378-380). In a unique type by Huviṣka, with the couple Ommo and Oesho (Umā and Śiva), Ommo carries a flower or a stylised cornucopia (Göbl 1984, no. 310). The monetary emissions of later Kuṣāṇa rulers are mainly characterised by the representations of the enthroned goddess Ardoksho, from Kaniṣka I to Vasudeva III (Göbl 1984, nos. 538-539, 541-545, 549-553, 556-568A, 569-596, 598-620, 780, 1015-1019, 1022-124A).

39 For the appropriation, adaptation and transformation of cornucopia and lotus, see, for instance, Diserens (1993), Carter (2010a) and Di Castro (2012b, 175-176; 2015, 277-278). A stylised flower/cornucopia is represented on some seventh century CE Sogdian ossuaries from Chorasmia associated with Anāhitā, who wears a typical Sasanian mural crown (Marshak and Grenet 2002, fig. 230); the cornucopia looking like a flower stem is very similar to the gold medallions depicting Hārītī. Moreover, the undulating hem of Hārītī's upper garment on both medallions is also very close to a rendition of similar garments worn by a goddess in a painting from Panjikant dated around 500 CE (Marshak and Grenet 2002, fig. 162).

who covered their bodies with ashes and performed sacrifices (Beal 1884, I, 113-114). On a number of seals from Kashmir Smast, Bhīmādevī is generally depicted as Lajjāgaurī, the 'shameless' goddess with legs spread, exposing her vulva next to a trident and a *liṅga* (Rahman and Falk 2011, 24-25, cat. nos. 07.04.01, 07.04.02, 07.04.04, 07.04.07, 07.04.09, 07.04.11-07.04.13, 07.04.15).[40] On the seals, the figure of Lajjāgaurī is also replaced by an enthroned matronly goddess with cornucopia similar to the Ardoksho images found on various Kuṣāṇa coins (Rahman and Falk 2011, 99, cat. nos. 07.04.13, 07.04.17; Göbl 1985, nos. 538, 541, 555, 780).

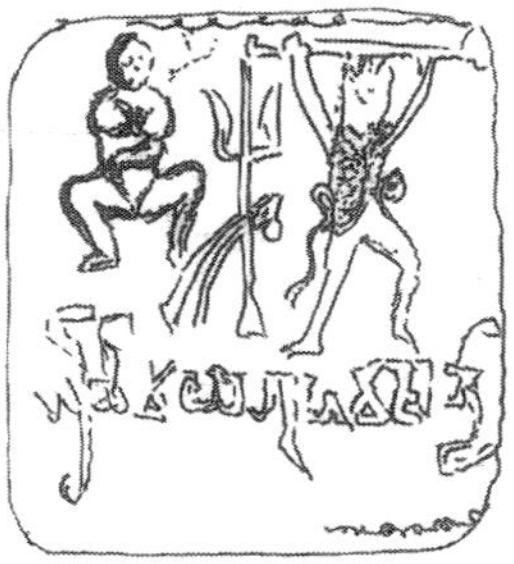

Figure 2.16: Seal with Lajjāgaurī from Kashmir Smast.

Figure 2.17: Seal with matronly goddess holding a cornucopia from Kashmir Smast.

The way of representing Bhīmādevī as the naked Lajjāgaurī, as well as the decently attired Ardoksho (or Hārītī), implies an appropriation of

40 On Lajjāgaurī, see also Bolon (1992). Interestingly, other non-Buddhist Gandhāran goddesses are associated with the trident. The so-called Hārītī from Sahri Bahlol (Kurita 2003b, fig. 488), with four arms holding a trident, a vessel, a child and a cup, can be considered in connection to śaivite contexts too (Di Castro 2015, 276-277). Siudmak (2013, 105-107, pl. 39) identifies this image as Māheśvarī. Kurita (2003b, fig. 489) refers to another four-armed goddess holding a trident, a cup, a sword, and a damaged object.

a local fertility cult by Hindus who respectively adopted both northern and southern visual traditions for the symbolic representations of this Śaivite goddess. Based on the evidence of the seals and other archaeological material from the temple of Maheśvara Śiva, the transformation of the original sacred cave of the local goddess into a *devī tīrtha*, a sacred place of the Śākta cults, occurred between the second and the fifth–sixth century CE.[41]

The Gandhāran process of appropriation and amalgamation that involved goddesses like Ardoksho, Nanā, Anāhitā, Tyche, Hārītī, Durgā and Śrī-Lakṣmī is visible on the seals from the Indo-Scythian period and a gradual syncretic transformation can be traced down to the composite votive statuettes from Swat and Kashmir during the fifth–sixth century CE.[42]

Figure 2.18: Seal with goddess wearing a loincloth and holding flower and cornucopia from Kashmir Smast.

The goddess and the lion

Bhattacharyya (1996, 43-44) makes reference to Vedic narratives related to the goddess Vāc who can also be described as 'naked' and can take the form of a lion, although it is not until the Maurya period (fourth–second centuries BCE) that a naked goddess is found represented on ringstones in association with lions (and other wild animals), lunar crescents and plant symbolism (Gupta 1980, 55, 57, 59, pls. 20b, 21c, 21c, 26a, 29c; Di Castro 2008, 33-35). For the association of a goddess with a lion it is possible to recognise some numismatic examples that precede

41 For the Śiva temple at Kashmir Smast, see Khan (2005); for the Śākta connections, see Bhattacharyya (1996, 75-76, 97-98, 121; 1999, 60, 120, 233, 312).

42 For the seal and statuettes, see, for instance, Diserens (1993), Srinivasan (2010), Rahman and Falk (2011, 07.02.01-07.02.05), Di Castro (2012b) and Siudmak (2013, 160, 180-183, pls. 61, 75).

the Kuṣāṇa period. A goddess, possibly a Yakṣiṇī, is depicted in Indian dress and holds a flower on the obverse of an Indo-Greek coin issued by Agathocles. The reverse of the coin depicts a lion (Bopearachchi 1991, pl. 7 nos. 14-19 series 10).

Figure 2.19: Coin of Agathocles with Yakṣiṇī and lion.

A late first century BCE coin of the nomadic ruler Sapadbizes displays interesting symbolic associations with the goddess Nanā/Nanaia. The obverse carries the ruler's portrait while the reverse presents a moon crescent over a lion with the legend 'Nanaia' (Mitchiner type 509).

Figure 2.20: Coin of Sapadbizes with lion and the legend Nanaia.

According to the evidence derived from the Kuṣāṇa inscription of Rabatak, Nanā was the supreme goddess of the Kuṣāṇa kingdom who conferred royal power upon Kaniṣka. On many Kuṣāṇa coins and seals Nanā is typically represented as holding a sceptre with a lion finial and a bowl. However, on a number of coins and seals she is also represented as riding a lion – and it is certainly not by a mere coincidence that during this period the Indian goddess Durgā was also represented either riding or standing on a lion.[43] The political character of Nanā becomes clear from the evidence discovered at the sanctuary of Māṭ near Mathura, where Kuṣāṇa dynastic statues have been found together with cultic icons apparently pertinent to a Śaivite milieu (Rosenfield 1967, 140-151; Fussman 1989, 198-199). The Royal Fortune of the Kuṣāṇa (see Note 7), along with other divinities who protected the royal dynasty, was worshipped in this important shrine. It is conceivable that a fragmentary sculpture from Māṭ depicting the lower part of a goddess standing on a lion is to be interpreted in relation to the royal cult of Nanā (Rosenfield 1967, 150, fig. 9; Srinivasan 1997, 291, pls. 20.23-24).

Does this represent a case of appropriation of a goddess like Pārvatī (Verardi 1983, 233), or rather Śrī (Fussman 1989, 198-199), by the Kuṣāṇa rulers for their dynastic rituals, or is this an Indian (Gangetic) manifestation of Nanā? In any case the ideology known to be connected to the Kuṣāṇa kingship would have facilitated the amalgamation of goddess imagery in the North West as well as in the Gangetic regions. It is intriguing to look at the similarities between early images of Durgā, whose *vāhana* (vehicle) is the lion and the Māṭ sculpture. An example is the Kuṣāṇa sculpture from the Berlin Museum where Durgā is standing on a lion holding a trident (Figure 2.13). Another image that can be compared to it is a fragmentary Gandhāran piece of which only the lion, part of the garment and feet are visible (Kurita 2003b, fig. 442).

With regard to Anāhitā and the lion, the Achaemenid seal previously mentioned points to noticeable conflations with other Near Eastern divinities (Figure 2.9). It is interesting to note that the second–third century CE author Aelian (*On the Nature of Animals* XII. 23) refers to a temple in Elam dedicated to Anaitis where tamed lions were welcoming the people who visited the shrine. Yet, in order to substantiate the adoption of the lion as a *vāhana*, a number of scholars have made the unsubstantiated assumption that the second century BCE silver disc from Ai Khanum depicting Cybele riding on a chariot pulled by lions,

43 On the Rabatak inscription, see Sims-Williams and Cribb (1995-96) and Fussman (2001). The goddess, also named Nano, Nonyo, Nanaia, Nanashao and Shaonana on Kaniṣka and Huviṣka coins, is generally depicted standing with a sceptre and often with a bowl; see Göbl (1984, nos. 27, 35-36, 54, 60, 80, 152-153, 165-167, 281-283, 300-303, 313-315A, 324-329, 358-361 (no. 359 Nanā on lion), 376-377, 660 (Nanā on lion), 776-779A, 805-810, 839-846, 884, 896-899). On Nanā, see Note 13 above, Rosenfield (1967, 73, 83-91), Mukherjee (1969), Ghose (2006) and Carter (2010b).

is the origin of the diffusion of this important symbolic feature of the Hindu goddess Durgā.

Figure 2.21: Silver disc with Cybele from Ai Khanum (National Museum, Kabul).

In reality it seems almost that Cybele has been 'appropriated' by modern scholars rather than by ancient artists.[44] The migration and appropriation of symbols can in certain cases also be perceived as a consequence of the migration of peoples, like the migrations of Greek and Macedonian colonists to Hellenised Bactrian centres. Although the Greek colonists might have carried images of the goddess Cybele to Ai Khanum, along with other cultic objects, the archaeological evidence seems to support the case that the cult of Cybele was not particularly popular amongst the populations living in the Bactro-Gandhāran regions in the late Hellenistic period. Without ruling out a possible role for the iconography of Cybele, it seems more likely that the much more popular goddess, Nanā on lion, had a significant role in shaping the traits of the Indian Durgā, in particular her association with lion and kingship rituals.

44 For the archaeological report describing the silver disc of Cybele, see Francfort (1984, 93-104). As for the modern interpretations, for instance, Joshi (1994) maintains that Cybele has exerted a deep influence on the formation of the iconography of Durgā; Ghose (2006, 98) reinterprets the silver artefacts as a manifestation of syncretic 'orientalised' goddesses; Pal (2009, 85-87) believes that Durgā's lion chariot was adopted from the classical world in Kashmir and looks at the disc of Cybele from Ai Khanum for a probable source. Very close to Ghose's position is Carter (2010b, 143) who, instead of Cybele, identifies the goddess from Ai Khanum as Nanā. It is highly speculative to derive an assumed diffusion of the cult of Cybele based only on one example; despite its importance, the artefact constitutes limited evidence that is not helpful in justifying the appearance of lion chariot iconography at a much later period.

Concluding observations

A few observations can be suggested when we discuss the process of transferral, adaptation and appropriation of ancient goddesses in Gandhāra. For example, a move towards a more private sphere of religiosity emerges when considering the seals discussed earlier. The notion of a poliadic goddess that represented political power and wealth, prosperity and protection of the state and its populations, typically exemplified by the classical goddess Tyche, became increasingly personalised and embodied different values of individual fortune, power and protection. This may also have had implications in the formation of personal protective divinities in both the Buddhist and Hindu contexts.

Despite uncertainties in establishing accurate identities for many goddesses, for instance the *nagaradevatā* of Puṣkalavatī, the goddess of the City of the Lotus, connections to Śaivite milieus cannot be lightly dismissed. This is also true in consideration of circumstances where Mediterranean, Mesopotamian, Bactrian, Inner Asian, Indian and local divinities, political and private spheres, each pertinent to different social groups, and historical conjunctures become entangled and overlap. From such a perspective it is also possible to see how the suggestive hypothesis by Verardi (2011, 308) gives reasons for the presence of the Durgā Mahiṣāsuramardinī in the last phase of the Buddhist monastery at Tapa Sardār near Ghazni.[45] In this case the appropriation in Vajrayāna circles of a Hindu goddess 'subjugated' by powerful Buddhist Tantric divinities related more to political factors rather than theological ones.

In conclusion, the vitality and persistence of the cult of the Kuṣāṇa goddess Nanā are remarkable when the long-term effects of the cultural and religious entanglements that occurred at the Indo-Iranian borderland are considered. Following the demise of the Kuṣāṇa rule, Nanā's popularity did not decline. After being integrated into the mediaeval Śākta movement, in modern times her cult is still significant in many areas of the Indian subcontinent. In addition to the more popular shrine of Hinglaj in Baluchistan,[46] mention can be made of modern-day shrines to Bibi Nani in Afghanistan as well. As Potts (2001, 31 and n. 81) asserts, this demonstrates the 'long period of profound influence' exerted by Nanā.

45 For Tapa Sardār, see Taddei and Verardi (1978, in particular pp. 47-58 for Chapel 23, where the image of Durgā was found) and the more recent Verardi and Paparatti (2005).

46 For the shrine of Bibi Nani in Baluchistan, see Jayakar (1989, 154-155), Bhattacharyya (1996, 87) and Shah (2009).

Bibliography

Ambos, C. 2003. 'Nanaja – eine ikonographische Studie zur Darstellung einer altorientalischen Göttin in hellenistisch-parthischer Zeit'. *Zeitschrift fur Assyrologie* 93: 231-272.

Bachhofer L. 1937. 'Pañcika und Hārītī – ΦΑΡΟ und ΑΡΔΟΧÞΟ'. *Ostasiatische Zeitschrift* 13: 6-15.

Beal, S. 1981 [1884]. *Si-Yu-ki: Buddhist Records of the Western World, Translated from the Chinese of Hiuen Tsiang (A.D. 629)*. Delhi: Motilal Banarsidass.

Bhattacharyya, N.N. 1996. *History of the Śākta Religion*. New Delhi: Munshiram Manoharlal.

Bhattacharyya, N.N. 1999. *The Indian Mother Goddess*, third enlarged edition. New Delhi: Manohar

Bolon, C. 1992. *Forms of the Goddess Lajjā Gaurī in Indian Art*. University Park: Pennsylvania State University Press.

Bopearachchi, O. 1991. *Monnaies gréco-bactriennes et indo-grecques: catalogue raisonné*. Paris: Bibliothèque Nationale.

Bopearachchi, O., C. Landes and C. Sachs (eds.) 2003. *De l'Indus à l'Oxus: archéologie de l'Asie centrale: catalogue de l'exposition*. Lattes: Association imago-musée de Lattes.

Boyce, M. 1982/2011. 'Ābān Yašt'. In E. Yarshater (ed.), *Encyclopædia Iranica*, http://www.iranicaonline.org/articles/aban-yast (accessed 30 March 2016).

Boyce, M., M.L. Chaumont and C. Bier. 1989/2011. 'Anāhīd'. In E. Yarshater (ed.), *Encyclopædia Iranica*, http://www.iranicaonline.org/articles/anahid (accessed 30 March 2016).

Broucke, P.B.J.F. 1994. 'Tyche and the fortune of cities in the Greek and Roman world'. In S.B. Matheson (ed.), *An Obsession with Fortune. Tyche in Greek and Roman Art*, 35-49. New Haven: Yale University Art Gallery.

Burkert, W. 1985. *Greek Religion*. Oxford: Blackwell.

Burkert, W. 2000. 'Migrating gods and syncretisms: forms of cult transfer in the Ancient Mediterranean'. In A. Ovadiah (ed.), *Mediterranean Cultural Interaction: the Howard Gilman International Conferences II*, 1-21. Tel Aviv: Ramot.

Bussagli, M. 1951. 'Royauté, guerre et fecondité: à propos d'une monnaie kuṣāṇa'. *Revue de l'histoire des religions* 140: 129-154.

Bussagli, M. 1984. 'Variabilità di valori nel "sistema" delle "coppie" in epoca kuṣāṇa e in Asia Centrale'. In L. Lanciotti (ed.), *Incontro di religioni in Asia tra il III e il X secolo d.C.*, 115-146. Firenze: Olschki.

Callieri, P. 1997. *Seals and Sealings from the North-West of the Indian Subcontinent and Afghanistan (4th Century BC–11th Century AD): Local, Indian, Sassanian, Graeco-Persian, Sogdian, Roman*. Napoli: Istituto Universitario Orientale, Istituto Italiano per l'Africa e l'Oriente.

Callieri, P. 2002. 'Regalità, guerra e fecondità: interpretazione iconografica della glittica del Nord-Ovest del sub-continente Indiano di età Kuṣāṇa'. In C. Silvi Antonini, B.M. Alfieri and A. Santoro (eds), *Oriente & Occidente: Convegno in Ricordo di Mario Bussagli*, 53-65. Roma: Istituti Editoriali Poligrafici Internazionali.

Carter, M.L. 1985. 'A numismatic reconstruction of Kushano-Sasanian history'. *American Numismatic Society - Museum Notes* 30: 215-61.

Carter, M.L. 2010a. 'The evolution of the Goddess with the cornucopia'. In P.Callieri and L. Colliva (eds.) *South Asian Archaeology 2007: Proceedings of the 19th Meeting of the European Association of South Asian Archaeology in Ravenna, Italy, July 2007* (BAR International Series 2133), 53-59. Oxford: Archaeopress.

Carter, M.L. 2010b. 'Nanā with crescent Kuṣāṇa numismatic imagery'. In E. Franco and M. Zin (eds.), *From Turfan to Ajanta: Festschrift for Dieter Schlingloff on the Occasion of his Eightieth Birthday*, vol. I, 141-150. Lumbini: Lumbini International Research Institute.

Colledge, M.A.R. 1977. *Parthian Art*. London: Paul Elek.

Cribb, J. 1990. 'Numismatic evidence for Kushano-Sasanian chronology'. *Studia Iranica* 19 (2): 151-193.

Czuma, S.J. 1985. *Kushan sculpture: images from early India*. Cleveland: Cleveland Museum of Art and Indiana University Press.

Dani, A.H., and B.A. Litvinsky. 1996. 'The Kushano-Sasanian kingdom'. In B.A. Litvinsky, Zhang Guang-da and R. Shabani Samghabadi (eds.), *History of Civilizations of Central Asia*, vol. 3, *The Crossroads of Civilizations: A.D. 250 to 750*, 103-118. Paris: UNESCO.

Di Castro, A.A. 2005. 'The barbarisation of Bactria'. In *Cultural Interaction in Afghanistan, c. 300 BCE to 300 CE* (Working Paper 5), 1-18. Clayton: Centre of South Asian Studies, Monash University.

Di Castro, A.A. 2008. 'Archaeology of the goddess: an Indian paradox'. In J.B. Bapat and I. Mabbett (eds.), *The Iconic Female. Goddesses of India, Nepal and Tibet*, 21-41. Clayton: Monash University Press.

Di Castro, A.A. 2012a. 'Graves, trees and powerful spirits as archaeological indicators of sacred spaces'. In A. Haendel (ed.), *Old Myths and New Approaches: Interpreting Ancient Religious Sites in Southeast Asia*, 237-251. Clayton: Monash University Publishing.

Di Castro, A.A. 2012b. 'Aspects of the Indian fortune'. In I. Mabbett (ed.), *Prācyaprajñāpradīpa: Professor Dr. Samaresh Bandyopadhyay Felicitation Volume on Early Indian History and Culture*, 172-184. Kolkata: Forum for the Felicitation of Professor Dr Samaresh Bandyopadhyay and the North American Institute for Oriental and Classical Studies.

Di Castro, A.A. 2012c. 'Hestia, a Tabula Iliaca and Poseidon's trident: Symbols' adaptations of some Bactrian and Gandhāran Divinities'. In E. Anagnostou-Laoutides (ed.), *ASCS 33 Selected Proceedings (2012)* [Proceedings of the 33rd Conference of the Australasian Society for Classical Studies], available online at http://www.ascs.org.au/news/ascs33/.

Di Castro, A.A. 2015. 'Goat heads and goddesses in Swāt, Gandhāra and Kashmir and connected problems'. In A.A. Di Castro and D. Templeman (eds.), *Asian Horizons: Giuseppe Tucci's Buddhist, Indian, Himalayan and Central Asian Studies* (Serie Orientale Roma, CVI), 263-295. Melbourne: Monash University Publishing.

Diserens, H. 1993. 'La statue de Brār (Kaśmīr) retrouvée'. *Arts Asiatiques* 48: 72-85.

Errington, E., Cribb, J. and Claringbull, M. (eds.) 1992, *The Crossroads of Asia: Transformation in Image and Symbol in the Art of Ancient Afghanistan and Pakistan*. Cambridge: Ancient India and Iran Trust.

Foucher, A. 1905. *L'art gréco-bouddhique du Gandhâra,* vol. 1. Paris: Imprimerie nationale.

Francfort, H.P. 1984. *Fouilles d'Aï Khanoum, III. Le sanctuaire du temple à niches indentées, 2, Les trouvailles* (MDAFA XXVII). Paris: De Boccard.

Fussman, G. 1988. 'Une statuette gandharienne de la déesse Śrī'. *Annali dell'Istituto Universitario Orientale* 48: 1-9.

Fussman, G. 1989. 'The Māṭ *devakula*: a new approach to its understanding'. In D.M. Srinivasan (ed.), *Mathurā: The Cultural Heritage*, 193-199. New Delhi: Manohar for the American Institute of Indian Studies.

Fussman, G. 2001. 'L'inscription de Rabatak, la Bactriane et les Kouchans'. In P. Leriche, C. Pidaev, M. Gelin and K. Abdoullaev (eds.), *La Bactriane au carrefour des routes et des civilisations de l'Asie central, 251-291*. Paris:

Maisonneuve et Larose.

Ghirshman, R. 1974. 'Un tétradrachme d'Andragoras de la collection de M. Foroughi'. In D.K. Kouymjian (ed.), *Near Eastern Numismatics, Iconography, Epigraphy and History: Studies in Honour of George C. Miles*, 1–18. Beirut: American University of Beirut Press.

Ghirshman, R. 1982 [1962]. *Arte Persiana: Parti e Sassanidi*. Milano: Rizzoli.

Ghose, M. 2006. 'Nana: the "original" goddess on the lion'. *Journal of Inner Asian Art and Archaeology* 1: 97-112.

Giuliano, L. 2004. 'Studies in early Śaiva iconography: (I) the origin of the *triśūla* and some related problems'. *Silk Road Art and Archaeology* 10: 51-96.

Gnoli, G. 1996. 'Note Kuṣāṇa: a proposito di una recente interpretazione di Pharro'. In *Convegno internazionale sul tema: La Persia e l'Asia centrale da Alessandro al X secolo (Roma 9-12 novembre 1994)*, 685-702. Roma: Accademia nazionale dei Lincei, Istituto Italiano per il Medio ed Estremo Oriente.

Gnoli, G. 1999. 'Farr(ah)'. In E. Yarshater (ed.), *Encyclopædia Iranica*, http://www.iranicaonline.org/articles/farrah (accessed 30 March 2016).

Göbl, R. 1984. *System und Chronologie der Münzprägung des Kušānreiches*. Wien: Österreichische Akademie der Wissenschaften.

Grenet, F., and B. Marshak. 1998. 'Le mythe de Nana dans l'art de la Sogdiane'. *Arts Asiatiques* 53: 5-18.

Gupta, P.L. 1980. *The Roots of Indian Art. Delhi:* B.R. Publishing.

Harmatta, J. 1961. 'Cušanica'. *Acta Orientalia Hungaricae* 11: 191-220.

Harmatta, J., *et al.* 1994. 'Religions in the Kusana Empire'. In J. Harmatta, B.N. Puri and G.F. Etemadi (eds.), *History of Civilizations of Central Asia*, vol. 2, *The Development of Sedentary and Nomadic Civilizations: 700 B.C. to A.D. 250*, 313-29. Paris: UNESCO.

Hoffner, H.A. 1969. 'The "City of Gold" and the "City of Silver"'. *Israel Exploration Journal* 19: 178-180.

Jayakar, P. 1989. *The Earth Mother*. New Delhi: Penguin.

Joshi, M.C. 1994. 'Goddess Cybele in Hindu Śākta tradition'. In B.N. Saraswaty, S.C. Malik and M. Khanna (eds.), *Art, the Integral Vision: A Volume of Essays in Felicitation of Kapila Vatsyayan*, 203-209. New Delhi: DK.

Khan, M.N. 2005, 'Kashmir Smast (Gandhara) and its religious significance: study based on epigraphic and other antiquities from the site'. In U. Franke-Vogt and H.-J. Weisshaar (eds.), *South Asian Archaeology 2003, Proceedings of the Seventeenth International Conference of the European Association of South Asian Archaeologists (7-11 July 2003, Bonn)*, 247-252. Aachen: Linden Soft.

Kurita, I. 2003a. *A revised and enlarged edition of Gandhāran Art I. The Buddha's Life Story*. Tokyo: Nigensha.

Kurita, I. 2003b. *A revised and enlarged edition of Gandhāran Art II. The World of the Buddha* Tokyo: Nigensha.

Le Rider G. 1967. 'Monnaies de Taxila et d'Arachosie', *Revue des Études Grecques* 80: 331-42.

MacDowall, D.W. 2007. 'Coinage from Iran to Gandhāra, with special reference to divinities as coin types'. In D. Srinivasan (ed.), *On the Cusp of an Era: Art in the Pre-Kuṣāṇa World, 233-266*. Leiden: Brill.

Marshak, B., and F. Grenet. 2002. 'L'arte Sogdiana (IV-IX secolo)'. In P. Chuvin (ed.), *Le Arti in Asia Centrale*, 114-177. Milano: Garzanti.

Matheson, S.B. 1994a. 'The Goddess Tyche'. In S.B. Matheson (ed.), *An Obsession with fortune: Tyche in Greek and Roman Art*, 19-33. New Haven: Yale University Art Gallery.

Matheson, S.B. 1994b. 'Catalogue of the Exhibition'. In S.B. Matheson (ed.), *An Obsession with Fortune: Tyche in Greek and Roman Art*, 107-118. New Haven: Yale University Art Gallery.

Metzler, D. 1994. 'Mural crowns in the ancient Near East and Greece'. In S.B. Matheson (ed.), *An Obsession with Fortune: Tyche in Greek and Roman Art*, 77-85. New Haven: Yale University Art Gallery.

Mitchiner M. 1975-1976. *Indo-Greek and Indo-Scythian Coinage*, 9 vols. London: Hawkins Publications.

Mukherjee, B.N. 1969. *Nanā on Lion*. Calcutta: The Asiatic Society.

Narain, A.K. 1957. *The Indo-Greeks*. Oxford: Oxford University Press.

Needham, R. 1975. 'Polythetic classification: convergence and consequences'. *Man*, new series 10 (3): 349-369.

Nougayrol, J. 1955. *Le Palais Royal d'Ugarit*, vol. 3. Paris: Imprimerie nationale.

Pal, P. 1986. *Indian Sculpture*, vol. 1. Los Angeles: Los Angeles County Museum of Art and University of California Press.

Pal, P. 2009. 'Durga in Kashmir'. In P. Pal (ed.), *Goddess Durga: the Power and the Glory*, 82–95. Mumbai: Marg Publications.

Panaino, A. 2000. 'The Mesopotamian Heritage of Achaemenid Kingship'. In S. Aro and R.M. Whiting (eds.), *The Heirs of Assyria*, 35-49. Melammu Symposia 1. The Neo-Assyrian Text Corpus Project, Helsinki.

Pope, A.U. (ed.) 1938-1939. *A Survey of Persian Art: From Prehistoric Times to the Present*. 6 vols. London: Oxford University Press.

Potts, D.T. 2001. 'Nana in Bactria'. *Silk Road Art and Archaeology* 7: 23-35.

Rahman, A. ur, and H. Falk. 2011. *Seals, Sealings and Tokens from Gandhāra* (Monographien zur Indischen Archäologie, Kunst und Philologie, Bd 21). Wiesbaden: Reichert.

Roller, L.E. 1999. *In Search of God the Mother: The Cult of Anatolian Cybele*. Berkeley: University of California Press

Rosenfield, J.M. 1967. *The Dynastic Arts of the Kushans*. Berkeley: University of California Press.

Sanderson, A. 2004. 'Religion and the state: Śaiva officiants in the territory of the king's Brahmanical chaplain'. *Indo-Iranian Journal* 47: 229-300.

Santoro, A. 2002. 'De dea turrita: La divinità poliade nell'arte del Gandhāra'. In C. Silvi Antonini, B.M. Alfieri and A. Santoro (eds.), *Oriente & Occidente: Convegno in Ricordo di Mario Bussagli*, 223-235. Roma: Istituti Editoriali Poligrafici Internazionali, Pisa.

Sarianidi, V.I. 1980. 'The treasure of the Golden Hill'. *American Journal of Archaeology* 84 (2): 125-131.

Senior, R.C. 2001. *Indo-Scythian Coins and History*, 4 vols. Lancaster and London: Classical Numismatic Group.

Senior, R.C. and R. Babar. 1998. 'Ancient India: a new king and a new deity'. *Newsletter of the Oriental Numismatic Society* 157: 13.

Shah, I. 2009. 'The Hinglaj Shrine, Baluchistan'. In P. Pal (ed.) *Goddess Durga. The Power and the Glory*, 188-197. Mumbai: *Marg Publications*.

Shayegan, R.M. 2004/2012. 'Hormozd I'. In E. Yarshater (ed.), *Encyclopædia Iranica*, http://www.iranicaonline.org/articles/hormozd-i (accessed 30 March 2016).

Shepherd, D.G. 1980. 'The iconography of Anāhitā'. *Berytus* 28: 47-86.

Sims-Williams, N., and J. Cribb. 1995-96. 'A new Bactrian inscription of Kanishka the Great'. *Silk Road Art and Archaeology* 4: 75-142.

Siudmak, J. 2013. *The Hindu-Buddhist Sculpture of Ancient Kashmir and its Influences*. Leiden: Brill.

Spycket, A. 1980. 'Women in Persian Art'. In D. Schmandt-Besserat (ed.), *Ancient Persia: The Art of an Empire*, 43-45. Malibu: Undena.

Srinivasan, D.M. 1997. *Many Heads, Arms and Eyes: Origin, Meaning and Form of Multiplicity in Indian Art*. Leiden: Brill.

Srinivasan, D.M. 2010. 'Śrī-Lakṣmī in early art: incorporating the north-western evidence'. *South Asian Studies* 26 (1): 77-95.

Taddei, M. 1962. 'Descriptive catalogue'. In D. Faccenna, *Sculptures from the Sacred Area of Butkara I (Swat, Pakistan)*, Part 2 (Istituto Italiano per il Medio ed Estremo Oriente, Reports and Memoirs, II.2). Roma: Istituto Poligrafico dello Stato.

Taddei, M. 1964. 'Descriptive catalogue'. In D. Faccenna, *Sculptures from the Sacred Area of Butkara I (Swat, Pakistan)*, Part 3 (Istituto Italiano per il Medio ed Estremo Oriente, Reports and Memoirs, II.3). Roma: Istituto Poligrafico dello Stato.

Taddei, M. and G. Verardi. 1978. 'Tapa Sardār second preliminary report'. *East and West* 28 (1-4): 33-135.

Tarzi, Z. 1976. 'Hadda à la lumière des trois dernières campagnes de fouilles de Tapa-è-Shotor (1974-1976)'. *Comptes-rendus des séances de l'Académie des Inscriptions et Belles-Lettres* 120 (3): 381-410.

Tucci, G. 1963. 'Oriental Notes II. An image of a devi discovered in Swat and some connected problems'. *East and West* 14: 146-182.

Verardi, G. 1983. 'The Kuṣāṇa Emperors as Cakravartins: dynastic art and cults in India and Central Asia: history of a theory, clarifications and refutations'. *East and West* 33 (1-4): 225-294.

Verardi, G. 2011. *Hardships and Downfall of Buddhism in India*. Singapore: Institute of Southeast Asian Studies; New Delhi: Manohar.

Verardi, G., and E. Paparatti. 2005. 'From early to late Tapa Sardār: a tentative chronology'. *East and West* 55 (1-4): 405-444.

Widemann, F. 2009. *Les successeurs d'Alexandre en Asie centrale et leur héritage culturel: Essai*. Paris: Riveneuve.

Wroth, W. 1903. *Catalogue of the Coins of Parthia*. London: British Museum Trustees.

Chapter 3

The Appropriation of the Goddess into the Purāṇic Narrative

Integration/Appropriation in the *Vāmanapurāṇa*

Greg Bailey

'Integration of culture' is a phrase used by some scholars to describe the function of the Purāṇas as a body of semi-popular literature within the amorphous frame of Hindu culture. Indian scholars, in particular, have conceived of the genre performing an integrative function at various levels of society. This could mean integrating religio-cultural ideas derived from low caste oral traditions to high caste oral/written texts, or justifying mythologically the entry of tribal deities (especially mother goddesses) into the pan-Hindu Sanskritic tradition, or, at a local level – exemplified in both *Jāti*- and *Sthalapurāṇas* – introducing local specific myths into the pan-Indian Purāṇic genre. In large part this has been a viable and ongoing process, because of the recitational tradition of Purāṇic narrative that has traditionally involved a mixture of Sanskrit and vernacular language performance before a local audience. In such situations, what were originally Sanskritic and non-Sanskritic ideas[1] are usually given equal signposting

1 The argument here may be seen as circular, for how can one tell what is Sanskritic or non-Sanskritic on the basis of a narrative composed in Sanskrit and usually not traceable back to contemporary vernacular sources? Of course Sanskrit is not just a medium of expression; it is also a cultural context socially grounded in the Brāhmin *varṇa*.

within a unifying devotional context buttressed by ritual and the telling of *kathās*, the narrative form making up a substantial part of the Purāṇic narrative.

Using this same logic of integration it has also been asserted (Chakrabarti 1992; Nath 2009) that the entry of the goddess into Sanskrit literature was facilitated by the Purāṇic genre. Evidence of goddess cults prior to the beginning of the Common Era can be found in Pāli literature, and the widespread worship of female *devatā*s in villages has been registered in literature for the past two millennia. As an example of the integration of the goddess, the *Devīmāhātmya* has often been mentioned (Coburn 1984), but for the integration theory to hold it would necessarily have to explain the emergence of other goddesses as well into the Purāṇic narrative. But there is a fundamental difficulty: where it is easy to trace the appearance of the goddess in any given Purāṇa, it is usually hard to find her appearance in earlier pre-Purāṇic literature in vernacular/Prakrit languages. I suspect the emphasis on the goddess as an example of appropriation follows the precedence in scholarship established by work on the *Devīmāhātmya* or a ferocious goddess only hinted at in earlier literature, and then integrated with Sanskritic male deities in that text by being given male epithets, including an avataric function. Taking away all of the Sanskritic material leaves us with a ferocious goddess conforming perfectly to the later image of the Tantric goddess who is both benign and malign.

References to the goddess are not particularly common in the *Vāmana Purāṇa* (hereafter *VāmP*), apart from a few prominent exceptions. However, there is a series of myths about the marriage of semi-divine women (admittedly a vague expression) with some royal figures, myths used to develop a series of arguments as to why Andhaka, subsequently a prominent devotee of Śiva, should not seek to marry Pārvatī, who is an important goddess in her own right. The marriages involve the linking of tribal women with figures associated with Brāhminical values and in that sense the difficulties these marriages raise can be seen as analogous to the process where the originally non-Brāhminical goddess is integrated into the Brāhminical pantheon of deities and panoply of myths. I contend that by studying these myths, as I have done in this chapter, insight can be gained into the manner in which originally non-Brāhminical goddesses have been integrated into the Purāṇic cultural system which is an overwhelmingly assimilatory process governed by Brāhminical imperatives.

Appropriation/Integration

Appropriation implies specifically intentional adaptation or adoption, whereas integration/assimilation is not necessarily intentional; it involves either conscious or unconscious adaptation or borrowing. Both seem to be applied mainly to the goddess and the cataloguing of sacred places, where many of these were originally pre-Hindu and associated with mother goddess worship (Kosambi 1962), and both words have technical connotations in the sense of implying that one group of people is taking something from another group, and in texts or performative productions end up presenting it as their own. Given the existence of a possible appropriation process, the Sanskrit tradition, dominated by Brāhminical disseminators and reciters, would represent the appropriating group, and all of the other localised and regional groups would represent the appropriated groups. Of course, this is simplistic, and constant interaction has occurred between both groups, neither of which is monolithic, and each continues to exist historically alongside the other. Given the extent to which the first group sought to universalise into a pan-Indian tradition transcending local cultures, they may be considered to have rescued from disappearance everything they considered of importance, or highlighted specifically localised features of religion and culture they considered to need incorporation into the Brāhminical tradition. During the early historical period (200 BCE – 200 CE), the representatives of this tradition regarded it as needing to have a broader cultural ambit, especially one reflecting the influence of devotional cults and the theological framework buttressing them. This process of appropriation may not have been of significance to the lower classes of society, not conversant in Sanskrit, but seen from above it was certainly a significant process of cultural incorporation, even if not explicitly recognised as such.

Many recent and contemporary Indian scholars of the Purāṇas have sought to ground the genre in a functioning process of integrating diverse cultural and religious elements into a whole larger than the combination of its individual elements. R.C. Hazra (1975, 5-7) was one of the first, using the words ‘absorption’ and ‘incorporation’ in regard to bringing material on Brāhminical Hindu rites and customs into mythological texts. For him, the Purāṇas were responding to the threat represented by Tantrism and Buddhism to Hinduism, taking up and excising some aspects of both of these in order to domesticate them and bringing acceptable aspects of both into the Brāhminical mould. A recent manifesto of this role of the Purāṇas is given by Pushpendra Kumar (2005, 46-47):

> The Purāṇas play a pivotal role in shaping the life and culture of Indian people and vividly describe a set pattern of social, monetary, geographical, political, philosophical, religious and educational systems. Along with this, all Purāṇas have presented the similar type of synthecism [*sic*]. This synthecism is logical and in accordance with the fundamental spirit of the Upaniṣads: 'This all is Brahman.'

And he goes on to argue that the Purāṇas play a major role in synthesising different cultural strands and traditions within the society.

More nuanced is V. Nath (2009, 170), who focuses intelligently on sacred places as important sites for the integration of different cultural and religious components:

> To coalesce such disparate material [as the different *tīrthas*], the Purāṇa composers adopted an extremely flexible and accommodative stance. They took cognizance of diversity in religious performance at the tīrthas and provided location for them by upholding the validity of variant forms of *lokācāra* and *deśācāra*.[2] They even recognized variants arising from the different contexts in which religious performances took place. These contexts ranged from *saṃskārika* (connected with the stages of life) to *pāramārthika* (dealing with spiritual aspirations) and *vyāvahārika* (which pertained to more worldly desires for children (or *putreṣaṇa*), wealth (or *vitteṣaṇa*), and other forms of material gain (or *lokeṣaṇa*).

But this is rather too general to allow insight into quite specific aspects of appropriation, which may well be regarded as a different cultural process than integration. Nath glosses the difference between appropriation and integration by using the words 'adopted an extremely flexible and accommodative stance,' and not taking into consideration active or passive accommodation, that is, appropriation or integration.

2 These words refer to conduct accepted generally (*lokācāra*) and conduct accepted locally (*deśācāra*).

One of the most eloquent of commentators on the subject of appropriation and integration, but essentially running the same line as Nath and Hazra, is K. Chakrabarti (1999, 57-58):

> The Purāṇas evolved out of an interaction between the Sanskritic and the many local traditions. But by the time the first phase of the composition of the Purāṇas was complete, it had already acquired an identity independent of its even notional Vedic moorings ... and the various 'little tradition' traits which the Purāṇas assimilated ... The cleverly manipulated cosmic model of the Purāṇic myths was constructed on the principle that it would rationalize and at the same time transform actions in everyday life ... The Purāṇas thus further relinquished their pretension of Vedism and reabsorbed the beliefs and practices of the exclusively local cults.

Appropriation is not a process involving forcible acquisition and integration into an existing tradition of originally extraneous material. Traces of opposition to the integration of non-Brāhminical ideas and practices occur in respect of the heterodox religions and perhaps Tantrism, though even Tantric practices are commonplace in late Purāṇas. Acceptance of beliefs and practices associated with mother goddesses was not resisted, but became part of the Brāhminical assemblage of practices as registered in the Purāṇas. This was inevitable in an agrarian society where mother-goddess worship is so strongly associated with the maintenance of fertility of the soil and of women. And it is this area that scholars have most focused upon. In taking up a commonly held view that the Purāṇas somehow provide a link between the learned elite and the non-Sanskrit masses, Chakrabarti (1992, 139) suggests:

> The prime technique employed by the Purāṇas for this purpose was to identify the countless deities worshipped in various localities with deities of similar features in the Sanskritic tradition. The most prominent example of such identification is the innumerable local goddesses who coalesced with Devī as different manifestations of the same Śakti. As the locale of Brāhminical culture expanded, fresh shrines and sacred centres of pilgrimage were designated in new areas in similar fashion. This process is elaborately exemplified in the Purāṇic texts.

Nath (2009, 178) points to an example of the assimilation of a folk goddess with Durgā:

> Another example of the same phenomenon is furnished by the cult of goddess Danteśvarī, who was installed at Jagdalpur by the Kākatīya chief who soon came to be regarded as her human agent and representative, and was accordingly held in great veneration by the tribal folk. The goddess later came to be identified also with the Purāṇic goddesses Mahādurgā and Kālī and consequently emerged as the apex deity of Bastar. Significantly, in both the above cases, the power and influence of the chiefs grew with the growing fame and popularity of the *tīrthas* [citing Singh 1993].

But the problem with all of these judgements is that, though they may be right, we do not have exact details as to how the process of appropriation, assimilation or integration takes place. In other words, what is the connection between a non-Sanskritic goddess being popular in a particular location and then being integrated into a Purāṇic narrative? Who makes the decision to integrate myths of the goddess into a particular version of the Purāṇa? Is it going to involve a complete set of myths about that goddess? And who reworks them to fit into a Sanskritic format? Samuel's (2008, 111) warning is prudent here:

> We should be careful about assimilating all goddesses of this kind into Lakṣmī, since as I shall argue later this process of assimilation, which is a characteristic feature of how Brāhminical religion came to work in later times, is actually part of what we should be studying rather than something to be taken for granted.

The question is whether the version of the goddess myth exemplified in such celebrated texts as the *Devīmāhātmya,* elements of which are also found in *Vāmana Purāṇa* 17-20, has become so formalised that all its appropriative/assimilatory elements have been removed or smoothed out. It is difficult to read behind the rather formulaic Sanskrit to discover the extent of appropriation, as arguably all Purāṇic literature is appropriated. Another problem concerns the extent to which the attempted marriage of the demon (as in the Andhaka myth, alluded to below) with the emergent goddess is replicated in non-Sanskritic texts and why this was taken over.

Was it to give the promoters of Purāṇic Hinduism a total view of what they wished to communicate? Or are we just being given a picture of Purāṇic process in which the end result is apparent and both the beginning and the process itself are substantially lost to us? This is definitely the view given by Chakrabarti and we can only agree with him, even in respect of the Bengali Purāṇas. Accordingly, does this leave us any room at all in which to move and does it tell us anything about 'appropriation' as a cultural process different from 'assimilation', a quality seemingly long identified with Purāṇic composition? Appropriation seems to be deliberate, integration not, but we only ever perceive these in hindsight (except in contemporary fieldwork), and it is usually fallacious to think we can recover the exact process associated with each.

On one view the Purāṇa constitutes a process completely devoid of originality of content, though not of organisation of this content, and it is in this operational aspect of the genre that possibilities of inclusion and exclusion can be found. Clearly the foundations for this appropriative/integrative process lie in the *bhakti* semantic frame (Bailey 1988), a process functioning as a filter through which all sorts of material from great and little traditions can be included.[3] Moreover, each Purāṇa seems to have several localisations it wants to stress and a mythic geographical context running counter to localisation, but undoubtedly including it.

The *Vāmana Purāṇa* as example

The *Vāmana Purāṇa* may have been composed between the ninth and tenth centuries (Rocher 1986, 241), and its contents mainly relate to devotional myths centred on both Viṣṇu and Śiva.[4] In addition, it contains the *Sarojamāhātmya* of twenty-eight chapters detailing the *tīrthas* of Kurukṣetra, but rehearsing the devotional myths surrounding Viṣṇu in his dwarf (Vāmana) *avatāra*. In respect of the assimilation/inclusion of

3 I am inclined to agree with Chakrabarti that the great and little tradition concepts are primarily scholarly constructs, easily mixed up in an indigenous cultural environment.

4 The chronology of this and other Purāṇas roughly replicates the dating from archaeology of the appearance of Hindu sculptures and images as suggested for Sanchi by Shaw (2007, 185): 'As shown in Table 12.1, apart from the previously published Mahiṣāsuramardinī and saptamātṛka examples at Udayagiri and Besnagar, very few Gupta period Brahminical goddesses were discovered during the survey. It is not until the post-Gupta period that they appear in significant numbers throughout the wider countryside'.

goddess narratives, the available material is restricted, though not entirely absent. It can be summarised into three categories:

1) Myths of the fierce goddess. These are restricted to Chs. 19-21 and are constituted by a version of the Mahiṣāsuramardinī myth where the goddess is produced by the combined fiery energy (*tejas*) of all the gods and is named Kātyāyanī (18, 8). It is a much truncated version of the narrative found in the *Devīmāhātmya* and the fierce goddess becomes Brāhminised as a result of all of the well known Brāhminical deities providing her with presents that give her fighting attributes (18, 9-17). Mahiṣa recognises her as a young unmarried woman (*kanyā*) (19, 21) and declares his wish to marry her. She responds positively to this, but only if he can pass the test of defeating her in battle (19, 34). This he tries and it leads to his killing. At 21, 51 she declares she will be reborn for the sake of the gods, therefore placing her activity within a modified *avatāra* framework. Was she assimilated into the Brāhminical superstructure even before incorporation into the Purāṇic narrative? Almost certainly yes!

2) *Tīrthayātrā* material in the *Sarojamāhātmya* and the minimum presence of the goddess. The presence of the goddess was conceivably played down here because of the centrality given to Vindhyācala in the Mahiṣa myths, where localisation is very obvious. In the other *tīrtha* passages it seems to be a case of movement from one to the other within the Kurukṣetra region or along the Sarasvatī river. At *Sarojamāhātmya* 36, 18-19, a number of goddesses including Durgā are mentioned and also at 55-56 (in Gupta et al. 1968), but elsewhere they are conspicuous by their absence.

3) Myths of intermarriage. These are quite different from the myth cited in section one above because the marriages are completed, always at the end of a very convoluted plot. I analyse these myths in detail here because they have not been studied before and may provide some clues as to how assimilation and integration, not appropriation, have taken place.

Chapters 63 to 66[5] narrate three myths, which I designate in the following ways:

---

5 I have used Kamboja's (1983) edition, which has different chapter numbers from Gupta's (1968) edition. The reason is that both include the *Sarojamāhātmya*, but Kamboja just numbers its chapters consecutively with what precedes and follows it, whereas Gupta allocates separate chapters to it. He begins his numbering of the *Sarojamāhātmya* at the end of Chapter 23 and begins the *VāmP* again at Chapter 24, numbering the *Sarojamāhātmya* separately as Chapters 1-28. This results in the Gupta edition numbering the chapters I have used from Kamboja 63-66 as 37-40.

- EMB (Embedding Myth)1: 63, 1-19; 66, 19-70, 96; Andhaka's wish to take Pārvatī as a wife, his failure and transformation into a devotee of Śiva.
- EM (Embedded Myth)1: 63, 20-37, 50; 65, 167; 66, 1-18; Daṇḍa's illicit desire for Arajā and his ultimate destruction.
- EM2: 63, 38-49, 51-86; 64, 1-79; 65, 1-167; Citrāṅgadā and Suratha.

This set of myths in fact deals with only one goddess, Pārvatī, as a woman who is entirely unavailable, yet is still desired by others. Where the embedding myth begins with Andhaka's forbidden desire for Pārvatī as its principal theme, the embedded myths are really arguments Prahlāda puts to Andhaka as illustrations to explain why he should abandon the course of action that would lead him to attempt to gain her as his wife. Myth is commonly used as argument in Indic literature.

What emerges thematically from each of the embedding myths is the contrast between forest and sacred ford (the city/village being rarely ever mentioned), between royalty and other, human and non-human, and, above all, between male and female. Mediating figures, such as sages, play an important role in communicating between different figures and causing movements in the narrated action, and arguably mediate different levels of culture and belief. Above all, sacred places and rivers are also relevant, perhaps as mediatory points where different levels of culture are conflicted, then integrated.

A minor, yet highly significant sub-text of these chapters is woman's adherence to Brāhminical values, as expressed through the regulated capacity of a woman to choose her own husband (or have sex) and for this to be denied. This corresponds on a sliding scale with the attitude women have towards suitors, beginning with Pārvatī who has no interest in her suitor Andhaka, Arajā who is not interested in Daṇḍa, Citrāṅgadā who is definitely interested in Suratha, and the others, all of whom are interested in their potential husbands, though scarcely knowing them. Pārvatī already has a husband, whereas Arajā is stridently not prepared to compromise, but Citrāṅgadā is given no choice. Let us note that Pārvatī, a Brāhminical goddess, is the first example used, and then she provides a model experienced by other semi-divine women who may not originally have been Brāhminical. In this sense, these myths do relate to the difficulties associated with the integration of the goddess in the Purāṇic narrative.

In EM2 other characters come into play and their relationship turns on thwarted desire, curses and eventual union with a husband. A close reading shows these narratives to be dealing with the resolution of problems through typical mediatory points: sacred places, holy men and devotional acts (to Śiva), the latter seemingly mediating across status positions. A summary of the myths, with a few passages directly translated, follows.

One day the demon Andhaka expressed his desire for Pārvatī and offered blandishments to anyone who would bring her to him so that he could marry her. Prahlāda quickly intervened warning him that dharmically, she is his mother and that Śiva and his hosts would need to be defeated before she can be won. This is not a possibility in his opinion, and he tells the embedded myth [EM1] of Daṇḍa and Arajā (63, 20ff) to make his point. 'Have you not heard, demon, how King Daṇḍa, a deluded man who desired the wife of another, was destroyed with his kingdom?' (63, 19). Daṇḍa became interested in Arajā, the daughter of his *purohita*, Śukra, when the latter was away performing a sacrifice for an *asura*. Arajā remained in Bhārgava's (= Śukra's) hermitage so the king entered, having dismissed all the servants. She rejoiced, regarding him as a brother (63, 29), except that he asked for sex (30), leading her to spell out the problems with these words: 'Stupid man, you are like a brother to me, yet you are steeped in bad conduct. According to the law, I am your sister. You are the pupil of my father' (32). But he persisted, taking an opportunistic view, knowing her father was away. In 36cd she appealed to the Brāhminical obligation, which states: 'Prince, I am unable to give myself to you, because for women there is no self-choice (*asvatantrāḥ hi yoṣitaḥ*).' And she warned that his kingdom would be destroyed because Śukra would curse him.

In response Daṇḍa introduced EM2 in order to persuade Arajā to have sex with him. Once Viśvakarman's daughter Citrāṅgadā (63, 40) went to Naimiṣa forest with her friends to bathe. As she was entering the water a king named Suratha saw her and was overcome with lust (43). She asked her friends if she could offer herself to him. But they declared the orthodox Brāhmin view that she was *asvātantrya* and that her father adhered to *dharma* (*dharmiṣṭha*) (44). But like Daṇḍa, Suratha was utterly overwhelmed by desire and at length she gave herself to him (63, 49). By analogy, Daṇḍa said Arajā should give herself to him (63, 50a).

Then she continued to narrate the consequences affecting Citrāṅgadā and Suratha. 'She gave herself of her own will (*svātantryāt*), in consequence of which her father cursed her: "Since you have abandoned the law due to your female disposition, stupid woman, and have given yourself, there will be no marriage (52-53ab).'" As a result (54) the Sarasvatī river swept the king thirteen *yojanas* away, his goal uncompleted. Citrāṅgadā was left for dead and fell into the Sarasvatī, going from there into the Gomatī, which in turn cast her into a huge forest.

Now Daṇḍa takes over again and says that at this point the Guhyaka Añjana came along (65), saw her and offered to take her to Saratha. But he directed her first to gaze upon Śiva, called Śrīkaṇṭha, located on the southern bank of the Kālindī (68). She performed austerities, then the ascetic Ṛtadhvaja came and asked who she was, and why she had come to the forest, himself realising something was wrong.

On hearing her response the sage became enraged and cursed Viśvakarma: 'Since his own daughter had to be given to another (*paradeya*) and yet the evil man caused her not to be united with her husband, then he must become a monkey (63, 75).' He then worshipped Śiva and told Citrāṅgadā to go to the sacred place where the seven Godavaris come together (77). There she must worship Śiva, and he predicted that two women would come: Devavatī who is daughter of the *daitya* Kandaramālin, and Nandayantī (Añjana's daughter). And a third woman would also come: Vedavatī, daughter of Parjanya, who we subsequently learn is king of the Gandharvas. They will meet where Mahādeva, called Hāṭaka, is located and Ṛtadhvaja predicts that Citrāṅgadā will achieve *saṃyoga* (union) (81). She went where she was instructed to go, engaged in austerities and worshipped Śiva. Finally the sage (Ṛtadhvaja?) wrote a verse on a slab saying that nobody can remove her suffering by his own courage (84-85). Then he went to Puṣkarāraṇya, near the Payoṣṇī river.

The next chapter (64) takes us back to EM1 and has Daṇḍa narrating the fate of Viśvakarman who, affected by the curse, immediately fell from Mt Meru, and dwelt on a forested mountain near Śālūkī river. He performed austerities, until one day he saw Devavatī passing by and grabbed her by the hand. Her father, Kandaramālin, lifted up his sword and attacked, at which point the monkey took the girl to Himavat mountain, but he saw the image of Śrīkaṇṭha on the Yamunā bank and an inaccessible hermitage there, where he placed the girl. Then he sank into the Kalindī whilst Kandara watched, believing his daughter had died. The monkey was carried away by the river to a place called Śivi, and, though desiring to go back to where Devavatī was located, he instead saw that Añjana, the Guhyaka, had come with his daughter, Nandayantī, and decided to follow them. He thought Damayantī was Devavatī, ran towards her and in fear she fell into the Hiraṇyavatī river (64, 16). Añjana saw her fallen into the river and sorrowfully returned to Añjana mountain, where he performed austerities.

Nandayantī was carried away by the Hiraṇyavatī until she came to a fig tree which had dreadlocks like Śiva (64, 20). She sat under a tree and heard a voice saying that a certain Jābāli was bound somewhere and that no one can free him. She spotted him (64, 20) and found that he too had been cursed by Viśvakarma to be held in the tree. Now he proceeded to tell her what events conspired to bring him to this situation, telling her that his father Ṛtadhvaja had previously lived in the city of Unmattapura where Maheśvara was located (64, 27). Whilst Jābāli was wandering he had met the monkey who accused him of taking Devavatī, whom he (Viśvakarman) had left in the hermitage. Then he cursed him to be bound in the tree. After that the monkey went back to Amaraparvata (64, 38–39).

Nandayantī then revealed her true identity to him and said that the sage Mudgala had predicted of her that she would become a queen (*iyaṃ narendramahiṣī bhaviṣyati*) (64, 42). The monkey then fell from the bank of the Hiraṇyavatī and, fearful of him, she threw herself into the river, saying 'I have been brought to this isolated spot by it' (64, 46). Now Jābāli told her to go to Śrīkaṇṭha on the bank of the Yamunā, where his father (Ṛtadhvaja) would come to worship at midday, and, if she made an offering to Śrīkaṇṭha, she would achieve prosperity. She went there and wrote another verse, asking when somebody would come and protect (*trātum*) her (64, 53). Then she went to the huge hermitage located at the Yamunā's tributary, where she saw Devavatī (56), and both women talked at length about what had happened to them. At this point Ṛtadhvaja arrived, saw what Nandayantī had written and went straight to the Ikṣvāku capital at Ayodhyā. He asked the king to free Jābāli and he sent his son, Śakuni, to complete the task. Eventually Ṛtadhvaja and Śakuni freed the boy, called Bharavāhī because he still carried part of the tree on his back, and went to the Sūryajā river (64, 79).

A new chapter (65) begins with the two women arriving at the Yamunā where they began worshipping Śrīkaṇṭha. Then the sage Gālava arrived at the same place, worshipped Śiva and asked the two women who they were. He invited them to go to the Puṣkara forest with him. It was the full-moon time of the month of Kārtika and a huge festival attended by many sages and kings, with the exception of Ṛtadhvaja, was taking place.

They plunged into the water at the sacred ford and saw a huge male fish being courted (*priyamānam*) by several female fish, but the male fish was outraged, criticising the female fish on the grounds that a man should lawfully have only one wife (65, 20-21). Nor could he bear the criticism of the citizens. In justifying their actions, the female fish used the example of Gālava, saying that he was in the water with two women around him. Ashamed at hearing this, Gālava stayed at the bottom of the water for a long time. Then the two women surfaced to find that all the citizens had gone, leaving only Citrāṅgadā (65, 28). Gālava resolved not to come up, but then Vedavatī arrived, born from Ghṛtācī, by Parjanya. She bathed in the water and then saw the three women, Devavatī, Nandayantī and Citrāṅgadā, standing on the banks of the river.

Then Vedavatī heard Citrāṅgadā's story and told how she, in turn, was brought forcibly to Puṣkara by the monkey who mistakenly thought she was Devavatī. Brahmā had previously predicted she would be the wife of Indradyumna (65, 49). Both then approached the other two girls (Damayantī and Devavatī). The four women remained living at the confluence of the Godāvarī and worshipped Śaṅkara, whilst Śakuni, Jābāli and Ṛtadhvaja wandered around looking for them (65, 56). They gave up and went to meet King Indradyumna at Sakala (58), informing him that Damayantī was missing, only to be informed by the king that a beautiful young woman of his had disappeared (62). He had cut down a mountain-like tree, then a young woman disappeared, and he went looking for her until he found a śaivite ascetic at Badaryāśrama (66-67). Asked his identity, he declared himself to be the son of Manu, brother of Ikṣvāku and king in Sakala (70-71). Both then went in search of the woman. Ṛtadhvaja advised them to go to the Godāvarī (65, 78) as the prince (Manu's son) had already seen Citrāṅgadā there.

Simultaneously Ghṛtācī was at Udayagiri searching for her daughter (Vedavatī). She reached the monkey and asked where her daughter was to be found. The monkey said he had kept her at a large hermitage near the Śrīkaṇṭha temple on the bank of the Kalindī river, but Ghṛtāci told him he had made a mistake, that she was Vedavatī, not Devavatī. Both then agreed to go the Kauśikī river, where the three *rājārṣis* were also going. Jābāli warned them of the presence of the monkey and Śakuni put an arrow to his bow, but Ṛtadhvaja refused to let him kill the monkey. Instead he requested the monkey to help them, which he did, and Ṛtadhvaja offered him a boon. Viśvakarman asked him to remove the curse he originally had placed on him, declaring himself now to be Tvaṣṭṛ, carpenter of the gods. Ṛtadhvaja predicted the boon would be finished when Tvaṣṭṛ produced a son from Ghṛtācī. Then they had a courtship on Vindhya Mountain (109).

Five people, Ṛtadhvaja etc., then reached Godāvara, at noon, and alighted from their chariots to have a rest. The horses began running around near the temple, the women heard their hooves and, curious, found the Hāṭakeśvara temple. Then they saw the men in the water of the ford (115ab); Citrāṅgadā saw Suratha bathing there and became aroused (115cd). They recognised Ṛtadhvaja and then Jābāli, and then sat down and recited a long *stotra* to Śiva (120). Many sages and kings came and saw the women eulogising Śiva. A whole series of verses follows describing how all the men and the four young ladies met each other, including bringing Añjana (131) from the mountain, Kandaramālin from the underworld, and Parjanya, the Gandharva king, from heaven.

Then Devavatī asked the monkey to bring Gālava, and he went and brought the four of them with him to the Hāṭakeśvara ford. When their daughters saw their fathers there, they had tears of affection in their eyes (141). Ṛtadhvaja told Citrāṅgadā the monkey was her father (144), but she was ashamed and wondered if it was her fault Viśvakarman had become a monkey. She offered suicide, but the sage stopped her and Ghṛtācī eventually gave birth to a son Nala, leading Viśvakarman to lose his monkey appearance. He summoned all the gods and Gandharvas and went to the *tīrtha* called Hāṭaka. Then Indradyumna asked Ṛtadhvaja to give Kandaramālin's daughter to Jābāli; Śakuni should marry Damayantī; Vedavatī was to remain as his wife and Citrāṅgadā would be the wife of Suratha (158-163). All were married in sequence (*evaṃ kramād vivāhas* ...), implying that everything is in order in the three worlds.

At 167 Daṇḍa brings the whole story to a conclusion and says to Arajā (168c-f) that she must give herself to him. Finally in Chapter 66 the dénouement of EM1 is reached and Daṇḍa's fate is sealed. Arajā began by saying she would refuse to give herself to him as this will save him from her father's curse, but Daṇḍa raped her despite her protests. He went back to his own city (*nagaraṃ nijam* 3d) after doing the deed. Eventually Śukra returned, cursing Daṇḍa and his kingdom. The curse was fulfilled and the gods eschewed Daṇḍaka forest and declared it a place of *rākṣasas*. Hence, at 66, 19-20, we return to the embedding myth with a recommendation from Prahlāda that even good people who try to marry the wives of others are reduced to ashes and suffer a massive defeat. But Andhaka was not moved, so Prahlāda continued by citing the words of sages and dharmic precepts, until eventually Andhaka was defeated in combat by Śiva and became his devotee.

Analysis

The embedding and embedded myths are framed by Andhaka's misconceived desire for Pārvatī, a desire ameliorated only when he transforms sexual desire into devotional love by becoming Śiva's most prominent devotee. The myth narrating this relates to the goddess in the important sense that she becomes the improper object of desire by a figure who could never have her, but it also reminds us of the inherent difficulty she has with her own husband Śiva, manifested most clearly in the string of problems she encounters in attempting to win him. But for the continuity between this and the embedded myths, we have to look to the context in which a woman/goddess is 'the wife of another' and the extent to which she has a male protector. A possible *śāstric* intertext is represented by the early verses of the famous ninth chapter (9, 1-10, and especially 9, 2-4ab) of the *Manusmṛti* where emphasis is consistently laid on the fact that women have to be protected by the men around them:

> Day and night men should keep their women from acting independently (*asvatantrāḥ*); for, attached as they are to sensual pleasures, men should keep them under their control (*ātmano vaśe*). Her father guards her in her childhood, her husband guards her in her youth, and her sons guard her in her old age; a woman is not qualified to act independently (*na strī svātantryam arhati*).
>
> A father is reprehensible (*yāpyo*), if he does not give her away at the right time (*kāle 'dātā*) (5,147-49, trans. Olivelle (2005, 190)).[6]

This sets the default position for the Brāhmin and invites comparison with the way unmarried women are treated in the embedded myths.

All of the five women, including here Arajā, are at a crucial time separated from their fathers, who should be protecting them at this crucial time when they are *yauvanā/kumārī*, or of marriageable age. What happens when they have no protection or just surrogate protection, which is what is provided by Ṛtadhvaja, the most orthodox of them all, and

6 Cf. MBh 13,021.012a: *nāsti svatantratā strīṇām asvatantrā hi yoṣitaḥ / prajāpatimataṃ hy etan na strī svātantryam arhati //*

by Gālava? Conflating the two embedded myths shows that Arajā and Citrāṅgadā are both under pressure to give themselves willingly – with no other explicit agent regulating their behaviour – to a king who appears to want them only for sex. Daṇḍa is overwhelmed by desire and is unafraid of Śukra's curse, and Suratha too is also overtly sexual in his approach, when Citrāṅgadā says to her friends 'This prince is being tormented by lust (*madanena*)' (63, 42). And she is prepared to accept this as a reason to offer herself to him (63, 43), a decision strengthened by his expression of his subjection to desire (63, 46-48).

She is the main female character of EM2 and it is she who repudiates (63, 44) the thesis of *asvātantrya* for women, whereas Arajā is absolutely firm in her acceptance of this dictum (63, 36), as are Citrāṅgadā's friends who attempt to restrain her from giving herself (63, 44; cf. 65, 36). Viśvakarman also reasserts the thesis when he curses her, stating angrily that 'She abandoned the law due to her female disposition' (63, 52). Not only is she cursed not to be married – she is cursed also not to have a son. And the cause of this is reiterated by Daṇḍa when he sums up with quite moderate language, in saying, 'As such because of her own independence she found herself in this plight' (63, 62ab), offering an argument seemingly in contradiction to his own desire to have Arajā. If this is difficult enough, the situation becomes more problematic when Ṛtadhvaja curses Viśvakarman: 'Since his own daughter had to be given to another (*paradeya*) and yet the evil man caused her not to be united with her husband, then he must become a monkey' (63, 75). When the event causing Viśvakarman's curse occurred, he was absent, in possible dereliction of his duty as a father, and Ṛtadhvaja is condemning him for not fulfilling the obligation of giving her away, when *dharma* required that she must be given away. Who is more at fault, Citrāṅgadā or Viśvakarman? Did Viśvakarman curse her because she disobeyed him? Surely not! Or is it because of embarrassment about his own absence when Suratha approached her and that she does not respect the Brāhminical view of a woman's role? In any case, he is taking the strong Brāhminical line in the case of his own daughter, not even investigating Suratha's suitability to be a husband.

The other women – Devavatī, Nandayantī and Ghṛtācī, at the end – are not placed in a position where they have to make a choice about themselves by themselves. But like the other two women they find themselves in a position where they are without protection in the sense required of the orthoprax Brāhminical view. Viśvakarman is associated with at least two of them and, in fact, abducts two of the women. Devavatī is brought to the forest where Viśvakarman is performing austerities and is seized (*prajagāha balāt*) (64, 6), seemingly without reason, by him in the presence of her father. He attempts to defend her but eventually goes back to his own world when he mistakenly believes Devavatī has been drowned in the Yamunā. With his next encounter the monkey is still travelling and meets the Guhyaka Añjana travelling with his daughter Nandayantī, and, thinking she is Devavatī, whom he apparently lost, runs towards her, but she too fell into the Yamunā (64, 16) and her father left, thinking her dead. She is washed away in the river and meets Jābāli, also cursed by Viśvakarman, who accused him, again mistakenly, of taking (*gṛhya*) Devavatī, about whom the text gives no mention in relation to Jābāli, who is still a boy. But of Nandayantī it was predicted by Mudgala that she would marry a king, after a period of trouble, and she too is seen by Viśvakarman wandering in the forest. As directed by Jābāli she worships Śiva, then by chance meets the real Devavatī. Both have essentially been placed in the same situation: both were to be given away by their fathers but this was stopped by Viśvakarman, the monkey, possibly a negative reflection on his failure to correctly give away his own daughter.

These two meet Citrāṅgadā at the *tīrtha* of Puṣkara where she waits alone, all the pilgrims having left. Devavatī and Nandayantī have also been abandoned by Gālava, who disappeared when it was implied these two women were his two wives. For no reason Vedavatī, a *gandharva* woman, appears and tells how she was chased up a tree by the monkey, thinking she was Devavatī. In fact he had committed an attempted act of violence against her, and this continued as he pushed the tree down with her in it into the ocean. All the onlookers were deeply disturbed because it had been predicted by Brahmā that she would become the wife of Indradyumna, Manu's son. But she was carried by the wind to Puṣkara. Vedavatī and Citrāṅgadā then meet up with the other two and go to the Saptagodavara hermitage.

Citrāṅgadā's centrality in EM2 is evident and makes the other three women seem incidental. Each is initially accompanied by her father, who loses her – again a case of poor protection? But are they really incidental? Despite their Brāhminical names, their fathers are neither gods nor Brāhmins, but demi-gods, possibly representing the three worlds in a spatial sense. Nor are the motives of the suitors of Devavatī, Vedavatī and Damayantī (who first appear at 38, 79-80) described in any detail. Their suitors seem to be of little importance and only really come into play at the end of EM2. Yet the fathers of the three women never seek to lose them, rather Devavatī and Nandayantī appear to be abducted by Viśvakarman. Suratha, Citrāṅgadā's potential lover, is washed away by the Sarasvatī, which eventually takes her as well. Separation is fundamental – emotional as well as physical – in all cases.

The status of the three women mentioned is further complicated by the roles Jābāli and Gālava play in EM2. Viśvakarman curses Jābāli to be imprisoned at the top of a tree, because he thinks he has taken Devavatī whom he had left in a hermitage. Is it really a counter-curse because he has been cursed by Jābāli's father to become a monkey? Monkeys are sometimes depicted in Sanskrit literature as lecherous, but this seems to go against the motive for Viśvakarman's curse of Citrāṅgadā, yet consistent with his wish to seize (64, 6, 7, 35 *grabh*) Devavatī. He accuses Jābāli of having seized (*gṛhya*) Devavatī, even when it is he who had really done so.

In the final analysis it is only when the Ikṣvāku king's son, Śakuni, is requested (64, 65) by Ṛtadhvaja to intervene that all good things come to fruition, implying the combination of the Brāhmin and *kṣatriya* as being fundamental for good polity, hardly a novel idea in ancient Indian political theory. This raises the question of the class affiliation of the other participants in this myth, a critical point if the question of appropriation is to be raised. Only the Brāhmin status of Śukra, Ṛtadhvaja, Jābāli and possibly Gālava seems clear. All the rest are either not Brāhmin or non-Brāhmin, except for the *kṣatriya* figures such as Indradyumna, Śakuni, his father and Daṇḍa. Lack of specificity is probably deliberate, if these myths are discourses performing an appropriative function.

It is the fathers of the three women, who are secondary to the principal female characters, who may fit the non-Brāhminical category most clearly, except that no *varṇa* status is assigned to them. Noticeably, all three return to their own worlds immediately they are separated from their daughters, a fact surely of significance. And what finally is the status of Viśvakarman, a god, cursed to become a monkey, who now lives in the forest, the location of tribal people?

The spatial arrangements developed in the embedded myths are significant, the more so since they are concentrated in terms of particular types of localities: forest, hermitage, river and sacred fords. The cartographic scenario operative is one where rivers break the landscape and constitute fields where transformations occur and the results of curses take place. Whether the gender specificity (mountains being masculine, forests neuter) of rivers as feminine is significant in this regard, I cannot say. Most of the action is then set within the forest wilderness, though this is becoming less so by the identification of sacred fords and the placement of hermitages. It is reminiscent of the acculturation of ancient India from about 200 BC onwards where the Brāhmins were used as the cultural advance guard of kings to develop a Brāhminical framework into which a particular, no doubt localised, form of kingship could be legitimised. Often this involved marriage alliances with tribal women (see the instance of the Pāṇḍavas, all of whom had a tribal as well as a *kṣatriya* wife), and I suggest this is what is happening in EM2.

And the sacred ford where Hāṭakeśvara (in the form of an image) resides is the place where all of the marriage arrangements come to fruition. A *tīrtha* is a meeting place for all kinds of conflicts, and Puṣkara and Saptagodāvara are the principal *tīrthas* having a bearing in this myth. Historically, many had a sacred function before being appropriated by Hindu and Buddhist interests. That is, they were associated with what today might be called the little tradition. And so they became places where different traditions could meet, places where the difference between tribal beliefs and practices, Brāhminical devotional practices and Buddhist practices, were glossed over by virtue of the sacrality of the location. Thus in the case of EM2 there is a meeting of men, *gandharvas*, *daityas*, *guhyakas*, gods, kings, sages and women of a variety of classes. And it is here where the integration of various practices might become most apparent. Everything is rectified in the devotional practices performed for Śiva in the *tīrthas* where he is present as Śrīkaṇṭha and Hāṭakeśvara. From this perspective it is clear the Brāhmins who composed and recited the Purāṇas were more concerned with presenting diversity within unity rather than describing the process whereby this occurred. They were not bothered with diversity. In truth, they welcomed it. Rather, they were motivated with bringing all local customs into a Brāhminical framework and letting them continue to exist.

Analysis of these myths is not easy, nor is it immediately apparent why they should be read as contributing to an understanding of appropriation/integration as a process. They turn somewhat on the identity of the women, all available for marriage, but only in the right circumstances, when their fathers give them permission to marry another. This is reflected in Arajā's refusal to break the dictum, known at least since Manu, that women cannot avail themselves of self choice, reflected also in Ṛtadhvaja, 'he who has the truth/law as his banner', cursing Viśvakarman when he had cursed Citrāṅgadā who should have been *paradeya*, rather than having to make her own choice. I read this as a statement that traditional family structures of authority have broken down or that they are not observed by some groups, in the way they should be by the Brāhmins who should be providing the lead. Only at the end, when all the fathers are present, can the women be given away in a manner acceptable to Brāhminical precepts. The self-choice (certainly not like the *svayaṃvara*) practised by Citrāṅgadā may have been the Brāhmins' view of a tribal woman's marriage, made worse by the fact that she is the daughter of a god. But it remains a mystery why Ṛtadhvaja cursed Viśvakarman for cursing her to be without a husband. Does Ṛtadhvaja, despite the meaning of his name, represent a modified form of marriage in the areas where Brāhminical practices are just beginning to penetrate?

Going back briefly to the first embedded myth it can be noted immediately that there is symbolism in the names of the characters: Arajā means 'absence of desire/impetuosity', Daṇḍa, meaning 'stick', could also convey the sense of 'penis', and Śukra can mean 'semen'. Suggestions of extreme positions being taken here are present in the names, and are confirmed by Daṇḍa's rape of Arajā and Śukra's subsequent total destruction of him. Nor do the embedded myths used by Daṇḍa justify the arguments he wishes to put to win Arajā. I read this as an indication that the myth is placed here to demonstrate unacceptable solutions to the problems being rehearsed in the second embedded myth. There an ascetic, Ṛtadhvaja, enables a situation to occur where fathers can give away their daughters in the appropriate manner, whereas Śukra denies this possibility to Daṇḍa. Brāhmins sought to bring political elites under some kind of control in regard to choosing marriage partners, and, in tribal regions, the use of prominent ascetics to broker marriages of economic or political convenience would have helped effect this control. Both embedded myths, with their contrasting outcomes, go some way to showing how this might be achieved, at least in the fluid world of myth.

Conclusion

Are the Purāṇas entirely appropriative? Is there anything in them not taken from elsewhere, anything other than their organisational structure? It is difficult to read through the Sanskrit to find something drawn from somewhere else in them. The argument for appropriation/integration can in part be read as an argument from silence, where male gods are rarely seen as appropriations because they are found so often in Vedic literature and the *Mahābhārata,* and a sense of continuity is favoured above all. No such continuity can be found in relation to the fierce or the benign goddess, though they do populate the *Mahābhārata*, without for all that playing an extensive role in any of the mythic narratives. And it is surely worth asking why it is that goddesses seem to be more the subjects of appropriation than gods?

Instead, are the myths alluded to in this chapter exploring the possibility of choice for women and telling how it can be integrated with the absence of such in the Brāhminical system? Certainly this is a prominent sub-text, yet does not exhaust the complexity of the themes in the myth. For the embedding myth is one of forbidden marriage on the male's part (as with the first embedded myth), and represents almost a confusion as to the role of the male, depicting kings (though not Brāhmins) as operating under no such rules as apply to high class women. I suspect that what is happening here is a realistic reflection that kings in outlying areas had to come to alliances with tribal people, partly by marriage, and that this enables the use of the *kṣatriya* form of marriage, that is, abduction. Epigraphical evidence shows this did occur. However, in the more reflective world of myths the Brāhmins can attempt to place limits on the social/marital behaviour of kings, whilst admitting the necessity for practical modes of integration of non-Brāhminical groups into the realm of Brāhminical kingdoms. It is in the achievement of this task that the meanings of these myths should be explored.

Bibliography

Bailey, Greg. 1988. 'The semantics of bhakti in the *Vāmanapurāṇa*'. *Rivista degli Studi Orientali* LXII: 25-57.

Chakrabarti, Kunal. 1992. 'Anthropological models of cultural interaction and the study of religious process'. *Studies in History* 8: 123-149.

Chakrabarti, Kunal. 1999. 'Divine family and world maintenance: Gaṇeśa in the Bengali Purāṇas'. In *From Myths to Markets: Essays on Gender*, edited by K. Sangari and U. Chakravarti, 56-81. New Delhi: Manohar.

Coburn, T. 1984. *The Crystallization of the Goddess Tradition*. Delhi: Motilalal Banarsidass.

Gupta, A.S., S.M. Mukhopadhyaya and A. Bhattacharya. 1968. *The* Vāmana Purāṇa *with English Translation*. Varanasi: All India Kashiraj Trust.

Hazra, R.C. 1975. *Studies in the Purāṇic Records on Hindu Rites and Customs*. Delhi: Motilal Banarsidass (First ed. 1940. Dacca: Dacca University).

Kamboja, J. (ed.) 1983. *Śrī Vāmanamahāpurāṇam*. Delhi: Nag Publishers.

Kosambi, D.D. 1962. 'At the crossroads: a study of Mother-goddess cult sites'. In *Myth and Reality: Studies in the Formation of Indian Culture*, 82-109. Bombay: Popular Prakashan.

Kumar, Pushpendra. 2005. 'The Purāṇas and National Integration'. In *Facets of the Purāṇic Wisdom*, 35-47. Delhi: Eastern Book Linkers.
Nath, V. 2009. 'Tīrtha: instrument of acculturation'. In *The Purāṇic World: Environment, Gender, Ritual and Myth*, 166-201. Delhi: Manohar.
Olivelle, Patrick (trans.). 2005. *Manu's Code of Law: A Critical Edition and Translation of the Mānava-Dharmaśāstra*. Oxford: Oxford University Press.
Rocher, L. 1986. *The Purāṇas*. Wiesbaden: Harrassowitz.
Samuel, Geoffrey. 2008. *The Origins of Yoga and Tantra: Indic Religions to the Thirteenth Century.* Cambridge: Cambridge University Press.
Shaw, J. 2007. *Buddhist Landscapes in Central India: Sanchi Hill and Archaeologies of Religious and Social Change, c. 3rd Century BC to 5th Century AD.* London: British Association for South Asian Studies; The British Academy.
Singh, K.S. 1993. 'Hinduism and the tribal religion: an anthropological perspective'. *Man in India* 58: 1-16.

Chapter 4

The Yakṣiṇī Devī of Mangaon

Appropriation of a Jain Goddess by Brāhminic Hinduism

Jayant Bhalchandra Bapat

As the editors point out in Chapter 1, an extreme form of appropriation can involve usurping or forcefully acquiring a custom, an artefact, a symbol, or an age-old practice by a dominant culture. In what I am going to describe below, Brāhminic Hinduism seems to have forcefully acquired a Jain Goddess, removed her from her shrine and converted her into the well-known Hindu goddess Durgā. She has been then installed into the adjoining Jain shrine by removing the main image in the shrine, that of a Jain Tīrthaṃkar.

In the course of my research on the non-Brāhmin temple priests of Maharashtra (Bapat, 2000), I came across a caste group called the *Jain Gurav*. Because of its contradiction in terms, the name fascinated me. Jainism, an ancient religion of Indic origin, is thought to predate Hinduism and the Jains certainly do not call themselves Hindu. The Guravs on the other hand are a class of Hindu temple priests in the non-Vaiṣṇavite temples of Maharashtra and the border parts of the neighbouring state of Karnataka.[1] As the two words most definitely do not sit together, I decided to collect some information about the Jain Guravs.

My task proved difficult and time-consuming. There were only a few references and all, except for one, were quite old. I summarise below what these references told me about the Jain Guravs.

The oldest reference is in the tenth volume of the *Gazetteer of the Bombay Presidency* (1880, 119). Enthoven (1922, Vol II, 33-34) used this source when he wrote:

1 For more on the Gurav temple priests, see Bapat (1993, 1998, 1999 and 2001).

> Jain Guravs resemble local Bráhmans in matters of religion and custom, though they have a system of division by *devaks.*[2] ... They abstain from flesh and liquor and do not take food and water from any Hindu caste, even from Bráhmans. They are mainly servants in the village temples which, though dedicated to Bráhmanic gods, have still by their side broken remains of Jain images. This, and the fact that most of the temple lands date from a time when Jainism was the State religion, support the theory that Jain Guravs are probably Jain temple servants who have come under the influence ... partly of Bráhmanism ... A curious survival of their Jainism occurs at ... festivals ... On these occasions, in front of the village god's palanquin, three, five, or seven of the villagers, among whom the Gurav is always the leader, carry each a long gaily-painted wooden pole ... the chief one, carried by the Gurav, is called the Jain's pillar, *Jainácha khámb.*

Russell and Hira Lal (1975, 175-181) quoted Enthoven and furnished identical information. Satoskar, (1979, 250-251) in his work on Goa, wrote:

> In Goa, there used to be a sub-caste of the Guravs called the 'Jain Gurav'. They were also found on the north of Goa in Malvan, Savantwadi and Vengurle. These Guravs belonged to the Jain religion but were worshippers of Hindu deities [translation from the Marathi by the author].

Kelkar (1981, 17), also writing in Marathi, echoed similar views. It is worth noting that the above references talk of the Jain Guravs only in the past tense.

The most recent and most informative mention of the Jain Guravs appears in the *People of India* series volume on Goa, edited by K.S. Singh (1993, 94-95). Unfortunately the authors here quote only from the 1901 census and from Enthoven (cited above). They also supply some additional information that appears to be more recent but do not provide the sources for that information:

2 Traditionally, Brāhmins decide their hierarchical status depending on their Gotra (the seer or ṛṣi they are thought to have originated from) identity. For the Guravs, it is the *devak* (god/godling or an object of worship such as a tree or animal) that decides their hierarchy.

> According to Enthoven (1922), there are five groups of Guravs, such as Śiva Gurav, Kadu Gurav, Lingayat Gurav, Jain Gurav and Bhavik Gurav. But according to informants from Morjim village in Pernem Taluka of Goa, there are only two sub-groups, namely Jain Gurav and Lingayat Gurav ... In Goa, only Jain Guravs are found. The informant also said that there were only seven households of Jain Guravs in Goa having only 35 members. Of these, four are in Pernem taluka, two in Salcete taluka and only one in Ponda taluka ... Jain Guravs have nothing to do with Jainism. According to Enthoven (1922), the Shaiva temple of Vangani in Malwan taluka (Sindhudurga District), is called Jain Rameshwar Temple, probably after the Jain builder and it may be that the Jain Guravs are descendants of Jains who had taken to Śiva worship under the influence of Lingayatism ... The Jain Gurav are not included in O.B.C. [other backward classes], S.C. [scheduled castes] or S.T. [scheduled tribes] categories by the Government. ... Jain Guravs say that they are higher in status than Lingayat Guravs in the hierarchy, but of late, matrimonial alliances between the two sub-groups have started. ... Jain Gurav worship at Mahadeo temple. They are strictly endogamous with clan/kul exogamy. The clan/kuls are Kaushik and Kashyapa, Atri and Ishwar ... The Jain Guravs think of themselves as equal to Brahmans. Other communities also think so. But the Brahmans think that the Guravs are inferior to them in hierarchy.
>
> ... Monogamy is strictly followed. Mangalsutra and toe-ring worn by the wife are symbols of marriage ... The (Jain) Guravs profess Hinduism. Their family deity is Lord Vishnu. The village deity is Ravalnath enshrined in the village temple ... A major festival called Morjai (Bhagavati) is held every year in November in the village temple where the Jain Guravs officiate ... Literacy among the Guravs is very high ... They do not avail themselves of employment under E.G.S. [Employment Guarantee Scheme].

In summary, then, these references suggest that, in the past, Jainism was a state religion in these parts. In Goa only are the Jain Guravs found. These Guravs have a Gotra identity are strictly vegetarian and do not take water even from the Brāhmins. Although they worship at Śiva temples, their family god is Viṣṇu. They are possibly descendants of Jains who took Śiva worship under the influence of Lingayatism. Finally, the references say that there are broken Jain images all over this region and in Śiva temples.

According to these references, the Jain Guravs were very few in number eighty years ago. My chances of finding them now were, therefore, very limited. In spite of that, I decided to pursue my investigation. This meant that I had to visit the coastal Konkan area of Maharashtra and, in particular, Goa. I started making inquiries from people who came from these areas and asked them if they had heard of any temples in the region that had the name 'Jain' associated with them. In Pune, considered to be the home of scholarship in Maharashtra, I struck luck. I found a retired couple called Kunte who have extensively studied temples in Maharashtra.[3] They gave me the names of five temples that had the word 'Jain' in them.

Many visits to the Konkan unfortunately proved futile. I was finally able to locate a handful of Jain Gurav families in Goa and shall discuss them in a forthcoming paper. However, during these travels, I discovered that although the Jain Guravs have long disappeared from these areas, a large number of vestiges of their erstwhile presence remain. This is particularly true of a small town called Mangaon in the narrow coastal strip of Maharashtra called Konkan. I have chosen to quote from the pages of my field diary to describe the course of events and my discovery of a Jain goddess who has now been converted totally to Hinduism and who is the main subject matter of this chapter.

---

3 Moreshwar and Vijaya Kunte, a couple from Pune, retired from their ordinary clerical jobs in their mid-fifties and decided to take up a novel pastime. Moreshwar has an old motorbike. He and Vijaya decided to visit every temple in the city of Pune on this bike. They would visit the temple, take its measurements, collect its history and folklore, and write it up in the local newspaper. Within six months they had completed charting every temple in Pune, small or big, and published their first book. They then decided to go further and tour the entire state of Maharashtra to collect similar data. Twelve years on, they have published over fifteen volumes on Maharashtra temples. They had heard about the Jain connection in many of the Konkan temples and gave me details of some of the ones I visited.

Diary Entries

January 4, 2007

The train arrived two hours late at 10 am at Kudal in the heart of Konkan. Mr Patwardhan, a friend of my nephew Jitu who had accompanied me, had come to the station to pick us up. He took us in his car to hotel Abhimanyu, the only reasonable hotel at Kudal. The claim to its three-star status could be contested, but it was clean. As per Indian tradition, there was only one double mattress, laid straight on the floor. We got the hotel to give us two single mattresses. They were still without any mattress bases, but that will have to do. The hot water in the room geyser[4] worked only between 6 and 7 in the morning. Thankfully, one of the many servants brought us hot water in buckets and we had our baths. Jitu had booked a car for us, and our driver by the name of Vijay was patiently waiting for us outside the hotel. We started at around 12 noon and took the road that went to the town of Kharepatan. I had been told that there was a Jain temple there. Maybe they would know about Jain Guravs. Soon we stopped at a village called Oros where we picked up a gentleman called Dwarkananda Dicholkar, the owner of Ramli Inn, a big motel. Dicholkar was kind enough to spend the day with us. His local knowledge would be useful for us. The three of us then went on to the village of Kankavali.

Here we met Madhav Kadam, chief editor for the Konkan area edition of *Taruṇ Bhārat*, a respectable Marathi newspaper. When I explained to him that I was after locating Jain Guravs and their temples, his response was that he had never heard of them. He was most helpful though and, after many phone calls, organized for his offsider Nandu Korgaonkar to meet us at Kharepatan. Kadam confirmed that there were many Jain households and a practising Jain temple in that town. Like me, he also thought that the Jains at Kharepatan would most probably know about the Jain Guravs. We left for Kharepatan and had lunch on the way: authentic Malvani pomfret and Surmai (two tasty fish varieties) thalis.[5] Although a bit hot, the food and particularly the fish were excellent.

We reached the Jain temple known as Chandraprabha at 2 p.m. The temple contained a standing Jain Tīrthaṃkar image. Exactly opposite the main entrance stood a decorated pillar that also contained a standing Tīrthaṃkar image [Plates 4.1 and 4.2].

---

4 From the Icelandic for hot spring (*geysir* literally, 'gusher') and now extended in British and Indian usage to mean a plumbed water-heater to fill baths, buckets etc.

5 A *thali* is a plate of rice, meat, fish or vegetable curries and pickes, etc. available at restaurants in Maharashtra at meal times. No second serves are available.

I interviewed the pujari of the temple, Pranaykumar Subhash Pandit. The information I received from him was as follows:

Konkan had a very large population of Jains in the past and there were many Jain temples in the area. Chandraprabha was the oldest Jain temple here and Pranaykumar's ancestors had been there for many generations as pujaris. The image inside the temple was that of a Jain Tīrthaṃkar.[6] Jain pujaris are called Pandits. It takes them three years to obtain training with an *ācārya* (Jain teacher) to be able to qualify as a Pandit at a Jain temple. Pranaykumar said that Jain Pandits like him were never called Jain-Guravs and he was surprised to hear the term. He did mention that the Lingayat priests in the Śiva temples in the area were called Gurav and that people often mistakenly identified these Lingayats with Jains. He postulated that this might have been the origin of the term Jain-Gurav.

From Kharepatan we went to Nardave, a two and a half hour journey. This was one of the four places suggested by the Kuntes for me to visit. We reached there at 5 p.m. and eventually managed to locate an old man called Dajee Patel who agreed to help me with my quest. Patel is a common Gujarati name and is most unusual in Maharashtra; Dajee said that his forefathers might have come to Konkan from Gujarat, and hence the typically Gujarati surname. Dajee used to be a schoolteacher and knew a lot of old history of the place. He knew the myth about the Ādi-Śankarācārya defeating Maṇḍana Miśra and Jains being thrown out of their temples or forcefully converted to Hinduism.[7] At the temple of goddess Ambādevī (Durgā), he showed me a number of images which he called Jain images. To me, however, they looked like Veeragul[8] images.

Not far from the Ambādevī temple, at the outskirts of Nardave, is the Viṭṭhalādevī temple dedicated to the goddess Viṭṭhalādevī. In the courtyard of this temple, there were a large number of scattered stone images. Daji told me that this temple also belonged to the Jains; it was taken over by Hindus and the Jain images were thrown out in the courtyard. While I saw a lot of partially carved stones in the courtyard, there was no way of identifying them as Jain images.

Dajee asked us to visit Kalsuli,[9] a village on the way to our destination, Kudal. He mentioned that there was a practising temple there called 'Jain Brāhmaṇa temple'. The Kuntes had told me about this as well. The name was

---

6 All Jain temples have an image of one of their Tīrthaṃkars (seers, liberated souls) which they worship. The Jains claim that there were twenty-four Tīrthaṃkars, the twenty-fourth and last Tīrthaṃkar being Mahāvīra (599-527 BCE).

7 I discuss this myth at the end of this chapter.

8 Veeragul or Veerkallu stones are stones carved in honour of warriors who have passed away during battles. These stones do not have any names but depict the valorous deeds performed by the warrior (Setter and Sontheimer 1982).

9 Pronounced '*Kaḷsulī*'.

interesting and once again a contradiction in terms, and I therefore took his advice. Kalsuli is a tiny village with no more than half a dozen houses scattered amongst small rice paddocks. There was a small *pan-bidi*[10] (betel leaf and Indian cigarette) shop on the main road and we enquired there about the Jain-Brāhmaṇa temple. The female owner of the shop was most kind and accompanied us all the way to the temple, which was a good 20-minute walk through rice paddocks. The temple was really old.

The ancient carved stone pillars now supported a newly tiled roof. Someone sent for the Gurav temple priest and he arrived within half an hour. It was now getting dark. Atmaram Gurav would have been around 50. He first of all lit a small oil lamp (Plate 4.3). Unfortunately it was the power load-shedding day in the area and there was no electricity. I took several flashlight photos in the dark interior and hoped that at least some of them would be okay. Atmaram told me that he belonged to a group of Guravs called the 'Ahimsak Gurav'. The word 'ahimsak' means non-violent, although in the context of his profession, strict vegetarian would be the more appropriate meaning. There were only a few dozen families of these Guravs in the region now. They are strict vegetarians and, although they do not belong to the Lingayat caste, lately there have been marriages between the two groups. Atmaram told me that his family had been the Guravs at this temple for generations. He did the evening puja in our presence. It was simply a matter of offering Haldi (powdered turmeric) and Kumkum (vermilion), some flowers and waving of the incense stick and lamp. The main image in the shrine was a Śivaliṅga. However, scattered around the sanctum were many more images and some of them did look very much like Jain ones with one Tīrthaṃkar in the sitting posture. However, they were badly eroded.

Atmaram did not however know anything about them; he just worshipped them all. He did, however, mention that the temple did belong to the Jains in the past and it was still called 'Jain Brāhmaṇa' temple. He was not sure what the word Brāhmaṇa in the name meant in this context. To him, it never had any connection with Brāhmins. When asked about this and the worship of the Jain Tīrthaṃkar-like images, his was the same argument that village folk in India use time and time again. 'I don't know why I do this. I am just following what my father taught me, who in turn was taught by my grandfather.'

A curious phrase that he repeatedly used in his worship of all the idols except the Śivaliṅga was, 'Oh Jain Brāhmaṇ God! Accept the offering'. He did not know the origin or the phrase, or the reasons for using it.

I could see that the trail was getting hot. This to me was the clearest indication yet of a Jain shrine being appropriated by śaivite Hindus. The main image was that of Śiva; the others displaced from the sanctum were Jain images. The

---

10 Pronounced '*pān-bidī*'.

story gave credibility to the myth about Śankarācārya destroying Jain shrines and allowing the Jains to worship some Jain images only if they converted to Hinduism. If the Śankarācārya was behind this, then, he being a staunch devotee of Śiva, the main image of course had to be the Śivaliṅga.

Atmaram told us to go to Bordave,[11] not far from Kalsuli, because there was a practising Jain shrine there. This would have been interesting in checking out the tell-tale signs of Brāhminic/Hindu influence and comparing it with the Chandraprabha Jain temple at Kharepatan. We reached the place at 8 p.m. The temple was closed but the pujari (pandit), who lived nearby, kindly opened it for us. The shrine has been recently restored and had a new white marble image of a Jain Tīrthaṃkar.

The pujari said that the temple had no connection whatsoever with Hindus and he was not a Jain-Gurav. His information once again confirmed what we had been told by the Pandit of the Chandraprabha temple, that there are a number of Jain temples in Konkan but they have no connection with any Hindu shrine. We returned to the hotel at 9 p.m. and had dinner in their lovely outdoor garden. Every spirit and beer was available and the fare included fresh local fish.

January 5, 2007

I got up at 5.30 am. Had a shower and performed Yoga. By the time the laid-back hotel guy provided us the breakfast, it was 8.45 am. Vijay, our driver, had already come downstairs. We left the hotel at 9 am and went straight to Poip, another visit suggested by the Kunte couple. Here we were looking for the Munjeshwar temple.

The temple is a few kilometres away from the town in dense bush on a hillock surrounded by paddy fields. We parked the car and walked up the hillock. As we entered the temple grounds, we could hear a cassette tape running, 'Oṁ, Namaḥ Śivāya" (Hail Śiva, Obeisance to Śiva). Someone had just lit an incense stick and an oil lamp. The major surprise though was the image. It was nothing like a Śiva image,[12] a Śivaliṅgam or a traditional image of any other Hindu god.[13] It was colossal and looked more like a life-size statue of a Yakṣa,

---

11 Pronounced '*Borḍave*'.

12 The god Śiva is represented either as his phallic emblem (Śivaliṅgam) or, rarely, as the dancing Nāṭarājan.

13 These colossal images, purportedly of Śiva or his assistants such as the Vetāḷa, are found only in the Konkan coastal area of Maharashtra and at Goa. I was unable to find them in the literature on Hindu, Buddhist and Jain iconography. David Templeman, Buddhist scholar and contributor to this volume, also commented that he had seen nothing like this in his work in India and Tibet. This seems to be a rich field for a scholar in Hindu iconography to investigate.

an important god for the Jains.[14] He was sitting in the Yogāsana posture and had a serene smile on his face. He had a large moustache. An ornate crown, depicting cobra heads all around, adorned his head. The pujari had put a large sacred thread on him (Figures 4.1 and 4.2).

I was taking a few photos when the current pujari, Laxman Shiva Naik, also called Sonji, walked in. He warned me against taking pictures because he said that the god was very short-tempered and did not like being photographed. Those who had tried to take pictures in the past had suffered great misfortunes. However, after hearing my explanation of the reasons for my visit, he gladly allowed me to take photos.

Naik said that he knew the image was that of a Jain god but he told me that it was worshipped as Śiva for as long as he could remember. This was supported by the fact that the temple was also called Jain Munjeshwar[15] or Jain Pashan[16] temple. It is a very popular temple and devotees who wish to seek assurances from the god about their problems and anxieties[17] often visit it. According to Naik, there used to be a Gurav at the temple many years ago but he left and was never replaced. Since then, Naik and his family, who are the Mānkaris[18] of the temple, come every morning and perform a simple puja. Next to the image,

14 For instance, the *Bharatiya Samskritikosha* (Indian Cultural Encyclopaedia [in Marathi]) describes the Yakṣa Maṇibhadra as follows: He is one of the most worshipped gods in Jainism. Jain merchants (Vaishyas) erected many shrines for him. Jain Āgamas mention that at Mithila and Vardhamanapura there were *Chaityas* erected in his honour. Padmavati near Gwalior (the present town of Pawaya) was a major place for the worship of Maṇibhadra. There are images of Maṇibhadra in the museums at Gwalior and at Mathura. Both of these are huge and show him wearing a Dhoti, a sacred thread and a crown which tilts back (Joshi 1970, 667-678 [translated by the author]). Another Yakṣa, Digambara Yakṣa Sarvahna, c. 900, is described as a Jain male attendant, and the figure looks remarkably similar to that of the Munjeshwar shown in Figure 4.1 (Norton Simon Museum 1975).

15 Pronounced '*Muñjeśvara*'.

16 The term *ishwar* (all powerful lord) is applied as a suffix to the names of all Śiva shrines, such as Aranyeshwar (Śiva in the forest), Vishveshwar (Śiva, the lord of the universe), etc. In Marathi, Munja is a term meaning a threaded Brāhmin who has passed away and wanders the earth as a fearsome ghost on the banks of rivers. He can also reside on banyan trees. The term Jain Pashan, meaning a Jain stone, is most interesting. It is also the subject of my investigation in this chapter. The Sanskrit word *pāṣāṇa* is also used in Marathi and has the same meaning, i.e. a stone.

17 This procedure is called '*gārhāne karaṇe*' in Marathi and is basically the same as '*kaul lāvaṇe*'. A devotee comes to the temple before undertaking anything important or to seek reasons and remedies for his/her misfortune. The pujari acts as a medium and conveys the appropriate measures to be taken.

18 Mānkari(s) (literally, one who is honoured) are given priority over others in their ranking in undertaking tasks at the king's court or associated with temples. Dictated by age-old tradition, these rankings are jealously guarded and passed on to the next of kin.

Figure 4.1: Munjeshwar.

there were idols of what Naik identified as a goddess, Viṣṇu and the god of the Gondhaḷīs.[19] To me, however, they all looked like Jain images.

Naik told us to visit the temple of the Vetāḷa a few hundred metres down the hill. This temple was in the hands of Ghadi[20] pujaris. The life-size image, identified as Vetāḷa,[21] was identical to Munjeshwar, except for the fact that it was standing. The pujaris had clad the image in a dhoti, but, without it, it was

19 A Gondhaḷa is a song and dance performance common in Maharashtra in honour of the goddesses, usually Bhavani, Ambabai or Renuka. The performer is called a Gondhaḷi (pronounced '*Gondhaḷī*') (see Bapat 2003).

20 Ghadi (pronounced '*Ghāḍī*') is a caste that came originally from the state of Karnataka. Their main function was sacrificing animals for the goddess and predicting the future. Their tutelary deity is Vyaṅkateśa, a synthesis of Śiva and Viṣṇu.

21 Pronounced '*Vetāḷa*'.

Figure 4.2: Vetāḷa.

totally naked and displayed a large phallus, visible through the flimsy dhoti. The Ghadi pujari came straightaway. He asked me what my Garahne[22] was. I gave him a hundred rupees and asked him to pray for the health and wellbeing of my family and the successful completion of my research. The pujari then put this in front of the Vetāḷa and prayed for us in Konkani Marathi dialect. After visiting both of these shrines, I formed the impression that the Munjeswar and Vetāḷa temples were once again strong indications of the appropriation of Jain temples by Hindus.

22 The Marathi folk term *garahne* (pronounced '*gārāhṇe*') literally means complaint or grievance. In Konkan temples, the term is used to seek fulfilment of particular wishes or removal of particular obstacles in the way of the devotee. The pujari of the shrine asks the devotee what his particular grievance is. He then seeks redress from the god on behalf of the devotee.

We left Poip and were on the way to Malvan when we passed a village called Rathivde. Jitu suddenly remembered that Shyam Dhuri, the author of the book, *Konkanatil Gavrhati* (Traditional Running of the Village in Konkan),[23] was from this village. We decided to look him up and were very lucky to discover that he was at home. Dhuri's was an interesting story. He had a really good job in Mumbai, but gave it up and came to his hometown with the sole purpose of doing research on the Gāvarhātī system and start renovation of the old Gangeshwar temple. Dhuri firmly believes that the main reason for the loss of the social order today is the demise of the Gāvarhātī system. When I asked him about the Jain-Gurav, he told me that the Jains were very much a part of the *Gavrhati* system but they were never Gurav. He had not heard of the Jain-Gurav. His guess was that the Jains may have been called Guravs simply because they were temple priests. He did, however, tell me that many Śiva temples in the area housed a stone called a 'Jain Pashan'. The old Gangeshwar[24] temple in the outskirts of the village was one such temple. In the middle of the village, there was a comparatively recent temple called the new Gangeshwar temple which had been renovated by the villagers. Dhuri was not in favour of these renovations; he maintained that the real Gangeshwar temple was the old one and it needed urgent attention. He then took us to both the temples.

I was keen to see the old temple because of its Jain Pashan. In the small entrance hall before one entered the sanctum, there was a stone image on the left. Dhuri said that this was the 'Jain Pashan'. It did not look like the image of a Jain Tīrthaṃkar and I was unable to identify it due to bad erosion. It is this totally neglected temple that Dhuri wants to renovate and bring back into community worship.

Dhuri told us to visit the Śiva shrine called Kunakeshvara[25] in a small village with the same name on our way back to Kudal. This temple, more or less in total ruin, provoked a sense of *déjà vu*. Iconographically, the image here looked almost identical to the images I had seen at Poip.

The temple's antiquity was evident from the huge stone pillars which were badly eroded. These pillars held a thatched roof, obviously a later addition. There were no walls. The temple was being used as storage for timber and other items by the villagers. At one end stood the huge image, which looked like a Yakṣa, identical iconographically and in its physical dimensions to the image of Vetāḷa at Poip. It was a standing, totally naked image and was being worshipped as Śiva.

---

23 *Konkanatil Gavrhati* (pronounced '*Konkanatīl Gāvarhātī*') can be loosely translated as system for the (smooth) running of the village. While the rest of the state of Maharashtra had the Balute system, the Konkan area had the *Gāvarhatī* system.

24 Pronounced '*Gaṅgeśvara*'.

25 Pronounced '*Kuṇakeśvara*'.

Figure 4.3: Kunakeshwar Image.

At the other end stood a huge anthill. Unfortunately there was no pujari here either. A young man from the next-door house came and told us about the temple. It had been in ruins ever since his childhood. The anthill was also held sacred and occasionally worshipped along with the image of Śiva.[26] These days there is a *jatra* (fair) once a year and that is the only time when a proper puja is performed.

26 In village folklore, an anthill has always been held sacred and represents the generative organ, Yoni, of mother earth.

Many people had told us about Pendur where there was a famous temple of *Santeri,* the goddess in her anthill form. They told us that next to the *Santeri* temple there were a large number of Jain images under a banyan tree. We therefore made Pendur our next stop. The shrine of *Santeri* is fairly large and, this being the *Santeri* festival, it was thronged with devotees. The huge anthill had been painted and covered with several garlands. There were a number of Shamans who were making offerings to the goddess on behalf of the devotees. I saw at least two people who were possessed and were surrounded by people asking them questions about their future. At the behest of these Shamans, various offerings were being made to the goddess.[27]

Everyone knew about the broken Jain images that were only a hundred metres away from the *Santeri* shrine. A thought came to my mind that the shrine may have belonged to them before they were removed and put under the large banyan tree.

These images were a sorry sight; there were a few Tīrthaṃkars, one without a head. A Yakṣiṇī image had coalesced with banyan roots that had engulfed her, reminding me of many of the Angkor Wat temples. The Yakṣiṇī was obviously worshipped still, as evidenced by the small silver swing that hung above her and the offerings of *haldi*, *kumkum* and fresh flowers.[28] Many people told me that such broken Jain images were scattered all over Konkan. It was now getting quite dark and we headed back to Kudal.

January 6, 2007

We woke up early; I had a shower, did my yoga and left the hotel at 7.30 am. A well-known Jain academic, Dr Tupkar, had told me to visit Mangaon which was a stronghold of the Jains in the past. Tupkar had said that the goddess Yakṣiṇī at Mangaon was in actual fact a Jain goddess. He had told us to visit one Mr Bhogar who is over 70 and a Jain Kasar[29] (manufacturer of glass bangles) by caste. We located his house without much difficulty and found both him and his son at home. They were very hospitable and we were treated to the

27 Possession is a fairly common phenomenon in many of the goddess temples in Maharashtra and in many other parts of India. It is said that, on special days, the goddess enters the body of a favourite devotee. Once possessed, the devotee is thought to be elevated to a supernatural shamanic plane and has direct contact with the deity. The person starts trembling uncontrollably and displays unruly behaviour. Those possessed also display psychic powers and are believed to be able to predict the future. The gathered devotees ask these Shamans questions about their welfare and are often given cryptic answers. Possession may last from just a few minutes to several hours.

28 This is common in folk Hinduism. Women who are unable to have children worship a local goddess and make a vow to make an offering of a small swing, often a silver one, to her image if they conceive.

29 Pronounced '*Kāsār*'.

Figure 4.4: Headless Tīrthaṃkar image.

mandatory traditional sweet, strong Indian Chay. I recorded an interview with Bhogar Senior. He told me that Mangaon was one of the several towns in the area in which there had formerly been a very large Jain population. There had been over ten households of Jain Kasars alone. The main temple in the town housed a Jain Tīrthaṃkar. There was another small shrine in the temple courtyard dedicated to the Jain goddess Yakṣiṇī. The worship of these deities was in the hands of the Jain-Guravs. There were more than a dozen houses belonging to Jain-Guravs in the temple precinct. However, they left the place one by one and the puja at the shrine came to *Kokaṇastha* Brāhmins.[30] He told me that his father had told him that the Jain Tīrthaṃkar used to be the main image in this shrine. However, the Tīrthaṃkar image was removed and shoved into the

30 Amongst Maharashtra Brāhmins, the *Kokaṇastha* Brāhmins are thought to be hierarchically superior to others, who are Deshastha, Karhade, Devrukhe and Gaud Saraswat.

left hand corner of the temple and the Yakṣiṇī image was brought in from the next-door shrine and installed as the main deity.

Bhogar senior insisted that a Yakṣiṇī had got to be a Jain deity; the Hindus have never worshipped her as a goddess.[31] He also told me to look for the 'Jainachā Khamb'[32] in a covered porch outside the temple. I did find it there.

The current pujari at the temple is a *Kokaṇastha* Brāhmin by the name of Konkar. Contrary to what Bhogar senior had said, Konkar insisted that Yakṣiṇī Devī was a Hindu deity. She appeared in the dream of his grandfather and instructed him to remove the Jain Tīrthaṃkar and install her image there. That is why the Tīrthaṃkar image was removed and put into one corner. Mr. Konkar does not worship this Tīrthaṃkar image, neither does anyone else. The puja of the goddess now consists of a regular Hindu puja with the daily chanting of parts of the *Durgā-Saptaśatī*.[33] I paid him Rs.100 for chanting on my behalf.

Konkar is in his late twenties. He told me that his uncle had the rights to the puja until ten years ago and that his wife might be able to tell me more about the history of the place and about the Jain Gurav. We were lucky that the lady in question was available and volunteered a lot of information. She said that she was brought up as a child in Mangaon. She distinctly remembers that in her childhood there was a very large number of Jains and Jain Guravs in the town. There were over a dozen households of the Jain Guravs close to the temple and they were the ones who had the right to perform worship at the Tīrthaṃkar and the Yakṣiṇī Devī temples. They were very staunch in their beliefs and were strict vegetarians. They refused to eat even at Brāhmin households and had a separate well for their water. She took us to the Jain well and also showed us what was left of their houses; just some stone foundations. She further showed us the Brāhmin locality, which was away from the Jain one, and the Brāhmin well also. Neither of the wells is in use now. Finally she took us a few hundred metres from the temple in the woods to where some broken Jain images and Pādukā[34] (carved impressions of feet) lay in the midst of nowhere.

31 Bhogar Senior's observations seem to be correct. Yakṣas and Yakṣiṇīs are hardly worshipped as parts of the Hindu pantheon. Hinduism did worship them in the distant past, but only as malevolent deities. They were worshipped so that they would not harm the devotee and would keep away from him.

32 Pronounced *Jainācā Khāmb*, meaning the Jain Pillar.

33 The *Durgāsaptaśatī* or just *Saptaśatī* (literally, 700 verses) is part of the *Devī Māhātmya* which itself is a part of the *Mārkaṇḍeya Purāṇa*. It contains 567 verses which are divided into 700 mantras and hence the name. These verses describe the myths and exploits of Kālī, Lakṣmī and Saraswatī, considered to be part of the same ultimate goddess, the Devī. It is common to chant parts of the *Saptaśatī* during the puja repertoire.

34 It is a common practice in India to worship stone impressions of holy men's feet. These carved images are kept in the sanctum along with images of gods and goddesses.

Figure 4.5: Jain Pādukā (right-hand side).

She did not know why, but the Jains left the town one by one and the worship eventually came to the Konkar family. She confirmed what the Bhogars had said to the effect that the Yakṣiṇī Devī was originally a Jain goddess.[35]

From Mangaon we went a long way to Nevati, and saw the Śivaji's fort there. The town of Khavane[36] is about two kilometres from Nevati. We had to cross the bay on a small raft to get to Khavane. This is the place for the shrine of Khavaneshwara,[37] a Jain Tīrthaṃkar being worshipped as Śiva. The sanctum has several Jain images within. The main image is of a Tīrthaṃkar. Other images include Jain goddesses. The pujari as well as an old man who has been a resident for many years told me the same story. There was no attempt here to hide the fact that a Jain Tīrthaṃkar was being worshipped as Śiva.

35 In Hinduism, Yakṣas and Yakṣiṇīs have always been looked upon as malevolent godlings. They do not have their own temples and are thought to be tree-dwellers. They are rarely worshipped. One exception is childless village women who worship Yakṣiṇīs, often in their form as autochthonous stones under trees, in order to conceive. On the other hand, they have had a more prominent presence in Jainism and Buddhism. In Jainism, Kuber is considered to be the king of Yakṣas, while the leader of the Yakṣas is Maṇibhadra. Maṇibhadra's images are invariably found in Jain temples. Jain works, such as Jinasena's *Ādipurāṇa* and Jain *āgama* literature contain details about the abodes and worship of the Yakṣas (Deshpande 1986, Chapter 8). For a detailed discussion of the Jain goddesses and the Yakṣiṇī cult in Jainism, see Nandi (1973, Chapters X and XI).

36 Pronounced '*Khavaṇe*'.

37 Pronounced '*Khavaṇeśvara*'. Īśvara is a name used normally for Śiva and Śiva temple names normally end with the suffix *-īśvara*. Examples are Karṇeśvara, Hareśvara, Viśveśvara etc.

Figure 4.6: Tīrthaṃkar worshipped at Khavaṇeśvara as Śiva.

The two men told me an interesting tale. The Jain images were being transported by sea by a Jain merchant when the boat got stuck in the shallow waters near Khavane. Śiva came into the dream of the merchant and the townsfolk and told them that he did not wish to go any further and that he should be worshipped by erection of a temple at Khavane.

Analysis and conclusion

My quest for Jain Guravs was more or less complete. My diary entries can be summarised as follows. Newspaper editors in the Konkan area had not heard of the Jain Gurav. There were many Jain households and temples in the area but none of them had heard of the Jain Guravs either. Pujaris in the Jain temples were called Jain-Pandits but they were never called Guravs. At least one temple, that at Kalsuli, had Jain images which were invoked as 'Jain-Brāhmaṇa images' by the pujari. In two places, Poip and Kunakeshwar, there were colossal images that did not look like the traditional Hindu ones; they looked more like Yakṣa images but were being worshipped as Śiva. Besides, the pujaris in both of these temples said that they knew that the temples were Jain temples in the past but were now practising as Śiva temples. There were several stones in and around Śiva temples in the area. These were identified by people as 'Jain Pashan'. In the courtyards and outskirts of most of the temples there were broken Jain images. At the Yakṣiṇī Devī temple, a large image of Tīrthaṃkar sat in one corner of the sanctum sanctorum without being worshipped and a smaller image of the goddess was being worshipped as Durgā. Finally, at Khavane, a Jain Tīrthaṃkar was being worshipped as Śiva.

Several questions come to mind after examining the literature and my diary entries:

1. Was Jainism a state religion in Maharashtra and particularly in the Konkan and Goa areas? Are there vestiges of Jainism in Maharashtra today?
2. Is there any evidence to show that Jains were converted to Hinduism and some of them became temple priests?
3. What was the hierarchical position of the Jain Guravs in Konkan and Goa?
4. Do Śiva temples carry a 'Jainacha Khamb' and other Jain artefacts in these areas?
5. Why were the Jain Guravs found only in the Konkan and Goa parts of Maharashtra?

Question four is the only one that can be answered in the affirmative. However, answers to other questions have been lost in antiquity. Recorded history of Maharashtra between the eighth and thirteenth centuries is surprisingly sparse in detail. We do, however, know some facts, which I discuss below.

Jainism in Maharashtra[38]

There is good evidence to suggest that Jainism was a prominent force, if not the state religion, in Maharashtra since ancient times. Maharashtra is often called the gateway to South India. Migration of Jain monks from North to South India through Maharashtra took place as early as the third century BCE. The earliest inscriptional evidence of their presence is found in the Jain cave at Pale[39] in Pune district. The cave is situated on the famous route passing through Nane Ghat.[40] The inscription in this cave quotes the first line of the Namokara[41] mantra, the most sacred mantra for the Jains. The first inscription in the Marathi language is dated 981 CE and is at Shravanabelagola, in the present-day Karnataka, near the left foot of the statue of the Jain Tīrthaṃkar Gomateshwara, the first human to achieve *moksha* according to the Jains.

Great dynasties such as Rashtrakutas, Kadambas, Chalukyas, Ratts, Kalachuris, Yadavs and Shilaharas ruled over Maharashtra. Many of these rulers were Jains. Kings of these dynasties built many forts, which had Jain temples within. Their remains are still found all over Maharashtra. Texts such as the *Śaṅkardigvijaya* (Vidyaranya, 1986) and the *Śivalīlāmṛta* (Shridharaswami, 1996) suggest that a large number of Maharashtrians were Jains in the past. Jain temples known commonly as *basti* are found all over Maharashtra and especially in the areas bordering the state of Karnataka. As can be seen from my diaries and photographs, there are broken and neglected images of Jain Tīrthaṃkars and Jain goddesses at many places in Maharashtra.

The demise of Jainism

Both Jainism and Buddhism were authentic alternatives to Vedic teaching and Brāhminism. Therefore, during the heyday of these two faiths, Brāhminism was at a low ebb. Traditionally the *kṣatriya* kings were the main hub of support for the Jains and Buddhists. However, between the

---

38 In spite of an extensive search, I was unable to find much in the way of Jain history in Maharashtra. I did get in touch with many Jain academics and scholars, such as Professor Tupkar, mentioned in the text above, and did an exhaustive search on the Internet. There are also several Jain blogs and Jain Internet sites. However, they are all silent about Jain history of Maharashtra and the demise of Jainism therein.

39 Pronounced *'Pāle'*.

40 Pronounced *'Nāṇe Ghāṭa'*.

41 Pronounced *'Ṇamokāra'*.

sixth and eighth centuries CE, the Alvar (Vaiṣṇavite) and Nayanmar (Śaivite) saints started a violent reaction against Jainism in the south, forcing the latter to move away to Karnataka, where there was support from the Ganga kings. In the seventh century, the anti-Jain preaching by the Śaivite saints such as Appar and Sambandar resulted in the massacre of 8,000 Jains at Madurai. According to M.S. Ramaswamy Iyengar, between the ninth and tenth century, the Jains lost prominence in the South, due to the systematic persecution and annihilation by the Alvars.[42] This paved the way for the total removal of all the traces of Jainism in the Andhra-Karnataka country as well. As Verardi comments:

> In order to survive, the Jains resorted to a sort of mimicry of the Brahman institutions and behaviours that, on one hand assured their survival, (but) caused their weakening and the almost total loss of their identity. Jinasena in the 8th century incorporated the sixteen samskaras of the Brahmans into the Jain system, almost in their entirety ... Sankara, who was the greatest apostle of orthodoxy and persecutor of heretics, appeared towards the end of the 8th century ... A class of 'Jaina Brahmanas' was introduced among the Digambaras, entrusted with the care of the temples and the performance of elaborate rituals ... Only on these terms were the Jains allowed to survive as a community (Verardi 1996, 226).[43]

The Jain Guravs, their disappearance and appropriation of Jain images

Who were the Jain Guravs? From the evidence seen above, they may have been Jain priests who were forcibly converted to Hinduism at the time of the Ādi-Śaṅkarācārya and, later, under the persecution of śaivite Brāhmins, who took over Jain temples and converted them to Śiva shrines. At this juncture, it is worthwhile looking at the myth concerning the Śaṅkarācārya because it involves Jains in one of its versions written in Maharashtra.

Legend has it that before the first Śaṅkarācārya was born in the seventh century, the ruling religions of India were Jainism and Buddhism

42 See Verardi (1996), citing Ayyangar (1922, 222-227).

43 I am grateful to my colleague, Andrea Di Castro, who alerted me to Verardi's scholarship in this area.

(Vidyaranya, 1986). Sanātana Dharma (the eternal religion which later became Hinduism) had all but disappeared and had given way to heretical teachings. Śaṅkarācārya, considered to be an *avatāra* (incarnation) of Śiva, was born to bring back Brāhminic Hinduism. He learned the scriptures at a very young age and debated the virtues of Sanātana Dharma with Jain and Buddhist scholars. He won every one of these debates and converted the Jains and Buddhists *en masse* to Hinduism. It is said, further, that he was also responsible for the massacre of thousands of Jains. Śaṅkarācārya preached non-dualistic religion and is known to have had a famous debate with the dualist Pandit Maṇḍaṇa Miśra. The latter lost and became a disciple of Śaṅkarācārya under the name of Sureśvarācārya.

Another version of this myth appears in chapter 15 of the *Śivalīlāmṛta*, a well-known work in Marathi attributed to Shridharaswami (1996).[44] In a fantastic flight of imagination, the *Śivalīlāmṛta* portrays Maṇḍaṇa Miśrā as a clever but devious Jain pandit who is given to having drinking orgies with none other than Saraswatī, the goddess of Knowledge. The Śaṅkarācārya wins the debate and Maṇḍaṇa Miśra becomes his disciple. The winner orders the total destruction of all of the Jain scriptures and their temples. Maṇḍaṇa Miśra begs the Ācārya to let the Jains keep at least one diacritic marker of the Jains. Śaṅkarācārya, in his largesse, allows them to keep one stone next to the Śivaliṅga in the temple and says that the stone should be called 'Jain Pashan' and worshipped as such (Bapat 2012). He also allowed one Jain book to be saved, the *Amarakośa* by the Jain Pandit Amarasinha.

It is interesting to note that this fantastic tale of Śaṅkarācārya's victory over Jainism comes from a Marathi poet-writer. It is only in Maharashtra that one hears of the Jain Gurav. It is also the only state where one finds a large number of Śiva temples with the Jain stone in the sanctum.

Given the literary references, facts ascertained from my travel diaries and the photographic evidence I have presented, one can now assemble the possible reasons for the departure of the Jains, and hence the Jain Guravs, from Maharashtra, along with the chronology of the process. Until the eighth century, the regions of Karnataka and Maharashtra were under one rule. The systematic oppression and annihilation of Jainism that happened in Karnataka would have therefore affected Maharashtra equally. Jains would have been killed or converted to Hinduism in large

44 Shridharaswami was an important and highly productive Marathi saint-poet who lived in the late seventeenth and early eighteenth century (1658–1729 CE). He wrote over 125,000 verses of poetry; the *Śivalīlāmṛta* was his last work.

numbers and their temples converted to Śiva shrines. Even their gods were hinduised and worshipped as such. The Jain goddess Yakṣiṇī at Mangaon was removed from her small shrine and installed in the main temple as Durgā. The Tīrthaṃkar in the main temple, on the other hand, remains in one corner of the main shrine totally neglected. He is never worshipped by the Brāhmin priest.

Those Jain temple priests who survived the massacre would have been required to worship Śiva in the newly converted shrine. The origin of the Jain Pashan in Śiva temples may go back to the time of the Ādi-Śaṅkarācārya in the eighth century, but the Brāhminic hierarchy would have been more than willing to continue the status quo centuries after that. The Jain Brāhmaṇa at the Śiva shrine at Kalsuli tells us a similar tale. Maybe he was a high priest in Jainism who is now remembered only as a stone in a Śiva temple. With the march of time, the Jain Guravs would have lost their 'Jain' memory and became mere temple servants or pujaris.

As I shall elaborate in a future paper, there are still a few village temples in Goa in the hands of a handful of Jain Guravs. They have the Śivaliṅga and also the Jain Pashan in the *sanctum sanctorum*. Although they worship both of these images, they do not know who the 'Jain Baba' is or why they worship him. They also do not know why they are called Jain Guravs. Their fate is no different to that of pujaris in many of the small shrines in India today. Although the Jain Guravs are not now persecuted for being Jains, the younger generation of these temple priests is not at all interested in keeping the tradition going in the face of abject poverty and chooses to leave the village in search of more attractive professions. No matter what your religion is, that is the fate of people in village India.

Bibliography

Ayyangar, M.S. Ramaswami. 1922. *Studies in South Indian Jainism, Part 1, South Indian Jainism*. Madras: Printed by Hoe & Co.

Bapat, Jayant Bhalchandra. 1993. 'The Gurav temple priests of Maharashtra'. *South Asia: Journal of South Asian Studies* 16: 70-100.

Bapat, Jayant Bhalchandra. 1998. 'A Jatipurana (clan history myth) of the Gurav temple priests of Maharashtra'. *Asian Studies Review* 22 (1): 63-77.

Bapat, Jayant Bhalchandra. 1999. 'The Devalaka myth in the Śivapurana: an early example of a Jatipurana?' *Journal of the Oriental Institute, M.S. University of Baroda* 49 (1-2): 85-117.

Bapat, Jayant Bhalchandra. 2000. '*The Shaiva Gurav Temple Priests of Maharashtra: A Problem of Hierarchy and Status*'. Ph.D. thesis, La Trobe University, Melbourne.

Bapat, Jayant Bhalchandra. 2001. 'The Jatipuranas of the Gurav temple priests of Maharashtra'. *International Journal of Hindu Studies* 5 (1): 45-90.
Bapat, Jayant Bhalchandra. 2003. 'Gondhala'. In *South Asian Folklore: an encyclopaedia*, edited by M. Mills; P. Claus; S. Diamond, 265–266. New York and London: Routledge.
Bapat, Jayant Bhalchandra. 2012. 'The end of the Jain-Gurav and the persistence of memory in the Śivalīlāmṛta'. In *Prācyaprajñāpradīpa. Professor Dr. Samaresh Bandyopadhyay Felicitation Volume on Early Indian History and Culture*, edited by Ian Mabbett, 137-151. Kolkata: Forum for the Felicitation of Professor Dr Samaresh Bandyopadhyay and the North American Institute for Oriental and Classical Studies.
Deshpande, S.R. 1986. *Bhāratīya Kāmaśilpa* [in Marathi]. Pune: Continental Prakashan.
Enthoven, R.E. 1922. *The Tribes and Castes of Bombay, Vol. 2*. Bombay: Government Printing Press.
Gazetteer of the Bombay Presidency, Volume X. Ratnágiri and Sávantvádi. 1880. Bombay: Government Central Press.
Joshi, Pandit Mahadeoshastri (ed.). 1970. *Bharatiya Samskritikosha*. Vol. 6. Pune: Bharatiya Samskritikosha Mandal.
Kelkar, R.N. 1981. 'Konkaṇ Prantātīl Gurav Samāj' [In Marathi (The Gurav community in the Konkan area)]. *Bharat Itihas Samshodhan Mandal Quarterly* 60: 17.
Nandi, Kamendra Nath. 1973. *Religious Institutions and Cults in the Deccan*. Delhi: Motilal Banarsidass.
Norton Simon Museum. 2012. 'Digambara Yaksha Sarvahna, c. 900' F.1975.17.07.S. http://www.nortonsimon.org/collections/browse_title.php?id=F.1975.17.07.S (accessed 13 July 2016).
Russell, R.V. and Hira Lal. 1916 (reprinted 1975). *The Tribes and Castes of the Central Provinces of India,* Vol.3. Patna: Rajdhani Book Centre.
Satoskar, B.D. 1979. *Gomantaka, Prakruti and Samskruti* [In Marathi] Vol.1. Pune: Shubhada Saraswat.
Setter, S., and Gunther Sontheimer (eds). 1982. *Memorial Stones* (IIAH Series No. 2, South Asian Studies No. XI/11). Dharwad: Institute of Indian Art History; Heidelberg: South Asia Institute.
Shridharaswami. 1996. *Shri Śivalīlāmṛta* (*Parayana va Phalashrutisaha*) Adhyaya 1-15 [in Marathi]. Mumbai: Dharmik Prakashan Samstha.
Singh, K.S. (ed.). 1993. *People of India*, Volume XXI, Goa. Bombay: Anthropological Survey of India and Popular Prakashan.
Verardi, Giovanni. 1996. 'Religions, rituals and the heaviness of Indian history'. *Annali (Istituto Universitario Orientale,* Napoli) 56 (2): 215-248.
Vidyaranya, Madhava. 1986. *Sankara Digvijaya: the Traditional Life of Sri Sankaracharya.* 3rd ed., trans. Swami Tapasyananda. Madras: Sri Ramakrishna Math.
Wikipedia. 2013. 'Jainism in Maharashtra'. http://en.wikipedia.org/wiki/Jainism_in_Maharashtra (accessed 31 March 2016).

Chapter 5

Appropriating the Inappropriate

John R. Dupuche

Many forms of appropriation – cultural, linguistic, social and so on – are studied in this volume of essays. Perhaps the form of appropriation that goes to the heart of all reality, however, is religious or metaphysical, which is precisely the focus of this essay. It studies the extreme act of appropriating the inappropriate, which, paradoxically, constitutes the ultimate method of attaining the universal mind, the mind of Devī herself.

The word 'appropriation', in its various cognates, 'inappropriate', 'expropriate', 'proper', 'improper', 'property', 'proprietor' and its additional meanings in the French word *propre* signifying 'clean', and 'self' are tackled in this essay. It seeks to show how all these varied meanings are reconciled in the overarching structure of the non-dualism (*advaita*) of Kashmir Shaivism which seeks to attain the ultimate state of 'resting in the self' (*svātmāviśrānti*). Only by this reconciliation of opposites can all things be truly liberated.

It will be shown that 'appropriation' does not mean domination, or elimination, despising or fearing. Quite the contrary, appropriation means that one truth is found in the other, one is a preparation for the other. The very title *Tantrāloka* 'Light on the Tantras', suggests the supremacy of Kashmir Shaivism whilst demonstrating the essential value of the other tantras.

This non-dualism (*advaita*) of Kashmir Shaivism raises many crucial issues, however. The limited and the unlimited: how can they be non-dual? How can the impure be pure? How can god and goddess be identified? Good and evil, pleasant and unpleasant, in short, all the forms of *sukha* and *duḥkha*: how are they one?

These incompatibilities are resolved, this chapter hopes to show, by Abhinavagupta (c. 975–1025 CE), the leading figure in this school, in his presentation of the Kula ritual in chapter 29 of his great work, the *Tantrāloka*, and in its thoroughgoing commentary by Jayaratha (c. 1225–1275 CE). In his *Tantrāloka* Abhinavagupta surveys all the *tantra*s of his day and reinterprets them according to the philosophical system of Trika in the form initiated by Vasugupta (875–925 CE) in his seminal work *Śivasūtra*. To put it very briefly, according to this system all reality is seen as threefold, Śiva, Śakti, human; subject, means and object of knowledge; action, mental constructs and the absence of mental constructs; the goddesses Parā, Parāparā, Aparā, etc. etc. This threefold structure, however, is shown by Abhinavagupta to be non-dual.

Among the vast number of *tantra*s examined in that encyclopaedic work, Jayaratha states that Abhinavagupta prefers the Kula tradition – 'he esteems more highly the guru who follows the Kula ritual procedure (*kulaprakriyā*) – because of [its] restfulness – in comparison with the guru who is devoted to tantra ritual procedure (*tantraprakriyā*)' (*TĀV* vol. 2, 31) – where the Devī has the central role.

Abhinavagupta must find his way through reefs and shoals, however. He must justify his teaching in face of the *Laws of Manu* and Brāhminic *dharma* and their strict sanctions against impure substances. He must show how the extremist Kula is worthy of consideration, in face of the need to keep it secret. He must show how his preferred ritual, the Kula ritual, is available to householders despite its origins in the exotic practices of the Kāpālikas. He must show how this material reality is real in contrast with a monistic version of the Vedantā, which sees this world as illusion (*māyā*). He will need to mitigate the essential divisiveness of the four *āśrama,* which place liberation (*mukti*) in opposition to the other three *āśrama,* and show how the Kaula practitioner can become liberated while still living (*jīvanmukta*). In achieving this, he must depart from the fundamental dualism of the school that prevailed in the Vale of Kashmir in his day, namely the Śaivasiddhānta, for which liberation consists in being only like Śiva, and so fundamentally other than Śiva (Sanderson 1988, 691). He does all this by showing how Devī appropriates everything, even the inappropriate.

The presentation in this essay is readily accepted by scholars in the field, but misconstrued extensively in popular *tantra* which eagerly uses the antinomian character and illicit substances to an end not intended by Abhinavagupta. Georg Feuerstein comments, 'This "California tantra,"

[is] based on a profound misunderstanding of the Tantric path. Their main error is to confuse Tantric bliss ... with ordinary orgasmic pleasure' (quoted in Urban 2003, 205). To which Hugh Urban (2003, 255) adds 'instead of the ideal of unity, order, or harmony, the late-capitalist aesthetic is one of physical intensity, shock value, immediate gratification, and ecstatic experience'. The 'Tantric sex' business in the West has made an 'abusive appropriation of the adjective "Tantric"' (White 2003, xiv). This essay seeks to re-appropriate the Tantric sexual tradition.

Tantrāloka 29 is a ritual text. It does not present a clear, systematic philosophical discourse but rather describes various ceremonies. By interspersing rubrics with occasional comments, by using symbolic gestures and code words with multiple layers of meaning (*sandhi*), Abhinavagupta and his commentator Jayaratha show how appropriation occurs. This chapter will try to unpack the bewildering welter of information by quoting relevant ritual texts and explaining the terminology. In this way a much needed systematic presentation will be provided out of material that is not systematic. It is a corrective to common misunderstandings that still exercise a powerful and fascinating effect on the modern mind.

Expropriating the traditions

What is the place of the Vedas, the *Laws of Manu*, and the wide variety of schools that tussled with each other in the Vale of Kashmir around the year 1000 CE? Other schools might seek to disprove their opponents' view by rational debate, but Abhinavagupta does not discard other views. Indeed, the very concept of non-dualism precludes any outright rejection of other traditions, even those it opposes. If all is non-dual, all must somehow cohere. This coherence is achieved by a process of expropriation. An example of this is provided in the first major ceremony of *TĀ* 29 where the practitioner withdraws his mind from the outer, lesser manifestations to reach the inner dwelling of the goddess.

> She who dwells within the kula which consists of a circle, i.e. of the mantras, the Perfected Beings, the subtle-breath and the instrument of consciousness, she who is consciousness, she who has been called Prabhvī (Sovereign): she, in this context, is Kuleśvarī (Mistress of the Kula). She [dwells] at the centre as Śrī Parā (the Illustrious Supreme One) and as Devī (*TĀ* 29.46b–47).

Having acquired the mind of *Devī*, the practitioner then moves outwards, in a contrary movement, since all the other traditions proceed out of the union of god and goddess as rays of light from their source – 'A stream of rays flows like sparks of fire from consciousness which has the form of a great splendour' (*TĀ* 29.50a). Thus the other traditions are not simply false. Rather, to the extent that they are distant from the source, they have less power and are less enlightening. As Abhinava says: '"Non-dual only, not dual" is Parameśitā's[1] command. The mantras given by the Siddhāntas and the Vaiṣṇavas etc., are therefore impure. Because they cannot bear so much splendour they are lifeless … ' (*TĀ* 29.74–75a).

Alexis Sanderson, in his meticulous study of the history of the Tantric tradition, shows this in detail. He points out that there is a clear trajectory (Sanderson 1988, 669) from the Vedas, through the Siddhānta tradition, the Left, Right, Mata, Kula, and Kaula traditions, to reach the Trika; 'Thus the Trika locates itself at the furthest remove from neutral "Vedic" orthodoxy' (Sanderson 1990, 50). The Trika is superior to the Kula ritual inasmuch as Trika is pure consciousness, without the need for ritual. Sanderson further notes that in this process, the *tantra*s progressively shift their focus away from the male deity to the female deity, from the *dharma* established by the god to the antinomianism inspired by the goddess. It is a trajectory from 'right' to 'left', from the licit to the illicit, from the ordered to the disordered.

Devī is triumphant, therefore, not by rejecting other traditions, but by lessening their importance. She shows she is superior to them by absorbing them. Each is given its place but she surpasses them by being their heart, their source and their purpose. They are simply a diminution of the totality of her revelation. Thus the Vedas and other traditions are not false; they are only inadequate and impotent.

Devī, the Appropriator

The Kula *tantra* tradition makes many extremist claims. It holds that Devī, and not Brahmā or Viṣṇu, is supreme; it postulates a non-dual position; it makes use of impure substances; it attributes overwhelming power to mantras; it has an antinomian character; it emphasises the primacy of energy; it holds to the reality of this world and so on. All these hallmarks of the extreme Kula *tantra* must be justified by an appropriate ontology, which is described in the following passages and the terminology of the system.

1 Parameśitā is another name for Śiva.

According to Kashmir Shaivism the ultimate reality is not 'That' (*tat*) as in the famous *tat tvam asi* ('Thou art That') of the Vedānta, but 'I' (*aham*). This basic viewpoint underlies the rituals, and the rituals in turn are designed to inculcate the sense of "I" in the practitioner.

The phoneme *A*, the first phoneme of the Sanskrit alphabet, represents Śiva, the foundation of all. The phoneme *HA* is, properly speaking, the final phoneme of the alphabet. By the rule of *pratyāhāra*, where the first and last phonemes of a series contain all that is found in between, the word *aham* signifies the beginning and end of all. It is the whole of reality in all its aspects, not disparate but identical, non-dual. All is 'I'.

Furthermore, the phoneme *Ḥ* (*visarga*), which is classed as the last of the sixteen vowels, represents the moment when all reality, symbolised by the thirty-four consonants of the alphabet, comes into existence. The very orthography itself is taken to symbolise this pregnant moment for *Ḥ* is written as ':' where the two dots represent the union of Śiva and Śakti. From their union, all reality proceeds; '*Ḥ* is the projection of reality' (Abhinavagupta 1975, 52).

Thus, the ultimate reality is the couple, Śiva and his Śakti, who are engaged in an eternal embrace, not divided but inseparate (*anavachinna*). As Jayaratha puts it, the world is 'the outflow from the pulsation (*sphāra*) of Śiva and Śakti' (*TĀV* vol. 7, 3295). From their relationship, indeed from the play (*krīḍā*) of their love-making, the world is emitted. All arises from them. This world is the vibration (*spanda*) of their intercourse. Countless manifestations, in the form of attendant (*āvaraṇa*) gods and goddesses likewise engaged in love play, surround the original couple. The whole universe is one vast field of love-making. Abhinava writes, again in the first major ritual:

> The swollen Śakti pours forth. Bhairava,[2] for his part, is overjoyed. ... A stream of rays flows like sparks of fire from consciousness which has the form of a great splendour. Within [the triangle] the set of twelve is to be worshipped and then the set of sixty-four or the set of four or whatever one desires. ... He should worship that same [stream] within [consciousness] as a group of deities. Māheśī, Vairiñcī, Kaumārī, Vaiṣṇavī are at the four cardinal points, while Aindrī, Yāmyā, Muṇḍā, Yogeṣī

2 The word *śiva* means 'auspicious'. The word 'Bhairava' refers to Śiva in his awesome and terrifying aspect. Accordingly, 'Bhairavī' refers to Śakti as the consort of Bhairava.

> are at the corners, starting from the north-east. The set of eight [goddesses is each with a bhairava] starting with Aghora and finishing with Pavana. Then, as regards this set of eight [couples], [each of them] is to be worshipped in turn in a paired state by contemplating the bliss of their union (*TĀ* 29.51-53).

Thus, Śiva and Śakti are the foundation and impulse of all the traditions and of all aspects of reality. The 'I am' which the practitioner realises is not separate from the whole of reality. 'I am' signifies equally 'I am all'.

The mutuality of Śiva and Śakti is different, however. Śiva is the inactive aspect of consciousness; Śakti is the dynamic aspect. The well-known phrase reads, 'Śiva without Śakti is a corpse.' This is true conceptually; it is also true orthographically. If the word *śiva* is written in *devanāgarī* script without the 'i', which symbolises Śakti, it reads as *śava* (corpse). Since Śiva and Śakti are present in all their manifestations, stillness and movement are found everywhere.

In all of this Bhairava, the fearsome form of Śiva, is inactive. Bhairavī is the active principle of the godhead. The title 'Bhairavī' is suitably connected with the low-caste sexual partner, the *dūtī*, who is fearsome since her shocking impurity will impel the practitioner to that supreme dimension of reality where there is neither pure nor impure. We shall see this in detail later.

Śakti is 'swollen' because she eternally emits both fluids and offspring. The goddess is author of reality. All reality is the emanation of her unbounded nature. The whole world is her radiance (*sphurattā*). She holds all things in her being, even the most opposed. All is proper to her, no matter what it may be.

This same idea is found in the term *kula*, which has several meanings: 'clan', 'family', 'woman'. For Abhinavagupta, it refers above all to Śakti: 'And the kula is the Śakti of Parameśa, his capacity, eminence, freedom, vitality and potency, mass, consciousness and body' (*TĀ* 29.4). *Kula* is thus the source of all; '*Kula*, the unsullied consciousness within the self-existent, is the universal cause' (*TĀV* vol. 7, 3294).

Mortal women are eminently appropriate symbols of Devī by reason of their bodies. The emission of fluids and the birth of children are the perfect expression of the constant fruitfulness of the goddess. But this has implications. Since every woman is the perfect symbol of Devī, to unite with the ritual sexual partner (*dūtī*) is to be in union with the goddess. To enter into the blissful experience of the *dūtī* is to be appropriated by Devī and to acquire supreme consciousness. Jayaratha quotes a pertinent text: 'And let him contemplate each [male and female joined in intercourse] in turn as having the form of Śiva and Śakti' (*TĀV* vol. 7, 3363). Highest knowledge is obtained more effectively in this way than through a guru, as we shall see.

Furthermore, her sexual organ is to be worshipped as the *maṇḍala* of all reality, extending from the high point of consciousness to the outermost circle of light (*TĀ* 29.130-132); '... the "mouth of the yoginī" is said by Maheṣī to be the principal circle. At that place this sacred oral [ritual] tradition [is celebrated]. From it, knowledge is obtained' (*TĀ* 29.124b-125a). Additionally, the woman is called *vāma* in its various meanings. Because she sits on the 'left' of her consort she is *vāma,* meaning 'left'; because she is a 'beautiful woman', she is *vāma,* meaning 'beautiful'; because she is antinomian she is *vāma,* meaning 'left' in the sense of 'sinister'; she is *vāma* because she 'emits' (*vamati*) products from her 'opening and closing central path' (in other words her vagina) (*TĀ* 29.122a). This combination of meanings is essential to the Kula ritual.

Śiva and his Śakti are expressed in the manifold variety of the world, but the human being is the finest expression of this variety. The human body is itself a *maṇḍala* consisting of an intricate yet organised set of faculties. These are arranged hierarchically into the 'principal *cakra*' (pronounced "chakra") (*mukhya-cakra*) and its sub-*cakra*s (*anucakra*) (cf. *TĀ* 29.105b-106a). The principle *cakra* is consciousness itself or, anatomically, the sex organ. The identification of the sex organ, particularly that of the woman, with consciousness, leads to a series of consequences in the sexual ritual described later in this chapter. The act of satisfying or satiating (*tarpaṇa*) the lesser faculties makes the higher faculties start to function; their 'wheel' (*cakra*) begins to turn. This process continues till consciousness, 'the principal circle', is manifest and acknowledged and ultimately worshipped; 'After drawing her close, after reverencing each other, having satiated each other, worship of the principal circle takes place by a process involving 'the inner part' (*antar-aṅga*)' (*TĀ* 29.104b-105a). All the *cakra*s and their functioning are the work of the goddess. All are her property.

The reverse process also occurs, for oscillation is an essential characteristic of the Kula ritual. Abhinavagupta puts it clearly:

> As a result, the pair, who are intensely agitated by the contact which occurs through being absorbed into the upper sacred

> place, agitates the sub-circles as well. The [sub-circles], in this case, are integrated with the [sacred place], they are not separate from it (*TĀ* 29.114–115a).

When supreme consciousness, the principal *cakra*, 'the upper sacred place', is attained, all the other *cakra*s are invigorated as well.

Śiva is commonly understood to express himself in five ways: emanation (*sṛṣṭi*); stability (*sthiti*); absorption (*saṃhāra*); concealment (*tirodhāna*); and grace (*anugraha*). Śiva does these things by his own freedom (*svātantrya*), but his free will is none other than the goddess. He freely conceals himself in his emanation, even to the state of becoming inert (*jaḍi*), dull, opaque and ignorant; and he freely reveals himself to the unenlightened by the gift of his grace, which too is the goddess.

The Śakti not only emits the world but she reabsorbs it as well, whence her 'dangerous' aspect. She seizes the practitioner and takes him into the absolute. All actively comes from her and all actively returns to her, so that she is called Kālasaṅkarṣiṇī, 'she who draws time to a close' (*TĀV* Vol. 7, 3339). She is Kālī, the fearsome goddess; she is Kālāntakī, 'she who is the end of time' (*TĀV* Vol. 7, 3300). She brings all to herself and therefore back to the god with whom she is united. There is a constant alternation.

The twofold process of emission and reabsorption is described by Jayaratha through the image of the woman who sits on the oil press and directs the turning of the wheel (*cakra*). This image is simple, yet has many meanings. The woman symbolises the goddess who governs this changing world. The turning of the wheel symbolises this transient world with its constant coming to be and ceasing to be. The pressure of the woman sitting on the wheel symbolises the impact of Śakti on the practitioner as she draws out from him, as from a grain of sesame seed, the finest 'oil' to be used in sacrifice. Jayaratha provides a relevant quote: 'The goddesses, who have no physical form, turning to him who does have physical form, abide within the body. They play with diverse attitudes (*bhāva*) since they long for the finest ingredients (*dravya*)' (*TĀV* vol. 7, 3309). He spells it out more fully:

> [Cakriṇī, the principal Śakti,] because the universe is placed within her womb, has the form of Kuṇḍalinī … When, out of her own freedom, she wishes to display the extent of duality, she … assuming the [limited] subjectivity of the body etc., … irradiates in every direction by means of whatever is 'blue',

> 'pleasant' etc. Then again, intending to bring the universe to rest in the self alone, she brings pressure to bear on the 'seed' (*bīja*) in order to separate the oil (*rasa*) from the husk; i.e. by a process of reducing the subjectivity which derives from the body etc. she draws out the essence of supreme consciousness … (*TĀV* vol. 7, 3337-3338).

This obscure passage is a good example of how difficult it is to understand the text without explanation. The *Cakriṇī* is given the title Kuṇḍalinī which comes from the word *kuṇḍala* ('ring' or 'circle'). The title is given because the goddess governs the cycle of emanation and dissolution. All things emanate from the goddess, and, in that sense, all come from her 'womb'. She freely emits the universe through all its levels down to the most limited and objective reality, which is customarily referred to as 'blue and pleasant'. The cycle continues, for the goddess also leads back to fullness of consciousness from which all came in the first place. She freely brings people to consciousness. She destroys their limited sense of self, which here is referred to as 'subjectivity' and brings them to unlimited awareness. This unlimited consciousness is the 'oil' which is worthy of the sacrifice. The now abandoned limited form of consciousness is the husk, which is useful only for feeding animals (*paśu*), that is those people who do not have divine consciousness. She presses the 'seed' because she is the principal agent in this process. The 'seed' refers to whatever method will lead to consciousness. Pressing the 'seed' can also refer to the ejaculation of sperm, as we will see more fully in dealing with the *dūtī*.

Devī is the cause both of the emanation and of the dissolution of the universe. Absorption, however, does not mean annihilation. It refers to the dissipation of that illusion whereby a person imagines that they are merely individual and time-bound. Absorption is the elimination of false understandings and the imparting of the enlightened mind where all is seen as the expression of the Śakti. Abhinavagupta is thoroughly realist. Reality truly exists and is objective but, in the moment of enlightenment, is also at last truly understood for what it is. The practitioner in turn becomes what he really is and understands himself fully. Essentially he is Śiva. Absorption is not a sort of infantilism or a reductionism. It is not rejection of matter, or flight into an ideal world. The Kula practitioner simply recognises that all reality is Śakti. Indeed, the *tāntrika* should constantly reflect that he is nothing in himself; he is only *śakti*s (energies); 'I am not, neither does another exist; I am only energies'. He should, in every circumstance, as a result simply of recollection, maintain that attitude of mind (*TĀ* 29.64).

Devī is wild, contrary. Truth and bliss are to be found in her ungovernable career. She appropriates all the rituals and all substances to herself, whether proper or improper. She is dangerous. Yet only here, in her train, can ultimate consciousness be found. She is omnipotent and communicates her power to her devotees. She is bliss itself and shares her bliss with those whom she chooses. She is found in the ordinary; she is extraordinary. Devī is the triumph of the feminine. All is properly hers.

Who appropriates whom? Devī and Deva

Abhinavagupta very often uses the phrase 'Śakti and Śaktimān' ('the one who possesses Śakti', namely Śiva).[3] In this way he indicates that there is no separation of the goddess from the god. She is his form. She is his consciousness, his energy. But is she paramount? The question is significant.

Devī's act of appropriating all reality to herself involves her being identified in turn with Śiva. This process is outlined by Abhinavagupta in his the study of pronouns 'I', 'you', 'he', 'she', 'it' (cf. Dupuche 2001, 1–16). He notes that objects are grammatically divided into masculine, feminine and neuter genders. The knowing subject (*pramātṛ*) observes objects ('he-she-it') and by so doing transforms them into 'you', which has no grammatical gender, and are seen as Śakti. By means of the same contemplation (*bhāvanā*), Śakti in turn is transformed into pure consciousness, 'I' (*aham*). Thus the act of contemplation transforms the observed object into the observing subject. The object is drawn to the subject and becomes the subject. The object, ceasing to be foreign and separate, becomes identified with the Self so that Śiva is the ultimate 'I' of all reality.

In other words, the practitioner, upon realising that his very self is none other than Śiva, occupies the centre point between the fluctuations of emission and reabsorption of the universe: 'Mentally projecting all the faculties such as seeing simultaneously, on all sides, into their respective objects and remaining at the centre …, you [O Śiva] appear as the one foundation of the universe' (*Kṣemarāja* 1982, 98). If he looks outwards he sees himself, since all is a projection of his own being. If he looks inward he sees all things since he is the foundation and essence of all

3 Cf. *TĀ* 29.108a, 114a, 119b, 154b, 246a.

beings. His 'eyes' are both open (*unmīlita*) and closed (*nirmīlita*); his view is both outward (*bahiḥ*) and inward (*antaḥ*). It is the 'attitude of Bhairava' (*bhairavamudrā*).

This attitude is expressed in sexual terms. Indeed, the purpose of the sexual rituals is to attain this frame of mind. Abhinavagupta puts it well: 'Moreover, having by his own nature become the sole lord of the kula, he should satiate the many śaktis by pairing [with them], he who possesses every form' (*TĀ* 29.79). Devī is the focus of Kula ritual, yet Śiva is the ultimate *tattva*; he is the thirty-sixth category in the list of categories whereas Śakti is thirty-fifth, and the last, in descending order, is earth (*pṛthivī*). Who is ultimate, Śiva or Śakti? They are both paramount but differently. Śiva is inactive, but this very inactivity of itself involves Śakti, for from the void of his being Śakti arises. He is paramount by being empty (*śūnya*); she is paramount by being full (*pūrṇa*). The ultimate reality is both empty and full. He who is without form 'possesses every form'.

Devī appropriates by means of her mantra[4]

The goddess is the self-illumination (*vimarśa*) of the god who is light (*prakāśa*). She is his self-awareness, which is his word (*vāc*). All mantras are expressions of that primal word. Therefore the effectiveness of a mantra (*mantravīrya*) is the proof of its closeness to Śiva. According to Abhinavagupta, that proof is shown not in the capacity to defeat enemies in battle or to win a bride, but in attaining the greatest gift – fullness of knowledge. Jayaratha puts it well in a quotation:

> The mantras mentioned in the tantras of the Siddhānta etc., are all impotent since they all lack the splendour of Śakti. The great mantras of the Kaula tradition, by contrast, are splendid with innate fire; they shine with a divine splendour, immediately causing conviction (*TĀV* vol. 7, 3293).

In the Kula ritual tradition there are three principal mantras – Parā, Mālinī, and Mātṛsadbhāva – which are the phonic form of the goddess. Indeed, the goddess and her *vidyā* are one. Parā is the supreme mantra of the Trika, consisting of the three phonemes *S, AU, Ḥ*. Mālinī consists of the fifty phonemes of the Sanskrit alphabet, but with vowels (considered to be male) and consonants (considered to be female), mixed in

4 Properly speaking, the phonic form of the goddess is the term *vidyā*, whereas *mantra* is the phonic form of the god. Generally, however, the word *mantra* is used for both.

together,[5] starting with *NA* and finishing with *PHA*, whence the abbreviated form *NA-PHA*. This combination of male and female bestows enjoyments. Mātṛsadbhāva, which can be translated as 'essence of the mother' or 'essence of the knowing subject', is the sound *KPHREṀ*, which grants liberation.

Jayaratha explains their various usages.

> In all ritual actions, Mālinī is distributed as follows: [Mālinī alone] is to be used for success; if the aim is for liberation, Mātṛsadbhāva is recited first, then [Mālinī], then Mātṛsadbhāva again; if the aim is for both [success and liberation], Parā is recited first, then [Mālinī], then Parā again (*TĀV* vol. 7, 3308).

The goddess and her phonic form are one and the same. To have the mantra is to have all the powers of the goddess and possess all that she is. Since the mantras have different values – Mālinī emphasises success or enjoyment (*bhukti*); Mātṛsadbhāva emphasises liberation (*mukti*); Parā gives both – the practitioner recites the combination that best achieves his purpose.

The *vidyā* cannot be given explicitly in written form, for then it loses its power. It can be truly acquired only in initiation, during which the disciple is absorbed by the goddess. But the *vidyā* is truly given to the initiate. Therefore he appropriates the Devī. Who appropriates whom? To have one is to have the other. The initiate and the goddess appropriate each other. To have her mantra is to have all she is, all her powers. He and she are one, just as she and her mantra are one.

Devī appropriates by means of initiation

In chapter 36 of the *Tantrāloka*, Abhinavagupta portrays the vast sweep of traditions that descend from Śiva. Śrīkaṇṭha (aka Śiva) is the guru of the three Perfected Beings (*siddha*), Āmardaka, Śrīnātha and Tryambaka. At Śrīkaṇṭha's command, these promulgate the dualist, dualist-non-dualist and the non-dualist Śaiva traditions respectively. Furthermore, Tryambaka himself has twin children, a son and a daughter who is called Half-of-Tryambaka or Ardhatryambakā. Her lineage, namely the Kula tradition, is appropriately called the 'three-and-a-half' tradition (*adhyuṣṭa-pīṭha*). The fact that the lineage is communicated through the daughter helps to explain the predominance of women in the Kula ritual.

5 For example, *N, Ṝ, Ṛ, Ḷ, Ḹ, TH, C, DH, Ī, Ṅ, U, Ū, B, K, KH, G, GH* etc.

The initiation ceremony, derived from the *Mālinīvijayottaratantra,* which is the foundational text of the immense *Tantrāloka*, reads as follows:

> After sprinkling the [disciple] with rudraśakti,[6] [the guru] should bring him before the god. After looking at the arms of the [disciple], [the guru] should set them on fire with rudraśakti. With the same [rudraśakti] he should place a flower in the hands of the [disciple], which have been smeared with sandal-paste. Having ensured that [his disciple's hands] are unsupported, [the guru] should reflect on them as being pulled by rudraśakti, which is a flame with the form of a hook. Then, after the [disciple] has spontaneously taken the cloth, he is blindfolded and he spontaneously drops the flower. From its fall [the guru] ascertains the kula to which the disciple belongs]. Then, after [the disciple] has uncovered his face, [the *rudraśakti*] makes [him] fall prostrate at the feet [of the goddess into whose kula he has been initiated] (*TĀ* 29.187b–190).

In other words, the guru blindfolds the disciple and places a flower in his hand while the disciple stands above a *maṇḍala* or *yantra* that sets out the various *yoginī*s and their families (*kula*), which are manifestations of the goddess. The guru projects Śakti into the disciple's arms who, when inspired to do so, lets the flower fall. The place where it comes to rest indicates the 'family' to which he now belongs. By being assimilated by the goddess into a *kula*, the disciple acquires all the powers (*siddhi*) and worlds (*bhuvana*) that belong to that *kula*. He is to worship the goddess of that clan and in return the goddess gives herself to him.

He has been appropriated by the goddess, but he in turn has appropriated the goddess. Not only does he have the typical eight powers (*siddhi*), such as minuteness (*aṇimā*), but, most importantly, he has the bliss (*ānanda*) that belongs to the Devī, which is the highest supernatural power.

The ceremony of initiation shows the predominance of the goddess. Although the guru is active and in some sense directs the energy, it is the goddess who actually initiates. The guru may direct the goddess to the disciple's arms but it is the *rudraśakti*, the phonic form of the goddess, who does the initiating.

6 The mantra *rudraśakti* is Mālinī, enclosed (*saṃpuṭa*) by either Parā or Mātṛsadbhāva.

In the *Ratnamālā,* which is one of the very large number of texts referred to and quoted in the *Tantrāloka* but which has not yet been retrieved, the goddess is similarly active but in a less spectacular fashion.

> [The disciple] ... stands upright before [the guru]. The guru who is composed of the Śakti should [then] reflect on the Śakti, which is all blazing, as going from the foot to the top of the head of the [disciple], burning his bonds. After that, when the [disciple] has sat down, [the guru] should reflect, step by step, on the [Śakti] as burning [the bonds], starting right from the cleansing of the base [and] terminating with the final cleansing of the top [of his head]. Having thus burnt ... all the categories etc., that are to be cleansed, he should meditate [on the Śakti] as merged in Śiva, whether in his simple or his composite form. [The Śakti,] which the yogī joins to the path, nourishes that which is of the same nature [as herself and] burns up anything else that belongs to a different class (*TĀ* 29.203–206).

The mantra is given to the disciple in initiation and cannot be used effectively without initiation. The disciple becomes one with the mantra; he becomes the *mantrī.* In reciting her phonic form he unites with her and all her powers. He takes on the mantra, becomes the mantra, is taken by the mantra. He, the mantra and the goddess are identical. Jayaratha explains: 'Therefore, one should not make the slightest distinction between the practitioner of the mantra [and] the mantra [viz. Śiva], the prāṇa which is identical with the [mantra-goddess] and the [limited] self' (*TĀV* vol. 7, 3351). The initiate, the mantra, the god, the subtle-breath, the goddess and her powers – all appropriate each other. The *mantrī* emits with his mantra and he reabsorbs all with his mantra. He has been initiated; he is now ready to perform the ritual.

Devī appropriates by means of ritual

The very many practices described in chapter 29 of the *Tantrāloka* are summed up in the daily (*nitya*) ritual. Devī is central to them all.

> After entering the hall of sacrifice rich with perfume and incense, facing north-east he should, by means of Parā or Mālinī, upwards and downwards, perform the cleansing which consists of 'fire' and 'growth', 'burning' and 'cooling'

> respectively, in due order. Or else [he may do this], with the mantra Mātṛsadbhāva. … Let him fill the vessel with ingredients[7] which are the fruit and the causes of joy. At that point, through an identity with the mantra that has been mentioned, he should bring himself to the state of Bhairava. Consequently, he should satiate the self with its multitude [of goddesses] in the circle and sub-circle, externally by sprinkling drops [from the ingredients in the vessel] upwards and downwards, and internally by drinking [the ingredients] (*TĀ* 29.18–23).

There are three basic steps in the ritual. The first consists in the practitioner transforming himself into Bhairava. This is done by placing (*nyāsa*) the *vidyā* of the goddess on the various parts of his body. It is first placed in an upwards-moving direction which signifies the 'burning up' of his whole person, that is the reabsorption of his whole person into consciousness in imitation of the offering that is consumed by the sacrificial fire. He then emanates his whole person by means of the same *vidyā*. In this way he is transformed by the goddess. His whole being is now her outer manifestation. He is defined in her terms. His individual and limited 'I' (*ahaṃkāra*) is the expression of the goddess from whom all comes and to whom all returns. More than that, his limited self is in fact Bhairava. He is truly able to perform the sacrifice, for only Śiva can fully sacrifice to Śiva.

The second step is to prepare the elements in the sacred vessel, whose nature and significance will be explained more fully in the next section when dealing with the 'improper' substances.

The practitioner has become Bhairava by means of the Devī and her phonic form. In this state he now satiates all the *śakti*s, from the greatest to the least, by giving them a share in the ingredients of the vessel. He satiates the internal *śakti*s by drinking, as Jayaratha explains with a quotation: 'The goddesses, who have no physical form, turning to him who does have physical form, abide within the body. They play with diverse emotions (*bhāva*) since they long for the finest ingredients' (*TĀV* vol. 7, 3309). In other words, the goddesses are active within the practitioner and cause him to experience many emotions and states of mind, such that he will move to the highest state of consciousness, which is the 'finest ingredient'.

7 These ingredients will be described in the following section. Their 'improper' nature is essential to the ritual.

Having reached the state where he understands himself as Bhairava, he then satiates the external *śakti*s by sprinkling the ingredients around him. He who is Bhairava thus shows the fullness of his power by reserving none. He shows the greatness of his being by being completely unconcerned with it. His whole focus is on the Devī and her entourage. They are the source and purpose of the ritual. His transcendence is shown by his use of 'inappropriate' substances.

Proper and improper

The *paśu* ('bonded animal') operates on the dualistic level, distinguishing between pure and impure, right and wrong. The *vīra* (hero), on the other hand, transcends such divisive concepts because his mind is non-dual in every respect. He shows this clearly by making use, in the second step of the daily ritual, of those very substances which the divisive mind considers to be improper. Typically such substances are called 'the hero's meal' (*vīrabhojya*) (*TĀ* 29.777a).

These forbidden substances are not the usual five Ms (*pañcamakāra*) of other Tantric rituals, but the three Ms of the Kula ritual, namely wine (*madya*), meat (*maṃsa*) and intercourse (*maithuna*) with impure and adulterous women.

These three elements are interrelated; 'Bliss is the supreme brahman and it resides in the body in three ways. Of these, two are aids, the other is the result, [all three] consisting of [bliss]' (*TĀ* 29.97). Jayaratha explains (*TĀV* vol. 7, 3355) that the two 'aids' are wine and meat. The 'result' is intercourse. All three lead to bliss. In other words, the consumption of the forbidden substances, wine and meat, the use also of beautiful things such as incense and flowers, satisfies the physical appetite and opens up the higher *cakra*s. This is because of the interrelationship of sub-*cakra* and principal *cakra*.

> Resulting from what is done by the one who possesses Śakti in the circle and sub-circle and in the 'subtle-breath'; resulting from taking the food which pours forth bliss and from external sources such as perfume, incense, garlands etc., there is a welling up of consciousness (*TĀ* 29.108).

The satisfaction of the lesser leads to the manifestation of the greater, so that there is a 'welling up (*ucchalana*) of consciousness', which is the non-dualist mind in all its fullness.

Wine (madya)

In the *Laws of Manu* 11.68, 91-98, 147-151 the use of wine is strictly forbidden so that Jayaratha goes to great length (*TĀV* vol. 7, 3299-3304) to show why the use of wine is legitimate. Note that he does not take the same care to show the propriety of using outcaste women.

Wine is to be preferred to the manufactured (*kṛtrima*) alcohols such as mead and whisky for it is natural and unprocessed.

> And [alcohol] is of two kinds: processed and natural. Of these, the processed is of three kinds: grain alcohol, mead and rum. However, the natural, the single produce of the grape, which is designated by the words 'Bhairavic' etc., surpasses [the other alcohols] to a supreme degree, which is the reason why he mentions [the alcohols which are made from] flour etc. (*TĀV* vol. 7, 3299).

This same preference for what is spontaneous is found in the choice of the guru, for the best guru is a person who is naturally gifted and 'not made' (*akalpita*), just as the highest forms of initiation[8] are those given directly by the goddess without the services of a human guru.

This reference to spontaneity shows that, while method and practice have their due place, the goddess is essentially free and acts as she pleases. She is under no one's control. She freely chooses to manifest or not to manifest herself, as in the cases where the initiation ceremony is ineffective. Spontaneity is evidence of Devī's freedom and supremacy.

Because wine is the spontaneous and natural product of the grape, it is considered to be the very self of god and goddess. To drink wine in the ritual context is to be identified with the divine pair; 'Alcohol is the supreme Śakti; wine is said to be Bhairava. The self (*ātmā*) is turned into liquid form since Bhairava is great-hearted (*mahātmanā*)' (*TĀV* vol. 7, 3299). Not only does the practitioner use the forbidden wine, but he adds other impure substances. Jayaratha explains with a quote: 'This lineage [of the Perfected Beings] is to be worshipped with ingredients that are both hated by people and forbidden according to the scriptures, that are both disgusting and despised' (*TĀV* vol. 7, 3298). He gives the recipe for the ingredients: 'Male semen, male urine, and menstrual blood, faeces and phlegm; human flesh, beef, goat's flesh, fish, fowl; onion and indeed garlic' (*TĀV* vol. 7, 3306). By using such a concoction, the practitioner

8 They are described in *TĀ* 13.130b–217.

shows that he transcends pure and impure, pleasure and horror, and all the dualities. Śakti is the source of them all. If he is to be united with her, he must not fear to take all her products into himself.

Meat (maṃsa)

While meat is one of the forbidden ingredients and is mentioned several times (*TĀV* vol.7, 3301, 3329, 3354, 3355, 3357), there is little detailed discussion of it in the presentation of the Kula ritual. It is found among the ingredients just listed. It is also used in a substitute form, namely a 'lamp' (*TĀV* vol.7, 3329).

Intercourse (maithuna)

The Kula ritual is explicitly sexual: 'The [*kaula* ritual] can in no way be successfully performed without a sexual partner' (*TĀV* vol. 7. 3353). The appropriation performed by the goddess reaches its apogee here, but it must be properly understood for it is subject to serious misunderstanding.

The *dūtī,* the ritual sexual partner, who is to be identified with Ardhatryambakā, the legendary founder of the Kula tradition, is the principal means by which the guru communicates the Kula tradition.

> To [the *dūtī*] alone … the guru properly transmits the substance of the Kula. And by means of the [mouth of the *śakti*], he transmits [the substance of the Kula] to men, in the manner which has been described (*TĀ* 29.122b–123a).

Jayaratha is quite explicit about the reason for this superiority: ' … because her central sacred space [that is, her vagina (*yoni*)] is spontaneously fully opening and closing, the śakti is superior to the [guru's] own body' (*TĀV* vol. 7. 3378).

Although in the ritual context, the guru will designate and consecrate the woman who is to be the *dūtī*, she in fact surpasses the guru precisely because of her body. His act of consecration does not confer superiority; it is simply an acknowledgment of the superiority she already has by nature. '[The guru] should ritually prepare [the *śakti*] because by her very being[9] she is superior to his own body' (*TĀ* 29.123).

---

9 The term *sad-bhāva* is translated here as 'by her very being'. The terms *kaula-sad-bhāva* and *kaulāmṛta* can also designate the *yoginī*'s sexual emission (White 1996, 138).

The guru may teach his disciple and initiate him, but it is the *dūtī* with her 'lower mouth' (*vaktra*) who will bring the disciple to consciousness. Whereas the guru must use words from his ordinary mouth, she brings him to consciousness by her very body.

> Because of that [superiority], i.e. because of the [superior] nature [of the *śakti*] which has been mentioned, the 'mouth of the yoginī' alone, which is synonymous with other ['mouths'] such as the Picu-mouth[10] etc., is said by the Lord Maheśvara to be the principal circle. At that very place this sacred oral [ritual] tradition ... is to be celebrated. As a result knowledge is received from it, i.e. the [disciple's] entire absorption into supreme consciousness takes place (*TĀV* vol. 7. 3379).

> The 'oblation' and the sacred oral tradition, the discriminating knowledge and the mating and the ceremonial of worship are located in the 'mouth' of the *yoginīs* (*TĀV* vol. 7, 3309).

A word of explanation is needed. The 'mouth', namely the vagina of the *yoginī*, is the focus. The 'oblation' is the sexual fluid that arises there; the 'sacred oral tradition' is passed down by means of this organ since the Kula ritual is deemed to come from Ardhatryambakā; 'the discriminating knowledge' is the experience of supreme consciousness which is achieved through the 'mating'; and the 'ceremonial of worship' is performed not in the Vedic fire-pit (*kuṇḍa*) but in the vagina of the sexual partner.

Abhinavagupta specifically notes that the women are chosen, not because of age or beauty, but because they are impure. Their husbands perform impure tasks: 'The husbands are an outcaste, a *kṛṣṇa*, a bowman, a butcher, a tanner, a eunuch, a bone-splitter, a fisherman, a potter' (*TĀ* 29.66).

The *dūtī* is morally adulterous and socially impure, totally *adharmikā*. Moreover, the intercourse is best undertaken when the woman is deemed to be physically impure by reason of her menses. In other words, the ritual is not concerned with romantic love or passion but with the rejection of the categories of pure and impure. In this way the *tāntrika* shows he

10 Śiva has six faces (*mukha*) of which the Picu-mouth, the lower face, is here identified with the female sex organ.

possesses the purity of non-dual consciousness and that he transcends the dualist mind which is the real impurity.

The social customs of medieval Kashmir valued the wife particularly in relation to sexual pleasure and to children, but the Kula ritual is not concerned with orgasm and progeny. Jayaratha explains it clearly.

> In this [ritual], however, the activity is not undertaken because of a desire for sexual pleasure in a worldly sense. Rather, [the activity is undertaken] ... because of the intensity of the absorption into the very nature of undivided supreme consciousness. ... If one's wife were indeed involved, there would be a danger of focusing on sexual pleasure (*TĀV* vol. 7, 3362).

The dutiful husband will engage in intercourse with his wife so as to achieve ejaculation and secure progeny. The focus is, therefore, on the ejaculation and its pleasure. The Tantric practitioner, on the other hand, is not focused on such things but on the consciousness that is experienced in the pleasure. The difference is significant.

The woman is the visible counterpart of Devī who is Śiva's consort, not his wife. The male practitioner and the *dūtī* seek to manifest in their own being the relationship of Śiva and Śakti. They become the divine pair, not as husband and wife, but as deity and consort.

The *dūtī* is an adulterous outcaste. Yes, but what is the really essential requirement? In leading up to the answer, Jayaratha gives verbal portraits of two women, the one highly erotic, the other very demure (*TĀV* vol. 7, 3357–3360), in order to show that no single woman can have all feminine qualities. Abhinavagupta then gives the answer: 'The characteristic quality of a śakti is that she is in no way separated (*anavicchanna*) from him who possesses her. Let him, therefore, bring [a *śakti*] of this sort, but without regard to castes etc.' (*TĀ* 29.100b–101a). The essential requirement is that she should be inseparate (*anavicchanna*). Her mind must show complete identification (*tādātmya*) with the practitioner. Only then will the coupling truly reflect the identity of Śiva and Śakti. Clearly, she is likely to be very different from her male partner in terms of intelligence, but the identification spoken of here is not in external matters such as social status or education. Identification refers to an inner disposition, namely the capacity to take on the unified mind of Śiva and Śakti.

Much is required of the male practitioner also. During the use of the three Ms with their pleasures he must retain his awareness of supreme consciousness.

> And it is said in the Triśirastantra: "He whose interior faculties are set on an unsullied foundation while in the midst of the set of six senses[11] becomes fully absorbed into the abode of Rudra." (*TĀ* 29.110b–111a).

Jayaratha explains.

> And so the person who is qualified for this [ritual] belongs amongst those great-hearted knowledgeable persons whose thought is undifferentiated. By putting aside their own fluctuating mental states, they attend to just one consideration: is the mind centred just on the non-duality of consciousness or not? (*TĀV* vol. 7, 3363).

The male practitioner takes part in the rituals, not in order to attain the divine bliss which he does not yet enjoy but in order to show that he already possesses it. This crucial point is made clearly by Jayaratha:

> ... the [set of three Ms] is to be utilised by the person who has entered upon the Kula path for the reason that he is in every way committed simply to manifesting his own bliss. [The set of three Ms] is not [to be utilised] out of greed. If that were the case, how would [the use of the three Ms] differ from worldly usages? (*TĀV* vol. 7, 3357).

By courageously rejecting the distinction between pure and impure, and showing that he does so by making use of impure substances, the *vīra* shows that his mind transcends human prejudices. He is not dual. Nothing is improper. All is equally appropriate to him.

The goddess reserves herself for such a 'hero'. She recognises him as one like herself, for she too is destructive, putting an end to all mental categories. She appropriates the *vīra* and in turn subjects herself to him. The hero and the goddess become one; they are Śiva and Śakti united in a lasting embrace.

The other goddesses of the clan (*kula*) also take delight in him. For that reason the *tāntrika* should visit the various sacred sites and enter into relations with the resident human *yoginīs* who are assimilated to the divine *yoginī*s who are themselves expressions of the supreme Devī. The appropriators are appropriated. These *yoginī*s will take part with him in

11 These six are the five faculties of knowledge (*jñānendriya*) and the mind (*manas*), which is the organising principle.

the sexual rituals and provide him with the menstrual and other fluids that he can use in his daily ritual as a substitute for an actual *dūtī* : 'Being conversant with such signs, if he tours around the sacred sites in search of super-natural powers, he will quickly acquire whatever is to be obtained from the "mouth of the yoginī"' (*TĀ* 29.40). The fluid that arises spontaneously in the context of pleasure is the symbol of the goddess and the bliss of her consciousness, and is thus considered to be most pure (*TĀ* 29.128a), even though the 'bonded animal' will view it as profoundly impure.

What has happened to sexual pleasure? Has it disappeared from the discussion? Yes, it has at this point, but the purpose of the Kula ritual is not primarily pleasure; the purpose is consciousness. If consciousness can be achieved by using substitutes, then pleasure is relativised. The attitude criticised by Feuerstein and Urban, as we have seen above, confused *tantra* and sexual pleasure. The fact that substitutes can be used is an important corrective to that mistaken view of *tantra*.

By consciously drinking it or placing it on his body, the practitioner is taken up into the goddess.[12] The emission, the *yoginī*, Devī and the practitioner are all appropriated one to the other. All this is secret. The *tāntrika* remains, according to Jayaratha's quotation, 'Secretly (*antaḥ*) a kaula, outwardly a Śaiva-[siddhānta], but publicly a follower of the Vedas' (*TĀV* vol. 3, 643 and 894).

In public, his conduct is socially correct. If, in the ritual context, the *tāntrika* ignores caste and *dharma* and uses the three Ms, he does so without wishing to disturb the social order, not out of respect for it but because it provides him with the means of acting illicitly. His impropriety is all the more powerful for being secret. He is no revolutionary.

The *dūtī* brings her devotee to consciousness in other ways as well. For example, she affects him by the sound of her voice, as when she cries out '*HĀ-HĀ*' during orgasm, which is an appropriation into the ultimate bliss of consciousness. 'As a result of savouring everlasting bliss, the [sound] '*HĀ-HĀ*' occurs in the throat [of the *dūtī*]. Coming into being of its own accord, it is a pleasurable utterance which perceives the category of sexual desire' (*TĀV* vol. 7, 3400). Note that the *tāntrika* focuses on the *dūtī*'s experience, not on his own pleasure. He takes pleasure in her pleasure. She experiences pleasure because of him but he focuses on her and

12 For a full discussion of the uses of the fluid, see chapter 4 'The Mouth of the Yoginī' in White 2003, 94-122.

so is taken into the *ānanda* of the goddess who is eternally in pleasurable union with Maheśvara.

> The inarticulate [sound, viz. *HĀ-HĀ*] which comes from the region of the heart between the breasts and ends at the lips, is [uttered] in the throat. After hearing [the inarticulate sound] between the two circles [viz. in the throat] ... when the agitation ceases, at that moment [all the audible forms of sound] vanish. And at that moment, Bhairava as sound [appears] ... It is called the supreme pervasion of the mantra (*TĀ* 29.158–160).

Being attentive to this sound and observing its arising and its disappearance, he is taken to the ultimate source of sound and becomes Bhairava.

We have reached the climax of the ritual. Being sound, the practitioner experiences universal pervasion (*vyāpti*). Abhinava puts it well: 'Recalling, in every action and in every place, the pervasion [of the mantra] in this fashion, being ever unattached, liberated-while-living, he becomes the supreme Bhairava' (*TĀ* 29.161b–162a).

Conclusion

The theme of appropriation is intimately tied to the notion of non-dualism. Monism allows only one reality; dualism posits realities that are ultimately irreducible. Non-dualism is essentially a negative term that rejects both monism and dualism and allows the many to be understood as identified in the most profound unity.

Taken to its ultimate conclusion, the Kashmir Shaiva version of non-dualism implies the identification of pure and impure, licit and illicit. The Kaula *tāntrika* deliberately uses the inappropriate to show that he enjoys full non-dual consciousness beyond all human constructs. He does so particularly through women who are Devī's most potent symbol. That is, he enjoys Devī herself who is the ultimate power since she freely emanates all and reabsorbs all.

While the *tāntrika* may seem to be the principal actor – along with his *dūtī* – it is in fact the Devī who, from the moment of initiation till the final outcome of the ritual, exercises her freedom. She shows her unbounded power precisely through turning the impure into a means of purity, that true purity which is consciousness. She sweeps away all human fears and prejudices and communicates her utter freedom. She appropriates all because she is all.

Abbreviations

TĀ *Tantrāloka* of Abhinavagupta, in Abhinavagupta 1987.
TĀV *Tantrālokavṛtti* of Jayaratha, in Abhinavagupta 1987.

Bibliography

Abhinavagupta. 1975. *La Parātrīśikālaghuvṛtti de Abhinavagupta,* translated by A. Padoux. Paris: E. de Boccard.

Abhinavagupta. 1987. *Tantrāloka; with the Commentary of Jayaratha*. R. C. Dwivedi and Navjivan Rastogi (eds). Delhi: Motilal Banarsidass.

Dupuche, John R. 2001. 'Person-to-Person: *vivaraṇa* of Abhinavagupta on *Parātriṃśikā* verses 3–4.' *Indo-Iranian Journal* 44: 1-16.

Dupuche, John R. 2003. *Abhinavagupta: The Kula Ritual as elaborated in chapter 29 of the Tantrāloka*. Delhi: Motilal Banarsidass.

Kṣemarāja. 1982. *Pratyabhijñāhṛdayam: the Secret of Self Recognition*, edited by Jaideva Singh. Delhi: Motilal Banarsidass.

Sanderson, Alexis. 1988. 'Saivism and the Tantric traditions'. In *The World's Religions*, edited by S. Sutherland, L. Houlden, P. Clarke and F. Hardy, 660–704. London: Routledge.

Sanderson, Alexis. 1990. 'The visualisation of the deities of the Trika'. In *L'image divine : culte et méditation dans l'hindouisme*, edited by A. Padoux, 31–88. Paris: Editions du Centre National de la Recherche Scientifique.

Urban, Hugh. 2003. *Tantra: Sex, Secrecy, Politics and Power in the Study of Religion*. Berkeley: University of California Press.

White, David Gordon. 1996. *The Alchemical Body: Siddha Traditions in Medieval India.* Chicago: University of Chicago Press.

White, David Gordon. 2003. *The Kiss of the Yoginī.* Chicago: University of Chicago Press.

Chapter 6

Ravidās and the Gaṅgā

Appropriation or Contestation?[1]

Peter Friedlander

The centrality of the river Ganga[2] (Ganges) to Indian civilisation can be seen in the words of Jawaharlal Nehru, the first prime minister of India after independence, who in his last will and testament said of the river:

> The Ganga, especially, is the river of India, beloved of her people, round which are intertwined her racial memories, her hopes and fears, her songs of triumph, her victories and her defeats. She has been a symbol of India's age-long culture and civilization, ever-changing, ever-flowing and ever the same Ganga (Nehru's will of 21 June 1954, quoted in Ghose 1993, 342).

In this chapter I will explore the relationship between the river Ganga, the goddess Ganga, and legends related to the medieval poet-saint Ravidās and examine how the terms 'appropriation' and 'contestation' might relate to exploring such relationships. I shall begin by showing that veneration of sacred rivers is one of the most ancient aspects of spiritual traditions found around the world. In India there has been a tradition of reverence for the sacred rivers as goddesses since an early period. The Ganges, or Ganga, is the foremost river of India; its deity, Mother Ganga,

1 This article uses sources in various languages and from various historical periods; no single system of spelling or diacritics can be appropriately applied to all the names used in translation. Generally, names of places, of deities, and of individuals living in modern times are left without diacritics, while technical terms and individuals named in primary sources have diacritics. The name 'Ravidās' is consistently used here. In a few cases, diacritics are offered as a guide to pronunciation (with the macron, as in 'ā', indicating a long vowel and 'ṅ' indicating the guttural 'ng' sound; 'c' indicates the palatal 'ch' sound).

2 Pronounced *Gaṅgā*.

holds a special place in the spiritual life of the majority of the inhabitants of India. I then explore stories about the goddess Ganga found in Hindu, Buddhist and ethnographic literature about Chamar[3] communities. I argue that veneration of the goddess was, and is, an aspect of the cultures associated with the Chamar communities of India. This leads to a study of how the goddess appears in stories about Ravidās, who has for more than 500 years been regarded as the foremost religious leader of the former untouchable leather-working communities of North India. I argue that Chamar communities' cultures have always involved the worship of the goddess, and Ravidās' relationship to the goddess Ganga should be seen as part of a process by which Chamar followers of Ravidās engaged in contestation over their rights to play a role in public and sacred spaces. I conclude that the relationship between Ravidās and his followers and the goddess Ganga is not an expression of appropriation but a manifestation of contestation within the public sphere.

What is 'appropriation'?

The term 'appropriation', especially in the context of cultural appropriation, is currently often used in discussions about cultures and communities. One possible definition is 'taking intellectual property, traditional knowledge, cultural expressions, or artefacts from someone else's culture without permission' (Scafidi 2005). Such a definition clearly relates to issues such as use of Aboriginal or Indigenous American art by people not from those communities. However, before such a term can be used of the relationships between cultural practices in communities in India, two questions need to be asked. The first is what previous debates there have been about this issue. The second is whether it is possible to define what a 'culture' means in relation to South Asian communities.

One longstanding model for understanding the relationships between South Asian cultural communities has been through the concept of 'great and little traditions' which is associated with the name of Milton Singer and his seminal work published in 1972. This model was originally developed during field work in the 1950s and 1960s by the Chicago school of scholars, such as Srinivas and Redfield, which led Singer to the view that South Asian cultures were made up of a mix of great traditions (a Sanskrit-based high-status tradition) and little traditions (local folk traditions based in vernacular languages). In this model the relationships

3 Chamar or camār; pronounced with the palatal 'ch' as in 'charmer'.

between the two traditions were described not in terms of appropriation but in terms of incorporation, or adoption, via movements towards great traditions through Sanskritisation and towards localisation through parochialisation. Later scholars have criticised these theories on a number of grounds, particularly because of their implicit hierarchy where the great Sanskritic tradition is privileged in relation to local traditions and because of problems in defining what constitutes a community or tradition. These gaps in the theory were identified by the 'Subaltern Studies' approach, developed in the 1980s by scholars such as Partha Chatterjee, David Hardiman and Ranajit Guha, for whom emphasising power and confrontation were crucial issues in uncovering the nature of the hegemony and the subaltern perspectives. It is notable that, with this discourse, the concept of 'appropriation' started to make an appearance in what was largely a rewriting of history which sought to move away from an essentialising view of Brāhminical tradition as the highest expression of Indic traditions, locating it instead in the subaltern and investing the subaltern with their own agency (Doron 2006, 346-347).

The further development of the use of the term 'appropriation' and a concept of 'cultural appropriation' were brought to prominence by the American cultural theorist George Lipsitz and argued for in his work on the appropriation of popular music (1994) in race relations in the United States. This idea has grown in currency in cultural studies and has now become a feature in the analysis of South Asian cultures.

When used as a tool for the analysis of contemporary phenomena, this approach has considerable merit, as it is possible to apply George Lipsitz's ideas and Susan Scafidi's definition to an analysis of cultural relations. Thus, authors such as Gwilym Beckerlegge are able to identify particular groups or individuals, such as Vivekananda and the Ramakrishna mission, and speak of the appropriation of their ideas by groups like the Rashtriya Swayamsevak Sangha (Beckerlegge, 2003). In such an analysis it can be seen that what was taking place was that ideas and symbols associated with one figure, in this case Vivekananda, were then used by figures from another movement in order to advance their claims for higher status for their group.

In a South Asian context we need to move away from Scafidi's definition of cultural appropriation. I suggest a tentative definition of appropriation should be 'a rhetoric used by higher caste communities to criticise the use of symbols by lower caste communities contesting their status in the hierarchy'.

I will further argue that a practice such as veneration of the Ganges in the form of the goddess Ganga cannot be seen as ever having been the exclusive possession of any one caste in South Asia. It was, and is, an aspect of a public sacred sphere which is then drawn on by different traditions, including Brāhminical, Epic Hindu, Buddhist and lower caste community traditions. Consequently, I argue that the label 'appropriation' should not be applied to the appearance of the goddess Ganga in legends associated with Ravidās, as this label springs from the rhetoric of higher caste criticism of lower castes. Rather, this association should be seen as part of the ongoing historic contestation between different caste communities for the rights of all caste communities to speak of and employ imagery from the public sacred space which the goddess Ganga inhabits.

This raises the question whether Scafidi's model of cultural appropriation is a productive model for understanding the relationships between caste communities and their cultures in pre-modern South Asian studies. I will argue in this chapter that it would be more productive to look at the relationships in terms of contestation between castes seeking to appear in contested public and sacred spheres.

The worship of sacred rivers and the goddess Ganga

Sacred rivers have been venerated since early times in many places around the world. For instance, the Celts venerated rivers and regarded them as the homes of goddesses (MacCulloch 1911, 183) and the ancient Egyptians venerated the Nile as a goddess called Anuket. In India there are also ancient traditions of the veneration of river goddesses and possibly the most ancient of these was related to the worship of the goddess Sarasvatī mentioned in the Rig Veda who was the goddess of the now lost river Sarasvatī (Srivastava 1979, 45).

The goddess Ganga is mentioned in the *Rāmāyaṇa* and the *Mahābhārata* in relation to the story of the *Gaṅgā-avatāraṇa,* describing how she descends to earth upon the locks of Śiva and then flows from the Himalayas along with her sister Yamuna (Srivastava 1979, 142 *et passim*). The most widely known version of this story about the goddess Ganga relates to a certain king called Sagara who, after two years of childlessness, retired from the world with his two wives, Keśinī and Sumati, to Mt Kailash, where he practised austerities. After some time the sage Bhṛgu granted his wish, but with the proviso that from one queen one son would be born and from the other, 60,000. They then returned to their kingdom and, as prophesied, one queen, Keśinī, bore a single son, and the other, Sumati, gave birth to a kind of mass that became 60,000 sons. Sagara then decided to carry out an *aśvamedha* ceremony and let loose a horse to wander throughout the land, establishing that wherever it wandered was the king's land and the king was a Cakravartin, a world conqueror. However, the horse ended up being hidden by the gods in the *āśrama* of the *ṛṣi* Kapila who dwelt on the eastern seashore. When the 60,000 sons arrived to claim the horse, they angered the sage and he burned them all to ashes with his gaze. It was then established that the sons would only be liberated when the waters of the Ganges reached them; however, this could not be realised in Sagara's lifetime and it fell to his son Bhagīratha to attain this goal. This he did by retiring from the world to the Himalayas where he practised austerity and, pleased by his efforts, the gods agreed to grant his wishes. Śiva agreed to catch the Ganges in his locks as the river descended to earth. Eventually, the Ganges then descended at Lake Manasarovar and separated into seven streams. Eventually the streams of the Ganges reached the eastern seashore and the 60,000 sons of Sagara attained liberation into paradise (Darian 1978, 17-19). There have been a number of depictions of this story, such as at Mamallapuram near Chennai, created by the Pallava kings in the seventh century CE (Darian 1978, 21-27).

There is also a famous story about the goddess Ganga as a mother, which relates to how once a certain king called Śāntanu met her in human form and took her to be his wife, but she agreed only on the condition he did not question her actions. Their life was perfect in all respects but one: at the birth of each of her first seven children, all male, she took the newborn son and cast it into the Ganges. When finally, at the birth of his eighth son, the king then could bear this no more and questioned her, she explained she was a goddess and had been cursed to bear seven sons in this manner, but that now she was released from the curse, and she disappeared (Darian 1978, 35-37).

During the Gupta period (c. fifth century CE), in temples such as those at Udaygiri, Ganga on her *vāhana* (mount, in this case a crocodile or *makara*) and Yamuna on her *vāhana* (a tortoise) began to be represented on either side of the doorways into Hindu temples (Srivastava 1979, 145). Representations of the goddess Ganga then continued on Hindu temples at their entrances and became a common feature in temple iconography.

Ganga in Buddhist tradition

The goddess Ganga was also venerated in Buddhist tradition and there are various accounts of this in the Buddhist *Jātaka* stories. In the *Kiṃchanda-jātaka* (no. 511) there is an account of how goddess Ganga manifested herself and spoke to a king who was fasting on the shore of the river Ganga. She explained to him she was the guardian of all the foods related to the river and granted him the boon of being transported to a grove of mango trees and being able to eat their fruits (Francis 1905, 1). In the *Mahāsuka Jātaka* (no. 429) there is also a story about a parrot king who lives in a mango tree on the shores of the Ganges; to test his devotion to the tree, the gods wither the tree, but the parrot refuses to leave it. Moved by this, Sakka grants the parrot's wish to have the tree restored, which he does by splashing Ganga water on it (Darian 1978, 35-37).

The legends of the Buddhist Siddhas also include a number of stories related to the goddess Ganga. For instance, the realised Siddha Virūpa is said to have once on the shores of the Ganga asked the goddess Ganga for something to eat and drink, but when she refused to give anything he then parted the waters of the Ganga and walked through her bed to the other shore (Dowman 1985, 46). In another variant of this account Virūpa wanted to cross the Ganges but could not pay the ferryman's fare, so instead he pointed at the river, causing it to reverse its direction of flow above that point, so that its waters parted; then he walked across through the river bed (Templeman 1983, 15).

Ganga in the life of the Chamar community

George W. Briggs wrote a study of the Chamar caste which he completed in 1920 and into which he incorporated both his own observations and observations from a variety of studies from the nineteenth century. He observed that sacred rivers, such as the Ganga and the Yamuna, received 'special consideration as great satisfiers of life' (Briggs 1920, 199). He also noted that goddesses and the Ganga formed a vital part of the cultural life of the Chamar community and were particularly prominent in relation to life-cycle rituals (*saṃskāras).* In many aspects of these observances Chamars shared with many North Indians commonly held beliefs about the importance of Ganga water in purification. This can be seen in the ritual of calling on Ganga to bless a marriage and the sprinkling of

Ganga water at marriage rituals (Briggs 1920, 75), giving Ganga water to a dying person (99) and immersing the ashes from a cremation in a tributary of the Ganga, or, if that is not possible, keeping them in a pot and taking them to the Ganga during *pitṛpakṣa* (103, 108). Rituals during the mourning period also often involve Ganga water, such as burying a mixture of Ganga water and food in a trench near the door on the third day after the cremation (108).

There are also some traditions that related to the magical power of Nona Chamarin,[4] a kind of witch figure who was widely believed in by people in the eastern areas of the states of Uttar Pradesh and Bihar. According to her story her magical powers came about because she had eaten from a cauldron she found floating in the Ganga containing the cooked flesh of Dhanvantari, the physician of the gods. Dhanvantari had been poisoned by Takṣaka, the king of snakes, and had told his sons to cook his flesh and eat it after his death in order to gain his magical powers. However, after they cooked his flesh, they were warned against eating it by Brahmā and so it was that it floated down the Ganga and was eaten by Nona Chamarin who, consequently, became a powerful sorceress with the power to cure snake bites (Briggs 1920, 185).

Ganga water also formed a significant part in purification rituals, such as those that needed to be carried out if a cat was inadvertently killed (Briggs 1920, 124), and in the case of smallpox when offerings of flowers, milk and Ganga water were made (139).

In regard to birth rituals, Briggs also noted the existence of a tradition that was clearly somehow part of a complex of practices that also relate to the myth of Ganga and Śaṃtanu. Before children were born, mothers would pledge (*manautī*) to make an offering of the child's hair to the Ganga if the birth was successful. Then at four or five days after the birth, or at six months, they would shave the infant and wrap its hair in a *pūrī* (unleavened deep-fried bread) and offer it to the river. Moreover, in some cases, while they were at the Ganga they would cast the baby momentarily into the river and then catch it up before any harm came to it, and they would do this seven times (Briggs 1920, 62).

Taken together these examples of reverence for the goddess Ganga and her waters point to the importance of Ganga in the lives of the Chamar community from which the followers of Ravidās are drawn.

---

4 Pronounced *nonā camārin*.

Ravidās and the goddess Ganga: witness, liberation and purification

Ravidās, also known in Hindi as Raidās, in Marathi as Rohidās and in Bengali as Ruidās, was a poet-saint of the *bhakti* tradition from the untouchable Chamar community. He was a younger contemporary of Kabīr, but the precise dates of both Kabīr and Ravidās have been a matter for much debate. There is a wide range of traditional dates, but contemporary scholarship suggests that Ravidās probably lived from around 1500 to 1550 CE.

Academic studies in Hindi on the life of Ravidās began in the 1950s with the work of Ramanand Shastri and Virendra Pandey (1955) and the earliest English language Indian studies were by Darshan Singh (1977) of Jullundur and by Darshan Singh (1981) of Patiala. Winand Callewaert and Peter Friedlander (1992) published a study that examined sources on his life and works from before 1700 CE. David Lorenzen and Winand Callewaert have also published a number of significant studies of Rajasthani hagiographic literature and of the hagiographies of Anantadas (Callewaert 1994; Callewaert and Sharma 2000; Lorenzen 1991). More recent works have included a group of papers by Joseph Schaller, James Lochterfield and others published in a work on untouchable saints edited by Eleanor Zelliot and Rohini Mokashi-Punekar (2005).

An argument put forward in a paper on the hagiographies of Ravidās (Friedlander 1996) was that representations of individuals in the hagiographic stories should be interpreted as indicating contacts between communities. In this paper I want to further extend that idea and argue that representations of locations in the stories should be considered in relation to the existence of story-telling traditions that once existed, and in some cases still exist, at those locations. Furthermore, this would indicate that these narratives about locations also imply that they indicate that Chamar community activities were involved in contestation about their rights to utilise these public spaces and their corresponding elements from the sacred sphere.

Included in stories about his life are a number of stories about Ravidās and the Ganga, and I want here to look at these stories in relation to the themes of witness, liberation and purification.

The story of the gift of the bracelet is first found in the account of Ravidās' life in a Sikh text, the *Pothī Prem Ambodha,* which dates from 1693 CE, when the tenth Sikh Guru Gobind Singh's court was at

Anandpur in the Punjab. This contains accounts of the lives of sixteen *bhagats* whose works are found in the *Guru Granth*, including Kabīr and Ravidās, as well as Mīrābāī (Sābar 1984). One of the stories in this account of the life of Ravidās is that Ravidās once gave a Brāhmin a coin to give to the Ganga and, when the Brāhmin tossed the offering into the river, the goddess Ganga manifested herself and gave a valuable gold bracelet to the Brāhmin to pass on to Ravidās. The Brāhmin was greedy, however, and gave the bracelet to his wife, which eventually led to the king being informed about the marvellous bracelet and the Brāhmin being asked to hand over a matching bracelet to make a pair, which he could not do. The king and the Brāhmin then came to where Ravidās was working, and when he was asked to go to the Ganga to ask the goddess for another bracelet he said that he did not have time to do so; instead he entreated the polluted water in the barrel in which he soaked leather, whereupon the goddess Ganga manifested her hand from the water trough and gave another bracelet to match that which she had previously given. It is notable that this story is clearly the origin of the well-known Hindi saying '*mana caṅgā kaṭhautī meṃ gaṅgā* (for the heart that is blessed, even in a water barrel the Ganga is manifest)'.

There are echoes here of many themes already introduced. The ways in which Chamars made offerings to the river Ganga, as in the related story of pledges made in relation to successful births, are echoed here with Ravidās' offering to the Ganga. Also the notion of the Ganga as witness to the greatness of her devotees, as in the case of the Buddhist Siddhas, is clearly evident here as her manifestation from the river's water proves Ravidās' connection to her even at a distance. Finally, the third theme, that of purification, is also evidently present here, since for the goddess Ganga to appear in an impure vessel is not a problem – she purifies all through her presence.

It is also possible to see in this story a narrative about Chamar communities being challenged by Brāhminical authorities over their rights to direct access to the Ganga in both its aspects as public sphere and sacred space. Indeed, the way in which at first the Brāhmin must mediate, from a distance, the offering to the Ganga, and then, because of his greed, he is stripped of this right by the king, would fit perfectly a narrative about contestations over the rights to make offerings to the Ganga on its shores.

It should also be borne in mind that the theme of the right to move freely in public spaces was, and is, a real one for Chamar communities who formerly were not allowed to enter some areas, particularly those that were ritually pure. The aspiration for the right to move freely in the city is a central tenet in Ravidās' verses and in his verse on the Sorrowless City (*Begampur*) it is one of the rights that Ravidās asserts that the liberated Chamar (*khalās Camār*) will have in his vision of society in an ideal city and where his community can 'wander around wherever they please, they stroll through palaces unchallenged' (Callewaert and Friedlander 1992, 126). The prominence of Persian vocabulary in this verse also points to an aspect of this context. The name of the city is partially based on a Persian word, *begum*, which in combination with *pur* can be taken to mean either 'sorrowless city' or 'queens city', or both; most of the terms related to social organisation in the verse, such as that for 'liberated' (*khalāsa)*, are also all drawn from Persian and Arabic. This suggests that this contestation for public space by Brāhmins and Chamars was taking place when the administration of the state was under Muslim control and administration.

The story of the test of the *śāligrāma* is another story found in the *Pothī Prem Ambodh* account of the life of Ravidās. It tells how the Brāhmins once complained to the king that Ravidās was worshipping a *śāligrāma,* an aniconic symbol of Vishnu, but that he had no right to do this. This then led to a contest before the king on the shores of the Ganga in which both Ravidās and the Brāhmins had to try to make a *śāligrāma* float on water. However, despite the Brāhmins cheating and using a fake wooden *śāligrāma*, their *śāligrāma* still sank. In the end it was Ravidās' real stone *śāligrāma* that, supported by the goddess Ganga from below, floated on the water like a duck whilst the Brāhmins' *śāligrāma* sank.

This story again points to the persistence of the themes of the goddess Ganga as witness and liberator. She bears witness to her devotees' greatness by her miraculous support of offerings, as with the babies in folk tradition noted by Briggs. She also clearly acts here as liberator from suffering, as she saves Ravidās from persecution by witnessing to his greatness. It is also evidently another story that focuses on contestation, of conflicting claims over the right to inhabit sacred spaces. Again, that the contest takes place on the shores of the Ganga points to the role of this location as both a physical public space and an idealised sacred space.

There were also numerous stories about Ravidās and the Ganga in Marwar that were current amongst untouchable community members in the nineteenth century. Some of these can be found in the account of the religious beliefs of Chamars and the Raigar community in the 1891 vernacular (that is, Hindi) census of Marwar carried out by the princely state along the lines of the British census of India. The vernacular census gave a variety of legends related to Ravidās. The first concerned how once Ravidās was working in the market in the Mandu area (Dhar District, Madhya Pradesh), making shoes, and some drops of water from his work splashed onto the clothes of a passing royal servant. The servant tried to wash off the spots but the stain would not go, so he sucked it, and became enlightened; and on this miracle the king became Ravidās's disciple.

The public market where the shoemakers were engaging in trade is the focal location in this story and also the first location in the story of the golden bracelet. I would suggest that this points to the presence at markets being one of the spaces being contested at this time by the Chamar community.

The second story is that Ravidās's personal deity was the goddess Ganga, who came in person to his house in the form of his daughter. When she was about to be married, the king of Chittorgarh, hearing of her great beauty, became infatuated and sent an army to fetch her, but when the army arrived the Ganges flowed out from Ravidās's water-trough and drowned the soldiers. This story has parallels with the story of the earth goddess Vasundharā in Buddhist tradition in South East Asia. According to these stories, when the Buddha was sitting under the Bodhi tree and had resolved to attain enlightenment, he was assailed by the armies of Māra. However, when he touched the earth as witness to his resolve to attain enlightenment, the earth goddess manifested herself and by twisting the tresses of her hair created a deluge of Ganges water, which swept away the armies of Māra. The similarities between this Buddhist story and the story about Ravidās just recounted suggest that the image of the goddess sending a deluge to destroy the armies of the unrighteous was found in a wide range of contexts.

The same source also mentions that the Raigars (Chamars) of Malwa and Rajputana believe that the Chambal River is the Ganges and that its source is the water-trough in which Ravidās steeped his leather hides. Furthermore, in Mandu it is mentioned that there was a stone statue that was worshipped by Ravidās, along with a pool he used, and that the water from it cured many diseases.

The theme of the purificatory role of Ganges water is one that features prominently in North Indian traditions, and the idea that water touched by a saint becomes transformed into a form of purificatory water like that of the Ganges is one that appears in a number of stories associated with Ravidās (Friedlander 1996).

A further story said that Ravidās had two wives; the children of one were Chamars and the children of the other were Raigars. The Raigars were Vaiṣṇava followers and worshipped the *śāligrāma*. In eastern districts they wore a sacred thread of raw cotton and their personal deity was the Ganga. They believed that whenever somebody held a great feast the Ganga emerged from the pots at the feast (Singh 1891, 528).

Unlike the previous stories mentioned, these stories do not relate to the actual river Ganga, as they are all set in Rajasthan and Madhya Pradesh. Nevertheless, like the earlier stories mentioned, they all focus on contestation within the sacred sphere for the rights of Chamar communities to practise their beliefs in the shared common space of public life.

Ravidās and the goddess Ganga in the twentieth century

The introduction of printing to North India in the mid-nineteenth century led to the beginnings of the creation of print cultures by groups such as the followers of Kabīr and Ravidās. By the 1860s Kabīr's followers had begun to publish works on Kabīr's life (Friedlander 2012a). The first life-story published by followers of Ravidās was published in 1911 and was called the *Ravidāsa Rāmāyaṇa* (Jatav 1911). Its author, Bhakshidas Jatav, was from Jahadpur in Merut district where dalit communities identifying themselves by the caste title *Jātav* were beginning to agitate for greater rights. Despite being called *Rāmāyaṇa,* it was actually an account of the life of Ravidās, but was composed in *dohā* and *caupai* metres in a Hindi like that of Tulsīdās' *Rāmcaritmānasa*. There is great prominence given in the work to the stories of the goddess Ganga and the bracelet and the competition on the shore of the Ganga with the Brāhmins over the right to worship the *śāligrāma*.

The next significant life of Ravidās was published in 1940 under the title *Bhagvān Ravidās Kī Satyakathā* (The true story of Lord Ravidās). Its author, Ramcaran Kuril (1882-1956), was from the leather-working communities of Kanpur. He had set up an organisation in 1917 for reform called the *Ravidās Kurīl Sabhā* (The Ravidās Kuril Assembly), and by the 1930s was the president of the *Ākhil Bhārtīya Ravidās Mahāsabhā* (All India Ravidās General Assembly) (Kuril 1940). Kuril's work not only gave great prominence to the stories of the goddess Ganga found in the *Pothī Premambodh* and in *Bhakshidas* but also included the stories related to Mandu that were first recorded in the nineteenth-century ethnographic and census accounts of the Chamars mentioned above.

The tradition of publishing works called *Ravidās Rāmāyaṇa* continued unabated and there were, and are, numerous such works. A typical example was that by Mahadev Prasad Simh from Ara district whose work was published at least twelve times from the Loknath Pustakalaya in Calcutta (Simh 1984). These *Ravidās Rāmāyaṇa* accounts all feature prominently the stories about Ravidās and the goddess Ganga within sets of narratives about Ravidās's struggles with Brāhmins, Sufis, Yogis and rulers for his rights (Friedlander, 2012b).

Taken together, these accounts of the life of Ravidās show how narratives about Ravidās and the goddess Ganga formed a significant part of what could be characterised as movements by followers of Ravidās who were contesting in the public sphere for their rights.

Ravidās temples and memorials on the Ganga today

The importance of these stories lies not only in what they can tell us about changes taking place at the time of Ravidās in the sixteenth century and in the early part of the twentieth century, but also in that they have a direct impact on contemporary society and politics in India and in Varanasi.

Followers of Ravidās had been prominent in agitations for equal rights for much of the twentieth century and followers of a teacher called Sant Sarwan Dass of Dhera Sachkhand Ballan came to Varanasi in the 1960s and had visions that a location in the South of Varanasi near Benares Hindu University had been the birthplace of Ravidās. This land was then bought and in 1965 construction of a temple on the site commenced; it was inaugurated in 1972 (Schaller, 2012). Under the administration of the government of Mayavati in the early 2000s, a number of other works were also undertaken in the area, as well as the Ravidās public gateway, Lanka, Varanasi in 1998. Subsequently another prominent monument to Ravidās was constructed as a park and memorial to Ravidās in the South of Varanasi at Nagwa; this monument, on the shore of the Ganga, was inaugurated by Mayavati in 2008. Accounts of Ravidās' life published by the Seer Goverdhanpur temple and available at the temple also feature quite prominently versions of the stories about Ravidās and the goddess Ganga (Suman 2009, 115-119 and 129-134).

There is a second prominent Ravidās temple in Varanasi in the north of the city. It was founded by the prominent Congress Party politician Jagjivan Ram, from the untouchable Shivnarayani community of Bihar.

He conceived of the idea of building a temple to Ravidās on the shore of the Ganga and bought a substantial block of land at Rajghat in 1976 in the north of Varanasi. It was at about this time that this location was determined to have been where Ravidās' debate with the Brāhmins had taken place after the goddess Ganga's gift of the bracelet. In 1982 work began on the 108-foot tall temple that is now a prominent feature of the Varanasi skyline (Rāmlakhan undated, 5-6). Among the activities of this group at the time was research into the works of Ravidās and stories about his life. In a 1988 pamphlet called *Raidās Gāthā* there is a detailed account of the story of Ravidās and the goddess Ganga and the bracelet, which on its last page identifies the exact location of the story as the site of the new temple at Rajghat (Simh 1988, 14).

The followers of the traditions focused both at Seer Goverdhanpur and at Rajghat now draw on the stories about Ravidās and the goddess Ganga in their contestations for public space on the shores of the Ganga and in their assertions of the role of Ravidās within the sacred sphere in Varanasi. This points to the importance of understanding the role of the goddess in the stories associated with Ravidās. To argue that Ravidās and his followers have appropriated the goddess Ganga would be to align the analysis with caste Hindu claims to exclusive rights over access to the public space of the shores of the Ganga and the sacred space of the Ganga. If, however, we follow the narratives of the stories themselves, we can characterise the relationship between Ravidās and the Ganga as one of contestation between different communities for the right to utilise and create spaces within the public and sacred spheres.

Conclusion

I would argue that what emerges from considering these stories about Ravidās and the Ganga from the Sikh accounts and the folk accounts from Rajasthan and Madhya Pradesh is that there was an interplay between the existing religious traditions of the Chamar communities which involved veneration of the goddess Ganga and traditions which developed around Ravidās. Furthermore, these narratives themselves form part of the ways in which communities who follow Ravidās, in the words of B.R. Ambedkar, 'organise, educate and agitate'.

There is no evidence whatsoever that the goddess Ganga was originally the possession of a particular culture, as she was venerated in multiple Indic cultures, Brāhminic, Epic, Hindu, Buddhist, and folk cultures of communities such as the Chamars. I would rather suggest that we need to regard the goddess Ganga as having been part of a public sacred sphere within which Indic religious cultures flourished.

It would therefore seem utterly inappropriate to try to directly apply Lipsitz's theories and Scafidi's ideas to argue that the goddess Ganga had been appropriated by Ravidās and his followers. To do this would be to ignore the inherent power hierarchies in South Asia and miss the ways in which the term appropriation is part of a high-caste rhetoric of criticism of lower-caste communities such as those of the Chamars. I would argue that, in his time, Ravidās and his followers were contesting for their traditional rights to venerate the goddess Ganga in ways that were already part of the culture of their communities. Furthermore, this now has a direct impact on how contemporary communities associated with Ravidās are contesting for their rights to establish sacred sites on the shores of the Ganga and build temples and monuments to their leader.

My conclusion is that these stories are representations of the continued existence of reverence for the goddess Ganga amongst the Chamar communities and representations of contestations over sacred and public spheres that developed during the period when Ravidās was one of the prominent leaders of the *bhakti* movement.

In the light of this conclusion, it deserves to be repeated that the relationship between the goddess Ganga and Ravidās cannot be characterised as appropriation, which is a term used in the rhetoric of higher-caste criticism of lower-caste communities, but should be regarded as part of a rhetoric of contestation by lower-caste communities. What these stories tell us is how the Chamar communities' veneration of the goddess Ganga formed part of a narrative about contestation between the Chamar caste communities and Brāhminical communities, which has been ongoing since the sixteenth century, for the right to access and inhabit the public and sacred spheres in India.

Bibliography

Beckerlegge, G. 2003. 'Saffron and Seva: the Rashtriya Swayamsevak Sangh's appropriation of Swami Vivekananda'. In *Hinduism in Public and Private: Reform, Hindutva, Gender, and Sampraday*, edited by A. Copley, 31-65. New Delhi; New York: Oxford University Press.

Briggs, G.W. 1920. *The Chamars*. Calcutta: Association Press.

Callewaert, Winand. 1994. 'Bhaktamals and Paracais in Rajasthan'. In *According to Tradition: Hagiographical Writing in India*, edited by W. Callewaert and R. Snell, 87-98. Wiesbaden: Otto Harrassowitz.

Callewaert, Winand, and Peter Friedlander. 1992. *The Life and Works of Raidas*. New Delhi: Manohar.
Callewaert, Winand, and Swapna Sharma. 2000. *The Hagiographies of Anantadās: The Bhakti poets of North India*. Richmond, UK: Curzon Press.
Darian, Steven G. 1978. *The Ganges in Myth and History*. Honolulu: University Press of Hawaii.
Doron, A. 2006. 'The needle and the sword: boatmen, priests and the ritual economy of Varanasi'. *South Asia* new series 29 (3): 345-367.
Dowman, K. 1985. *Masters of Mahāmudrā*. Albany: State University Press of New York.
Francis, H.T. (trans.). 1905. *The Jātaka*, Vol. V. London: Luzac for the Pali Text Society.
Friedlander, Peter. 1996. 'The struggle for salvation in the hagiographies of Ravidās'. In *Myth and Mythmaking,* edited by J. Leslie, 106-123. London: Curzon Press.
Friedlander, Peter. 2012a. 'Kabīr and the print sphere'. *Thesis 11* 112 (2): 45-56.
Friedlander, Peter, 2012b. 'Ravidās'. In *Brill's Encyclopedia of Hinduism, vol. IV*, edited by Knut A. Jacobsen *et al, 371-378*. Leiden: Brill.
Ghose, Sankar. 1993. *Jawaharlal Nehru: a Biography*. Delhi: Allied Publishers.
Jatav, Kaviratan Bhakshidas. 1911. *Ravidās Rāmāyaṇa*. Meraṭh: Candūlāl Maṭrūlāl.
Kuril, Ramcaran. 1940. *Bhagvān Ravidās Kī Satyakathā*. Kānpur: Kṛṣṇa Pres.
Lipsitz, G. 1994. *Dangerous Crossroads: Popular Music, Postmodernism, and the Poetics of Place*. London; New York: Verso.
Lorenzen, David. 1991. *Kabīr Legends and Ananta-Das's Kabīr Parachai*. Albany, NJ: State University of New York Press.
MacCulloch J.A. 1911. *The Religion of the Ancient Celts*. Edinburgh: T. & T. Clark.
Rāmlakhan. undated. *Guru Ravidās Mandir, Kalpana, Nirmaṇ*. Dilli: Ravidās Smarak Sosaiti.
Sabar, Jasvant Siṃh. 1984. *Bhagat Ravidās Srot Pustak*. Aṃritsar: Guru Nanak Dev Yunivarsiti Prais.
Scafidi, S. 2005. *Who Owns Culture? Appropriation and Authenticity in American Law*. New Brunswick: Rutgers University Press.
Schaller, J. 2012. 'Ravidāsīs'. In *Brill's Encyclopedia of Hinduism,* vol. IV, edited by Knut A. Jacobsen *et al, 500-506*. Leiden: Brill.
Sastri, Ramanand and Virendra Pandey. 1955. *Sant Ravidās Aur Unkā Kāvya*. Jvalapur, Haridvar: Ravidās Āśram.
Singer, M. 1972. *When a Great Tradition Modernizes: an Anthropological Approach to Indian Civilization*. New York: Praeger.
Simh, Babu Mahadev Prasad. 1984. *Ravidās Rāmāyaṇa*. Kalkatta: Shrī Loknāth Pustakālay.
Simh, Shukdev. 1988. *Raidās Gāthā*. Vārāṇasi: Ravidās Smārak Sosaitī.
Singh, Darshan. 1977. *Sant Ravidas and His Times*. Delhi: Kalyani Publishers.
Singh, Darshan. 1981. *A Study of Bhakta Ravidas*. Patiala: Punjabi University.
Singh, Hardayal. 1891. *Mardumśumārī Rāj Mārvāḍ*. Jodhpur: Jodhpur State.
Srivastava, M.C.P. 1979. *Mother Goddess in Indian Art, Archaeology and Literature*. Delhi: Agam Kala Prakashan.
Suman, Chain Ram. 2009. *Miracles of Jagatguru Ravidāss Ji*. Seer Goverdhanpur: Shri Guru Ravidāss Janam Sthan Mandir.
Templeman, D. 1983. *The Seven Instruction Lineages*. Dharamsala: Library of Tibetan Words and Archives.
Zelliot, Eleanor, and Rohini Mokashi-Punekar (eds). 2005. *Untouchable Saints: an Indian Phenomenon*. New Delhi: Manohar.

Chapter 7

The Goddess Chinnamastā's Severed Head as a Re-Appropriation of the Cosmic Sacrifice

Ian Mabbett

(The Tantric adept) should conceive of himself [that is, intensely visualise himself] in the form of Bhaṭṭārikā Vajrayoginī ... of yellow colour, carrying in her left hand her own head severed by herself with her own *kartri* [sacrificial knife] carried in her right hand. Her left arm is raised up while the right is lowered. She is without clothing, and her right foot is advanced while the left is bent down. He (the adept) should also conceive of the streams (of blood) gushing forth from the (headless) trunk as falling into (the goddess's) own mouth and into the mouths of the two Yoginīs on either side of her.

He should also conceive of the two Yoginīs to (her) left and right, the green[1] Vajravarṇanī and the yellow Vajravairocanī, both of whom carry the *kartri* and the *karpara* [*skull*] in their hands.[2] Each has one leg advanced, the other bent down, and they have dishevelled hair. On both sides, between the two Yoginīs and in the intervening space, there is an exceedingly

1 *Śyāma* means, literally, of a dark hue, swarthy, but is often used for dark green.

2 The original is laconic and indicates only obscurely which hand holds which object. Vajravarṇanī, who is green, has a knife in her left hand, a skull in her right; Vajravairocanī, who is yellow, has a skull in her left hand, a knife in her right.

> horrifying cremation ground (Bhattacharyya vol. 2, 1928, 452-453; translated by present author).[3]

This iconographic description of the Buddhist goddess Vajrayoginī, in her decapitated form as Chinnamuṇḍā ('She with severed head'), comes from the *Sādhanamālā,* a Tantric text dating from about the twelfth century. Perhaps better known is the Hindu equivalent, Chinnamastā, a name with the same meaning: *masta* means 'head'; *muṇḍa* means 'bald head', or 'head' in general. The iconography of the two goddesses is virtually identical. To some extent they have a shared origin. The following shorter iconographic description of Chinnamastā, from a late text listing goddess mantras for meditation purposes, adds the important detail that the goddess is to be visualised as treading upon the bodies of the god and goddess of love, who are copulating:

> I worship the noble Chinnamastā who … holds in her left hand her own head, which is severed, has dishevelled hair, (and) an open mouth which is drinking her own blood from (her) throat, who is stationed on Rati and Smara [= Kāma, god of love], who are engaged in sexual intercourse, (and) is filled with joy upon seeing her companions Ḍākiṇī and Varṇinī (Mahidhara, *Mantramahodadhi* 6.6, in Bühnemann 2000, 108; Mahidhara 1992).

Here the name Chinnamastā will be used for convenience to stand for both herself and her Buddhist twin Chinnamuṇḍā, though it needs to be understood that in the indigenous explanations of iconographic symbols, Buddhist doctrines are introduced to explain the iconography of Chinnamuṇḍā and Brāhminic doctrines that of Chinnamastā.

Goddesses, both in Tantra and in regional popular traditions of India, frequently assume terrifying and violent aspects, and are frequently depicted in art and iconography as trampling on or beheading demonic foes, but there is something particularly gruesome about Chinnamastā

3 *Bharṭārikāṃ Vajrayoginīṃ … pītavarṇāṃ svayameva svakartri-kartita-svamastaka-vāmahastasthitāṃ dakṣiṇahastakartrisahitāṃ, ūrdhvavistṛtavāmabāhum, adhonamitadakṣiṇabāhuṃ, vāsaḥśūnyāṃ, prasāritadakṣiṇapādāṃ saṅkucitavāmapadāṃ, bhāvayet. Kavandhānniḥsṛtyāsṛkdhārā svamukhe praviśati, apare ubhayoḥ pārśvayoginyor-mukhe praviśati iti bhāvayet. Vāmadakṣiṇapārśvayoḥ śyāmavarṇa-Vajravarṇanī-pītavarṇa-Vajravairocanyau vāmadakṣiṇahastakartrisahite, dakṣiṇavāmahastakarpparasahite, prasāritavāmapādaprasāritadakṣiṇapāde saṅkucitetarapāde muktakeśyau bhāvayet ubhayoḥ pārśvayoḥ, ubhayor yoginīpramadhye antarīkṣe atibhayākulaṃ śmaśānaṃ bhāvayet.*

(or Chinnamuṇḍā – both have the same disturbing images); she cuts off her own head, which she holds in one hand, while three streams of blood from the severed neck flow into her own mouth and into those of her attendants. Symbolic explanations of such violent scenes are available in plenty, and they mostly decode the horrific images as tokens for various aspects of spiritual enlightenment and the means to attain it; but it remains to be explained why, along the path of purification and insight, such disturbing images should be selected as tokens. In a study of one particular Chinnamastā portrayal, Karel van Kooij asks, 'Why should these ethical values be rendered in such an extremely shocking and violent way?' (van Kooij 1999, 250).

How should this question be answered? It is not straightforward and depends a great deal upon our assumptions and methods in looking for the answer. In the article just cited, van Kooij sets about the task of bringing greater precision to the explanation of Chinnamastā's significance by focusing on a miniature painting from Kangra dating from around 1800. He places it in its context as a product of courtly art, requiring to be judged according to the criteria appropriate to it, which are largely aesthetic, influenced by a martial ethos. He distinguishes this from the priestly and theological standards that would apply to the judgment of such other objects of study as Tantric texts. So, in his view, attention must be given to the proper context. He sees little value in interpretations that force the Indian material into a mould supplied by modern theories likely to have little relevance, such as the theories of Jung or Freud (van Kooij 1999, 257).

As far as it goes this is certainly sound method within the disciplines of history and indology. We should look at the object of historical study in its immediate context, analysing it as a particular sort of creation belonging to a particular place and time.

Sometimes, however, to understand the meaning of a religious image or text as fully as possible, we need to ask wider questions and look at a broader context. If we interrogate closely the creators, viewers and readers of such disturbing images within their (often Tantric) context, we are given plenty of explanations of the symbolism of severed heads, blood, skulls, knives and so forth. In each case the symbol represents an abstraction of Brāhminic or Buddhist doctrine which the adept is to contemplate serenely on the road towards enlightenment. The iconographic features are tokens seemingly more or less arbitrarily chosen to represent abstractions belonging to teachings about meditation practice; but the puzzle remains why these tokens should appear to be so deliberately evocative of violence. Chinnamastā/Chinnamuṇḍā, with her confronting iconography – most especially her severed head – represents a disposition towards violent imagery that is pronounced in many cults, including popular cults of goddesses as well as Tantric ones. It is surely legitimate to investigate the chosen object of study as a feature of an enlarged historical setting, perhaps extending into the *longue durée*. Here the chosen focus is on the severed head, and the object is to consider its significance within the Indian religious tradition. We shall look at it in a broader context than that of any one text or representation.

The process of re-appropriation in religious change

To achieve this broadening of the context, we need first to make a short digression into broad theory in the study of religions. This is necessary here in order to make sense of the way in which the iconography of Chinnamastā will be discussed below. What this chapter will propose is that Chinnamastā's gory head belongs as a late term in a series of images that have emerged in different periods of Indian religious history. These images, it will be suggested, are successive embodiments of a particular cosmological theme. This notion of the continuity of cosmological themes is not essentially novel; it can be found in much indological scholarship of earlier generations, especially in France, as we shall notice further below. Here, however, we are looking at the goddess in question from a more modern perspective.

For this purpose it is useful to distinguish the relatively volatile rise and fall of particular religious doctrines and movements from the more persistent structures of cosmological belief that persist within the world-views of society at large, commonly transmitted through oral tradition.

Most religious groups or teachings construct from elements in these deeper currents their own relatively sophisticated system of explicit cosmological belief, but the underlying repertoire of ideas about the structure of the universe persists in the background, slow to change. The elements elaborated by specific religious teachings are adapted to the goals of the teachers who propound them, but in whatever new dressing, they incorporate continuity with the worldview and folk beliefs of the encompassing society.

For example, the rise of Buddhism deliberately rejected the place of gods in the old Brāhminic system, but did not abolish them; it accepted their existence as migrating beings like the rest of us, shorn of the majesty accorded them in the Vedic tradition, while popular beliefs in a multitude of *yakṣas*, *nāga* spirits and other local gods and spirits lurking in the natural environment remained integral to the assumptions drawn on freely by Buddhist teachers to illustrate their parables. Again, the belief in *karma* can itself be argued to be a broad feature of popular tradition, to which Brāhminism, Buddhism, Jainism and the other schools had to adapt their teachings in different ways.

In every case, the retention of old cosmological notions, frequently adapted to new forms in compliance with specific religious teachings, marks a process of re-appropriation of folk cosmology. People who adopt new beliefs need to define and interpret them within an enduring framework supplied by their pre-existing worldview. The adoption of sometimes challengingly novel dogmas by a population familiar with an older worldview positively requires some elements of continuity in order to make sense of new teachings within an ordered mental universe. The more revolutionary the new creed, perhaps, the greater the need for old and familiar features to figure like stage props in the scenery.

If we describe the case in this way, we are doing no more than to apply a commonsense perspective to the processes of evolution driving changes in Indian religious traditions. From the point of view of new schools and teachings, old ideas are appropriated and transformed; from the point of view of the ordinary people caught up in the changes, the old ideas are re-appropriated and fitted out to accommodate new customs, rituals and beliefs.

The same processes used to be differently described, in ways that commonly look outdated now, by earlier generations of scholars, particularly those writing in French. A striking example is Paul Mus' *Barabudur* (1935), which in a long introduction condenses a total view of the history of Indian religious thought and imagery as an explanation of the Javanese temple studied in its chapters. More recently, but in a similar tradition, Madeleine Biardeau's *Hinduism* (1989) argues for the powerful thematic unity of the whole religion. Scholars such as these looked upon Indian religion as an integrated organic system, almost as a soul with a personality. For Paul Mus, Indian civilisation as such was a unitary agent acting upon history, and it seemed necessary to him to explain everything that called for an explanation by deriving it orthogenetically from the logic of the civilisation's own intrinsic nature. The result was often a *tour de force*, but the method could not prevent mistakes.

However, we should not jump to the conclusion that all such scholarship is old-fashioned and fatally flawed, holding no interest for us. On the contrary, it is remarkable how often the conclusions reached by Mus (and others like him) still hold value. To see why, we need mentally to replace the explanatory concept of the enduring soul of a civilisation with that of the sluggish subterranean current of folk cosmology outlined above. *Motifs* from pre-existing structures of folk belief are constantly called upon by people's religious imagination, in times of change, to support the sense of a continuing framework of familiar truths about the enduring nature of the universe. The *motifs* will often need to be adapted to new forms, but they will retain their structural role. This is in fact just what Mus says about the principles to be followed in identifying continuities of meaning in different successive images; each, in its own context, must have the same function as the others do in theirs.[4] In assessing Mus' argument, we should allow for the wide erudition and sound intuition that often guided his judgment.

The reason why it is appropriate to draw attention to the place of folk cosmology in the methods followed by such writers as Paul Mus is that, at the end of our discussion of the interpretation of Chinnamastā's symbolism that follows here, we shall have occasion to profit from Mus' claims to detect a single series of cosmogonic symbols, all connected with sacrifice, running from the Vedas through many subsequent centuries. Chinnamastā's severed head will fit into the series.

Some explanations of Chinnamastā's symbolism

We can now return to the iconography of Chinnamastā herself and the ways in which it is interpreted within Indian tradition. The most conspicuous feature is the severing of her head, releasing from the neck three spouts of blood which enter her own mouth and those of her two attendants. Perhaps the main Tantric interpretation appeals to the system of transcendent anatomy associated with Kuṇḍalinī yoga. Kuṇḍalinī, the serpent spirit, lies in her latent state coiled at the base of the spine. In the passage to enlightenment gained in meditation, the adept incites her

4 See Mus (1968, 560). Cf. Mabbett (2006, 121), paraphrasing Mus' method: 'On ne peut pas déclarer que des images trouvées dans des sources différentes incarnent un seul motif persistant sauf s'il est possible de démontrer que chacun, dans le système décrit dans son propre contexte, possède la même fonction'.

to awake and stretch up vertically along a central vertical channel that passes through a series of nodes (*cakras*) situated at various points in the body. Spiritual enlightenment comes when her head reaches the topmost node (*sahasrārā*) which is invisible and located just above the skull. Two channels, which are passages for subtle winds or breaths (the media *par excellence* of spiritual energy), are twined around the central channel, and the adept is said to be able to incite Kuṇḍalinī to rise by the manipulation of these subtle breaths. This system, which has long been familiar to students of Indian religion, is deeply embedded in Tantric tradition and provides a template for visualisation techniques in many aspects of meditation practice. It lends itself neatly to the interpretation of Chinnamastā's blood-spouting neck: the removal of her head marks the ascension to full enlightenment (in one account, the ballistic force of Kuṇḍalinī's passage to enlightenment blows off her head); and the three streams of blood, giving life and sustenance to her and to her two attendants, represent the subtle winds or breaths. There is much more to the mythology that has grown in texts and oral traditions, but this much is enough to display the abstract and spiritual focus of the Tantric symbol system. The image contemplated by the practitioner in meditation is to be experienced as a vehicle of passage from the world of illusion (or, in Buddhism, absorption in the narrow interest of the illusory individual self) to freedom from ignorance and union with the absolute (or *nirvāṇa*). The apparently gruesome character of the image (in the eyes of some outsiders) plays no obviously important part in the exercise.[5] The whole focus of the meditation is upon the rarefied elements of a spiritual quest. This is what matters here.

Other aspects of the image receive similarly ethereal and other-worldly explanations. Buddhist versions often depict Vajrayoginī as standing upon the body of Kālī. This evinces an elaborate network of mythical correspondences linking Vajrayoginī to 'Black Kālī', to the extent that the two are often regarded as alternative forms of each other, but, in the context of Chinnamuṇḍā, the posture of the goddess is seen as representing her victory over time, or over entrapment in the round of rebirths. In Hindu

5 This statement complies with a deliberately naïve outsider's view. In Tantric soteriology, the gruesomeness is of a piece with the adept's purposeful adoption of behaviour and routines of life that violate normal standards of propriety and wholesomeness. Salvation must begin with wholehearted acceptance of the here and now, including its superficially most repellent aspects. This approach is to some extent characteristic of the ascetic tradition dating from the time of the *śramaṇas* in general. However, the point here is that textual prescriptions commonly offer abstract and innocuous-looking explanations of the disturbing symbols, as mentioned below.

Plate 4.1: Pillar opposite the shrine.

Plate 4.2: Standing Tīrthaṃkar image in the shrine.

Plate 4.3: Atmaram Gurav at the Kalsuli Jain Brāhmaṇa Shrine.

Plate 4.4: Goddess coalesced with the ficus tree.

Plate 4.5: Several Jain images engulfed by the ficus tree.

Plate 4.6: Yakṣiṇī Devī with Jain Tīrthaṃkar on the left.

Plate 10.1: Illustration depicting the type of deity to which Jomo Yangri Chugmo belongs.

Plate 10.2: Yangri Chugmo on her turquoise dragon. Tsuri Temple, Yolmo. Photo courtesy Zsoka Gelle.

Plate 11.1: Ekveera Devi temple at the entrance to the Karle Buddhist chaitya. In the foreground is a tank that has recently been enlarged. Photo courtesy Sanjay Ranade.

Plate 11.2: Contemporary photograph showing the five steps leading into the Ekveera Devi temple. Photo courtesy Jayant Bhalchandra Bapat.

Plate 11.3: Image of Ekveera Devi wearing the silver mask. Photo courtesy Jayant Bhalchandra Bapat.

versions, the goddess typically stands upon the bodies of Kāma (or, in Vaishnavite contexts from mediaeval times, Smara), and Rati, respectively the god and goddess of love. Standing upon some other being is unambiguously a symbol of dominion. In this case the copulating couple represents the energy of erotic love which Chinnamastā's enlightenment has enabled her to transcend; as David Kinsley (1986, 175) puts it, she 'takes life and vigor from the copulating couple, then gives it away lavishly by cutting off her own head to feed her devotees'.

Other features are given standard Tantric interpretations. She rolls her three bloodshot eyes; this indicates that 'she is the knower of the past, present and future' and her all-encompassing perception means that 'nothing escapes the vision of Vajrayoginī; therefore the ego has nowhere to hide.' She haunts the charnel ground, which with its evocation of death and transience stands for the dark and confusing round of rebirths born of ignorance and karma, 'the basic space in which birth and death, confusion and wakefulness arise' (Trungpa 1982, 239).

She carries or wears a number of sinister accoutrements: the *kartri* ('agent of cutting or destruction') or sacrificial knife (which in Hinduism represents the destruction of the illusion of a separate self, or in Buddhism the 'hook of mercy' offering salvation from the round of rebirths); a rosary made of skulls; a necklace of bones (these both representing the conquest of death and time); a serpent worn in place of the (Brāhminical) sacred cord (*upavīta*) (denoting the achievement of immortality, as the snake sloughs off its skin); and the Tantric staff (*khatvaṅga,* originally a weapon, adapted as a pilgrim staff and in Buddhism associated with the bodhisattva Padmasambhava).[6] In one way or another the details of iconography evoke death, violence, and the impermanence of all that is conventionally prized, and to the practitioner they mean that Chinnamastā has transcended such things. The conventions of the symbolism are familiar from much of the array of fierce goddesses belonging to the Hindu Mahāvidyās.[7]

The spectacular part played by blood in Chinnamastā's imagery demands a comment. Blood figures quite frequently in the myths of the ten Mahāvidyās and of Indian warrior goddesses across the board, and have been discussed by Wendy Doniger (1980) in the course of an examination of the symbolism of menstrual and other blood in texts from the Vedas onwards. She suggests that there came to be a complex relationship

6 On these accoutrements, see particularly Benard (1994, 107-108).

7 On the Mahāvidyās, see Kinsley (1997).

between blood and milk; mythically or cosmologically speaking, blood (which in itself is possessed of 'demonic' characteristics) is at the origin of 'female seed' (*rati*), but in its transformation it passes through a dangerously unstable intermediate state – 'To drink blood directly is demonic' (Doniger 1980, 42). But a delicate liminal stage separates blood from semen and breast-milk – 'Milk is made from blood, yet blood pollutes and endangers, while milk purifies and engenders' (Doniger 1980, 43). The demonic and the divine lie dangerously close alongside each other, illustrating the tension between purity and pollution, between the light and dark sides of the divinity, which can turn into each other. This analysis alerts us to ways in which we may understand the spouts of blood from Chinnamastā's severed neck; they are redolent of violence, danger and darkness, yet they have within them, under the influence of divine power, potential to create, nurture and maintain.

Sacrifice

These qualities – creation, nurture and maintenance – inevitably evoke the notion of the religious sacrifice, which is fundamental to the narrative implicit in the evolution of Indian cosmological ideas from early times.

Chinnamastā's symbolism cannot be adequately comprehended only by assessing her various attributes severally. The imagery of sacrifice is seldom far from the symbolism of the myths of deities, and, in the case of this goddess, it is clear that the sort of sacrifice evoked by her myth is no tame ritual. It is deliberately violent, even shocking. Whatever the resonances of the ingredients of folk cosmology evoked by the iconography of the goddess, it is clear that they have sinister and violent aspects. Sacrifice is designed to lead to renewal, protection and nurture for the sacrificer, but it carries at its heart a confrontation with desperation and fear, for the greatest rewards must come only after paying the greatest price. The creation of the world itself is the supreme sacrifice, and the sacrifice that brings the world into being must be a cataclysmic ordeal.

The work of J.C. Heesterman deserves to be mentioned above all. For him, violence is conspicuous in the culture reflected by Vedic sacrifices precisely by the way in which it is denied, inverted and sanitised. In *The Broken World of Sacrifice* (Heesterman 1993), he distinguishes rigorously between sacrifice and ritual. In his view, ritualism, as evolved by the composers of the Vedic scriptures, represents a denaturing and sterilisation of earlier sacrificial practices that were violent and agonistic. In the earlier stages, sacrifice was an affair for warriors, full of danger and sometimes leading to death. In the sanitised rituals of the succeeding age represented by the Vedic scriptures, the violence and danger were removed and sacrifice came to be represented by the merely symbolic actions of Brāhmins. Heesterman compares this change to the alteration of a football into a sort of choreographed display with only one team and no competition (Heesterman 1993, 2, 3, 76).

This theme of sacrifice as a way of channelling violence finds counterparts in other relatively recent writings (Girard 1972; Burkert 1983; Vidal et al. 1994). Such arguments serve to suggest, at least, that we will do well to keep in mind the psychology of violence lurking in the social and cultural background. Those who originally found the image of Chinnamastā compelling lived in societies where people were more likely to be familiar with the reality of physical atrocities, jets of blood and actual beheadings than we are today, and such things had far more resonance in the imagery that constituted the vocabulary of culture.

The cosmic sacrifice

In the dark side of the goddess, we can detect, in extreme form, a theme or *motif* that might well lurk continuously and pervasively within a culture's worldview, even when orthodox religious teaching does not make it explicit. This is the notion of religious enlightenment as the product of sacrifice, where what is sacrificed is the self, which must undergo a violent and thoroughgoing purification and renewal utterly destructive of the contaminated past life.

Such a notion is readily superimposed upon cosmological beliefs about the creation and destruction of the world. This applies to the core Brāhminic tradition which accords authority to Vedic ritual and belief. According to this tradition the cosmos is periodically renewed in a sacrifice whereby the cosmos is generated from the primordial man (*Puruṣa*). No detailed examination of the history of sacrifice in Indian religion can be undertaken here, but familiarity with the topic may well suggest that, through the concept of sacrifice, the cosmos and the personal self are conflated, each an image of the other, and that this correspondence, more than a poetic metaphor, lurks as a permanent potential in images that recur again and again in different forms throughout the history of Brāhminic and Buddhist religion. Such at least, as we shall notice below, was the principle adopted in some of his writings by Paul Mus (on which see Mabbett 2006).

According to this principle, sacrifice gives expression to a worldview in which both the world and the individual seeker after enlightenment must undergo cataclysmic and agonising processes of reconstruction and renewal.

Sacrifice and decapitation

J.C. Heesterman, exploring the links between Vedic sacrifice and the concept of the severed head, emphasises the Vedic origin of a notion of cosmic sacrifice that unfolds in an unending process of rebirth and renewal, disintegration and re-integration: 'The sacrifice is a cosmos which is violently broken up to be put together again' (Heesterman 1967, 24). P. Pal (1981) applies this idea of the constant renewal of creation in sacrifice directly to Chinnamastā herself, where he insists on the sacrificial reference of the image of the goddess's blood feeding her two attendants; he sees this as the mark of a 'munificent' goddess, like Annapūrṇā, goddess of food. The universe is renewed symbolically through the cycle of giving and receiving, and the munificent goddess participates through her bounty in the cycle, the 'primal sacrifice and renewal of creation' (Pal 1981, 82). Kinsley similarly emphasises the embodiment in Chinnamastā of the cosmic cycle of birth, death and nourishment. Unlike many other goddesses, such as Kālī and Durgā who demand the sacrifice of their heads from their devotees, she provides nourishment for others, but she, like them, confronts her worshippers with the inevitability of death (Kinsley 1986, 174-175).

So it is not surprising that the theme of decapitation should not be peculiar to Chinnamastā. It finds echoes in many Indian myths, and indeed in other traditions elsewhere. We cannot here do justice to the literature upon the subject of beheaded, or headless, divinities, which is represented by many traditions, Tantric and otherwise. Old folk traditions since early times have often produced types of goddess sculptures without a head, notably Lajjāgaurī (Bapat 2008). Pre-eminent among stories related to Vaiṣṇavism is the episode involving the beheading of Reṇukā by Paraśurāma on the order of Jamadagni, replete with mythical implications (Desai 2008). Pre-eminent among stories related to Śaivism is the episode of the beheading of Gaṇeśa by Śiva (Courtright 1985). Especially in tantra, there are many examples of goddesses, or other great beings, losing their heads.

Such myths range widely in place, time and religious context. One lesson deserves to be drawn here from consideration of the class as a whole: cases of divine decapitation often appear, from the bald facts of their narration, to be punishments, yet we cannot go far into the intricacies of their symbolism without discovering that their subjects are often not the passive victims of tragedy but themselves authors of a transcendent narrative. They can even be their own fully responsible executioners, decapitating themselves in order to demonstrate a higher truth, that of transcendence of the world of seeming reality by the wisdom of insight.

One story from outside India deserves to be noted here because of its reference to blood as a sacred fluid that can turn white, perhaps doubling as milk or sperm if we apply the code suggested by Doniger for Indian myth, as was noticed above. This is the episode of the death of Siti Jenar, the Sufi mystic in Java who was executed in the sixteenth century (Johns 1961, 46-48). His reputation as a teacher, professing to speak for God yet failing to observe the law or attend the Friday prayers, brought him to the attention of the ruler, the Sunan Giri, who sent for him to account for his unorthodox behaviour. On the first summons, he refused to go to the ruler, saying that Siti Jenar was not there; only God truly existed. The following summons was, therefore, addressed to God, but was met by the reply that only Siti Jenar was there. In the upshot, after both God and Siti Jenar were commanded to appear before the ruler, the Sufi mystic was beheaded on the order of Sunan Giri; but his blood ran red, then turned white and recited the confession of the faith ('There is no God but God, and Muhammad is his messenger'). Subsequently the voice of Siti Jenar was heard saying 'What does death matter? If one places his trust in any other unity than that of the All-Highest he will be disappointed and not attain his goal' (Johns 1961, 48).

Here the victim of the beheading appears to be truly the victor through his access to a divine realm. Closer to the tradition to which Chinnamastā belongs, a legend that acquired currency in mediaeval literature may be cited in illustration of the same idea. It is the story that the Buddhist teacher Nāgārjuna, celebrated in later centuries as a *mahāsiddha*, was immortal, but, having promised a boon to an ambitious prince who sought to compass his death by a ruse, willingly cut off his own head with a blade of *kuśa* grass (*Kathāsaritsāgara* 41.9 ff. (Somadeva 1915, 188)). Supernatural beings who can behead themselves at will are not strangers to Tantric lore; sometimes they can just as freely put their heads back again, thereby robbing the phenomenon of some of its gruesomeness. Here is an episode from Tāranātha's *Life of Kṛṣṇācārya*:

> The Mahacarya Kāṇhapa's female disciples attained siddhi too. When the acarya arrived in the south in Mahārāshṭra, two sisters lived there – the eldest was called Mekhala and the youngest Kanakala …
>
> On another occasion in Bengal, during the reign of King Lalitacandra, when the Mahacarya had seen that the time was right for converting the King, the two girls emerged from a throng of people surrounding the acarya, and paying homage at his feet said, "By the grace of the Guru we have attained the very highest and greatest of goals, and now we wish to fly off to the heavens. However, before that we will be happy to do whatever the acarya requests us to do." The acarya replied, "Well then, cut off your heads and offer them to me." The girls drew from their mouths well-tempered swords of wisdom and cutting off their heads without any hindrance at all, offered them into the Guru's hands. Facing backwards, they danced off, rising higher and higher on the heavenly paths, finally disappearing into rainbow light. The goddess Śrījñānā had also previously manifested a miracle similar to this and even rākṣasas and ḍākinīs in their ordinary bodily forms started to demonstrate it in considerable numbers. As an antidote to this activity, Vajravarāhī herself appeared in that form, with her head severed, and it is said that this miracle appeared frequently thereafter amongst her siddhas (Tāranātha 1989, 62-63).

Vajravarāhī is a form of Vajrayoginī. Tantric siddhas and deities were known to be capable of removing and replacing their heads by use of the 'sword of wisdom', which could vanquish the illusion of a narrow personal self and deliver one from the round of rebirths. Their feats of self-sacrifice were demonstrations of the transcendent illumination bestowed by their insight.

For us today, the act of beheading cannot fail to evoke the ferocious dispatch of a sacrificial victim, whose death is in some way the removal of an obstacle to the well-being of the sacrificing individual or community. Yet we observe again and again that the god, goddess or supernatural figure thus dispatched is not exactly a victim but the master of the whole situation. Violence is not incidental to the religious drama; it is

Figure 7.1 The female siddhas Mekhalā and Kanakalā, who cut off their heads with the sword of wisdom. Line drawing courtesy David Templeman.

integral, and its savagely agonistic context is still evoked for the beholder, even when the ritual act of sacrifice is tamed into the almost playful acrobatics of Mekhalā and Kanakalā who cheerfully cut off and replace their own heads.

Here it may be suggested that the symbolism of the head has a richer and deeper significance than is generally recognised: within it may lurk the spiritual enlightenment which, defying the principle of Gödel's theorem, can account, and indeed is the source, both for itself and for the rest of the body, or of creation. This was in effect argued many years ago by Paul Mus in his indological writings (in particular, Mus 1962 and 1968).

Mus' explanation of his thinking began with his interpretation of verse 12 in the famous Vedic hymn 10.90, which links cosmic creation with the sacrifice of the primordial man, Puruṣa. We need not dwell on the detail of his translation, which has not generally been followed since his time and is debatable,[8] but, regardless of its aptness to the originally intended meaning of the verse, the conclusions he drew can be applied to the subsequent course of Hindu-Buddhist mythopoeia with some cogency. His point is that, whereas at the creation of the world the inferior three orders of humanity (the *kṣatriya*, *vaiśya*, and *śūdra*) were brought into being anew, the Brāhmin, which was the head of Puruṣa, pre-existed eternally and was always available to initiate successive re-creations of the world.

Here, Mus detected an enduring theme inspiring myth and iconography in many subsequent forms. He exploited sources from the Brāhmaṇas to early Mahāyāna Buddhism in order to demonstrate the probable continuity of a particular *ensemble* of ideas concerning the origin and maintenance of the universe, proceeding from a constant interaction between what has already been created and the process of present creation. Cosmic renewal requires that something should exist even beyond the limits of what can be conceived of or named; there must be a transcendental source. The hymn to the creation of the world from Puruṣa begins cryptically with the assertion that Puruṣa covered the earth on all sides and extended beyond it by ten 'fingers' (*aṅgula*, that is, a finger's width, or a measure equal to ten barley-corns): '*sa bhūmiṃ viśvato vṛtvā / atyatiṣṭhad daśāṅgulam*' (*Rig Veda* 10.90.1). Mus explored later sources supporting the conclusion that this claim identified Puruṣa, and especially his mouth, as the conduit, manifest in the world, for the action of the transcendent and ineffable source of the universe.

This conception supplied the corpus of Indian religious myth with a powerful *motif* that, over the course of history, worked its way into the popular consciousness as a knot of ideas about the supreme source of divine power and consciousness. Human aspiration after divine illumination seeks direct apprehension of the holy (*darśan*), which is embodied pre-eminently in the divine word, in speech, in the mouth of the creator. So the head of Puruṣa, or of Brāhmā, is in a special category quite distinct from the rest of the world, for the rest of the world is creation in the passive sense, while creation, as an active force, is the eternal source, coming from the mouth or the head.

8 On this see Mabbett (2006, 120-121).

The body of Indian religions maintained this idea and elaborated it in various ways. Mus detected even in the iconography of the Buddha a direct continuity of the same images, for the *uṣnīṣa*, the protuberance on the Buddha's head, is not just a coil of hair (as it is usually represented in statuary) but an opening to the realm of the sacred – just as, in Vedic myth, the sun is a sort of trapdoor opening out upon the upper three-quarters of the universe. (We may naturally think too of Kuṇḍalinī reaching the *sahasrārā*, or Chinnamastā's head lifting off, or as it were opening out, to allow the union of celestial and terrestrial realms.)

In accordance with this analysis, it is possible to infer the cosmological principle that the universe is constructed upon a vertical scale, and that all these images – the head of Puruṣa from the chin up, the *uṣnīṣa* of the Buddha, and the summit of a stupa or temple, among other appropriations – represent the ineffable infinite above the whole of creation. As Mus wrote: 'Faut-il se résumer? Je dirai que Puruṣa finit là où le Bouddha commence' (Mus 1968, 560). Puruṣa comes to an end where the Buddha begins.

This is the point where Mus' inferences may begin to look like fanciful over-interpretation to today's reader, for we know that he sought to subordinate everything to the logic of a religious civilisation's orthogenetic evolution, and that is far from the sorts of assumptions made by social sciences nowadays. But this does not mean that Mus is necessarily wrong. The continuities of folk cosmology supplied much of what scholars like him sought in the enduring essence they attributed to Indian, or Hindu, civilisation. The whole series of terms which can be seen as symbols for painful death and glorious resurrection in a cataclysmic cosmic sacrifice – from the dismemberment of Puruṣa to the severing of Chinnamastā's neck – can also be seen as successive re-appropriations of traditional ideas from popular belief, serving at each point to express to the worshipper or adept the same message of spiritual renewal.

Puruṣa always lurks in the background as the symbol *par excellence* of the devotee's own self, the sacrifice, and the creation or renewal of the cosmos. By sacrifice one becomes one with the supreme *ātman* or Being itself. Such a sacrifice is no tame ritual to be casually undertaken; it is a personal holocaust confronting the devotee with all his own demons. The goddess, by cutting off her own head, shows (figuratively) how it is done. The streams of blood from her severed neck embody the passage from the demonic to the pure and life-giving, nurturing and sustaining those who take refuge in her.

Bibliography

Bapat, Jayant Bhalchandra. 2008. 'The Lajjāgaurī: mother, wife or *yoginī*'. In *The Iconic Female. Goddesses of India, Nepal and Tibet*, edited by Jayant Bapat and Ian Mabbett, 79-111. Clayton: Monash Asia Institute.

Benard, Elisabeth. 1994. *Chinnamastā: The Aweful Buddhist-Hindu Tantric Goddess*. Delhi: Motilal Banarsidass.

Bhattacharyya, Benoytosh (ed.) 1925-1928. *Sādhanamālā* (Gaekwad's Oriental Series). 2 vols. Baroda: Oriental Institute.

Biardeau, Madeleine. 1989. *Hinduism: the Anthropology of a Civilization*. Delhi: Oxford University Press.

Bühnemann, G. 2000. *The Iconography of Hindu Tantric Deities*, vol. 1. *The Pantheon of the Mantramahodadhi*. Groningen: Forsten.

Burkert, Walter. 1983. *Homo Necans: the Anthropology of Ancient Greek Sacrificial Ritual and Myth*, translated by Peter Bing. Berkeley: University of California Press.

Courtright, Paul. 1985. *Gaṇeśa: Lord of Obstacles, Lord of Beginnings*. Oxford: Oxford University Press.

Desai, Rashmi. 2008. 'When Reṇukā was not a goddess'. In *The Iconic Female. Goddesses of India, Nepal and Tibet*, edited by Jayant Bapat and Ian Mabbett, 65-78. Clayton: Monash Asia Institute.

Doniger, Wendy. 1980. *Women, Androgynes and other Mythical Beasts*. Chicago: Chicago University Press.

Girard, René. 1972. *La Violence et le Sacré*. Paris: Grasset. (English translation by Patrick Gregory: *Violence and the Sacred*. Baltimore: Johns Hopkins University Press, 1977.)

Heesterman, J.C. 1967. 'The case of the severed head'. *Wiener Zeitschrift für die Kunde Süd- und Ostasiens* 11: 22-43.

Heesterman, J.C. 1993. *The Broken World of Sacrifice: an Essay in Ancient Indian Ritual*. Chicago: Chicago University Press.

Johns, A.H. 1961. 'Muslim mystics and historical writing'. In *Historians of Southeast Asia*, edited by D.G.E. Hall, 37-49. London: Oxford University Press.

Kinsley, David. 1986. *Hindu Goddesses: Visions of the Divine in the Hindu Religious Tradition*. Berkeley: University of California Press.

Kinsley, David. 1997. *Tantric Visions of the Divine Feminine: the Ten Mahāvidyās*. Berkeley: University of California Press.

Mabbett, I.W. 2006. 'L'indologie de Mus: sociologie ou cosmologie?' In *Paul Mus (1902-1969): L'espace d'un regard*, edited by D. Chandler and C. Goscha, 117-128. Paris: Les Indes Savantes.

Mahidhara. 1992. *Mantra Mahodadhih*, edited and translated by Ram Kumar Rai. Varanasi: Prachya Prakashan.

Mus, Paul. 1935. *Barabadur: Esquisse d'une histoire du Bouddhisme fondée sur la critique archaéologique des textes*. Hanoi: Imprimerie d'Extrême-Orient.

Mus, Paul. 1962. 'Du nouveau sur Ṛgveda 10.90: sociologie d'une grammaire'. In *Indological Studies in Honour of W. Norman Brown*, edited by Ernest Bender, 165-185. New Haven, Ct: American Oriental Society.

Mus, Paul. 1968. 'Où finit Puruṣa?' In *Mélanges d'Indianisme à la mémoire de Louis Renou*, 539-563. Paris: Boccard.

Pal, P. 1981. *Hindu Religion and Iconology*. Los Angeles: Vichitra.

Somadeva (attrib.) 1915. *Kathāsaritsāgara*, 3rd ed., edited by W.L.S. Pansikar. Bombay: Tukāram Jāvaji.

Tāranātha. 1989. *Life of Kṛṣṇācārya/Kāṇha*, translated by D. Templeman. Dharamsala: Library of Tibetan Works and Archives.

Trungpa, Rinpoche Chognam. 1982. 'The Vajrayoginī shrine and practice'. In *The Silk Route and the Diamond Path,* edited by D.E. Klimburg-Salter, 226-240. Los Angeles: UCLA Art Council.

van Kooij, Karel. 1999. 'Iconography of the battlefield: the case of Chinnamastā'. In *Violence Denied: Non-Violence and the Rationalization of Violence in South Asian Cultural History,* edited by J.E.M. Houben and K.R. van Kooij, 249-274. Leiden: Brill.

Vidal, D., Gilles Tarabout and Eric Meyer. 1994. *Violences et non-violences en Inde.* Paris: Ecole des hautes etudes en sciences sociales.

White, David Gordon. 2003. *Kiss of the Yogini: 'Tantric Sex' in its South Asian Contexts.* Chicago: University of Chicago Press.

Chapter 8

The Appropriation of Durgā

Pratish Bandopadhayay

Everything in Kolkata (Calcutta), the capital of West Bengal in India, stops for a week to celebrate the annual religious and social festival of *Durgā Pūjā*. It is a calendrical ritual observed during the *śuklapakṣa* ('waxing fortnight') of the lunar month of *āśvina* (September-October) known as *navarātrī* ('nine nights'). From the sixth day to the tenth day of *navarātrī, Durgā* is worshipped in temporary shrines called *pandal*s[1] as *Daśabhujā* ('one with ten arms') *Mahiṣāsuramardinī,* the destroyer of demon Mahiṣāsura. Along with her, *Sarasvatī, Lakṣmī, Kārtikeya* and *Gaṇeśa* are worshipped as her four children. *Durgā Pūjā* today has multidimensional aspects, including social, religious, cultural and family functions. Although a purely Hindu religious ritual, *Durgā Pūjā* acts as a catalyst for many cultural events like musical functions, drama, painting exhibitions and literary meetings. The decorations of the *pandal*s with their show of light and dazzle transform the dull and mundane background of an ordinary narrow street into a world of fantasy, splendour and relief. *Durgā Pūjā* and its *pandal*s have been used as a social platform to introduce new concepts and norms. Many different sections of the community have used *Durgā Pūjā* to promote their own agenda, and the chief purpose of the present chapter is to bring out the sheer variety of purposes, pursued by many groups, to which the ritual has historically been put. This will serve to emphasise the intricacy of the dynamics propelling the history of a religious ritual.

Durgā worship in Bengal

It is believed that the present form of *Durgā Pūjā* in Bengal was initiated in 1583 by Ramesh Shastri, the family priest of the Bengali *zamindar* Raja Kangsanarayan (Rodrigues 2003, 16). Prajnanananda points to the Bengali myth that recalls how *Durgā Pūjā* was set up by the Tantric

1 Temporary marquees made of bamboo and cloth constructed specially for the *puja*.

Ramesh Shastri, the *kulapurohit* (family priest) of Raja Kangsanarayan Roy of Tahirpur, as the means of the latter's redemption (Prajnanananda 2002, 348). This popular Bengali story narrates the important role Raja Kangsanarayan played in the process of removing Sulaiman Khan Karrani and, later, his son Daud's sultanate of Bengal and bringing Bengal under Akbar's Mughal Empire. The invasion, subsequent collapse of the Sultanate and the eventual establishment of the Mughal Empire in Bengal, Bihar and Orissa resulted in many deaths and miseries. Kangsanarayan wanted to partake in some form of religious ceremony to redeem himself from the sin associated with his active participation in the process. He organised a meeting of eminent pandits for advice on a suitable religious ceremony. During this meeting Ramesh Shastri proposed that Kangsanarayan perform *Durgā Pūjā* and agreed to compose the *Durgā Pūjā paddhati* ('instructions on how to perform it'). Kangsanarayan is said to have performed the *Durgā Pūjā,* as instructed by Ramesh Shastri, in a very lavish way, and spent eight and a half *lakh* (850,000 rupees). From this very first public *Durgā Pūjā* by Kangsanarayan, the ceremony became a political object when his neighbour Jagatnarayan, a zamindar from a neighbouring town of Bhaduriya, is said to have spent even more, nine *lakh* (900,000 rupees), to worship *Durgā* as *Basanti Pūjā* (Durgā worship in Spring).

The *Durgā Pūjā* of the aristocrats and the *Zamindar*s

The annual *Durgā Pūjā,* organised by the rich Bengali aristocrats in their houses as a family event, used to be the centre of attraction for the local neighbourhood. The event in many ways influenced the social norm of the community. These *pūjās* and associated festivities were used by the aristocrats to establish their leadership and social power in the community by providing a major impetus for many social and cultural activities locally. Some of these traditions and communal activities still continue in traditional family *Durgā Pūjās*. Roy describes the ongoing *Durgā Pūjā,* and its community support in the village of Matiyari in the district of Nadia, which was started in 1663 CE by the Biswas family (M. Roy 1985, 35). Similarly, Kar's description of the *Sandhipūjā*[2] at the *zamindar*'s

2 A particular part of the *Durgā Puja,* at the point of confluence of the eighth and ninth day of the lunar cycle, known as *Sandhipuja,* is regarded as the highlight of the festivity. During these rituals 108 lamps, 108 lotus flowers and animal sacrifices are often offered.

house at the end of the eighteenth century demonstrates the influence of these aristocrats on the local population:

> In those days, all the families performing *Durgā Pūjā*s would prepare all the requirements for the *Sandhipūjā* and wait for the sound of the cannon fire from the *zamindar*'s house. The firing of the cannon signalled that the *Sandhipūjā* at Sobhabazar Rajbari, the residence of zamindar of Sutanati, had started. This would immediately start the *Sandhipūjā* rituals of sacrifices and *āratis* at all other *Durgā Pūjās* (Kar 1999, 20; translated by the present author).

Durgā Pūjā post Palashi

The structure and the scale of *Durgā Pūjā* in Bengal changed dramatically from 1757 when Nabakrishna Deb, a Bengali aristocrat, organised a large *Durgā Pūjā* to celebrate the British win at Palashi (Plassey). The *pūjā* was organised in place of a thanksgiving church ceremony to celebrate Robert Clive's victory in the battle because the only church in Kolkata at that time was destroyed by Siraj-ud-Daulah. From this time onwards, *Durgā Pūjā* became a focus for the rich Bengalis to flaunt their status rather than an annual family religious festival.

Kar gives a vivid description of the involvement of Robert Clive in the *Durgā Pūjā* performed by Munshi Nabakrishna Deb:

> Clive, although a Christian and against idol worship, purely for his own benefit, became a Hindu-lover and sent one hundred rupees and many baskets of fruits to the Nabakrishna's *Durgā Pūjā*. For the benefit of the administration and trade, English in this country created a group of favour seeking servant groups centring on the *Durgā Pūjā*. For Nabakrishna, *Durgā* was only an excuse; pleasing Clive was his main intention. Many used to refer to Nabakrishna's *Durgā Pūjā* as the 'Company *pūjā*'. Nabakrishna was the first Bengali from Kolkata who invited a real *Sāheb* to his own home (Kar 1999, 44–45; translated by the present author).

The rich *zamindar*s, *jagirdar*s and r*aja*s of Bengal converted *Durgā Pūjā* ceremonies into special functions where the English could be invited to participate. These aristocrats made these functions as lavish as possible by including music, dance, drinks and food to make them remarkable. Because of the competitions between different *zamindars* in terms of novelty, lavishness and grandeur, *Durgā Pūjā* soon became an important milestone in the social calendars of the British officers and the Bengali aristocrats. Holwell in 1766 described *Durgā Pūjā* as 'the grand general feast of the Gentoos' where Europeans were treated by the host with food, flowers and entertainments (Holwell, cited by B. Ghosh 1999, 310). From this point onwards *Durgā Pūjā* changed from a family event to a communal event, which, in turn, transformed this religious festival into a social ceremony.

The *Durgā Pūjā* was often used by the British as a tool for public relations. For example, John Chipps, the first Commercial Agent of the East India Company, regularly organised *Durgā Pūjā* at his official residence in the village of Surul near Shantiniketan in Bengal until his death in 1828. Although the *Durgā Pūjā* at Chipps' residence was a low-key affair, everyone in the village used to get new clothes and a full meal on the day of *Mahāṣṭamīpūjā* (Sripantha 2005, 350).

Figure 8.1: Line drawing of Durgā Pūjā in Kolkata at Sobhabazar Rajbari.

Baroyāri and *Sārvajanīna Durgā Pūjā* and the Independence movement

In 1790 twelve friends in the Bengali town of Guptipara in the district of Hoogly started a community *Durgā Pūjā* (A. Ghosh 2000). Their *pūjā* was financed by donations collected from the community and all the community members were invited to participate (R. Roy 2011, 168). This type of community *pūjā* became known as *baroyāri pūjā*.[3] In 1918 the *baroyāri pūjā* started in Bagbazar, Kolkata and since then this has been the most dominant form of *pūjā* in Bengal. Through *baroyāri pūjā, Durgā Pūjā* moved from the restricted circle of the elite *zamindar* families into the wider sphere of the common man. The *Durgā Pūjā* in Bengal was thus transformed from a religious family affair to a festival of religious extravaganza by the Bengali elites to a major annual community social and cultural festival.

The Indian freedom movement influenced the format of the community *Durgā Pūjā* in Kolkata and the involvement of the general public in the festivities. In 1926 Atindranath Bose initiated the first *sārvajanīna* ('everyone's') *Durgā Pūjā* where anybody, irrespective of their caste, creed or religion, could participate in the festivities (Ray 2006, 241). This change was deliberately introduced in *Durgā Pūjā* as a counter to hostility between Hindus and Muslims, seeking to promote among them a feeling of unity against the British. In 1882, novelist Bankimchandra Chattopadhyay (Chatterji), in his famous *Ānandamaṭh,* described three images of Mother India, clearly anthropomorphised as a goddess figure, to the disciples (*santān*) as the symbol of the nation:

> Gigantic, imposing, resplendent ... this is our Mother India as she was before the British conquest ... This is what our Mother India is today ... she is in the gloom of famine, disease, death, humiliation and destruction ... Bright, beautiful, full of glory and dignity – this is our Mother as she is destined to be (Chatterji 2006, 61-62).

Ānandamaṭh was very influential in the Bengali community as it combined nationalism and religious vigour. In the last quarter of the nineteenth century, *Durgā* in Bengal became a synonym for Mother India, and the Independence movement became the movement to free Mother India.

3 *Baro* is the number twelve, and *yār* means 'friends'.

Bagchi (1990) argues that the symbol of motherhood as a representation of nationalism was required to encompass the political, social and religious streams of colonial Indian society.

Members of the Independence movement used *Durgā Pūjā* as a front for their meetings and for training freedom fighters in the use of weapons. The *birashthami* ritual[4] became one of the central religious rituals of various contests involving dagger work, martial arts, wrestling and boxing. The training of freedom fighters in the use of various arms was conducted under the guise of religious rites under the very eyes of the British. In 1906, the Anushilan Samiti, an organisation committed to militant nationalism, organised a unique *pūjā* at their office in north Kolkata where, in place of the clay images, a cache of arms – spears, swords, daggers, falchions and sticks – were used as the objects of worship. Many eminent names on the British 'wanted' list, such as Sri Aurobindo, Bagha Jatin and Jatindramohan Thakur, attended the *pūjā* (Ganguly, n.d.).

In 1926 Atindranath Basu, the founder of the Simla Byām Samiti *sārvajanīna pūjā,* dedicated the organisation to the cause of freedom movements. In 1939 Netaji Subhas Chandra Bose, then president of the Indian National Congress, inaugurated the *Durgā Pūjā* of the Simla Byām Samiti and was associated with a number of other *pūjā*s, including the Kumortuli *sārvajanīna pūjā* and the Bagbazar *sārvajanīna pūjā* (being secretary of both in 1938 and 1939). The Bagbazar *sārvajanīna pūjā* was famous for its elaborate *birashtami* celebrations. During the non-cooperation movement against the British, arrests became widespread and the British banned the Simla Byām Samiti *pūjā* between 1932 and 1935.

Between the 1930s and 1947 the patriotic nature of the *Durgā Pūjā pandal*s became more and more pointed and *Durgā* herself took on a new persona, as the *avatāra* of Bhāratamātā (Mother India). The famous battle cry of *vande mātaram,* originally composed by Bankimchandra Chattopadhyay in the late nineteenth century, was successfully utilised to unite people of all races and creeds in one fundamental goal of freeing Mother India.

The Bengali writer, Sunil Ganguly, recalls a *Durgā Pūjā* in his childhood:

4 A ritual performed during the *Astami Pūjā*, initiated in 1902 by Saraladebi Caudhurani to honour heroes (McDermott 2011, 58).

> [I]n Faridpur ... at *Durgā's* feet lay a sahib in military gear – khāki uniform, spiked boots, rifle slung over the shoulder. The Devi, flashing fury from her three eyes, had clutched a tuft of auburn hair. Her mount, the rampant lion, was tearing at his abdomen. Close by, in place of Kartik and Ganesh, stood Subhas Chandra Bose, in dhoti-Punjabi and khadar cap and an unsheathed sword in his hand.
>
> The word spread, and the atchala (eight-pillared hall without walls) was soon brimming with villagers from afar. In place of the customary 'Durga ma ki jai' (Victory to Goddess Durga), a spontaneous chorus arose in Subhas Bose's name (Ganguly, n.d.).

But this *pūjā*, remembers Ganguly, was short-lived. Three days later, the *pūjā* was stopped by the authorities and the image was seized. Village residents had to make do with worshipping *Durgā* using just the symbolic water pot (*ghaṭ*).

The use of *Durgā Pūjā* as a symbol of Indian heritage and identity was used effectively by the Indian freedom movement as a powerful tool in dealing with the British. In 1915 at the initiative of some freedom fighters, *Durgā Pūjā* was performed at the Rajshahi jail. As Bhupendranath Dutta recalled:

> The chief secretary to the Bengal government, Sir Hugh Stephenson, granted permission to host the *puja* in association with the jail staffers and sanctioned an amount. A pandal was set up right outside the prison gate. Many dignitaries of the city, including the jail superintendent, paid a visit to the *puja*. By arrangement with the jailer, the state prisoners were allowed to go out and receive guests. On *Ashtami* the patriots treated about 1,200 fellow inmates to *luchi* [a form of deep-fried bread] and sweets. Jogeshchandra Chattopadhyay recalls how at the same jail, in 1918, a white goat was sacrificed to the *Devi*. The significance of the sacrifice lay in the colour of the goat skin, as the British were largely referred to as 'Whites' (Ganguly, n.d.).

In the same source it is reported that Netaji Subhash Chandra Bose, after a hunger strike at the Mandalay jail,

> managed to wrest permission from the government to hold *Durga Pūja* in Burma ... At Jilji Jail women patriots in the freedom movement like Santi Das, Banalata Dasgupta, Indusudha Ghosh and Bina Das also invoked *the Mother.* Rabindranath Tagore's drama, Tapati, was staged to celebrate the occasion (Ganguly, n.d.).

Durgā Pūjā since Independence

After Indian Independence in August 1947 *Durgā Pūjā pandal*s were decorated with the tricolour and the *Devī* was worshipped as Bhāratmātā. The freedom fighters took active roles in the festivities, and patriotic songs were played. The rituals have only become more popular in the years since Independence. Bengalis are deeply attached to their *Durgā Pūjās*, even though their religious significance and importance are often missed by the general public.

In 1945, there was a major change in Kolkata in the way *Durgā* idols and the *pandal*s were used for the *Durgā Pūjā.* Both the designs of the idols and the *pandal*s became objects of art. Sculptors like Ramesh Chandra Pal, as well as creating new idol designs, also dictated to the organising bodies how the idols should be used for *Durgā Pūjā.* The conditions he created for the use of idols included specifications for the *pandal*s and their lighting, the need to involve properly trained priests for the religious rituals, and for the type of music to be played through the public address systems in the *pandal*s. The sculptor even specified the type of dress the organising committee should wear while welcoming visitors to the *pandal* (Agnihotri 2001, 88).

Since the 1980s, Kolkata has witnessed a deliberate effort to revive the traditional Bengali designs for the idols, *pandal*s and decorations. With this shift in the emphasis on the artistic sides of *Durgā Pūjā*, corporate giants like Asian Paints and others initiated various sponsorship programmes. The annual *Durgā Pūjā* contest 'Sarada Sammelan', sponsored by Asian Paints, offers awards in categories, such as for the best *pandal*s, the best decorations, and the best lighting. Today, *Durgā Pūjā* in Bengal has become an occasion for spectacular extravaganza, glamour and pomp, with elaborate stylised interiors, carefully executed by trained artists and costing a fortune (iBangla 2012).

In Kolkata local communities spend very large sums of money to decorate their *Durgā Pūjā pandal*s in unique ways to impress the judges with their novelty and splendour in the hope of winning the award for best *pandal* each year. Some of these *pandal*s look so realistic that, until you get very close, it is hard to imagine that only a week earlier a street corner, which now looks as though it must be a world-famous landmark, looked drab and dilapidated.[5] Tripura's royal palace, Birla Planetarium in Kolkata, Kamakhya Temple in Guwahati, Sun Temple of Konarak, the snow-capped hills of Kashmir, the Bombay High court, a Buddhist temple in China and Kashmir's Dal Lake have all been depicted in various *pūjā pandal*s. *Durgā Pūjā* in Kolkata has become more innovative in its presentations and themes.

*Durgā Pūjā pandal*s and the idols of today also have strong political or social messages. *Durgā* might occasionally resemble a Bollywood heroine and the demon *Mahiṣāsura* some well-known reprobate. In 2001 the police in Calcutta were ordered to destroy the idol in a case where *Mahiṣāsura* had a remarkable likeness to Osama bin Laden (McDermott 2011, 145). Climate change and global warming, India's moon mission Chandrayaan-1 and the tragedy of the terror attack in Mumbai on 26 November 2008 have all been portrayed in *pandal*s through decorations and lighting. Today artists responsible for the Durgā Pūjā *pandal*s offer complete packages to create a unique ambience, arising from the design of the interiors, the entries and exits, the lighting, the music and everything else.

Political use of Durgā Pūjā in Bengal

Durgā Pūjā has become a powerful political tool in Bengal. There was a political upheaval in Bengal during 2010 and 2011 when the Communist Party of India (Marxist) (CPI(M)), which had been in power for over twenty years, was thrown out by the Trinamul Congress Party (TMC). The Santosh Mitro Square *Durgā Pūjā* in north Kolkata, renowned for its unique themes and as the biggest crowd-puller in the state, celebrated its seventy-fifth year in 2011 and its *pandal* had a very strong political message. It was modelled on Writers Building, the seat of power of the CPI(M) government in Bengal, with the theme *'Dori dhore maro taan/ raja hobe khaan khaan'* ('Pull the rope and the king will fall') leaving little to the imagination as to its intended message ahead of coming elections. It is worth noting that one of the main organisers of this community *pūjā* was a prominent Congress leader of the city (S. Roy, 2010a).

5 For an overview, see S. Ghosh (2000)

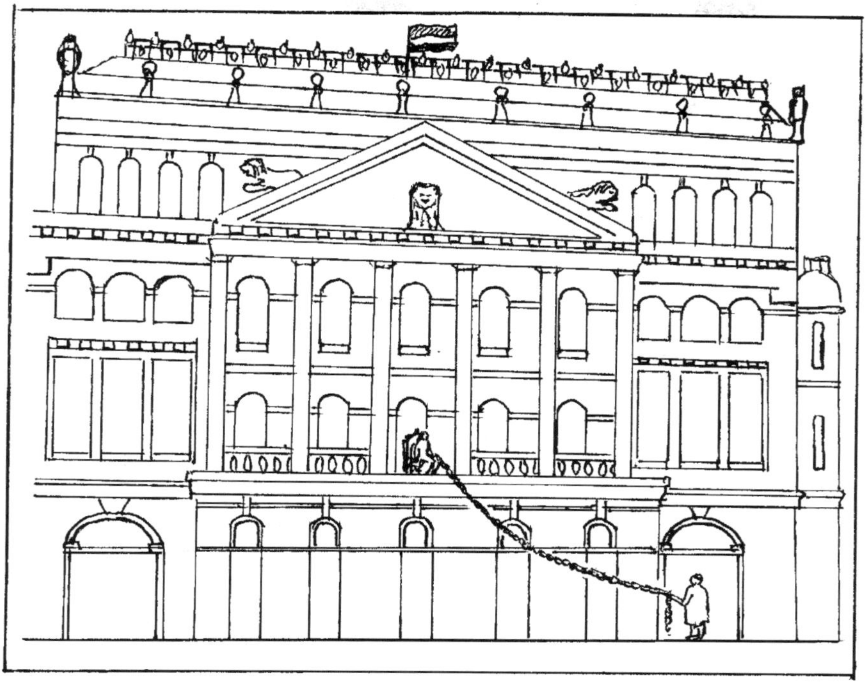

Figure 8.2: Line drawing of Durgā pūjā *pandal* at Santosh Mitro Square in north Kolkata.

Because of the changes to the power base in the municipality elections in 2010, the organisation of the annual *Durgā Pūjā* festivals at different communities was also thrown in chaos. For example the TMC-run municipality in Bansberia Hooghly used environmental pollution as the reason to stop the traditional *Durgā Pūjā* organised by the Nabamilan Mahila Samiti, which for years was supported by the CPI(M) leaders (Datta 2010). With the CPI(M) losing the municipal elections at Tarakeshwar in May 2010, the *pūjā* organising committee, previously run by CPI(M) leaders and councillors, was taken over by TMC members who brought in sweeping changes to many of the *Durgā Pūjā*s in that area. Some local *Durgā Pūjā*s established for many years were stopped; others had their venues changed while some were subjected to new rules and regulations. The TMC also proposed a new format for celebrations to include a nationalistic flavour in the *Durgā Pūjā*s with Tagore's 150th birth anniversary as the theme. Deshbandhu Club near Tarakeshwar station held its *pūjā* for the first time with TMC patronage. The *pandal* was built in the shape of a dragon, decorated with a giant cut-out of TMC leader Mamata Banerjee (Banerjee 2010).

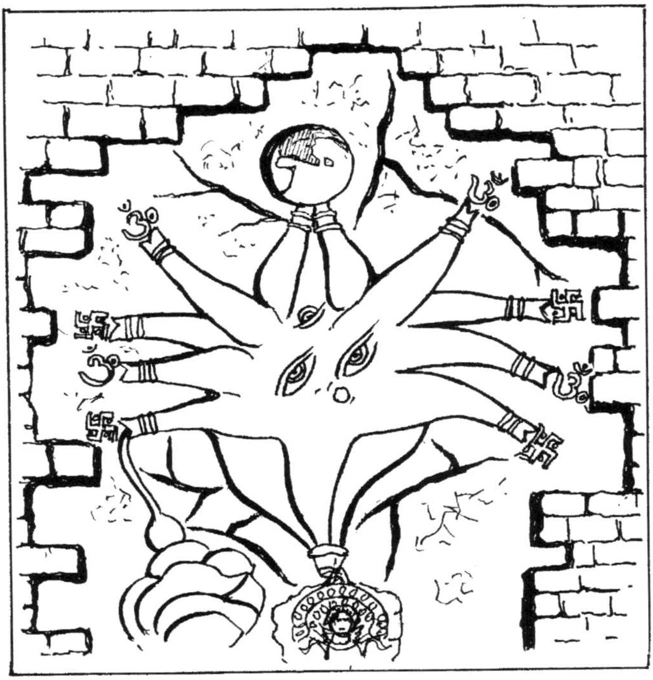

Figure 8.3: Line drawing of the sculpture designed by Mamata Banerjee for Bakulbagan *Durgā Pūjā* 2010.

In 2010 the TMC turned the *Durgā Pūjā* into its biggest public relations exercise by being an active participant in organising *Durgā Pūjās* at various localities. The TMC's publication *Jago Bangla* was printed in larger numbers than usual during the 2009 *Durgā Pūjā*, carrying a picture of Goddess *Durgā* on the cover sketched by the TMC leader Mamata Banerjee (Nagchaudhary 2009).

Mamata Banerjee exploited the possibilities of the *Durgā Pūjā* to the utmost. On 11 October 2010, she inaugurated the eighty-third Bakulbagan *sārvajanīna Durgā Utsav* community *pūjā* with M.K. Narayanan, the Governor, as the chief guest (S. Roy 2010a). Mamata Banerjee had chosen this community *pūjā*, close to her Kalighat home in south Kolkata, to showcase her talent by designing the idols and decor of their *Durgā Pūjā pandal*. The oval-shaped *pandal* was constructed out of bamboo and tarpaulin according to her sketches and was decorated with paintings she had done. The *pūjā* theme was based on the concept of Śiva as transcending time (*mahākāl*). The idol used for the *Durgā Pūjā* at Bakulbagan was a break from the tradition. The *Durgā* idol was depicted as the Dharitri

Figure 8.4: Line drawing of Mamata Banerjee and actress Debashree Roy at a *pūjā pandal* in Kolkata.

Maa ('mother earth'). The idol as conceived by Mamata Banerjee was an abstract depiction of ten hands holding the earth. Unlike the traditional image of *Durgā* with different weapons in her ten hands, the ten hands in this abstract depiction held no weapons; instead, '*Om*' and the swastika alternated, to convey the message of peace (D. Sengupta 2010).

In reply to the traditional *Durgā Pūjā* Bijoya Sammilani organised by the outgoing CPI(M) government of Buddhadeb Bhattacharjee, Mamata Banerjee used *Durgā Pūjā* in an effort to counter her anti-industry image by inviting dignitaries to a great post-*pūjā* get-together, which included more than 150 prominent names in industry, industrial houses and chambers, as well as foreign diplomats (*Mamata meets industry* 2010).

Although CPI(M) officially does not believe in religious festivities, the tradition of selling books during *pūjā* by CPI(M) is over half a century old. Hundreds of bookstalls have been set up in or close to the *pūjā* pandals to disseminate traditional Marxist literature.

Since its election success in Bengal in 2010, TMC has started to emulate the concept of bookstalls during *Durgā Pūjā*. In 2010 TMC set up more than 200 *Jago Bangla* stalls at different *Durgā Pūjā pandal*s in Kolkata, which sold about twenty titles written by their leader, Mamata Banerjee, as well as various articles by important literary personalities such as Mahasweta Devi, Debabrata Bandopadhyay and others on the land acquisition debate in West Bengal. There have been reports of pitched battles between TMC and CPI(M) supporters over the setting up of bookstalls near *Durgā Pūjā* locations (Singh 2010).

Durgā Pūjā and its underlying messages

Durgā Pūjā has been used to convey various underlying social or political messages. For example, the *Durgā Pūjā* organised by the Santhals in the village of Sulunga in the Birbum District of West Bengal follows their tradition of commemorating the actions of their tribal leaders Brojo Murmu and Durgā Murmu, who rose in revolt against the British. It is believed that over 100 years ago the two leaders decided to initiate *Durgā Pūjā* to invoke *śakti* to help them overthrow the British. The Santhals in general do not follow Hindu rituals and the *Durgā* worship in this case did not include any traditional Sanskrit mantras, but the prayers offered to the goddess were in Bengali: *'maa, fosol jeno bhalo hoy/gramey sobai jeno bhalo thake'* (Mother, let there be a good harvest, may all in the village be happy). As part of the *pūjā*, a white goat is sacrificed which they believe symbolises a *gorā sahib* (white man) (S. Roy 2010b).

*Durgā Pūjā pandal*s are decorated to highlight various social or political messages as shown by the following two examples. The first example shows the feeling of nationalism and a sense of anger at the 2008 terrorist attack in Mumbai by the inclusion of Bhāratmātā in front of the main *Durgā* idol. The second example shows the *Durgā* idol in the Mohammad Ali Park *pandal*, which expresses community outrage against the government. It purports to show that, because the government has failed to protect the citizens from lawlessness such as robbery, murders and corruption, they are praying to *Durgā* to fight these anti-social elements in the form of the demon *Mahiṣāsura*.

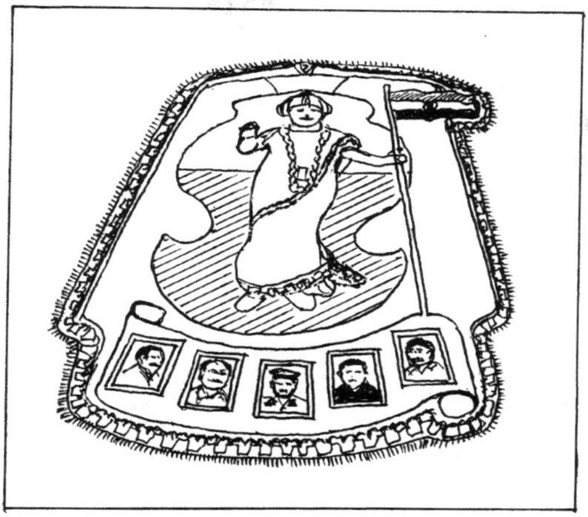

Figure 8.5: Floor flower decoration at a Durgā Pūjā *pandal* at Karhad, Maharashtra on the theme of the Mumbai terrorist attack of 26 November 2008.

Figure 8.6: Durgā Pūjā celebrations in Kolkata. In this modern representation, instead of the conventional *Mahiṣāsura,* the demon Durgā is fighting is the robbery, murder and corruption of a lawless society.

In 2007, Behala Notun Dal celebrated *Durgā Pūjā* as Banadebi ('forest goddess') and the *pandal* included 10,000 square feet of lush greenery containing trees such as ashokas, peepals and bels. This novel concept was designed to raise awareness of forest conservation (*Puja organisers* 2010).

In 2010, in the Maoist-affected Jharagram area of West Bengal, the *Durgā* idol was unique in being represented as an *Adibashi* (aboriginal) *avatara* carrying the flags of all the political parties striving for peace, together with the message '*Sarbodol uddyoge ashuk shanti, barta onno Durgār*' (This other *Durgā* promotes peace initiatives from all the parties).

Figure 8.7: Line drawing of Narendra Modi performing *shastra pūjā* in 2009.

The worship of *Durgā* can also have military overtones arising from the presence of various weapons and associated stories from the *Mārkaṇḍeya Purāṇa* and her incarnation as *Mahiṣāsuramardinī*. Weapon worship as part of *Durgā Pūjā* is still practised in many parts of India today. For example, recently at the headquarters of the Jharkhand Armed Police (JAP) in Ranchi, *Durgā Pūjā* was performed by worshipping weapons such as the AK47 rifle and other firearms, instead of the idol of Goddess *Durgā*. On the ninth day of the *navarātrī* JAP security personnel sacrificed goats to appease goddess *Durgā* and prayed for their safety and power to fight their enemies (Where arms are worshipped 2010).

In 2009 Narendra Modi, then Chief Minister of Gujarat, performed a *shastra* (weapon) *pūjā* at his official residence at Gandhinagar. As part of the ritual, various modern weapons, including AK47 rifles and machine guns, as well as primitive arms such as swords, axes and clubs, were worshipped during *navarātrī* (Narendra Modi prays 2009).

Figure 8.8: Line drawing of the poster depicting Congress President Sonia Gandhi as goddess *Durgā*.

Use and misuse of '*Durgā*' as a descriptive

Durgā as a descriptive is often used to describe a lady who is unique and brave. For example, Atal Behari Vajpayee, the leader of the Jan Sangh Party, after the Indian victory in the 1971 war with Pakistan, compared Prime Minister Indira Gandhi to goddess *Durgā* (*Indira Gandhi was a woman with guts* 2011). In 2006 the Congress Party of India sought to woo Trinamul Congress's firebrand leader Mamata Banerjee by hailing her as the 'political *Durgā* of West Bengal' (T. Sengupta 2009). The All-India Congress Committee General Secretary, Margaret Alva, stated that it was especially sad that the 'political *Durgā*' had been humiliated at the time of *Durgā Pūjā* (Bengal's 'political Durga' 2006). In 2010, a court in Muzaffarpur in Bihar summoned Congress President Sonia Gandhi to appear before it in connection with a complaint alleging that her depiction as Goddess *Durgā* in a photograph published in a newspaper and on posters was an 'insult to Hindu religion' (Bihar 2010).

Conclusion

It is in such cases that the concept of 'appropriation' demands especially to be applied; a particular group or interest will claim that it has privileged access to a particular status, image or ritual, and resents the claim upon it of another party. Each side regards the other as illegitimately seeking to monopolise, or to steal, the valued object. Yet in the present case it must be obvious that this political contest is simply the most recent twist in a long record of religious competition and aspiration. The rituals celebrating Durgā have been existence for many centuries, but the parties in contest are always changing. This multifaceted character of religious communities in their interactions with their social and political environment deserves to be emphasised in a volume of studies directed to the ways in which Indian goddess cults have been adapted, interpreted, even manipulated in the service of disparate interest groups, intentionally or otherwise. A broad-brush picture of the cult of Durgā can accommodate only a few actors, or interest groups, such as the Brāhmin world view and Bengali folk religion; either of these might be described as 'appropriating' the myths and rituals of the other in certain senses. However, the more closely we analyse the dynamics of the history of the celebration of Durgā in Bengal, the easier it is to see that there have been many interests, many motivations and many walks of life involved in the successive adaptations of the cult. So the question of who took what from whom can be answered in many ways, and we need to realise that the story of the *Durgā Pūjā* cannot be adequately encompassed by a single narrative of appropriation, or anything else – it is a constantly changing kaleidoscope.

Bibliography

Agnihotri, A. 2001. *Kolkātār Pratimāshilpirā.* Kolkata: Ananda Publishers.

Bagchi, J. 1990. 'Representing nationalism: ideology of motherhood in colonial Bengal'. *Economic and Political Weekly* 25: WS65-WS71.

Banerjee, Falguni. 2010. 'Winds of change blow over Hooghly Pujas'. *Times of India*, 27 September. http://timesofindia.indiatimes.com/city/kolkata/Winds-of-change-blow-over-Hooghly-pujas/articleshow/6632906.cms? (accessed 6 April 2016).

'Bengal's "political Durga" being humiliated' 2006. *Express India*, 26 September. http://www.expressindia.com/news/fullstory.php?newsid=74500 (accessed 6 April 2016).

'Bihar: Court summons Sonia Gandhi over controversial posters' 2010. NDTV, 17 July. http://www.ndtv.com/cities/bihar-court-summons-sonia-gandhi-over-controversial-posters-424064 (accessed 6 April 2016).

Chatterji, Bankim Chandra. 2006. *Ānandamaṭh*, translated from Bengali by Roy Basanta Koomar. Delhi: Orient Paperbacks.

Datta, Uttam. 2010. 'Trinamul halts festival backed by Left Leader'. *The Telegraph, 12* October. http://www.telegraphindia.com/1101012/jsp/bengal/story_13047742.jsp (accessed 6 April 2016).

Ganguly, S. n.d. 'From Courtyards to Street Corners.' Available from Onlinedarshan.com. Accessed 14 July 2016.

Ghosh, A. 2000. 'Spaces of recognition: *puja* and power in contemporary Calcutta'. *Journal of Southern African Studies* 26: 289-299.

Ghosh, B. 1999. *Kolkata Saharer Itibritta.* Kolkata: Bak Sahitya.

Ghosh, S. 2000. 'Creating new myths: Post-puja reflections'. *Economic and Political Weekly* 35, 94-96, 2012. See also 'Durga Puja: the largest outdoor art festival on earth'. http://iBangla.weekly.com/durgapuja.html (accessed 6 April 2016).

iBangla. 2012. 'Durga Puja: The largest outdoor art festival on earth'. Accessed 16 April 2014. Available from http://ibangla.weebly.com/durgapuja.html

'Indira Gandhi was a woman with guts: Thackeray' 2011. *Indian Express*, 19 October. http://archive.indianexpress.com/news/indira-gandhi-was-a-woman-with-guts-thackeray/862103/ (accessed 6 April 2016).

Kar, N. 1999. *Banglar Durgutsav.* Kolkata: Neel Publications.

'Mamata meets industry leaders in a post-puja event' 2010. *The Hindu*, 2 November. http://www.thehindu.com/news/national/other-states/mamata-meets-industry-leaders-in-postpuja-event/article864982.ece (accessed 6 April 2016).

McDermott, R.F. 2011. *Revelry, Rivalry and Longing for the Goddesses of Bengal: The Fortunes of Hindu Festivals.* New York: Columbia University Press.

Nagchoudhury, Subrata. 2009. 'Mamata puja avatar now leaves CPM praying'. *Indian Express*, 28 September. http://www.indianexpress.com/news/mamata-puja-avatar-now-leaves-cpm-praying/522361/0 (accessed 6 April 2016).

'Narendra Modi prays to guns' 2009. NDTV, 29 September. http://www.ndtv.com/article/india/narendra-modi-prays-to-guns-9265 (accessed 6 April 2016).

Prajnanananda, S. 2002. *Mahisasuramardini-Durga (Theoretical, Historic And Research Discussions).* Kolkata: Ramkrishna Bedanta Math.

'Puja organisers on buy-a-theme spree' 2010. *Times of India*, 20 September. http://timesofindia.indiatimes.com/city/kolkata/Puja-organisers-on-buy-a-theme-spree/articleshow/6588170.cms (accessed 6 April 2016).

Ray, R. 2006. *Kolkatar Bichitra.* Kolkata: Deb Sahitya Kutir.

Rodrigues, H. 2003. *Ritual Worship of the Great Goddess: the Liturgy of the Durgā Pūjā with Interpretations.* Albany, NY: State University of New York Press.

Roy, M. 1985. *Roopey Roope Durga.* Kolkata: Amar Bharati.

Roy, R. 2011. 'Guptiparar pratham baroyari durgapujo'. In *Mahishasurmardini Durga.* Kolkata: Dev Sahita Kutir.

Roy, Sabyasachi. 2010a. 'Mamata hand behind Durga Puja design', *The New Indian Express*, 15 September. www.newindianexpress.com/nation/article301833.ece?service=print (accessed 6 April 2016).

Roy, Sabyasachi. 2010b. 'Santhal Durga Puja symbolises revolt against British'. *Thaindian News*, 6 October. http://www.thaindian.com/newsportal/uncategorized/santhal-Durgā-puja-symbolises-revolt-against-british_100439815.html (accessed 6 April 2016).

Sengupta, Debaleena. 2010. 'Mamata turns puja designer'. *Business Standard* Oct 14. Accessed 19 April 2014. Available from: http://www.business-standard.com/india/news/mamata-turns-puja-designer/411411/.

Sengupta, Tamal. 2009. 'Mamata Banerjee: Durga of West Bengal'. *Economic Times, 17 May.* http://articles.economictimes.indiatimes.com/2009-05-17/news/28465463_1_mamata-banerjee-trinamool-congress-assembly-seats (accessed 6 April 2016).
Singh, Shiv Sahay. 2010. 'Politics finds a puja gateway through books'. *Indian Express,* 17 October. http://www.indianexpress.com/news/politics-finds-a-puja-gateway-through-books/698569/ (accessed 6 April 2016).
Sripantha. 2005. *Kolkata.* Kolkata: Ananda Publisher.
'Where arms are worshipped during Durga Puja' 2010. *News Jharkhand*, 16 October. http://newsjharkhand.com/Topstories.asp?Details=2100 (accessed 6 April 2016).

Chapter 9

From a *Śaktipīṭha* to *Kuladaivata*

The Appropriation of Goddess Jogāī of Ambe

Madhavi Narsalay

In India, the process of appropriation in order to elevate the social status of certain sects and clans is age-old. It applies to the adoption of religious symbols, texts, shrines and deities. In the Brāhminical caste-hierarchy, the social status of a particular community is intimately related to its religious practices. This chapter intends to chart the process of appropriation of the goddess Ambe Jogāī by the *Kokaṇastha* Brāhmin community. It contributes to the theory of appropriation by showing how the adoption of shrines and deities is entwined with the history of a community's changing social status. It will be necessary to give particular attention to the association of divine manifestations with particular sites, such as centres of pilgrimage, *śaktipīṭhas* and *kuladaivata* (clan deity) shrines.[1]

The rise of religious shrines as centres of pilgrimage is depicted through the *sthalamāhātmya*s (narratives about the importance of religious places) and *devatāmāhātmya*s (narratives about the greatness of a deity or deities), which have found their due place in the Purāṇic tradition. The *sthala* and *devatā māhātmya*s are significant for understanding the factors that

1 A *śaktipīṭha* is a shrine erected on a particular spot where the bodily organs of Satī, the consort of Śiva, fell after she immolated herself. In a larger sense, it is regarded as a seat of power, celebrating creative, protective and destructive powers of a female deity. A *kuladaivata* is a deity especially favoured and worshipped for these powers by a particular caste group. All major religious shrines become centres of pilgrimage over a period.

contribute to the rise of specific godheads in the context of ongoing social, economic and political changes. Further, *māhātmyas* and other allied literature indirectly provide information about the progression or regression of marginalised social groups vis-à-vis the dominant social group, their interaction with each other, and the evolution of tradition in this social process. Along with *māhātmya* literature, data procured through cultic texts, epigraphic and historical evidence and oral traditions contribute to mapping as well as tracking religious changes. These various sources in combination help us to form some idea of the social processes of adaptation, appropriation, acculturation and assimilation.

As Schneider (2003, 217) says, 'Appropriation practice involves the "appropriation" of ideas, symbols, artefacts, image, sound, objects, forms or styles from other cultures, from art history, from popular culture or other aspects of manmade visual or non visual culture'. The apparatus of ideas, symbols and so forth constitutes an explicit framework for the legitimisation of social authority, whereby a dominant group has preferential access to religious material for dissemination of ideas within the power structure of the society. By easy access to materials and tools of religious power, the dominant social group establishes its legitimacy and credibility within a social framework. The subordinate social groups accept and give consent to this process without any resistance. This lack of resistance should not be regarded as willingness on the part of the subordinate social groups, rather it is the supremacy wielded by the dominant social group and the subjugation of the subordinate social groups to it. This gives an essentially negative connotation to appropriation. In the Indian context, the social framework encompasses caste and sub-caste hierarchy, ethnic conflicts and patriarchal structures of the society and, given this background, such appropriations occur frequently.

With this viewpoint, this chapter studies the goddess Ambe Jogāī, and a religious shrine dedicated to her. Ambe Jogāī, also known as the Yogeśvarī (see Figure 9.1), whose main temple is situated in the Ambe *taluk* of Beed district of Maharashtra, has been regarded as the *kulasvāminī* (clan, or family, goddess) of many *Kokaṇastha* (those who live in the Konkan region) Brāhmin families.[2]

2 It is a tradition in Hindu families to worship specific gods and goddesses for generations and these deities are known as family gods (*kulasvāmin*) or family goddesses (*kulasvāminī*). Besides these deities, village deities (*grāmadevatā*) are also worshipped. The worship of family and village deities has gathered significance due to migrations of communities and/or families from one place to another. This worship is undertaken to establish allegiance to one's own roots in spite of being uprooted.

Figure 9.1: Line drawing of Goddess Ambejogai

The *Kokaṇastha* Brāhmins are a sub-caste of the Maharashtrian Brāhmins.[3] Although located all over Maharashtra, they trace their origin to the Konkan, the coastal strip region of Maharashtra. The temple of Ambe Jogāī is over 350 kilometres away from Konkan, which is very surprising because a clan goddess would traditionally be expected to be very close to where the community lives. There is no other apparent linkage of the *Kokaṇastha* Brāhmin sub-caste with goddess Ambe Jogāī. Also, the *Kokaṇastha* Brāhmins have traditionally been very poor. Most families have lived on small pieces of land, barely large enough to survive on, and continue to do so. They certainly have not had the resources to travel to such a distant place. What then is the reason for them to choose a clan goddess so far away? That is the question this chapter seeks to answer.

Let me therefore start with the mythical origin and the background of the *Kokaṇastha* Brāhmins. Their origin myth states that the sage

3 A detailed account of the *Kokaṇastha* Brāhmins has been published by the well-known Marathi historian, V.K. Rajwade; see M.S. Dixit (2003, Ch.1).

Paraśurāma, one among the seven immortals (*cirañjīvins*) in Hindu mythology and the destroyer of the *kṣatriya* caste twenty-one times, created this community to look after the religious activities in the Konkan region, a region also created by him. The *Kokaṇastha* Brāhmins are also known as *Citpāvana* Brāhmins. Mythologically, there are multiple theories about the etymology of the word *citpāvana*. The word means 'purified from the pyre' and is derived from the Sanskrit words *citā* (pyre) and *pāvana* (pure); it can also mean 'pure-minded' if its derivation is linked to the Sanskrit word *citta* (mind). *Cit-pāvana*, that is 'a corpse saved from the funeral pyre', can be read as a figurative epithet that condenses into one word the long history of these peoples' almost miraculous survival from the fire of Buddhistic persecution (Karve 1928, 95-97).

The *Kokaṇastha* Brāhmins prefer to call themselves *Citpāvana*s, perhaps because it elevates the caste from restricting itself within the geographical boundaries of the Konkan region. The etymological analysis identifies the caste as 'purified', but indicates that earlier some impurity was associated with this sub-caste and, as a result of deliberate efforts, the impurity has been eradicated, and may even imply that this sub-caste has a non-Brāhminical origin.

The *Citpāvana* sub-caste arose to power and prosperity during the regime of the *Peśvā*s when the Marathas were ruling the Deccan. The *Peśvā*s, who were the chieftains of the Marathas, themselves belonged to the *Citpāvana* community. In this chapter, I propose that at Ambe, the local tradition of worshipping the goddess as mother goddess was subordinated by the dominant ruling caste by appropriating the deity into its fold and also regarding her as a virgin goddess. The local culture in present times also worships her as a virgin goddess, as no *maṅgalasūtra*[4] is offered to her. Thus, she is no longer worshipped as a mother goddess but as a virgin goddess at Ambe.

In this chapter I explore the factors that contributed to this religious appropriation, and begin with the history of the temple and the evidence suggesting that the goddess was viewed initially as a mother before the involvement of the *Peśvā*s.

4 In Maharashtra, as in many other parts of southern India, a black bead necklace called the *maṅgalasūtra* has traditionally been the diacritical mark of a married woman, instead of the wedding ring in Western culture. During the worship of a goddess who is a consort of a male god, the devotee customarily offers a *maṅgalasūtra* to her as part of the worship regimen.

Epigraphic and historical evidence of Ambe Jogāī and her temple

The earliest detailed historical record is that of an epigraph in Sanskrit of the Yādava king Singhaṇa (13th century CE) and his general Kholeśvara which mentions the reconstruction of a temple dedicated to the goddess Yogeśvarī and the grant of the village Taḷaiṇī to it. The inscription commences with the salutation to the god Vighnarāja (Ganesh) in a prose formula. It also refers to the important conquests of Singhaṇa and his general (Shastri 1972, 37-48). Although the major portion of the record consists of a grandiloquent eulogy of Kholeśvara and his master Singhaṇa, the main object of the inscription is to record the rebuilding of the temple by Kholeśvara and the grant of a village for the temple of Yogeśvarī at Āmrapura. This clearly indicates the importance of the Śakti cult at the time.

It appears that the Yoginī cult was worshipped, revered and feared in this region before the time of Kholeśvara. Also, the goddess Yogeśvarī was considered to be closely associated with these Yoginīs. We get a clear-cut reference to this in the inscription in Marathi of the king Udayāditya at Ambe, dated 1144 CE, which refers to the place as Ambā and states that the thunderbolt staff (*vajradaṇḍa*) of the Yoginīs may befall one who might obstruct or revoke the grant made by Ratnadeva, the subordinate of Udayāditya (Kalegaonkar 2009, 12).[5] Tantric analogues suggest that this term signifies a staff topped by the *vajra*, the thunderbolt emblem.[6] This inscription mentions land and other material endowments made by Ratnadeva in favour of a temple of Śiva with the name Bhūcaranātha (the lord of those who move about on the earth), which is located in the caves in the periphery of the Ambe Jogāī goddess shrine. Though the grant is for the temple of Siva, the inscription proclaims that anyone who violates the site will have to face the wrath of the Yoginīs.[7] According to Dikshit (2010, 61), the word Yoginī is in the plural and it either hints at the sixty-four Yoginīs or stands for one Yoginī with the plural denoting

5 According to Dikshit (2010, 60), Mahāmaṇḍaleśvara Udayāditya was a vassal of the early Yādavas. Deshpande (2010, vol. 1, 71) considers him to be one of the kings belonging to the Parmar dynasty.

6 Dehejia (1986, 181) mentions an image of a Yoginī in the Madras Museum holding a *vajra* in her hand.

7 The mention of Yoginī/s appears in the inscription as follows: *lopī teā yoginnīncā vajradaṇḍu paḍe* (if this donation is discontinued the thunderbolt of the Yoginī/s would fall on the person/s).

respect. It is the earliest record of the Yoginī cult from this place and is therefore of immense importance for our study.

One can thus see that in 1144 CE there was important evidence for the presence of the Yoginī cult. Such cults were linked to the concept of the virgin goddess. This may also mean that virgin goddess worship was a feature of the reconceptualisation of an old mother goddess cult to suit the incoming *Kokaṇastha* Brāhmins.

The present temple of Yogeśvarī was built by Nagoji Trimal and Shyamji Bapuji in 1720 CE. It is difficult to establish if the duo was *Kokaṇastha*. However, one cannot forget the fact that this era witnessed the rise of *Peśvā* rule in Maharashtra. It is, therefore, very likely that they were *Kokaṇasthas*.

In the following pages, it will become apparent that the Ambe Jogāī site was home to a religious tradition with a number of ingredients emphasising different aspects of the goddess, upon which, after the Peśvā rule was established, the local incumbent priests could draw in order to adapt the cult to changing circumstances.

Textual references to Ambe Jogāī

Textual sources in the form of the Purāṇas are replete with narratives about the evolution and worship of the goddess, the earliest extant text being the *Devīmāhātmya* occurring in the *Markaṇḍeya Purāṇa* (400–600 CE). The text extols the exploits of the goddess identified as Ambikā or Durgā in liberating the world from the tyranny of a number of demons. The goddess, though addressed as Ambikā (little mother), is unmarried; nevertheless, she is referred to as one existing in the form of a mother amongst all living beings.[8] This is perhaps the first time that one sees the historical dichotomy and the ambivalent character of Ambe Jogāī. The *Harivaṁśa* (100–400 CE), a supplement of the *Mahābhārata* recording the legends of Kṛṣṇa, refers to the goddess as '*kaumāram vratam āsthāya tridivam tvam gamiṣyasi*', which means that the goddess, having undertaken (literally, placing herself in) the vow of virginity, will enter the heaven (*Harivaṁśa* II. 2. 46). In a eulogy to the goddess, the text says that the goddess represents celibacy amongst virgins and marital bliss amongst married women (*Harivaṁśa* II. 3. 13).[9] This indicates that the

8 *Markaṇḍeya Purāṇa* 85. 31ab: *yā devī Sarvabhūteṣu matṛrūpeṇa saṁsthitā I.*

9 *Harivaṁśa* II. 3. 13cd: *kanyānām brahmacaryatvam saubhāgyam pramadāsu ca I.*

concept of goddess exhibiting a dual form, that is, of a virgin and mother, at the same time is not new to the tradition.

We shall now discuss the Puranic sources for the goddess Yogeśvarī. Textual references to goddess Yogeśvarī at Ambe are to be found in the *Yogeśvarī Māhātmya*, which consists of thirty chapters and is traditionally regarded as the source book for the goddess at this place. It is a part of the *Bhaviṣyottara Purāṇa*, which is itself an appendix to the *Bhaviṣya Purāṇa*. Scholars have placed the upper and lower limit of the *Purāṇa* between 500 and 1200 CE (Hazra 1975, 6). The *Yogeśvarī Māhātmya* is a *sthalamāhātmya* describing sacred places in and around Ambe Jogāī. This text mentions the Mother Goddess[10] taking an incarnation as a Yoginī or Yogeśvarī, who destroys the demon Dantāsura. Whether this Yoginī or Yogeśvarī was a virgin goddess or not is unclear in the text, which indicates the text's ambivalence about the nature of the goddess. Further, the text narrates various myths regarding a number of sacred places.

At present no Sanskrit version is available.[11] There are two publications on the Yogeśvarī, both published in the town of Ambe Jogāī. The first, entitled *Śrī Yogeśvarī Māhātmya Darśana* and compiled by Lakshmanrao Kalegaonkar, gives a verse rendering of the first chapter of the *Yogeśvarī Māhātmya* in Marathi, but gives no information about how Kalegaonkar obtained the Sanskrit *Yogeśvarī Māhātmya*. On my visit to Ambe Jogāī and upon my inquiries in other parts of Maharashtra, I was unable to obtain a Sanskrit copy of the text.

Another extant text is a free rendering in prose of the *Yogeśvarī Māhātmya* in Marathi by Dr Harihar Matekar, published by Sri Yogesvari Devasthana. It is to be noted that the surname Matekar is not in the list of *Kokaṇastha* Brāhmins. In the introduction, Dr Matekar thanks Kamalakarrao Chausalkar, Secretary of Sri Yogesvari Devasthana, for providing him with a manuscript of the *Yogeśvarī Māhātmya* (Matekar 2003, 7). On referring to the *Bhaviṣyottara Purāṇa*, which is an appendage to the *Bhaviṣya Purāṇa* (500 and 1200 CE), there is no *Yogeśvarī*

10 The word *ambā* means mother. Pārvatī as the *mother* is known as Ambā or Ambā-Bhavānī. In the Purāṇic tradition, she is the one who then becomes Mahākālī, Mahālakṣmī or Mahāsarasvatī. Goddess Mahālakṣmī at Kolhapur in Maharashtra is actually Pārvatī, the consort of Śiva. She holds a Śivaliṅga on her head.

11 Kalegaonkar has translated the first chapter of the *Yogeśvarī Māhātmya* in verse form into Marathi. It refers to Yogeśvarī as the goddess who destroys the demon Dantāsura. In this task, Yogeśvarī appeared with an entourage of Yoginīs (Kalegaonkar 2009, 5).

Māhātmya in the text. This indicates that the text is a self-proclaimed appendage to the *Bhaviṣyottara Purāṇa*. The *Yogeśvarī Māhātmya* mentions a Marathi poet-saint, Mukundarāja, who existed in 1200 CE (Ajgaonkar 1957, 5) and his encounter with a king named Jaitrapāla. As per the chronology of Yadava kings, Jaitrapāla was his contemporary (Deshpande 2010, vol. 1, 63). But there is no inscriptional evidence of the encounter between the poet and the king. This *sthalamāhātmya* does not contain any reference to the relationship between *Kokaṇastha* Brāhmins and the goddess. It does not refer to any historical activity such as the rise of Islamic power in the region or the visit of some historical personality to this place. It is possible to date the text between 1300 and 1600 CE. It also does not describe the goddess as a virgin; rather, here she is Reṇukā, the mother goddess. The text narrates:

> There was a Brāhmin named Reṇuka who lived in the Dravid region and was dejected. He went to Ambāpura in order to have the glimpse of Mahādeva. He gave up worldly pleasures and there performed severe penance to propitiate Mahādeva. Mahādeva became pleased and decided to give him a boon. The Brāhmin said that Reṇukā was his *kuladevatā*. He wished to see her. Therefore, Śivānī (Pārvatī) in her form of Reṇukāmbā, who was residing at Ambā, appeared before him (Matekar 2003, 66-67).

It is clear, therefore, that there are inconsistencies in the text in the designation of the goddess; first as the Mother Goddess (Ambā), then as Yoginī/Yogeśvarī, whose status is unclear, and finally her identification with Reṇukā, again as the Mother Goddess.

According to the Tantric tradition, Yoginīs are an important aspect of Hindu female divinity. They are groups of goddesses, usually between seven and sixty-four in number. The *Devībhāgavata* (VII. 28) states that they are the manifestations of the Mahādevī, the highest principle in the universe. It is believed that Yoginīs frequent the temple of Kālī and arrive there with swords and severed heads (Nagaswamy 1982, 26). Some of the sixty-four Yoginīs are said to have bird heads: parrot, hawk, peacock, eagle, pigeon or owl. The Tantric practice of *śava-sādhana* (worshipping the goddess while the practitioner is seated on a corpse) requires the practitioner to worship the sixty-four Yoginīs with vegetable offerings (Kinsley 1998, 197 and 204). Dehejia (1986, 11) regards Yoginī as a female counterpart of Yogī. Just as a man who follows the path of Yoga as a bodily and spiritual discipline and becomes a master in that science, acquiring certain powers in the process, is a Yogī, the woman who follows this path is a Yoginī.

The *Yogeśvarīkavaca* from the *Rudrayāmalatantra* is regarded as an important device for propitiating the goddess. It addresses the goddess as Yoginī and not as Yogeśvarī. In order to understand the contextuality of the *Yogeśvarīkavaca* and the *tantra* text, one needs to understand that this text is a dialogue between Ānandabhairava and Ānandabhairavī about propitiating Yogeśvara (Śiva) for gaining material and metaphysical pleasures. It contains passages discussing the worship of *kumārī*, a virgin, to achieve certain powers.[12] The *kumārī* in this text is Yoginī and here we may recognise a link with Yogeśvarī as *kumārī,* the virgin goddess. She is another form of Mahābhairavī, whose male consort is Bhairava, for the *Rudrayāmalatantra* is the dialogue between Bhairava and his consort Bhairavī, wherein Bhairavī is revealing her form as a *kumārī.* The couple is known as Ānandabhairava and Ānandabhairavī, as well as Mahābhairava and Mahābhairavī. This indicates the dual nature of the goddess, as virgin and consort, in the Tantric literature as well.

The *Rudrayāmalatantra* also gives a Yogic dimension to the worship of the Yoginī. It describes the Yoginī seated in the *Khecarī Mudrā,* in the form of Vāyu and sitting in the lotus posture (II. 6. 17). Etymologically, *khecara* means flying in the sky, which figuratively stands for Vāyu (air). While attaining a metaphysical state, the aspirant becomes as light as air; therefore, in the text, Yoginī is regarded to be the form of Vāyu. This usage only indicates her metaphysically elevated status. *Khecarī Mudrā* is a Yogic practice wherein the practitioner places his tongue above the soft palate and into the nasal cavity. Here, the Yoginī has a metaphysical, spiritual and enlightened aspect. Therefore, the goddess is associated with Yogic practices. The Mudrā also refers to the *Khecarī Cakra* which is an elaborate circular formation of Yoginīs, which may be visualised as an expanding or unfolding lotus flower with a Yoginī seated on each of its many petals (Dehejia 1986, 44-45). She

12 *Rudrayāmalatantra* II. 6. 92-93: *Kanyā sarvasamṛddhiḥ syāt kanyā sarvaparantapaḥ I / homam mantrārcanam nityakriyām kaulikasatkriyām I / nānāphalam mahādharmam kumārīpūjanam vinā I / tadardhaphalam nātha prāpnoti sādhakottamaḥ I (Lit: The virgin stands for all prosperity; the virgin stands for great penance in totality. Therefore offerings, incantations, worship, regular rituals and Śakta practices should be undertaken. An excellent worshipper obtains half of many fruits and secures half of dharma if worship of the virgin is not undertaken.)*

is represented as a virgin, who is none other than Ānandabhairavī, one of the narrators of the *Tantra* text (II. 6. 28-33).[13] Bhairavī, the fierce one, is one among the ten *mahāvidyā*s who has many forms. Kinsley points out that Bhairavī embodies the principle of destruction. She is the feminine aspect of Bhairava, the fierce one. The commentator on *Paraśurāmakalpasūtra* (1250 CE), a Tantric work written in an aphoristic style, imagines a poetic and fanciful etymology that the word 'Bhairavī' is derived from the words *bharaṇa* (to create), *ramaṇa* (to protect) and *vamana* (to emit or disgorge), thus underlying the cosmic functions of the goddess (Kinsley 1998, 172-175).

The Tantric tradition depicts Yoginī in three forms – virgin, consort and destroyer. The Tantric tradition represented in the *Rudrayāmalatantra* is accepted by the shrine of Ambe Jogāī. Present devotees of Jogāī are advised to read repeatedly the *Yogeśvarīkavaca* (armour of the Yogeśvarī), a part of *Rudrayāmalatantra,* in order to propitiate the goddess.[14]

The Tantric tradition of Kashmir is reflected in the *Rājataraṅgiṇī* of Kalhaṇa, which mentions Yogeśvarī as a goddess (I. 331-333). It refers to a lovely Yogeśvarī capturing king Baka as an offering to a circle of goddesses (*devīcakra*). At another place in the *Rājataraṅgiṇī,* (II. 98-108), Dehejia (198, 72) observes that the words Yogeśvarī and Yoginī are used as synonyms.

In conclusion, it would, therefore, appear that the nature of Ambe Jogāī, as reflected in textual sources, is, at best, ambivalent. The Puranic tradition projects her as the mother goddess, as described by the *Yogeśvarī Māhātmya*. At Ambe Jogāī she is regarded as a form of Ambā, the mother goddess.[15] On the other hand, the Tantric tradition would like to see her as a virgin.

13 *Rudrayāmalatantra II. 6. 33a-b: kumārī yoginī sākṣāt kumārī parādevatā* (Lit: Kumārī is verily yoginī, Kumārī is the supreme deity).

14 This information was shared with me in March 2009 by Shri Sadanand Waman Naik, University Printing Press, Mumbai University. He handed over a pocket-sized copy of the text and asked me to translate it. Professor Sunder D. Khadke, Assistant Professor at the Kholeshvar Mahavidyalay, Ambe Jogāī, also confirmed that devotees of Jogāī read this particular text. It is believed to be extremely powerful, as it is capable of solving the reader-devotee's difficulties.

15 The *Yogeśvarī Māhātmya* I. 43: *mārgaśīrṣa śuddha paurṇimesī* [on the full moon day of the month of Margasirsa] *ambā avatarilī mūlapiṭhesī* [Ambā incarnated at the original place]; I. 70 *jethe ambā yogeśvarī* [where Ambā Yogeśvarī] *dantāsurāsi saṅgrama karī* [fought with Dantāsura] *te sthāna ambāpurī* [that place in Ambāpuri] *trilokī prasiddha jāhale* [which became famous in the three worlds].

Ambe Jogāī: A melting pot

In the early medieval period, there were cultural and political upheavals in this region of Maharashtra, which was under the sway of the Rāṣṭrakūṭa dynasty from the sixth to the ninth century CE (Altekar 1934, 19-21). Dantivarman, the Rāṣṭrakūṭa founder-ruler, had conquered the entire region after a series of battles. The Rāṣṭrakūṭa dynasty was followed by the Cālukyas and the Yādavas, until the region came under Muslim rulers. The Marathawada region was politically and economically significant because the Baleghat trade route, which opened at the coastal regions of Konkan, was situated in this zone. Any ruler who controlled this region could wield his influence and control up to the Deccan and Southern region at one end and the coastal region at the other. There were significant religious developments in this area during the medieval period. According to Anamika Roy (2004, 89), the royal families of the Paramāras (800–1305 CE), Candellas (831–1569 CE) and Kacchapagatas (1000–1200 CE) worshipped the Yoginīs for territorial gain. In the same manner, they were worshipped by other kings in this region, which may well be why the Udayāditya inscription threatens the wrath of the Yoginī if the land grant is obstructed.

The Nātha tradition

This area was also a centre of the Nātha tradition, which has Matsyendranātha (Macchindranātha) as the founder and Gorakṣanātha (Gorakhanātha) as its leading proponent. Mukundarāja, the first Marathi poet-philosopher, lived in this area and has his *samādhi* (memorial stone) at Ambe Jogāī. Author of the well-known Marathi work *Vivekasindhu*, Mukundarāja belonged to the Nātha tradition (Joshi 2004, 99). An account of Mukundarāja is narrated in the *Yogeśvarīmāhātmya*. The account says that there was a *siddha* (person of spiritual and occult powers) named Mukundarāja performing penance at a mountain named Mukunda in a place called Aśvadarī at Ambe Jogāī. Many sages sought refuge in him, because a king named Jayantapāla, alias Jaitrapāla, was inflicting tortures on them. The king spread unrighteousness (*adharma*) everywhere. He had an ambition to obtain occult powers and, therefore, summoned practitioners of sacrifices and scholars of different branches of learning, among others. Once, when he was performing a sacrifice, a young boy arose from the flames and said that the king could get powers if he served sages. The king invited the sages and gave them food to eat and asked them to give him powers. The sages said that they were not aware of such powers and that only a person who controls his senses can attain spiritual elevation. Angered, the king tortured the sages by making them grind Bengal gram in a grinding stone. The sages prayed unto the goddess Yoginī. Yoginī thought of Mukundarāja, who was at Kāśī.[16] When Mukundarāja warned the king to mend his ways, the king ignored him and got a giant grind-stone for the sages to grind Bengal gram. But a miracle took place and the grinding stone started following the king. The king realised his mistake and changed his behaviour (Matekar 2003, 69-71). One of the prominent aspects of Nātha worship tradition was the Tantric worship of Śakti (Briggs 2009, 63, 77) and, given his mention in the *Yogeśvarīmāhātmya,* it is likely that Mukundarāja had a close connection with goddess Ambe Jogāī.

It would also appear that the goddess Jogāī may have been worshipped in the Tantric tradition at least in the time of Mukundarāja (twelfth century CE).

Ambe Jogāī: a *śaktipīṭha*?

*Purāṇa*s such as the *Devībhāgavata* and *Kālikāpurāṇa* elaborately detail the origin of *śaktipīṭha*s. It is said that, after the immolation of Satī, Śiva was inconsolable and moved helter-skelter with the corpse of Satī. Later on, the body parts fell on the earth, and the places where they fell became *pīṭha*s (sacred seats) of the Mother Goddess. According to D.C. Sircar (2004, 7), she is represented as constantly living in these places in some form, along with a Bhairava (a being in the form of her husband Śiva). Any *śaktipīṭha* is regarded as a conscious *jāgṛta* (abode) of the Mother Goddess. The claimed number of *śaktipīṭha*s in the Indian sub-continent varies from four to 108. It is significant that the works that describe *śaktipīṭhas,* namely the *Purāṇa*s and *Tantra* texts, do not mention Ambe Jogāī as one of them. Hers is a *śaktipīṭha* outside the traditional list (Prabhudesai 2005, 277-278).

The *Yogeśvarī Māhātmya*, the narrative eulogising the magnificence of the goddess, does mention the sacrifice of Dakṣa, wherein Satī immolated herself.[17] But the *Māhātmya*, in Chapters 24-27, says that the Yoginī

16 There is some discrepancy in the account here about the whereabouts of Mukundarāja.

17 The text records the role of poet-saint Mukundarāja in controlling the king Jayantapāla, which clearly indicates that the text is no earlier than the twelfth century CE.

played the role of destroying the sacrifice. She also consumed blood in the sacrifice and was accompanied by Kṣetrapāla, Guhyaka and Ḍākiṇī, the minor tutelary gods with both benevolent and maleficent qualities. The entire episode of Dakṣa's sacrifice occurred at Ambe Jogāī, declares the text. It is to be noted that Satī is different from Yoginī. Here Yoginī appears to be a godling, assisting in the destruction of the sacrifice. The Puranic tradition is hinting at the Tantric tradition which points to the destructive nature of Yoginī.

Such proclamations employed in the *Sthala* and *Devatā Māhātmya*s are a deliberate attempt to heighten the significance of a place of worship. Further evidence reiteratimg the Śakti and Śiva relation is constituted by the representation of Yogeśvarī in the Kailasa temple at Ellora. In the Andhakavadha panel at Ellora, Śiva is shown with eight arms and has pinned down Andhaka with his trident. The goddess Yogeśvarī is squatting on the ground, holding in her hand a cup in which she catches the blood as it trickles down (Rao 1997, 193). This panel hints at the Tantric links of the goddess, but there is no definite proof to identify her with Pārvatī.

Chapter 1 of the *Yogeśvarī Māhātmya* mentions the goddess destroying a demon named Dantāsura. He was an atrocious ruler of Āmrapura (the Sanskrit name of Ambe) and was slain by the Yoginī. This narrative of the goddess killing the demon is very commonly employed across different *Māhātmya*s on goddesses.[18] It indicates that the nature of the goddess is not true to the concept of *śaktipīṭha*. Rather, it is the *pīṭha* of the Śāktas, the worshippers of Śakti and Śiva. Narrative literature and iconographic representations of Yogeśvarī depict the goddess as having both protective and destructive qualities.

The Śaiva and Śākta developments in this region are also significant. A glance over the sacred places in and around Ambe Jogāī indicates that this place was a stronghold of both Śaiva and Śākta worship. The shrines of Kālabhairava, Agnibhairava, Mahārudra, Nāganātha and Nāradeśvara indicate the strong Śaiva connections of this place. The Western Calukya regime, which took over from the Raṣṭrakūṭas, marks the rise of the Śaiva sect. Thus Tantric and epigraphic sources indicate that Ambe Jogāī is a confluence of the Nātha, Śaiva and Śākta worship. The Puranic tradition through the *Yogeśvarī Māhātmya* showed the development of the goddess as a protective mother and the Tantric

18 The *Karavīra Māhātmya*, which eulogises the goddess Mahālakṣmī of Kolhapur, mentions the goddess slaying a demon named Kolhāsura.

tradition projected her as a virgin. However, later, during *Peśvā* times, this tradition changed the goddess's character from a *śaktipīṭha*, the seat of a Śakti worshipped by all, to the *kuladaivata* (clan goddess) for the *Kokaṇastha* Brāhmins.

As already noted, *śaktipīṭha* literally means a seat or chair of Śakti, which stands for divine power exemplified by a dynamic female principle. *Śaktipīṭhas* are geographical places identified with shrines of goddesses across the Indian peninsula. They are associated with the *pīṭha* legend, which links them to the Dakṣa sacrifice wherein Satī, Śiva's wife, immolated herself. Śiva picked up her corpse and her body parts fell at various geographical locations and gave rise to *śaktipīṭhas*. In the case of Yogeśvarī, the *māhātmya* (Chapters 25-27) shows its allegiance to the Dakṣa sacrifice by stating that Ambe Jogāī is the location where the sacrifice of Dakṣa took place. This seems to be an obvious attempt by the writer of the work to affirm the place as a *śaktipīṭha*.

In a *śaktipīṭha*, Tantric practices like the worship of the goddess by *pañcamakāras* ('five Ms'), namely, *matsya* (fish), *maṁsa* (meat), *mudrā* (parched grain), *madya* (liquor) and *maithuna* (sexual intercourse), are practised either in the real sense or in the symbolic sense. Although the abovementioned essentials of left-handed *tantra* are not practised at all at Ambe Jogāī, the strong roots of such Tantric tradition are evident in this place, as evidenced by the mandatory chanting of the *Yogeśvarīkavaca* during the worship regime. It may be that, when the goddess was appropriated as the *kuladaivata* by the dominant sub-caste of the Brāhmins to whom the *Peśvās* belonged, these practices were discontinued.

Jogāī, the Mother Goddess

It can be seen that historical, epigraphic and Sanskrit textual references indicate that the Yogeśvarī shrine of Ambe was not a *śaktipīṭha* in its true sense. It was an abode of the confluence of Nātha and Śaiva-Śākta traditions. This indicates that she was either the Mother Goddess, displaying the functions of a protective mother, or the tutelary deity of the region. A linguistic analysis of the name 'Ambe Jogāī' unfolds a different aspect of the goddess, namely as as a fertility deity. The word Ambā itself indicates her motherhood. The Marathi word for the goddess is Joga-āī, and *āī* in Marathi stands for mother, which means that she is the mother of Jogis, that is, Yogins. At Ambe Jogāī, her original shrine, known as 'the maternal home of Jogāī' (*Jogāīche māhera* in Marathi), is ten kilometres from the present temple, in a place known as Reṇāgiri. This place has a temple of Reṇukā situated fifteen feet from the shrine. Reṇukā, the Mother Goddess, has her main temple at Mahur, also in Maharashtra, and there are many shrines of Reṇukā scattered in and around the Deccan region.

Another phonetically similar goddess is Joguḷāmbā. The suffix *ḷa* in Dravidian languages, especially in Telugu, is a plural possessive suffix, so she is the mother of Yogis. According to tradition, the shrine of Joguḷāmbā at Alampur in Andhra Pradesh is a *śaktipīṭha*, being the point where Satī's upper jaw fell off after her immolation. A shrine of the headless goddess named Bhūdevī, alias Lajjāgaurī, is also located within the periphery of the temple. The head has been worshipped as Yellammā and the torso as Bhūdevī (Bolon 1997, 26). The myth of Reṇukā, whose head was axed by her son Paraśurāma and later restored by his father Jamadagni, is narrated to explain the origin of this shrine. Dhere (2004, 46) cites references from Telugu works and argues that Reṇukā is the same as Yellammā which is the same as Joguḷāmbā. He further argues that these are all the names for the Mother Goddess and they symbolise fertility. *Joguḷa* in Dravidian languages stands for cradle songs, so she becomes the Mother Goddess alias Reṇukā (Dhere 2004, 45-46). There is a possibility that the word Jogāī has its origins in the Telugu word Joguḷāmbā, who is the fertility goddess identified as Reṇukā. The proximity of the shrines of Reṇukā and Jogāī (original) shows the interconnection of these fertility goddesses and indicates the earth-mother nature of Jogāī.

Jogāī and Reṇukā are identified in oral tradition. Songs of goddesses sung while undertaking a vow of begging are known as *jogavā*. One *jogavā* mentions Jogāī being called Reṇukā (Ranade n.d., 9):

> O Jogāī, mother Ambābāī,
> I ask for Jogavā by using vermillion.
> You have eight weapons in your hand,
> Laughter shines on your face,
> You have applied cooling ointment,
> Dear mother! You are the delicate Reṇukā.

Thus, linguistic analysis and the songs project Jogāī as Reṇukā, the earth mother.

Gunther Sontheimer (2006, 11) has pointed out that Jogāī of Ambe features as one among the mother goddesses for the Dhangar caste. He further mentions other Jogāīs getting married to gods like Siddhanātha and Kāḷabhairava. He discusses the elevation of Mhasobā (buffalo god), a godling, to the level of Kāḷabhairava who marries Jogubāī/Jogāī/Yogeśvarī (that is, Durgā) (Sontheimer 2006, 30-31). This identification of Jogāī, alias Yogeśvarī, as Durgā is based on the myth of goddess Durgā killing the buffalo demon Mahiṣāsura. The buffalo demon changed into a godling in order to marry Jogāī in the enactment of the metamyth of Durgā killing Mahiṣāsura. This relationship is also envisaged by Asko Parpola (1992, 275-276) and Dange (1996, 431). Some families of the *Kokaṇastha* Brāhmins worship goddess Durgā Yogeśvarī situated at Guhagar in the Konkan region of Maharashtra.

Sontheimer (1997, 28-29) cites a number of instances wherein Yogeśvarī is married to Kālabhairava; she is his first wife, whereas the second is the local goddess. Khaṇḍobā, the god of Jejuri and the *kulasvāmin* of many families in Maharashtra, irrespective of their castes, is known as Mārtaṇḍa Bhairava. Sontheimer (1997, 222 and 273) identifies the two wives of Khaṇḍobā, namely Mhāḷsā and Bāṇāī, as Yogeśvarīs. This is a folk depiction of the Tantric reference to Yogeśvarī, wherein she is identified with Ānandabhairavī, the consort of Ānandabhairava as stated in the *Rudrayāmalatantra* (II. 6. 28-33). In the context of Yogeśvarīs as consort goddesses, it needs to be noted that the *Kokaṇastha* Brāhmins do not claim every Yogeśvarī as their *kuladaivatā*. They worship only that Yogeśvarī situated at Ambe, indicating that the appropriation is not of any Yogeśvarī, but only of a specific Yogeśvarī situated in Ambe.

Jogāī and the *Kokaṇastha* Brāhmins

The *Rāmakṣetravarṇana* (description of the *Rāmakṣetra)* of the *Sahyādrikhaṇḍa,* a self-proclaimed appendix to the *Skanda Purāṇa,* refers to the land reclamation by Paraśurāma in the Konkan region of Maharashtra.[19] The opening line of the manuscript is *'sriskande sinhyādrikhaṇḍe uttarārdhe svāyambhuve … rāmakṣetravarṇanam'*, which means that *Rāmakṣetravarṇana* is a portion belonging to second half of the *Sahyādrikhaṇḍa* of the *Skanda Purāṇa*. The portion mentioned by Dhere is not available in editions of *Sahyādrikhaṇḍa* compiled by

19 This manuscript fragment is held in the personal collection of Dr R. C. Dhere, a well known researcher in the folk culture of India.

J. Gerson da Cunha (1877) and by Gaitonde (1972) and appears to be a separate manuscript. However, neither Dhere nor Gaitonde gives any other details of the manuscript. The eleventh chapter of this work says that Reṇukā, along with her family of Yoginīs, visited Paraśurāma. As the text mentions Reṇukā accompanied by Yoginīs, her nature becomes similar to that of Pārvatī as far as her motherhood aspect is concerned. Paraśurāma eulogised her and requested her to reside in this region and be the chief goddess of this clan (*kuladevatā*) of the Brāhmins settled in this region. He directed the *Brāhmins* to worship her for progeny. In this work Paraśurāma has addressed her as Yogāmbā, Yogāmbikā and Ambujamātṛkā (mother with a lotus, the symbol of fertility) (Dhere 2004, 46).[20] This is the clear-cut link between Yogāmbā–Jogāmbā–Jogāī and the *Kokaṇastha Brāhmins.* Thus one aspect of Ambe Jogāī is motherhood. The functional similarity between both these goddesses is probably the reason for Ambe Jogāī's addition in the *Kokaṇastha* pantheon. If we follow Dhere's thesis, we can see that the nature of the goddess either as a mother or a virgin is ambivalent amongst the *Kokaṇastha* pantheon.

The above discussion of the nature of the goddess highlights the following points:

A. Yogeśvarī, alias Jogāī, of Ambe displays a dual nature – that of a Mother and that of a virgin.

B. Manuscript evidence identifies her with Reṇukā, the earth-mother. Linguistic analysis supports this identification.

C. There are other shrines of the Jogāī goddess scattered through Maharashtra. At these places, the goddess is married with Bhairava/Kālabhairava or Mhaskobā/Mhasobā.

Contemporary tradition believes that Yogeśvarī of Ambe is a virgin goddess only. The factor strengthening this belief is the mythology of the goddess, transmitted only through oral tradition, regarding her broken marriage described below. Tantric, Puranic and even epigraphic sources are surprisingly silent about the broken marriage of the Yogeśvarī of Ambe.

20 Incidentally, there is a temple of Reṇukā behind the temple of Paraśurāma at a place known as Peḍhe Paraśurāma, alias Loṭe Paraśurāma (Kunte 2007, 31).

Myths of the broken marriage

Oral tradition in the form of myths and songs points to a different nature of Ambe Jogāī. She is regarded in these myths as a virgin goddess, whose marriage was broken, or, rather, she procrastinated in her marriage. I discuss below four of these myths.

The first of these myths, pertaining to the marriage of Yogeśvarī, is not recorded in any Puranic and Tantric texts, which implies that it is circulated only through oral tradition. The narrative expounds that the marriage of Yogeśvarī was fixed with Vaijanātha/Vaidyanātha of Paraḷī (Śiva in one of his *Jyotirliṅga* forms at Paraḷī, situated approximately 100 kilometres from Ambe Jogāī). Yogeśvarī arrived with her wedding paraphernalia at the place named Ambe.[21] The wedding procession of Vaidyanātha had already started. But a rooster, who was supposed to indicate the auspicious time *(muhūrta),* crowed before time. Vaidyanātha wrongly thought that the *muhūrta* had been missed and returned to Paraḷī. It was Yogeśvarī who caused the rooster to crow before time and disappoint Vaidyanātha. Thus, she remained a virgin and settled at Ambe. Even today, locals show the place where Yogeśvarī had settled with the wedding party. There is a temple of the original seat of Yogeśvarī situated within ten kilometres from the main temple site. Near the original place is a temple of goddess Reṇukā. This place is regarded as the *māhera* (maternal home) of Jogāī.

The second version of the myth says that she is goddess Durgādevī situated at Guhagar in the Konkan region, almost 350 kilometres away from Jogāī, whose marriage was fixed with Vaidyanātha of Paraḷī. As she did not want to get married, she deliberately made the rooster crow some hours too early to deceive Śiva and thus avoided marriage. After this she returned to Guhagar. This goddess is also known as Jogeśvarī, the Prakrit equivalent to Yogeśvarī. At this shrine, the goddess assumes two forms daily. In the morning, she is a married woman, who is the consort of Vyāḍeśvara/Vāḍeśvara of Guhagar, and in the evening she takes the form of a virgin, Kumārikā. This myth is enacted through a ritual. She is clad in a sari during morning times and in the evening wears *parkar-polke*, a type of garment worn by young unmarried girls in Maharashtra. Durgā

21 When I visited Ambe Jogāī, on 24 September 2010, I asked Professor Sunder Khadke, Kholeshwar College, why the goddess is associated with *Kokaṇastha* Brāhmins. He narrated the first and fourth of the myths recounted here.

as Mahiṣāsuramardinī is a virgin, but, as a form of Parvatī, is also the Mother Goddess.[22]

The third myth mentions that the entire wedding paraphernalia of Yogeśvarī went from Advire in Konkan to Ambe. But, as the goddess did not agree to marry Vaidyanātha of Paraḷī, he cursed her to remain a virgin and the entire party to be converted to stone. At present, in Ambe Jogāī, a place with a large number of stone sculptures is shown and is said to represent the bridal party at the time of the broken marriage.

The fourth myth popular in oral tradition is as follows. After Paraśurāma fashioned the *Kokaṇastha* Brāhmins out of the dead found on a ship, no Brāhmins were willing to have a matrimonial relationship with them. It was then agreed that girls from Ambe Jogaī would be given to them in marriage. As a mark of gratitude for this gesture, *Kokaṇasthas* would regard Ambe Jogāī, the virgin goddess, as their *kulasvāminī.* Besides, during the ritual of *boḍaṇa,*[23] performed after any auspicious incident occurs in the family, a *kumārikā* will play an important role. It is evident that this myth is popular at Ambe Jogāī.[24]

As mentioned before, these myths are of folk origin. Kalegaonkar (2009, 21) gives a detailed account of the how the goddess obviated her marriage.

> Tripurasundarī[25] spent most of her childhood in the Konkan region. Her marriage was decided with Vaijanātha/Vaidyanātha

22 When I visited Guhagar on 8 November 2010, the second and third myths recounted here were narrated by Dr Anand Khare, a member of Durgadevi Devasthan Fund, who feels that the Durgādevī of Guhagar is supposedly the *kuladaivata* of *Kokaṇastha* Brāhmins, for the goddess did not settle at Ambe Jogāī, but she returned to Guhagar. According to him, as *Kokaṇastha* Brāhmins migrated from Konkan to the plateau (*deśa* in Marathi), they accepted Ambe Jogāī as their *kuladaivata*, because Ambe is touched by the 'sacred feet' of the goddess Durgādevī.

23 *Boḍaṇa* is a ritual performed among the *Kokaṇastha* Brāhmins after marriage, childbirth or the thread ceremony. It involves a minimum of five married women and one virgin (*kumārikā).* An image of the goddess Annapūrṇā is placed in a container and, in accordance with the instructions of the *kumārikā*, milk, clarified butter, curds, honey and sugar are added and mixed with the image. The procedure stops after the *kumārikā* is satisfied. Some of this mixture is consumed by the family members as *prasāda* and the rest is offered to a cow.

24 Professor Khadke believes that *boḍana* is a thanksgiving ritual performed by the *Kokaṇastha* Brāhmins in memory of the good deed of the people of Ambe Jogāī rendered to them by giving their daughters to them in marriage.

25 Tripurasundarī is a new goddess emerging in this framework. In brief, she is a goddess understood to be a combination of the trio Durgā, Lakṣmī and Sarasvatī. She is one among the *Daśamahāvidyās* and is supposed to be sixteen years old.

> of Paraḷī. Tripurasundarī, who undertook yogic practices, remembered her earlier birth in which she was Pārvatī married to Mahādeva/Śiva. Śiva worshipped Rāma, but Pārvatī was not in favour of it. She decided to put Rāma to the test. After the abduction of Sītā, Rāma was desperately searching for her. Pārvatī took the form of Sītā and hid herself behind a tree. Seeing Sītā, Lakṣmaṇa got elated, but Rāma recognized her and called her 'mother'. Humiliated, Pārvatī returned to Śiva. But, Śiva began to revere her as the wife of his favourite deity Rāma and lost marital interest in her. Tripurasundarī remembered this insult; she had no interest in her wedding. The entire wedding retinue went from Konkan and camped at a distance of 15 miles near Paraḷī, on the banks of the river Jayantī. Vaijanātha arrived at the wedding place. But Tripurasundarī took a lot of time to get ready for the marriage. Meanwhile, the auspicious time was missed by her and the rooster crowed. The wedding had to be called off. Tripurasundarī rejoiced and decided to stay at the place, i.e. Ambe, and she became Ambe Jogāī. Vaijanātha, who was angered after the incident, cursed the entire wedding retinue to be converted into stone images. When Yogeśvarī[26] stayed at Konkan, she was the *kuladaivata* of the *Kokaṇastha* Brāhmins. Her changed place of residence did not alter the faith of the *Kokaṇastha* Brāhmins in her. They continued to worship her in spite of the change in her residence (Kalegaonkar 2009, 22-25).

Apart from the four myths, there are some songs in the oral tradition that mention the broken marriage of Ambe Jogāī (Matekar 2003, 101). One of them says:

> Under the canopy of the sky and on tarmac of the ground
> My Jogāī remains deprived of the marriage unbound.
> My compassionate Joga-māī, why she is so angry?
> Swallowed her Lord, who was devotion hungry.

My study of Yogeśvarī can be represented through figure 9.2.

26 In this narrative, Kalegaonkar has shifted suddenly to the use of the word 'Yogeśvarī' rather than 'Tripurasundarī'. It seems to me that he has used the word Tripurasundarī rather loosely in this narrative.

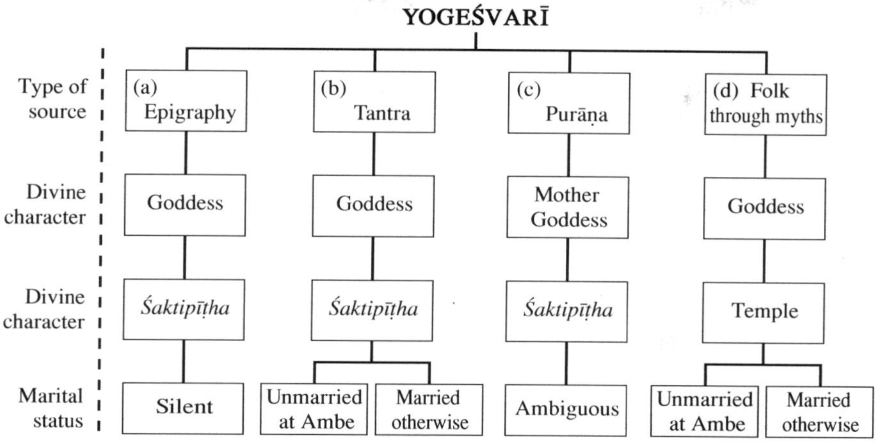

Figure 9.2 The purāṇic and mythological status of Goddess Ambejogāī.

By studying the various strands (a, b, c, d in the diagram provided here) emerging out of the study of Yogeśvarī, the ambivalent nature of the goddess becomes evident. The epigraphic sources accept Yogeśvarī as a *śaktipīṭha* but are silent about her marital status. The Tantric tradition regards Yogeśvarī as a *śaktipīṭha* but underline her as unmarried at Ambe and married elsewhere. The Puranic tradition reveres Yogeśvarī as a mother goddess, but is ambiguous about her marital status. Lastly, the folk traditions consider Yogeśvarī's shrine as a prominent religious place but reiterate her marital status as married elsewhere, but unmarried at Ambe. The diagram clearly indicates strong points of agreement between the Tantric tradition and folk tradition regarding the nature of Yogeśvarī as a virgin in the geography of Ambe and as a consort elsewhere.

The virgin status of the goddess Yogeśvarī or Jogāī is an isolated case that is geographically specific. It is the folk tradition of myths, supported by the Tantric tradition, that has contributed to the virgin status of the goddess.

The myths of the broken marriage of Ambe Jogāī and her virginity, transmitted through oral tradition, and their conspicuous absence in religious texts and historical data, suggest a gradual transformation in the nature of the goddess. Religious texts and historical data show the adaptation of this goddess in multiple texts, but the oral tradition indicates the movement of this goddess in a specific Sanskritised Brāhminic direction. It indicates the migration of a goddess along with migrating people. Here the goddess has not migrated in a physical form, but identical myths in two different regions have served the main purpose of the migrating

Kokaṇastha Brāhmin community, which was to find a means to elevate themselves in the Brāhminic hierarchy.

The first myth is of local origin. It shows the movement of the goddess within the periphery of the shrine, but a critical point of this myth is the presence of a site of goddess Reṇukā, the mother goddess, indicating an inter-relationship discussed earlier in this chapter.

The second myth indicates the travel and return of a goddess from the coast to the plateau. It also indicates the dual form of the goddess, as a virgin in the evening and a married woman in the morning.

The third myth indicates travel but no return and adds the motif of a curse.

The fourth myth mentions migration of girls from Ambe Jogāī, due to marriage. It also underlines the acceptance of this goddess as the main deity of the community situated far away from the goddess's home town. This myth opens up a few different scenarios:

A. It underlines the later addition of this goddess in the *Kokaṇastha* religious fold;

B. It indicates the lower status of *Kokaṇastha*s in the Brāhminic hierarchy;

C. It indicates that girls have migrated from Ambe Jogāī to the Konkan region for the purpose of marriage;

D. It sanctifies the position of the *kumārikā* in the *boḍaṇa* ritual.

Since Jogāī herself is regarded as a *kumārī*, the young girl present during *boḍaṇa* replicates her. According to Dixit (2003), this ritual is a remnant of ancient fertility cults. The custom of *boḍaṇa* is also prevalent among *Kokaṇastha* people who worship the goddess 'Ambābāī' (Ambā means mother goddess of the fertility cult). In several Citpāvana families, the *boḍaṇa* ritual is performed after childbirth; in some families it is even performed following the successful delivery of a cow in the animal shed. Dixit and others have also attempted to trace the ritual in practices of non-Vedic traditions of Maharashtra as well as in the Tantric tradition described in the *Merutantra*, but has not noted the role of the *kumārī* in the *boḍaṇa* ritual. The process of continuously adding milk and milk products stops only when the *kumārī* is gratified (Dixit et al, 2003, 94-95).

The oral tradition of *aratis* sung at the culmination point of *pūjā* during the *boḍaṇa* ritual mentions Yogeśvarī, one of which follows:

Victory to thee, O Mother Yogeśvarī,
I perform the *āratī*, you bestow good fortune.
We have filled *boḍaṇa* for happiness and peace.
Young girl (*kumārī*) and married women are very happy.
We have bathed you in milk, sugar, honey, curds and clarified butter.
We salute you again, may you give us blessings.
We fill *boḍaṇa* when the family line is extended (after the birth of a son).
We give offerings of *puraṇa* (sweet dish made of Bengal gram), pulses, sweet porridge.
We gratify the young girl (*kumārī*) and see Ambā in her.
O Ambā visit us again. Bless us for prosperity. Forgive our mistakes and take me (who has sought refuge at your feet) in your womb (Bhide 2011, 19).

The myth of the broken marriage is identical to the myth about the goddess Kanyākumārī, whose marriage was also fixed with Śiva. Śiva did not turn up at the right time. The marriage broke and the goddess remained a virgin. A similar myth of broken marriage is also attached to the goddess Mahālakṣmī of Dahanu in the Thane district of Maharashtra. The motif of the goddess getting angry and settling in a particular place distant from the proposed groom is seen in all the three cases.

Mythologies across cultures have incorporated virgin goddesses in the pantheon of deities.[27] In Hindu tradition, Śaiva-Śākta traditions referred to by Tantric texts such as the *Rudrayāmalatantra* indicate virgin worship (*kumārikā-pūjā*). Virgin worship is classified in two ways: a girl who has not attained puberty; and a youthful unmarried girl. Durgā, the slayer of the demon Mahiṣa, was a virgin in the second sense. Her virginity indicates unmanifested and dormant fertility. Sukumari Bhattacharji (1970, 164) has explained the dual nature of Durgā; Durgā, referred to as Pārvatī, is the mother goddess. Thus virgin worship in the Puranic tradition does not refer to a young girl before puberty. Tantric tradition gives

27 Artemis, the Greek goddess, is portrayed as a virgin. Zeus had granted her the boon of eternal virginity. She is also regarded as the goddess of childbirth. Also in Greek mythology, Athena and Hestia are regarded as virgin goddesses. Diana, in Roman mythology, was known as the virgin goddess of childbirth and women. Diana, Minerva and Vesta, three maiden goddesses, swore that they would never marry. It is worth noting that, even though they were virgins, mythology depicts them as goddesses responsible for childbirth.

significance to girls from age one to sixteen. The *Rudrayāmalatantra* (II. 6. 94–102) mentions worshipping such virgins and the fruit attained after the ritual; according to this text, a young, unmarried girl of sixteen is called Ambikā and is identified as Yoginī.[28]

The relationship of Jogāī with Citpāvanas (*Kokaṇastha*) Brāhmins

The *Citpāvanas*, who claim their place of origin as Guhagar in the Konkan region, worship a goddess named Durgādevī, situated at Guhagar. She is not worshipped in the form of an aniconic stone, but is embodied in an iconographic image possessing multiple hands and slaying a demon, namely Durgā-*mahiṣāsuramardinī.* But she is regarded as the consort of Vyāḍeśvara, the *kuladaivata* (family-god) of the *Citpāvana*s, and at times she is mentioned as Durgā-Vyāḍeśvarī, whose second epithet is Jogeśvarī. This goddess is dual in nature, being a virgin in the evening and a married woman in the morning.[29] In the first myth of broken marriage recounted above, it is Durgādevī from Guhagar who breaks her marriage with Vaijanātha/Vaidyanātha of Parali, as claimed by the oral tradition.

The *Sahyādrikhaṇḍa* mentions the origin of *Kokaṇastha,* alias *Citpāvana, Brāhmins.* It is said that Paraśurāma created them from dead bodies and directed them to perform religious rites for this region. *Śataprasnakalpalatikā*, a work discussing the origin of castes in Maharashtra, mentions *Citpāvana*s as among the lowest in the caste hierarchy of the Brāhmins.[30] Historical records of medieval Maharashtra indicate the rise of this community during the Peśvā rule. Initially, *Deśastha* Brāhmins were the office-bearers during the rule of Śivājī, the founder of the Maratha rule in the Deccan. But, after the rise of the Peśvā Balaji Vishvanatha Bhat, from the Konkan region, the centre of power shifted from *Deśastha* to *Kokaṇastha* Brāhmins. However, the *Deśastha*s, in their capacity as *joshi*s and *kulkarni*s (maintaining records of land and of villages), still controlled power at the micro level. The strife between these two communities was fuelled during the Peśvā rule, when the Peśvās were denied the right to use the Godāvarī Ghats at Nasik

28 *Rudrayāmalatantra* II. 7. 33ab: *kumārī yoginī sākṣāt kumārī parādevatā.*

29 An interesting parallel to this is the headless goddess Lajjāgaurī. Although she is portrayed iconographically, as a perpetual virgin, she is also considered to be the same as Bhūmātā, the Mother Goddess (Bapat 2008, 87).

30 This work is available in only in manuscript form and has been shared with me by Shri Deepak Gore. It deals with the rituals and rites, as well as the origin, of the Brāhmins. It was written by one Madhava in early eighteenth century.

(Kumar 2004, 37). *Deśastha* families have three patron family goddesses, Saptaśṛṅgī, Mahālakṣmī and Tuḷajā Bhavānī. Other goddesses worshipped, if any, are affiliated to these three. These are the three and half *śaktipīṭha*s located in Maharashtra.[31]

The goddesses of *Kokaṇastha*s were the minor goddesses from the Konkan region. In an attempt to elevate the community to be on par with the *Deśastha* community, Jogāī of Ambe must have been appropriated as the deity of *Kokaṇastha*s. This gave an independent identity and an elevated status to the migrating community. The documents of the Marathas during the Peśvā rule include an exchange of letters noting religious, political and social developments and upheavals with the Peśvā family; these letters indicate that the Peśvā, Madhavarao I, visited Ambe Jogāī in March 1772 (Gune 1996, 412). He was not keeping well. He went to Pandharpur and Tulajapur and visited Ambe Jogāī on the way. The place has been mentioned along with Pandharpur and Tulajapur in Peśvā records and indicates the importance given to Ambe Jogāī by the Peśvā family. This region was under the rule of the Nizam of Hyderabad and was known as Mominabad. Therefore, very few *Kokaṇastha* families migrated to this region. Records indicate that four families migrated to Beed (Kunte 2007, 586). Among them was Chintaman Kanitkar who was the *jahagirdar* of this region. The Kanitkars worship Vyāḍeśvara and Ambe Jogāī as their clan deities. An oral communication has revealed that two *Kokaṇastha* families from Ratnagiri settled at the Ambe Jogāī village around 1930-40.[32] This settlement occurred through the increasing religious activity of *Kokaṇastha* Brāhmins over the last century. The *Kokaṇastha* Brāhmin community has recently started building a guest-house for the community as more and more people are visiting this place with improvements in transport and communication. It is regarded as mandatory for the families of *Kokaṇastha* Brāhmins, whose *kulasvāminī* is Jogāī, to visit and seek blessings of the goddess and invite her to attend auspicious events such as marriage and the thread ceremony.

When I studied specific *kulavṛttānta*s (family records) of families with Ambe Jogāī as their *kulasvāminī*, I found that families with the same

31 The reason for the use of the term 'half *śaktipīṭha*' is unclear. One explanation is that according to Yoga and Tantric philosophy, Shakti manifests itself in the form of *Kuṇḍalinī* in our body. It is described as a female serpent that sleeps in the *Mūladhara Cakra,* turning its body into three and half folds. These three and a half folds of Kuṇḍalinī are compared with the four seats of Śaktis in the four *śaktipīṭha*s of Maharashtra.

32 Conversation with Shri Ganesh Joshi, Ambe Jogāī, 12 December 2011.

surnames did not necessarily worship the same goddess. For example, the Bapat *kulavṛttānta* mentions Ambe Jogāī, Yogeśvarī of Guhagar and Yogeśvarī of Kalambaste as *kulasvāminīs*. These two deities appear to be different because they are housed in different shrines. However, since the names are similar, Bapat families living in the periphery of Guhagar and Kalambaste prefer worshipping Yogeśvarī of Guhagar and Yogeśvarī of Kalambaste.

Jogāīs in the Konkan region

I shall now discuss the temple of Jogāī at Pirandavne in the Ratnagiri district, which was built by Shankarbhat Sathye in 1687. He installed a marble effigy of the goddess in the temple and the reason is mentioned as being that, because the original place of Jogāī is far off, it was difficult to visit it on a regular basis. Along with the Sathye families, this goddess is worshipped by the Gondhalekar, Dharu, Govande, Bhave, Bapat and Ghanekar families. The temple has been rebuilt and a new statue in black stone has been installed. 'She is the same Jogāī from Ambe, but has been shifted only to facilitate regular worship', testified the *Gurav pujārī*. The image of Jogāī here wears the *maṅgalasūtra*, a symbol of marriage in Hinduism. A temple of Someśvara is located in the temple complex. The *maṅgalasūtra* and the temple of her lord within close proximity suggest that this may well be the beginning of appropriation of the local goddess Jogāī on a micro level.

Another Jogāī or Jugāī located at Ratnagiri is the guardian goddess of this city (Kunte 2007, 408). Her temple complex has an effigy of her male consort, Bhairī (the Prakritised form of Bhairava). This evidence goes hand in hand with the literary reference in the *Rudrayāmalatantra* that she is the consort of Bhairava. It also supports Sontheimer's thesis about Jogāī/Yogeśvarī having been married to Bhairava. Surprisingly, this Jogāī is not worshipped by the *Kokaṇastha* Brāhmins at all. This would indicate that Jogāī as a goddess was not generally appropriated. It was the appropriation of one particular Jogāī, namely Yogeśvarī of Ambe, because of identical myths of broken marriage occurring in two different regions. The significance and sanctity of the shrine since ancient times contributed to its appropriation by the ruling Peśvas.

Chapekar (1938, 117-119) was of the opinion that there is no connection between Ambe Jogāī and *Kokaṇastha*s. He arrived at this conclusion from statistical evidence of 1100 *Kokaṇastha* families out of which only fifty-nine mentioned Jogāī as their *kuladevatā*. These families had settled in the Deccan. However, one point grossly ignored by Chapekar is that many families refer to Jogāī in combination with Vyāḍeśvara. Joglekar (2013) refutes Chapekar's argument and says that 'about 80% of Chitpavans have Vyadeshwar and Yogeshwari as Kulswamy and Kulswamini'.

It is evident that there was large-scale migration of the *Kokaṇasthas* to the Deccan during the Peśvā rule. The Peśvās had given a grant to the temple for offering the midday meal to the goddess (Kalegaonkar 2009, 29). This contributed to the popularity of the goddess as the *kuladaivata* of *Kokaṇastha* Brāhmins. Regular visits to the family-goddess situated in the place of origin were not possible, owing to difficult terrain and uncertain political conditions as the area of Ambe was under the rule of the Nizam of Hyderabad. I suggest that the nature and identical myths of two goddesses situated in far-off places are other reasons for the acceptance of Ambe Jogāī as the goddess within the *Kokaṇastha* pantheon. Besides, the nature of the family-goddess is defined in the *Skandapurāṇa*. She is the Yoginī, established for the protection of the *Brāhmins*, for the welfare of the people, and for extending the lineage. The *Purāṇa* says that such a goddess is called *kuladevī*.[33]

Practices prevalent at the Ambe Jogāī temple

Śaktipīṭhas in Maharashtra and elsewhere in India have been known to make blood offerings to the goddess,[34] but such practices are not in vogue for the goddess Ambe Jogāī. This is consistent with the fact that the goddess is the clan deity for Brāhmins who are strictly vegetarians. Those who regularly worship the goddess bearing a basket, a garland and lighted lamp are known as *ārādhī/ārādhinīs*. These worshippers dance in the procession of the goddess every Tuesday and Friday (Kalegaonkar 2009, 29). On Friday, the procession starts with an attractive palanquin of the goddess with her image in the outskirts of the temple. She is seated either on

33 The *Skandapurāṇa Brahmakhaṇḍa, Dharmāraṇyamāhātmya* X. 106-107: *rakṣaṇārtham hi viprāṇām lokānām hitakāmyayā / gotrānprati tathikaikā sthāpitā yoginī tathā / yasya gotrasya yā śaktirrakṣaṇe pālane kṣamā / sā tasya kuladevīti sākṣāt tatra babhūva ha.*

34 Offerings of goats are given to the goddesses Tuḷajā Bhavānī and Saptaśṛṅgī of Vani. The male and female worshippers, who are released in the name of the goddess, are called *jogtī, ārādhī, bhutye,* etc. They carry the emblems of the goddess, which are in the form of a garland of shells *(cowrie)*, symbolising the vagina, and a basket (*parḍī*), having the effigy of the goddess. The basket is a miniature world of the goddess. The worshippers ask for *jogvā* (offering of food or money) in the name of the goddess.

a lion or on an eagle. The *ārādhī* and *ārādhinī*s proclaim 'glory to the goddess'. The procession of the goddess takes place on the full moon days of the months of *Āśvina*, *Kārtika*, *Mārgaśīrṣa* (approximately October-December) and *Māgha* (approximately February). Temple authorities claim that no individual is permanently dedicated to the goddess, either willingly or forcibly. According to oral information, the rituals associated with the goddess include chanting of the *Śrīsūkta* , recitation of the *Devīmāhātmya* and *Navacaṇḍihoma* (fire sacrifices accompanied with the chanting of the *Devīmāhātmya*), and autumn and spring *navarātri* celebrations. *Boḍaṇa*, *kumārikāpūjana* for the *Kokaṇastha* families, is also a part of the worship-service offered by the temple.[35] It is considered mandatory for the *Kokaṇastha* families worshipping Ambe Jogāī as the *kuladaivata* to visit the place and offer worship-service to the goddess after auspicious ceremonies, such as the thread ceremony and marriage, and after childbirth. Feldhaus suggests that the story establishes the connection of the *Kokaṇastha*s with the place far inland on Deśa (Deccan plateau). The goddess's trip is enacted in the lives and imaginations of the *Kokaṇastha* Brāhmins again and again through their visit to this place (Feldhaus 2003, 118-119). All of the above rituals also denote the Brāhminical type of worship addressed to the goddess. *Kumārikā* worship is performed in certain families of Brāhmins who are other than *Kokaṇastha*, but it is not undertaken as a ritualistic procedure like that of *boḍana*. This ritual is performed by the *Kokaṇasthas* exclusively.

Initially, Yogeśvarī, the shrine of goddess Ambe Jogāī, was a centre of multiple religious cults and amorphous in nature. One may observe that this centre was a combination of Nātha and Tantra tradition. The Puranic narrative tradition added the element of protective mother goddess, one who destroyed the demon Dantāsura. This Puranic narrative is similar to that of the *Karavīramāhātmya* and the *Mumbādevīmāhātmya*. These *māhātmya*s are smaller versions of their archetype, the *Devīmāhātmya*, wherein the exploits of the Goddess have pan-Indian Brāhminical recognition. The goddess is eulogised as the destroyer of Mahiṣāsura, and here Yogeśvarī is praised because she slays Dantāsura. The narrative has a supra-national location, although individual episodes have regional significance. The place Jayantī, where the narrative supposedly occurred, is regarded as the certain centre of the earth, easily accessible to all the

35 I am indebted to Sunder Khadke, Associate Professor, Kholeshwar College, Ambe Jogai, Dr Sharad Hebalkar, Bharat Itihas Sankalan Samiti, and Principal Dr Kisan Pawar, Lokamanya Tilak College, Valavani, Beed, for this information.

sages residing in Naimiṣāraṇya.[36] Such narrative techniques employed in *Sthala* and *Devatāmāhātmyas* heighten the significance of the place of pilgrimage. Here, the regional identity merges into pan-Indian religious identity.

The elevation of any temple is distinguished by three characteristics: daily performance of *pūjā*; recognition by all castes; and more than local importance (Eschmann *et al.* 1978, 125ff). These three characteristics are visible in the case of Ambe Jogāī. Patronage by the *Peśvās* enjoined at this shrine led to Brāhminisation of this temple. This also reveals the problematic and complex dynamics of appropriation. The case of Jogāī becomes distinct because Brāhminisation has worked on two levels. Firstly, it took the goddess out of her local contexts; secondly, acceptance of this goddess elevated the status of a community. As discussed earlier, the *Kokaṇastha* Brāhmin community was facing severe discrimination within the sub-caste hierarchy. This socio-political motivation behind the appropriation of the goddess as the *kuladevatā* of the *Kokaṇastha*s brought the deity within the ambit of royal patronage. Historical, epigraphic and written tradition underlined the supernatural, benevolent and maleficent aspects of the goddess. The oral tradition of identical myths of broken marriage merged the identity of Durgādevī of Guhagar and Ambe Jogāī as one goddess. The *Kokaṇastha* Brāhmins who migrated to the Deccan found access to the shrine of Ambe Jogāī far easier than to shrines of their deities located in Konkan.

Development of a temple as a leading centre of worship is a process which involves cross-fertilisation of various religious and cultural forces. The effigy of the goddess is in the form of an aniconic stone. As Bolon (1997, 68) rightly points out, 'Tribal shrines usually contain aniconic symbols in the form of stones, sticks, pots etc.' The aniconic form of Yogeśvarī at Ambe Jogāī has not changed, but she has been given a pair of eyes, lips, a *kumkum* (vermillion) mark on the forehead etc. Eschmann, Kulke and Tripathi (1978, 91) write, 'The first requirement of an anthropomorphic image is certainly a head.' Therefore, the aniconic stone has partial anthropomorphic elements superimposed on it. This process is not restricted to the aniconic stone only. The other shrines of goddess Yogeśvarī have the goddess in anthropomorphic form. It is claimed that this is in accordance with the *Rudrayāmalatantra,* which describes the goddess as beautiful, endowed with sword, basket, gold ornaments,

36 The river Jayantī flows through Ambe Jogāī. In the *Yogeśvarīmāhātmya*, the place is identified with the river.

plough and a pestle.[37] The Yogeśvarī temple at Pirandavane is said to have these implements, which have been designed in accordance with the advice of the Śaṅkaracārya of Shringeri.

Dynamics of appropriation

As I have mentioned before, appropriation can be a journey of any object, entity or concept away from its origin. Historical, epigraphic and literary traditions directing Jogāī to be a mother goddess have been removed from their original context and the nature of the goddess has been encrypted. What emerges on the surface is her virginity due to the broken marriage preserved through oral tradition. This oral myth and some excerpts from the Tantric tradition have been recontextualised in accordance with the requirement of the dominant ruling class. A feminist interpretation of this myth of broken marriage has recently been advanced by Kalegaonkar (2009, 8), who argues that Jogāī refused to marry her groom in order to maintain her individual identity.

The preferential access to religious material by the dominant ruling class during the Peśvā rule paved the way for this change of identity of the goddess. The recontextualisation of the goddess was deliberately intended to establish the supremacy of the ruling caste in the Brāhminical hierarchy. As the goddess did not belong to the group of three and a half *śaktipīṭhas*, which were (and still continue to be) of prime significance, sub-castes or subordinate castes did not object to this change. It must have become easy to reconstitute matriarchal imagery in a renewed set-up. The socio-political motivation behind her modified form must have been explored by the dominant ruling caste of Brāhmins, rather than exploited within intersecting power trajectories. In this process her regional and religious identification as a Śākta mother goddess was relegated to the background and she was reconstituted as a virgin goddess within a renewed Brāhminic power framework. The co-existence of myths within diverse regions worked as a tool for this cultural appropriation and elevated the goddess from her temporal and spatial constraints as a local mother goddess to a revered *kuladaivata* of the then dominant ruling class.

37 Plough and pestle indicate the agrarian roots of the goddess and justify her original nature as mother goddess.

Acknowledgements

The author expresses sincere thanks to Professor Sunder Khadke, Dr Sharad Hebalkar, Dr Kisan Pawar and Dr Anand Khare for their valuable input and is indebted to Dr McComas Taylor and Dr Jayant Bapat, both from Australia, for sharing their insights.

Bibliography

Ajgaonkar, J. R. 1957. *Prācīna Marāṭhi Santakavi* [in Marathi]. Vol 1. Mumbai.

Altekar, A.S. 1934. *The Rashtrakutas and Their Times (*Poona Oriental Series no. 36). Poona: Oriental Book Agency.

Bapat, Jayant Bhalchandra. 2008. *'The Lajjāgaurī: mother, wife or yoginī'*. In *The Iconic Female: Goddesses of India, Nepal and Tibet,* edited by J.B. Bapat and I.W. Mabbett. Clayton, Monash Asia Institute.

Bhattacharji, Sukumari. 1970. *The Indian Theogony: A Comparative Study of Indian Mythology from the Vedas to the Puranas*. Cambridge: Cambridge University Press.

Bhide, Vasudha. 2011. *Citpāvana āṇi Citpāvanī* [in Marathi]. Pune: V. Bhide.

Bolon, Carol Radcliffe. 1997. *Forms of the Goddess: Lajja Gauri in Indian Art*. New Delhi: Motilal Banarsidass.

Briggs, George Weston. 2009. *Gorakhnath and the Kanphata Yogis*. New Delhi: Motilal Banarsidass. (First published in Kolkata, 1938.)

Chapekar, N.G. 1938. *Citpāvana* [in Marathi]. Pune: Arya Sanskriti Mudranalaya.

Cunha, J. Gerson da. 1877. *Skandapurāṇāntargatam Sahyādrikhaṇḍam*. Bombay.

Dange, S.A.1996. *Towards Understanding Hindu Myths*. Delhi: Aryan Books International.

Dehejia, Vidya. 1986. *Yogini Cult and Temples: A Tantric Tradition*. Delhi: National Museum.

Deshpande, Brahmanand. 2010. *Dakṣiṇacya Madhyayugīna Itihāsācī Sādhane* [in Marathi]. 4 vols., edited by G.H. Khare and re-edited by B. Deshpande. Pune: Bharat Itihas Samshodhak Mandal.

Dhere, R.C. 2004. *Lajjāgaurī* [in Marathi]. Pune: Shree Vidya Prakashan.

Dikshit, M.G. 2010. *Dakṣiṇacya Madhyayugīna Itihāsācī Sādhane* [in Marathi]. Book IV, edited by G.H. Khare and re-edited by B. Deshpande. Pune: Bharat Itihas Samshodhak Mandal.

Dixit, J; Joshi, A; Dixit, R. 2003. *Chitpavanism: a tribute to Chitpavan Brāhmin culture: the way we were.* Pune: Encyclopedia Maharashtrica, Dixit Publishers.

Dixit, M.S. 2003. 'Citpāvanāncī sāmājika mūḷa piṭhīkā, madhya va sadyasthitī'. In *Āhmī Citpāvana-Kokaṇastha*. Pune: Neelakantha Prakashan.

Eschmann, A., H. Kulke and G. Tripathi. 1978. *The Cult of Jagannatha and the Regional Tradition of Orissa.* New Delhi: Manohar; Heidelberg University South Asia Institute.

Feldhaus Anne. 2003. *Connected Places: Region, Pilgrimage and Geographical Imagination in India*. New York: Palgrave Macmillan.

Gaitonde, V.D. 1972. *Skandapurāṇāntargatam Sahyādrikhaṇḍam*. Bombay: Katyayani Publishers.

Gune, V.T. 1996. *Survey and Calendar of Marathi Documents 1600-1818.* Calcutta: K. P. Bagchi and Company.

Hazra, R.C. 1975. *Studies in the Puranic Records on Hindu Rites and Customs*. Delhi: Motilal Banarsidass. (First ed. published in Dacca, 1940.)

Joglekar, A.V. 2013. 'Kulvrutta'. www.chitpavan.net/html//Kulvrutta.htm (accessed 20 February 2013; no longer available at this URL).
Joshi, P.N. 2004. *Nāthasāmpradāya: Udaya va Vistāra* [in Marathi]. Pune: Anjali Publishing House.
Kalegaonkar, Laksmanrao. 2009. *Śrī Yogeśvarī Māhātmya Darśana* [in Marathi]. Ambe Jogai: Ratnakar Prakashan.
Karve, Irawati. 1928. 'The Chitpavan Brāhmins: a social and ethnic study' M.A. thesis (Abstract in *Research in Sociology, 95-100.* Delhi: Indian Council for Social Science Research, 1989).
Kinsley, David. 1998. *Tantric Visions of the Divine Feminine*. Delhi: Motilal Banarasidass.
Kumar, Ravinder. 2004. *Western India in the Nineteenth Century*. London: Routledge. (First ed. published in 1968.)
Kunte, Moreshwar. 2007. *Devadarśana: Jilhā Ratnāgirī* [in Marathi]. Pune, privately printed.
Matekar, Harihar. 2003. *Śrī Yogeśvarī Māhātmya* [in Marathi]. Ambe Jogai: Yogeshvari Devasthan.
Nagaswamy, R. 1982. *Tantric Cult of South India*. Delhi: Agama Kala Prakashan.
Parpola, Asko. 1992. 'The metamorphoses of Mahisa Asura and Prajāpati'. In *Ritual, State and History in South Asia: Essays in Honour of J.C. Heesterman*, edited by A.W. van den Hoek, D.H.A. Kolff, and M.S. Oort. Leiden: Brill.
Prabhudesai, R. P. 2005. *Devīkośa* [in Marathi]. Pune: Anjali Publishing House.
Ranade, U. n.d. *Śrīdevī: Jogave, Gāṇī va Āratīsaṅgraha*. Pune: Shree Yogeshvari Prakashan.
Rao, Gopinatha T.A. 1997. *Elements of Hindu Iconography*. Vol II, Part I, Delhi: Motilal Banarasidass. (First published 1914.)
Roy, Anamika. 2004. 'The myth of the Great Tradition and Little Tradition perspectives'. In *Indian History*, edited by A.K. Sinha. New Delhi: Anamika Publishers.
Schneider, Arnd. 2003. 'On "appropriation": a critical reappraisal of the concept and its application in global art practices'. *Social Anthropology* 11 (2): 215-229.
Shastri, Ajay Mitra. 1972. *Yadava Inscriptions from Ambe Jogai* (Vishveshvaranand Indological Series 56). Hoshiarpur: Vishveshvaranand Vedic Research Institute.
Sircar, D.C. 2004. *The Śākta Pīṭhas*. Delhi: Motilal Banarasidass. (First ed. published in 1973.)
Sontheimer, Gunther-Dietz. 1997. 'Some incidents in the history of the god Khaṇḍobā'. In *King of Hunters, Warriors, and Shepherds: Essays on Khaṇḍobā*, edited by A. Feldhaus, A. Malik and H. Bruchner. New Delhi: Manohar.
Sontheimer, Gunther-Dietz. 2006. 'Forest and pastoral goddesses: independence and assimilation'. In *Feminist Approach to Religion*, edited by Subhadra Channa. New Delhi: Cosmo Publications.
Tagare, G.V. 1980. *Śrīkaravīra Māhātmya*. Kolhapur: Shivaji University.
Tripathi, Bhagirathprasad. 1980. *Rudrayāmalatantra* [in Sanskrit]. Varanasi: Sampurananand Samskrit Vishvavidyalaya.
Tripathi, Bhagirathprasad. 1998 (1985). *Śrīharivaṁśapurāṇam*. Delhi: Nag Publications.
Tripathi, Bhagirathprasad. 2008 (1983). *Śrīmārkaṇḍeyamahāpurāṇam.* Delhi, Nag Publications.

Chapter 10

The Female Protector of Yolmo's Hidden Land

David Templeman

According to Tibetan belief it is well known that certain 'hidden lands' exist, scattered as they are throughout much of the Himalayan region and the plateau of Tibet. Where are these 'hidden lands,' what function do they fulfil, why are they 'hidden' and how do they manage to remain sequestered? In examining these questions some focus will necessarily be upon the female *protectrices*, the local goddesses who sometimes act as gatekeepers to such lands and maintain them against those seeking inappropriate entry.[1]

A further aspect of these intriguing figures which I wish to pursue briefly in this chapter is the occurrence of similar figures with analogous functions in the old Iranian culture, a civilisation with which Tibet almost certainly had contacts in the sixth to ninth centuries CE. In positing this link I suggest that there is some *prima facie* evidence to believe that such female protective deities as the female protectors of hidden lands might be part of a far more wide-ranging cultural phenomenon than has been recognised up to now. In the cases of both Tibet and Iran, we may note that female, local, cultic goddesses have been suborned into their revised roles as subsidiary protectors of a more recent major religious system, that of Himalayan Buddhism, while at the same time being permitted to retain much of their earlier, cultic power and awesomeness.

The place: locating Pematsal / Yolmo Gangra

This preliminary study focuses on just one 'hidden land,' that of Pematsal (Tibetan: *padma tshal*), the so-called 'Lotus Grove'. Pematsal is also known

1 In a more contemporary nightclub terminology they might be referred to as 'door bitches of the hidden lands'.

as Yolmo Gangra (Tibetan: *yol mo gangs ra*) and is located approximately fifty kilometres north of Kathmandu, the capital city of Nepal. It sits in the region of Yolmo and the land runs parallel with a tributary stream that leads into the Trisuli river. The valley is an area well trodden by trekkers over the last forty-five years or more. However, according to the superimposed conditions of entry and survival there which delimit that site as a 'hidden land', none of those trekkers are likely to have even seen it in their expeditions. Even if they had caught a glimpse of the actual valley, according to local belief they would have been utterly unable to recognise it for what it actually was.

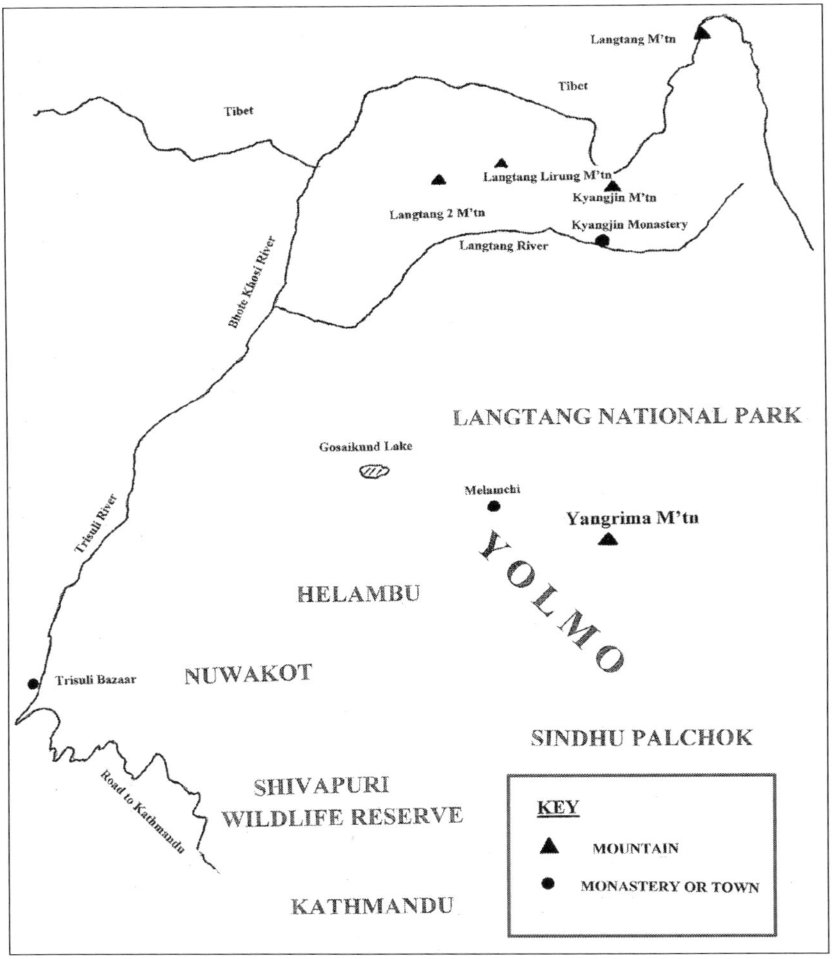

Figure 10.1: Map of Langtang/Helambu.

The mythical foundations of a 'hidden land'

The 'hidden land' of Yolmo Gangra was said to have been established sometime in the seventh to eighth century by the great culture hero Padmasambhava, who is said to have come originally from the area of Tokharistan in the north of what is modern-day Afghanistan. He is believed to have subdued the local autochthonous, and frequently malicious, deities and converted them to Buddhism so that they would act as a corps of protectors of that hidden land. This act of subjugation and conversion was performed by him in many other areas of the Himalayas, but for the purposes of this chapter I only focus on the specific area of Yolmo.

These lands were intended to remain as places of tranquillity and safety, where crops grew spontaneously, strife and war were unknown, life was long and disease-free and religion was able to be practised without any hindrance whatsoever. To ensure that the lands were not entered for purely adventitious purposes and that their actual location and entry points remained secret, many such places were 'sealed' through Tantric ritual and this sacred secrecy has been perpetuated through the placement of various gatekeepers, all of whom had been those previous malicious local deities who had been subjugated by Padmasambhava.

The location of such lands and the conditions of entry to them were intended to have been revealed by certain 'site-revealers' at various future times when the existing social and political conditions would necessitate access to such places. There exist many instances of refugees from political or religious strife seeking access to hidden lands in Tibet, but tragically perishing in abject circumstances because the mystically sealed 'entry doors' to the lands were unable to be opened, even by the skilled lamas leading them there. An early example is found in Bacot (1912), who encountered the remnants of precisely such a pitiful group, most of them dead through starvation, because their lama was unable to locate the secret portal to the land (Tibetan: *gnas*) of *Padma-bkod*, referred to by Bacot as Népémakö (Place of Arrayed Lotuses).

As for Yolmo Gangra, the subject of the present chapter, it remained secret and apparently inviolate until the latter part of the seventeenth century CE when it was revealed by the Tibetan site-discoverer, Rigzin Nyida Longsel (Tibetan: *rig 'dzin nyi zla klong gsal*), who died in 1695.

Texts concerning Yolmo Gangra

Franz-Karl Ehrhard (1997) has thoroughly explored the various literatures which describe the origin myths, the various routes into, and the layout of Yolmo Gangra and has discussed them. In this work he has noted the existence of a certain text named the Chötin Norbu Doshal (Tibetan: *mChod sprin nor bu do shal*) which translates as 'The Cloud of Offerings, a Jewelled Necklace', which Ehrhard had been unable to identify at the time of writing. Purely by chance I managed to find a handwritten manuscript (possibly seventeenth to eighteenth century) which appears to have come from Yolmo and contained two texts containing the name 'Cloud of Offerings' within their titles.

These texts are: 'Béyül Yolmo Gangray Nédag Jomo Yangri Chugmö Chötin' (Tibetan: *sBas yul yol mo gang ra'i gnas bdag jo mo dbyangs ri phyug mo'i mchod sprin*), *'The Cloud of Offerings to the Presiding Deity of the Region, Jo Mo dByangs Ri Phyug Mo, Mistress of Gang Ra, the Hidden Land of Yol Mo'* (abbreviated title: *'Mistress of Gang Ra'*) (13 folio sides); and "Né Pematsal gyi Gosung Lhamo Chötin' (Tibetan: *gNas padma 'tshal gyis mgo bsrungs lha mo mchod phrin*), *'The Cloud of Offerings to the Doorkeeper of the Land of Pematsal'* (3 folio sides).

It will be noted that the Tibetan title of each text contains the expression 'Chötin' ('Cloud of Offering') and it might be reasonably assumed that they are of a similar type to the as yet undiscovered manuscripts referred to by Ehrhard (1997). Whether these texts form part of a 'Chötin ('Cloud of Offering') literary genre' I am unable to say at present. I am reasonably certain that they were written in Yolmo and reading shows that they clearly relate to the 'Hidden Land' of Pematsal/Yolmo Gangra. They are products of a quite unsophisticated and possibly local scribe, whose attempts at spelling complex ritual words sometimes vary as much as the spelling 'richl' does from 'ritual'.

'Primitive' underlays to a more recent Buddhism?

In my preliminary translation of these two texts I have found extremely detailed descriptions of the local deity known as Jomo Yangri Chugmo, the presiding *protectrice* of the valley. The texts also contain descriptions of the local *tsen* (*btsan*) demons and others, all of whom act as protectors or as outriders in the retinue of certain other protectors.

These descriptions are supported with some extremely violent iconography and some rather gruesome sentiments expressed towards supposed enemies of the Buddha's doctrine. I was immediately intrigued by this juxtaposition of the supposedly primitive, raw substratum with a more pacific and insightful Buddhist description. I say 'supposedly primitive' here because there is absolutely no evidence to support the contentious view that the range of violent, earth-born, blood-lusting and malevolent deities which are found in the texts are, in fact, of any greater antiquity than the advent of Buddhism to the area. Certainly, they might *appear* to be older because of their immediate connection to soil and blood, and our innate sensibility might insist upon the equation 'simpler = older'. However, such an equation may not be taken as fact under any circumstances. It remains simply a presumption and an assumption until the primacy of the violent and 'earthy' has been actually demonstrated consistently over many examples of similar materials from the same cultural area. More often than not, the violent aspects of such texts are couched within the confines of an overpoweringly Buddhist terminology and sentiment that effectively mask this possibly earlier and more ostensibly violent attitude. In this particular text this apparently 'primitive' material shone through and permitted the reader a somewhat different view of how those local deities, supposedly subjugated in the seventh–eighth centuries by Padmasambhava, *might* have actually appeared in both their form and demeanour before the advent of Buddhism and its tendency to smooth over the rough and inconvenient aspects of such deities.

So my assumption here is that, although their demeanour and form might not necessarily have preceded the advent of Buddhism, these violent and aggressive figures are portrayed in the way that they were imagined to have existed. This does not necessarily suggest that they in any manner possessed a greater antiquity *per se*, but definitely does regard them as being mental creations, as artefacts embodying the fears, aspirations iconographies, etc. of that early period.

Political territory and the geography of 'hidden lands'

It is from the sixteenth century that a certain process in certain sub-Himalayan areas, including Yolmo, may be clearly seen evolving. We may accurately date many of the texts that describe the paths to hidden lands of Yolmo and the nature of the protectors to the hidden lands, because their authors are particularly well-known identities in the area. From those discoveries emerges an overview of the process of the expansion and the actual opening up of such hidden lands into areas sometimes quite peripheral to other, existing focal points of power.[2] In other words, it might be suggested here that the post-sixteenth-century rapid expansion of 'hidden land discovery' was in part also a process of colonisation of new territories by those who were the patrons of the site-discoverers themselves. This process also reflected the inexorable advancement of the Nyingmapa (*rnying ma pa*) tradition throughout certain Himalayan areas.

The awesome[3] goddess, Jomo Yangri Chugmo

In the first of the texts to be considered below, 'The Cloud of Offerings to the Presiding Deity of the Region, Jo Mo dByangs Ri Phyug Mo, Mistress of Gang Ra, the Hidden Land of Yol Mo' (hereafter 'Mistress of Gang Ra'), we find important details concerning the process of 'revelation through composition' of the work itself. The work was composed by the sixteenth-century Nyingma (Tibetan: *rNying ma*) yogi named Ngagchang Shakya Zangpo (Tibetan: *sNgags 'chang shakya bzang po*) who was a renowned hidden land site-revealer. He was given detailed information about the various hidden lands in the Yolmo area by Rigzin Chogden Gonpo (Tibetan: *Rig 'dzin mchog ldan mgon po*). This by no means suggests that the actual contents of the text dated to the sixteenth century but rather allows us to attribute its contents to a timeless period. This sense of timelessness arises largely because of the continually reincarnated lineage of masters who were responsible for the transmission of the details of the land and its denizens who passed on the same types of story from one generation to the next. Hence, although doubtlessly a sixteenth- to seventeenth-century piece of writing, the contents more than likely extend back much further than that relatively recent period.

The land of Pematsal over which Jomo Yangri Chugmo presides possesses four gates, each facing one of the cardinal directions.[4] It is to

2 In fact, as Ehrhard (1997, 340-341) notes, these sites extended as far east as Bhutan, from where several of the texts dealing with the hidden sites in Yolmo, far to the west, originated.

3 Here I follow both the spelling and the intention of the word 'aweful' as discussed by Benard (1994).

4 The eastern gate points to Nyanang (Tibetan: *gNya' nang*), the western one to Mangyül (Tibetan: *Mang yul*), the southern one to Yolmo Gangra in the land of

the southern 'gateway', which faces towards 'Yolmo Gangra in the Land of Nepal', that our attention is immediately directed, because that is the portal protected by the awesome and wrathful Jomo Yangri Chugmo herself.

Jomo Yangri Chugmo enters the first of the two texts referred to above in several contrasting ways. Firstly she is described as being 'good and noble, possessed of a most beautiful bodily form, whitish-red in colour and wreathed in a radiant light' ('*Mistress of Gang Ra*' 2). She possesses the virtues one might expect from such a person and is dressed in silk brocades and the most costly and precious ornaments. In this form, pacific and beautiful, she might not be out of place represented in an image located on a Buddhist altar. We find her holding a precious rosary and several other symbols which reflect her Buddhist status. These attributes include that of bringing down a shower of *siddhi* powers upon those who retain their Tantric vows. Indeed, her name in translation means 'The Wealthy Lady of the Melodious Mountain' and this clearly reflects the mild and concerned attitude reflected in her Buddhist gentility. As to any 'pre-Buddhicisation' name as a demoness which might have attached to her, it is entirely possible that it has been forgotten locally, as I have failed to discover it within the body of the text. This name might be recalled among the ritual specialists of Yolmo who, although using this invocation, might have other texts at their disposal that might indeed shed light on any earlier name she might have possessed.

However, after a few verses of this type of admittedly fairly routine Buddhist description, we find that the textual descriptions of her change into a completely variant type. She appears in the heavens, riding a turquoise-blue dragon and attended by flashes of red lightning. She is flanked by her outriders, who comprise 100,000 Menmo (Tibetan: *sman mo*) demonesses, as well as countless *tsen* (Tibetan: *btsan*) malignant goblins and Nyen (Tibetan: *gnyan*) bringers of sickness. She is the uncontested mistress over all these creatures, who act as both her emissaries and her attendants. When travelling through the heavens they accompany her, riding on goats, wild yak, sheep and antelope, amidst flashes of lightning and fanned cosmic flames. The text then goes on to describe Jomo Yangri Chugmo in even more unrestrained and challenging terms:

Nepal (Tibetan: *Bal po'i yul gyi Yol mo gangs ra*) and the northern gate towards Gungtang (Tibetan: *Gung thang*) or, in another version of the text, to Palmotang (Tibetan: *dPal mo thang*) (Ehrhard 1997, 344).

In this land of *Yol mo*, surrounded as it is by mountains,
To those people who break their *samaya* vows,
In this period of great wrathfulness,
You will be (clearly) seen as a fearsome woman, black in colour.
You are possessed of long black hair which hangs down and sways like a willow tree.
You see with your three eyes, which are (always) open and raised upwards.
Your mouth is open and your sharp fangs snarl.
In your right hand are demon's snares.
Your left hand holds forth a sack containing various illnesses.
As for your retinue, you are surrounded by 100,000 demonesses,
All of them wearing the clothes of noble ladies.
As for those people who break their *samaya* vows
You open the neck of that sack of contagious illnesses and
Various illnesses of both humans and cattle may be seen inside.
May those who break their *samaya* vows have their lives cut off!
('*Mistress of Gang Ra*', folio 4)

Later in the text we find a series of chastisements aimed at those people who maintain their obdurately anti-Buddhist stance or who break their Tantric vows. For such people Jomo Yangri Chugmo promises that she will deliver punishment from a selection of the following horrendous possibilities:

- the demonic devouring of one's flesh
- a two-year infestation of one's cattle
- expulsion from one's own landholdings
- infestation by Gegs (Tibetan: *bgegs*) hindering demons
- ensnarement in the lassos of demons to await further punishment ('*Mistress of Gang Ra*', folio 7) (see Plate 10.2).

When not reflecting herself in either Buddhist or demonic form she may also manifest as something altogether more alluring.

The text says that in her adopted form as a sixteen-year-old maiden, her beautiful ornaments tinkle together as she moves and that her beautiful attendant maidens sway around her. There is a clear sexual sentiment hinted at in these few verses and this sense of attractiveness is just as important as her more orthodox and attractively innocent Buddhist manifestation referred to earlier or her more terrifying form.

This combination of allure and threat recalls the description of the troupe of *ḍākinīs* located in the far north-west of India, who were said to have been encountered by the eleventh-century CE Buddhist *mahāsiddha* Kṛṣṇācārya. In the hagiography recorded by the scholar from Mustang, Kunga Drölchog (*Kun dga' grol mchog*) in the sixteenth century he notes of these enigmatic women that some were

> ... very old ... their masses of white hair streaked with blonde, and (which) were decorated with nits, like salt sprinklings. One ... even had a beard ... (In contrast) ... others were youthful bodied ... and he became completely fascinated by their great beauty, and especially the nipples of their huge, firm and heavy breasts, their tawny hair, their many glistening decorations ... which ornamented their tresses like the various types of necklaces of radiant, fresh heavenly flowers belonging to the gods themselves. They were bedecked, all of them, most beautifully in sparkling white human bone ornaments ... these ... naked girls had hanging from them whole flayed human skins which they wore as aprons (Kunga Drölchog, F. 5B-F 6A).

This combination of highly alluring personal beauty and grave threat, manifested especially through the *ḍākinī*'s human bone and flayed skin adornments, recalls the duality of Eros and Thanatos, sexuality and destruction, discussed with such insight by Sigmund Freud (1922). This combination of attraction and threat is also of importance in the context of Jomo Yangri Chugmo in her wider context, for, as we shall note below, these same elements are also shared by the Iranian *pairika*.

The perfect land of Yolmo Gangra

In this relatively short text we also find a brief description of what the ideal land of Yolmo Gangra appears like to those who are able to enter it. In this hidden land, perfected since time immemorial by Padmasambhava's vow and the co-option of the local spirits and deities, we find a place where enemies are prevented from entering, all one's servants and subjects are happy, everyone turns spontaneously towards Buddhism, the minds of all are imbued with compassion, all impediments to life are neutralised, all demonic forces are expelled, no adventitious 'friends' are permitted to enter, there are neither rainstorms nor mud, where only harmless animals are to be found, and where birds and even fledglings are protected from all harm. Furthermore, the text informs us that

> In this absolutely extraordinary land
> There are no armies and neither are there means for discord.
> In this place there exists no civil strife and all disagreement is pacified.
> Wild brandishing of cudgels is fully resolved
> And a person's body, speech and mind are completely transformed.
> Those inimical beings and others, who have harmed their *samaya* vows, are utterly cut off at the root.
> Magical powers are miraculously created there,
> And the most excellent gifts act as counters to any
> calamities.
> All thoughts and wishes are fulfilled exactly as one desires.
> There, one exerts oneself to attain the one thing which is desired – the *siddhi* powers ('*Mistress of Gang Ra*', folio 8).

Change of place: the pre-Zoroastrian *pairika* goddesses

The Iranian *peri* or *pairika*[5] have sometimes been referred to as local cultic witches. In much the same manner as Jomo Yangri Chugmo might appear as a tranquil, beatific deity and also as an horrific and malevolent one, so too the *pairika* can transform themselves at will, depending upon circumstances. Mary Boyce says of them that they are

> ... a class of female supernatural beings of malicious character, who seek to beguile and harm mankind – some of them witch-like in character, but in general more powerful than witches ... these wicked beings could work evil at any time ... other *pairikas* it seems took on human form, and some made themselves enchantingly beautiful (Boyce 1975, 85-86).

This combination of the hag and the seductive beauty is one of the factors which might link the *protectrice* of Yolmo with a wider cultural

5 *Pairika* is more or less the origin of the English word 'fairy'. Paradise = *pairika desha* = 'Land of the *pairika*'.

world, specifically that of Iran. The cult of the *pairika* may be found in the pre-Zoroastrian period as well as to this day, especially in Chitral in the north-west of Pakistan and in the Wakhan area of Afghanistan.[6] The *pairika* are said to inhabit the highest mountain peaks and live in vast crystal palaces that cannot be seen by mortals. Although Jomo Yangri Chugmo does not appear to manifest in any forms other than the tranquil and the threatening, the *pairika* may also adopt an animal role, inasmuch as they may adopt the form of the antelope so commonly found in the western Himalayan regions. Local people often report that when they see a herd of antelope, they are uncertain whether they are in fact a flock of *pairika* or a potential food supply. The *pairika* in antelope form may also tempt those lost in the mountains into dangerous situations, but equally often can give them warmth, succour and access for temporary shelter into their crystal citadel.

In much the same manner that Jomo Yangri Chugmo acts as a gatekeeper to the hidden land wherein one might find a perfect realm in which to practise one's religion, so too the *pairika* act as protectors of the entry door to the Iranian Paradise. It seems that the *pairika* act as protectors of both the Zoroastrian and the pre-Zoroastrian paradise realms for in the Hindu Kush region much pre-Zoroastrian belief is intermingled with Islam and *pairika* belief is widespread. Like Jomo Yangri Chugmo, the *pairika* combine allure and threat and, like her, they also possess a clearly defined soteriological role. The *pairika*, either singly or in flocks, guard the bridge that is said to connect the realm of after-death experience and the perfect paradise realm. The *pairika* guard not only this Chinvat bridge but the approaches leading up to it. So, rather than acting simply as gatekeepers and sentinels to the deceased's first steps on the bridge, the *pairika* actually patrol the areas that must be crossed to even draw near to it. In this role they may be likened to the guardian protectors (male or female) who serve as deflectors of the unworthy and the unready in the case of Yolmo.

Several other sections in the larger volume containing the text of the 'Mistress of Gang Ra' deal with these outriders and palladiums of the goddess herself and these will become the subjects of a subsequent paper.

---

6 A tragedy in a mountaineering expedition in the Hindu Kush region in the late 1970s attests to their currency. A Japanese climber is said to have heard the siren-call of the *pairika* from the peak his expedition was climbing and, walking out of his tent to find them, he fell off the mountain. The expedition was subsequently abandoned (Personal communication, Mr Gerry Virtue, Sydney, 1998).

The final section of this chapter does, however, discuss the poetic motifs employed in the descriptions of these figures as a prelude to that paper.

The *pairika* generally appear as attractive maidens and, having determined the worthiness of the deceased in terms of the sum of his or her good and bad deeds, they attract the spirit in the direction of, and assist it onto, the Chinvat Bridge. This is no guarantee whatsoever that one has been soteriologically successful. Once the deceased is actually on the bridge, the *pairika* ensure that it varies the bridge's breadth according to the relative spiritual 'health' of the deceased, rendering it either easier or impossible to pass over it as it alters from broad and easy to the narrowness of a single human hair. However, all this can alter in an instant, for, if the *pairika* becomes at all irked (or in certain cases, just bored) with the subject on the bridge or simply out of a sense of malignant spite, she can immediately assume the form of a vile and terrifying hag and in this form she literally terrifies the deceased off the bridge, consigning them to the everlasting hell-realms.

I contend that in this role assumed by the *pairika* as both seductive temptress and agent of terror we can see certain elements described above in the make-up and the demeanour of Jomo Yangri Chugmo, as well as in various other female *protectrices* of Himalayan *lieux saints*.

Outrider attendants to the goddess: the Drala (*sgra lha*)

In a particularly poetic description of one of the classes of attendants, who act as outriders to Jomo Yangri Chugmo, the Drala (Tibetan: *sgra lha* ('enemy gods')), we find the following 'song' evocation of these protectors and their powers. In this powerful piece of ritual poetry, intended to be sung or chanted rather than simply read, again we find much that appears 'primitive' and 'pre-Buddhist'. These aspects include most prominently the malevolent imprecations hurled at vow-breakers. Other such ostensibly 'early' features might also include the alliterative sounds at the end of several lines where the words enunciated may represent the sounds that are made in the air by the wielding of weapons and the various swirling activities of the Drala. On the other hand they may well be simply a series of joyous sounds to express the ebullience of the outriders as they careen across the mountains. Examples of similar employment of alliteration are certainly well documented aspects of early Tibetan writing dated to pre-eleventh-century texts excavated at Dunhuang and epic and folk writings of a similar period.[7] However, as discussed above, the presumption of antiquity, which might appear *prima facie* to be emotionally appealing, is yet to be demonstrated as such satisfactorily. Indeed, if the passage's final few lines were an integral part of the original text, they would appear to run counter to much of the rambunctious and rollicking 'earlier' sentiment so prevalent in the rest of the song. On the other hand, if we discount their being an integral part of the text in its original form, then perhaps they are in fact a later interpolation or an effective summation of the intention of the song's overall Buddhist sentiment added later on. The translated extract reads:

> Hum! At the time that *samaya* vows are broken the Drala arise.
> Riding blue-coloured horses … *sha ra ra*,
> This great military throng of (medicinal?) nāgas … *thib se thibs*,
> Wearing turquoise coloured armour which blazes with shimmering light … *lam se lam*,
> With poisonous vapours steaming from their *shang* bells … *mtho ro ro.*
> From their mouths bubble forth noxious diseases … *bun se bun.*
> From the blue coloured birds swirling above in great numbers comes the sound … *thib se thibs*
> Behind come blue coloured dogs … *breng se brengs*
> And there is a glowering blue light billowing over everything … *khyi li li*
> And as if by magic there is a threatening blue sky above all this.
> The king of the nāgas draws in his breath in semi-lungfuls, and
> The breath of the enemies is swiftly sucked out.
> The nāgas use their poisons as a scourge
> And are seen swirling around as if in leprosy-infected blood.
> The leprosy (text reads: *mdzes*) is seen to be like a buffeting wind.
> Various swelling diseases (text reads: *skya* for *skya rbab*) are seen to be like a buffeting wind.
> Cancerous tumours (text reads *'bras* for *'bras nad*), palsy (*'khol),* blindness (*mig med*) and *dpal,*
> Abscesses (*g.yan pa*), ulcers (*lhog pa*), thirst and
> Scrofula (*shu ba*) all whirled together without a gap between them.
> Make up an offering of the piled up hearts and lives of the enemy!

7 For examples, see Dotson (2009) and Thomas (1948 and 1957).

Cut off the enemy's bondsmen and wealth at the root!
May you fully perfect all your Buddha activities!
King of the Nāgas, kill all vow-breaking enemies and smash their lives utterly!
Thus are the words of exhortation.[8]

Perhaps it is precisely in that sense of enigma illustrated in the above quotation that we should approach the *cultus* of Jomo Yangri Chugmo. More specifically, through the linking of the apparently 'wild' primitive substratum of the locale and its cultic denizens with far more elegant and refined Buddhist aspirations, we may discover that in such apparent tension Jomo Yangri Chugmo becomes what we make of her *precisely through what we bring to her*. She can be at one and the same time demoness and protectress of a hidden land, aided as she is by bloodthirsty cohorts, as well as being, in her more tranquil forms, mother, lover, friend, helper and amanuensis to those seriously seeking the Hidden Land of Yolmo. Perhaps in her competing and multivalent forms we can see something of her underlying complexity. In her more direct and forthright aspects she is, like all beings, far more human than we might imagine.

Bibliography

Bacot, J. 1912. *Le Tibet révolté: vers Népémakö, la terre promise des Tibétains, suivi des impressions d'un Tibétain en France*. Paris: Hachette.
Benard, E. 1994. *Chinnamasta: The Aweful Buddhist & Hindu Tantric Goddess*. Delhi: Motilal Banarsidass.
Boyce, M. 1975. *A History of Zoroastrianism*. Vol. 1. The Early Period. Leiden: E.J. Brill.
Dotson, B. 2009. *The Old Tibetan Annals: An Annotated Translation of Tibet's First History*. Vienna: Austrian Academy of Sciences.
Ehrhard, F-K. 1997. 'A "hidden land" in the Tibetan-Nepalese borderlands'. In *Mandala and Landscape: Emerging Perceptions in Buddhist Studies,* edited by A.W. Macdonald. Delhi: D.K. Printworld.
Freud, S. 1922. *Beyond the Pleasure Principle*. London: Hogarth Press.
Templeman, D. 2016 (forthcoming). *Alternate Voices: Kunga Drolchog's Life of Kṛṣṇācārya: Translation, Commentary and Critical edition of Text.* Śāntiniketan, W. Bengal: Viśva Bharati University.
Thomas, F.W. 1948. *Nam, an Ancient Language of the Sino-Tibetan Borderland.* London: Oxford University Press.
Thomas, F.W. 1957. Ancient Folk-Literature from North-eastern Tibet. Berlin: Akademie-Verlag.

8 This text is from an untitled document bound in with the texts dealing with Jomo Yangri Chugmo, but unfortunately missing its first few pages. The colophon reads: 'I the terma master rGyal mtshan have been encouraged to conjoin this text known as the *dGongs pa kun 'dus* to the text the *Triple Nāga Cloud Offering* by Padma Thod 'phreng rtsal. Happiness! Sarvamaṅgalam!'.

Chapter 11

Ekveera Devi and the Son Kolis of Mumbai

Have the Kolis Appropriated the Karle Buddhist *Chaitya*?

Marika Vicziany, Jayant Bhalchandra Bapat and Sanjay Ranade

This is our sixth paper on the religious beliefs and practices of the Kolis, one of the three indigenous tribes of Mumbai.[1] Our work on the Kolis has been a voyage of discovery over the last eight years. The original questions and suppositions have been successively rejected, replaced or modified by new ones. At first we studied Mumbadevi, thinking that she was the *essential* Koli *Devi* (clan-goddess) (Vicziany and Bapat 2009). When that proved to be no longer the case, we turned our attention to the tribal goddesses we successively discovered in the Koli villages (Koliwadas) of Mumbai (Vicziany and Bapat 2008; Ranade 2008 and 2009; Bapat 2010; Appendix below). These tribal goddesses are worshipped alongside many other gods, goddesses, gurus, contemporary Indian leaders, water spirits and venerated fishermen who have drowned whilst fishing, the traditional labour of the Kolis. Most recently, we have discovered that the Kolis in two of Mumbai's Koli villages venerate Muslim saints as well (Vicziany, Bapat and Ranade 2013). In our work so far, the locus of Koli religious practice has been the family home or village in Mumbai. This paper, in contrast to all the previous ones, traces the involvement of the Son Kolis in the worship of their tribal clan goddess Ekveera,

1 The Agri and Bhandari are the other two indigenous tribes with a long history of settlement in Mumbai.

whose main shrine is located outside Mumbai near Lonavla, north of Pune, in the Western Ghats or western mountains that divide Mumbai from the Maharashtrian plateau (Figure 11.1). Of course, Ekveera is also worshipped in the home, but the frequent private and community pilgrimages to Lonavla play a unique role in forging Koli solidarity whilst simultaneously linking the Kolis to the Maharashtrian tradition of devotional pilgrimages.

Our argument in this chapter is that, first, the Kolis have appropriated the tradition of *bhakti* or devotional Hinduism in which pilgrimage plays an important role. Second, the object of their pilgrimage to the Ekveera temple has involved them appropriating the sacred hill on which the ancient Karle Buddhist cave is located. That cave is often referred to as a 'temple' but the correct terminology is *chaitya,* or prayer hall. It is a magnificent structure cut into the rocks that form the Western Ghats mountain range in the Mumbai hinterland. The word 'temple' implies the worship of gods or goddesses and their companions, but the image at the end of the *chaitya* is a structure called a '*stupa*', which symbolises the enlightenment of the Buddha and his teachings (Snodgrass 1985). Throughout this chapter, therefore, we refer to the misnamed Karle Buddhist Temple as the Karle Buddhist cave or *chaitya*. Of course, its magnificent carvings bear no resemblance to any naturally formed cave, but the terminology serves to distinguish it from the Ekveera Devi Mandir, or temple, situated immediately in front of it.

Third, we argue that the Son Kolis are involved in other appropriations, including claims to the special status given to the Mahadev Kolis as Scheduled Tribes. This last appropriation means that it has become increasingly difficult to differentiate the Son Kolis from the Mahadev Kolis, and our informants were reluctant in interviews to say which subtribe they belonged to. Does the actual tribe name matter? We say it does, because until now the devotional practices of the Son Kolis and Mahadev Kolis have been different in various ways, although this is now changing with the emergence of a cross-tribal Koli community.

What do we mean by appropriation?

The term appropriation can be used in many ways – to assert an identity by active participation in something; to assert claim to pre-eminent power over something; or to demand to be acknowledged as having some status. Our previous work on the Son Kolis has documented the syncretic religious traditions and practices that define their spiritual world. In the creation of this syncretic amalgam, the Son Kolis have drawn widely on many religious traditions in India. Perhaps this reflects their indigenous origins in Mumbai, where they have lived for so long that their culture could hardly ignore the many centuries during which migrants arrived and brought new ideas with them. The notion of the Kolis 'appropriating' *bhakti*, along with the sacred hill on which the Karle *chaitya* is located, points to something different. On the one hand, this 'appropriation' continues the tradition of cultural borrowing and adaptation, but, on the other hand, the extent to which the Son Kolis have travelled to a religious site outside of their Mumbai villages and asserted their presence on the Karle Hill is unique.[2] It is this uniqueness that compels us to employ the new description of 'appropriation'. We use it as a marker for why the worship of the clan goddess Ekveera differs from other forms of syncretic religious evolution that have defined the lives of the Son Kolis in the last 200 years.

Finally, we note that some aspects of the cultural appropriation that we are about to speak of in the case of the Son Kolis are not unique to them – for example, the *bhakti* movement has been taken up by many Indian castes and tribes, high and low. However, we need to remind ourselves that appropriation is not the only possible cultural response to the much vexed question of social hierarchy in Hinduism. Ambedkar, for example, decided 'not to die a Hindu' and led a mass conversion movement of untouchables out of Hinduism into Buddhism in 1956 prior to his death (Mendelsohn and Vicziany 1998: 77, 79, 81, 116-117). That conversion movement continues today and is a model of how not to 'appropriate' but rather reject Hinduism in its multiple manifestations. The Son Kolis have not done this, so the nature and reasons for their 'appropriation' is an important part of understanding modern India.

Kolis and the appropriation of *bhakti*

We do not know when the Son Kolis of Mumbai appropriated *bhakti* devotional Hinduism, but it has now become a very important part of their religious life. The appeal of *bhakti* is easy to understand since, from the time of its appearance in the thirteenth century or perhaps earlier, *bhakti* was defined by its use of popular, vernacular languages rather than

2 Narsalay, writing on the *Kokaṇastha* Brāhmins in this volume, has shown that these Brāhmins adopted a local cult far away from their home. The case of the Son Kolis shows an interesting parallel here.

Sanskrit. Until the nineteenth century, Sanskrit was the language of the small privileged elite of high castes, especially Brāhmins. This meant that low castes and tribal people in India were excluded from any textual or oral learning based on Sanskrit. But the arrival of the *bhakti* movement from about the thirteenth century onwards reduced the monopoly of the high castes and those who knew Sanskrit. The knowledge that ordinary people had of Hindu religious thought and ideas after that time no longer depended on the teachings of Brāhmins who had interpreted for everyone else. The *bhakti* movement was, therefore, revolutionary. The use of commonly spoken languages in religious worship gave ordinary people direct access to religious knowledge. Although the *bhakti* movement borrowed heavily from the myths, legends and epics of India (including the *Ramayana* and *Mahabharata)*, the religious teachers of *bhakti* developed their own interpretations of the gods and goddesses in a manner that projected them as humanised rather than idealised gods. As a result, the Hindu classics became very popular and of greater importance within the teachings of Hinduism. Many of the *bhakti* teachers were themselves of low caste, but many were also Brāhmins. Chokha Mela the fourteenth century Maharashtrian saint, for example, was from the *Mahar*[3] dalit labouring caste and Tukaram was a *Mali*[4], or from the gardening caste. What all the saints shared was a love for the common man.

The other important feature of the *bhakti* movement was that the devotional practices of the followers were inclusive of all social groups and strongly opposed to social hierarchy. As such the *bhakti* movement threw up powerful egalitarian role models for oppressed social groups, especially because many of the *bhakti* poets were from low castes. After their death, the *bhakti* saints became objects of veneration. The Son Kolis of Mumbai, by virtue of being a tribal community, are one of many low social groups attracted to the *bhakti* cult.

An important part of the *bhakti* rituals that the Kolis have also appropriated is the religious procession or pilgrimage. Many of these processions involve pilgrims (*warkaris*) travelling on foot for hundreds of kilometres between their homes and the temples that house the divine icon they venerate. Sometimes the images in the temples are also taken out and carried in processions around the town or towards a nearby river for ritual bathing. The appearance of the divine image in public allows huge numbers of ordinary people to absorb the 'light' (enlightenment)

3 Pronounced *mahār*.

4 Pronounced *māḷī*.

that the deities exude (*darshan*).[5] Traditional or Brāhminical Hinduism, by contrast, until recently, excluded untouchables, tribals and other low castes from seeing images of the gods or goddesses by preventing these 'lowly' social elements from entering Hindu temples. The sacred space and the sacred light (*darshan)* were the preserve of socially privileged elite castes; only these people benefited from the special grace that falls on devotees who sight the image. Officially, the exclusion of ritually polluting tribes and castes from Hindu temples has been outlawed in modern India, but, in practice, it often continues in subtle ways. The shrines frequented by the *bhakti warkaris* typically allow access to the inner sanctum, but there is simply not enough space for this to happen during the most important religious festivals. So the earlier practice of taking the religious images on procession has grown tremendously in its importance as thousands upon thousands of devotees participate in these pilgrimages and the grace and power of the image can then be shared by all.

The key shrines of the *bhakti* movement in Mumbai and Maharasthra typically house images of the favoured gods and goddesses and at their entrances there are often smaller shrines (*samadhis)* that house the ashes of the important *bhakti* teachers, philosophers, poets and singers, such as Dnyaneshwar, Tukaram, Eknath and Chokha Mela. The processions to these shrines on auspicious days of the religious calendar involve thousands of *bhaktas (*devotees), at times up to a million or more, winding their way for weeks along many roads towards the object of their devotion, which could be either the shrine of a deity, or the *samadhi* of a deceased saint, or both. One feature of the processions is that the pilgrims carry symbols representing the feet (called *paduka*[6]) of the *bhakti* teachers and saints[7] who have gone before them as pilgrims. In this way, the *warkaris* commemorate the memories of the *bhakti* philosophers.

For the Kolis, participation in the pilgrimages has become an increasingly important part of their beliefs and practices. Figure 11.1 shows the most important sacred sites that are the key pilgrimage destinations between Mumbai and Pandharpur for hundreds of castes and tribes, not

5 The importance of 'seeing' the divine image is discussed by Eck (1998).

6 Pronounced *pādukā*.

7 In Hindu thought, the feet of a deity or saint are considered highly sacred and carry great importance. To hold on to the feet of the object of devotion signifies extreme humbleness and the desire on the part of the devotee to stay physically close to the deity.

only the Kolis.[8] These sites are not linked into a single pilgrimage cycle for the Kolis because the sacred nature of these places probably evolved separately for the Koli communities. Each of these is discussed in the following paragraphs, beginning with the popular *bhakti* sites of Jejuri and Pandharpur. The Ekveera Devi site, by contrast, has a more limited social attraction bringing in mainly the Kolis and the Chandraseniya Kayastha Prabhus (CKPs)[9], while the adjacent Karle *chaitya* and its associated structures have been reclaimed as a Buddhist site by the dalits of Maharashtra.

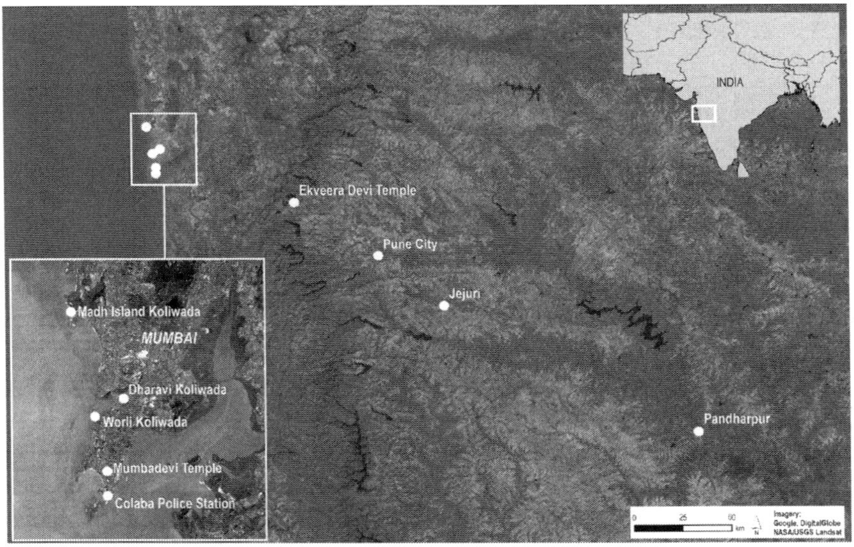

Figure 11.1: Koli sacred pilgrimage sites in Maharashtra: the Ekveera Devi Mandir, Jejuri and Pandharpur. Also shown are the key Koli temples that we have studied so far: Mumbadevi, Khadadevi, Dharavi, Worli and Madh Island. (Figure by Dr Uri Gilad, 7 May 2016)

The shrine to Vithoba, or Vitthal, at Pandharpur combines the essential characteristics of Vishnu and Shiva (Feldhaus 2011, xiv), which makes him especially appealing to the Kolis who embrace so many religious traditions. Vithoba began as a god of the pastoral communities of India but, as Dhere shows, became 'elevated' to such an extent that high castes (even Brāhmins) claim him as theirs (Feldhaus 2011, xiv-xv; Dhere 2011, chapter 13). For many Hindu pilgrims, Vithoba possesses many of the

8 The distance from Mumbai to the Ekveera Devi Mandir is 100 kilometres, from Ekveera to Jejuri 108 kilometres, and from Jejuri to Pandhapur 163 kilometres.

9 The CKPs claim to be high caste Kshatriyas.

qualities of a mother goddess, something that makes him highly compatible with the tribal goddesses that the Kolis have traditionally worshipped (Dhere 2011, chapter 12). Hence Vithoba, like Ekveera, is the embodiment of unqualified motherly love. As Dhere (2011, 233) notes, the transformation of Vithoba into an image of motherhood was achieved by the *bhakti* saints, such as Namdev.

The Shaivite god Khandoba is another important object of pilgrimage and worship for the Kolis who travel to Jejuri for his blessings. In a survey that we conducted in October 2009 we noted that more than half of the Son Kolis of Mumbai worship Khandoba, who expresses the dangerous (*kadak*) side of Shiva. Khandoba needs to be appeased with animal sacrifices and vows (Stanley 1977, n. 31), especially by newly married couples hoping to conceive children. In the past, sacrifices probably occurred within the temple at Jejuri, but today this is no longer allowed.[10] Yet the powerful imagery of Khandoba remains a potent factor in the spiritual life of the Kolis, including those who have migrated abroad.[11] In the homes of the Son Kolis, the worship of Khandoba is counterbalanced by the much softer adoration of Ganesh, the remover of all obstacles.

In addition to the Kolis' involvement in the rites at Pandharpur and Jejuri, the quintessential Koli pilgrimage is that from Bombay to the

10 The persona of Khandoba reflects the essence of the *bhakti* traditions of inter-community sharing and tolerance: his two wives come from two different socio-economic classes and he also has a special relationship with the Muslims of Maharashtra. At the Jejuri temple, the centre of the Khandoba cult, the man who led Khandoba's horse for many years during the pilgrimage procession was a Muslim who reported that Khandoba was his personal God while Allah was his family god (Stanley 1977, n. 45). In many of the 600 Khandoba temples of western India, the Muslims constitute an important body of worshippers. According to Stanley (1977, 31), Khandoba is 'one of the most widely worshipped gods in the Deccan, where he is regarded as the premier god of *sakaama bhakti* (wish-granting devotion) and one of the most powerful deities responsive to vows (*navas*)' (Stanley 1977, 31). Khandoba's magical potency stems from his incorporation of the characteristics of an Indian Sun God with those of an Indian Moon God (Stanley 1977, 33). According to Mate (1962, 15), the Kolis are especially attracted to the Moon God side of Khandoba and participate in great numbers in venerating the god during the Maghi full-moon day. The combined light–dark side of Khandoba also commonly expresses itself in the possession of the pilgrims as they dance their way to the river at Jejuri to celebrate *Somavati Amavasya* by dipping the image of Khandoba into the water (Stanley 1977, 38-39). It is also worth noting that according to at least one popular Khandoba society based in Pune, Khandoba had at least five wives including a Muslim from the oil-pressing caste (Khandoba.org 2016). On other aspects of Khandoba, also see Sontheimer (1986; 1989; 1997).

11 Interview with a female Koli professional migrant, Sydney, 2 May 2013.

Ekveera Devi Mandir, or temple, near Lonavla, a distance of about 100 kilometres. It is at the Ekveera Devi shrine that the Son Kolis from Mumbai's Koli villages[12] gather in a way that is not possible within the metropolis. As they undertake their journey, the pilgrims sing and dance the *bhakti* songs that blare from the loud speakers attached to the CD players in their cars, SUVs and auto-rickshaws. The Kolis have appropriated the ritual form of the *bhakti* pilgrimage while asserting their unique character in the selection of the songs (*bhajans*) that they sing in praise of their clan goddess Ekveera. Depending on the mood and personal preferences of the pilgrims, songs to other Koli cultural icons, in particular Shirdi Sai Baba[13] and the Hindu God Krishna,[14] are interspersed with praise of Ekveera.

During pilgrimages, when the devotees attain a high level of consciousness, some undertake special vows to become better persons by promising to abstain from meat and alcohol, perform extra *pujas* (devotional ceremonies), undertake regular pilgrimages, fast regularly and live modest, non-violent lives. The Maalkari *sampradaya* (sect), that has very strict vows, is one of many that some Kolis devote themselves to. In contemporary Mumbai, adopting the vow of non-violence represents a strike against communal hatred and militancy. Many *warkaris* adopt special names as part of their vows. Even Muslim names are acceptable, if one's devotion can be demonstrated by this means.[15]

12 The Koli Research Project at Monash University has studied closely five Koli temples in Mumbai, but has also identified many others. Five years ago we estimated that Mumbai had about twenty-three Koli temples, but the latest count, using various definitions, is forty-one. This will be documented further in a forthcoming paper on the number of Koli Temples of Mumbai and the evolution of the city and its social groups.

13 For Sai Baba's biography, see Rigopoulos (1993). Many devotees believe that this nineteenth-century guru was reincarnated as [Satya] Sai Baba, India's most famous contemporary guru, who died in 2011 (*ABC News* 2011).

14 The growing importance of Krishna worship for Mumbai's Son Kolis is to be further explored in forthcoming papers by Sanjay Ranade (on singing the Devi) and by Marika Vicziany and Jayant Bhalchandra Bapat (on the religious beliefs and social practices of the Koli diaspora).

15 One regular pilgrim to Pandharpur adopted the name Swami Arabi to demonstrate that there was no separation between Hindu and Muslim: Swami is a Sanskrit word meaning a religious teacher, or Lord, and Arabi is a name for someone from Arabia. By using them together he demonstrated that he held no hatred in his heart for Muslims. In his own words: 'I say there is no Hindu, there is no Muslim, there is no caste, there is only God' (Youngblood 2003, 291). Earlier in his life, this pilgrim had been recruited by the Hindu nationalists into an anti-Muslim hate campaign, but by the time he met Youngblood he had decided that his old attitudes were totally opposed to a movement based on love and devotion.

Finally, we note that the *bhakti* rituals also act as powerful reminders of Koli heroes who fought against British colonial rule. The great Koli warrior-hero Raghu Bhangare (son of the Koli rebel commander Rama Bhangare who led the revolts against the British colonial authority in 1828-29) adopted the garb of a *warkari* or *bhakti* pilgrim – he grew his hair long, smoked marijuana, worshipped the mother goddesses of western India and offered prayers to Vitthal at Pandharpur (Hardiman 1995, 117). His demeanour was that of a *gosavi* (holy man), a popular image as powerful as that projected by Mahatma Gandhi when he adopted the dress and lifestyle of a Hindu *Sannyasi* (mendicant) as a way of galvanising a mass movement. According to Hardiman (1995, 117),

> As a devotee, Raghu was popularly believed to enjoy divine protection in his revolt. He always carried two silver charms in a tiger skin bag slung over his shoulder ... It is likely that his band carried small *murtis* [images] of a variety of divinities, who were believed to provide protection.

Disguised as a devotee (*bhakta*) and often living in temples, Raghu was able to frequently escape capture. His eventual imprisonment by the British in January 1847 is explained by the Kolis as caused by his decision to shave his hair and beard in order to make the pilgrimage to Pandharpur disguised as a Vaishnavite pilgrim. He was particularly vulnerable on the day of his capture as he had not yet appeared before Vitthal and so 'at that moment [was] particularly exposed, unprotected and powerless' (Hardiman 1995, 188). The fact that Raghu was a Mahadev Koli in no way weakens his appeal to modern Son Kolis, for reasons we discuss towards the end of this chapter.

Ekveera Devi and the appropriation of Karle hill

As noted at the outset of this chapter, we stumbled upon the importance of Ekveera Devi after discovering that, in addition to the village-specific tribal goddesses the Kolis also had a clan goddess that brought all the Koli sub-tribes together into a mass communal form of worship well beyond the limits of the city of Mumbai. In September 2009, alongside other small shops located on the path leading to the Ekveera Devi Temple outside the Karle Buddhist *chaitya*, we set up a booth calling for volunteers to explain to us why they were visiting the site. A total of twenty-seven Koli pilgrims spoke to us about their religious views. We asked them about their beliefs regarding village, personal and clan gods and goddesses. Of twenty-seven pilgrims, five (19%) said that they no longer believed in the village deities, six reported that their village deities were *avatars* (reincarnations) of Shiva or Vishnu, and two said that their village deity was Ekveera (see Appendix).[16] Only thirteen Kolis, less than half, named a traditional tribal goddess as their village deity (see Appendix).

The relative decline of the Koli tribal village goddesses and the rise of deities that are followed by the wider Hindu communities is even stronger than this if we include several Kolis who told us that their most important personal deity or the deity to which they pray each day is a guru like Sai Baba or Swami Samartha, a nineteenth-century guru belonging to the Dattatreya *bhakti* sect.

On the other hand, the decline of the traditional village goddesses of the Son Kolis appears to have been counterbalanced by the growing importance of the clan deity of the Kolis, namely Ekveera Devi, 'the brave one'. As Dhere (1978, 111) has noted, Ekveera is only one manifestation of the mother goddess who is such an important part of folk tradition in western India. For some Son Kolis, Ekveera Devi is an *avatar* of the Hindu goddess Renuka, but for most Kolis she is really the goddess Bhavani, a ferocious *avatar* of Parvati, Shiva's consort.[17] Luckily, Bhavani also takes pity on the weak, so she is also known as the 'merciful one'. Bhavani's power is reinforced by her close association with Shivaji, the seventeenth-century Maratha king and warrior who defeated the Mughal armies. According to local oral traditions, Bhavani gave Shivaji a special sword with which he fought his way to victory. Bhavani is also the slayer of Mahishasura, the demon; in this way she is closely associated with the Hindu goddess Durga. The oldest extant Bhavani temple dates from the twelfth century and is at Tuljapur, in the district of Osmanabad in southern Maharashtra. Here Bhavani is represented by a metre-high rock sculpture that is armed to the teeth,

16 Ekveera Devi is the clan deity of the Kolis but this does not mean that she is also an important deity in the Koli villages. Ekveera Devi transcends family and village; hence only two respondents reported that she was their village goddess.

17 'Eka' is the Sanskrit word for one and 'veera' means a brave female; thus, Ekveera Devi is the Brave One. Ekveera could also mean 'one who has produced a brave son'. Interestingly, for some Kolis, the words 'brave one' refer to the son of Ekveera. In this paper we have reported on current Koli beliefs, but by this we do not wish to imply that the Sanskritic or Brāhminical names for the Koli goddesses take historical precedence over their original names, whatever these may have been. The worship of the mother goddesses by the Kolis is much older than Hinduism.

with many of her arms holding a weapon while the eighth arm holds the head of Mahishasura (Mate, 1962).

The Kolis worship Ekveera Devi for the same reasons that they worship all their other deities at their domestic and village shrines. However, the act of coming to Lonavla requires extra effort, so the rituals at the Ekveera temple are believed to be more efficacious. One 73-year-old Koli resident from Worli said, 'to cut the child's hair people go to the goddess Ekveera. People offer goats and rams. Everybody gives what they can' (Interview, 21 January 2008).

A 29-year-old mother confirmed that she too had visited the Ekveera temple on the occasion of *javal*,[18] the ceremony to celebrate the first cutting of her son's hair (Interview, 21 January 2008). She also prayed in the Sacred Heart Church near her village, touched the feet of the goddess Golphadevi in the Golphadevi temple and offered a *thali* (plate) of coconut, a blouse and *oati*[19] to Golphadevi and Ekveera Devi (Interview, 21 January 2008).

Seeking the goddess's blessing before marriage is another reason for making the pilgrimage to Lonavla. According to a 27-year-old unmarried Koli gym instructor from Worli, the community worshipped both Ekveera and Khandoba:

> We touch their feet before marriage and I go to the goddess to express my feelings. I prefer Ekveera. Her face has a unique form. I have gone there several times … maybe 50, 100 times. Our feet just carry us to her. People from our community have made arrangements to stay there. We have bungalows (Interview, 27 January 2008).

One prominent Koli politician from Mumbai was unable to meet us on one occasion in January 2013 because he had to rush to Lonavla in order to present his son's wedding invitation to Ekveera Devi. Ekveera had to

18 *Javal* (pronounced *jāvaḷ*) is one of the traditional sixteen rites that a male Hindu undergoes. Called 'tonsure' in English and *cūḍākarman* in Sanskrit, it involves removing all a child's hair between the age of two and three. The hair is shorn by a barber, and the priest chants *mantra*s for a long life. Sometimes the shorn hair is offered to some gods and goddesses, but, in most places, it is thrown away. The ceremony symbolises the separation of the life of the child from the time he was dependent on his mother to a new life (with new, strong hair) that he also shares with his father. *Cūḍākarman* is, essentially, a weaning ceremony that promotes obvious patriarchical values.

19 *Oti* (*bharaṇe*) is a woman's fertility ritual in which a married woman has a whole coconut, some coloured rice and some fruit placed into her lap. The coconut symbolises the womb.

be invited first, and only then could all the other invitations be posted out. To do otherwise was to court marital or other disasters in future.

The Ekveera Devi temple sits immediately before the Karle *chaitya* which dates from about 225–200 BCE (Interview with archaeologists, Archaeological Survey of India, 19 July 2012). The Karle cave is related to two other cave *chaitya* at Bhaja and Bedsa (dating from 250–225 BCE and 200–150 BCE) which, like Karle, have been cut out of a rock face. These three rock-cut structures used to form a pilgrimage triangle in pre-colonial times and simultaneously belonged to a trading route that linked the Deccan plateau behind the Western Ghats to the coastline of the Mumbai hinterland (Kosambi, 2009). The passing trade was an essential source of donations and grants to the temples and monks who sold their ritual services and artisanal products to merchants, bankers, and bullock cart drivers making their way to the coastal ports (Nagaraju 1981, 12, 26-27; Kosambi 2009), including some which are now located 'inland' and no longer form part of the river-sea routes, thanks to siltation.

The sacred hill on which the Karle *chaitya* sits has sixteen other caves that appear to have belonged to the one Buddhist complex which probably continued to evolve even after the Karle *chaitya* was completed in the early second century BCE. But when did the modest Ekveera Devi temple at the entrance to the *chaitya* first appear? Who built it and by what processes have the Kolis insinuated themselves into controlling this temple and other parts of the sacred Karle hill site?

The connection between the Ekveera Devi Mandir and the Karle Buddhist *chaitya*

Understanding the way in which the Son Kolis have appropriated the Karle site requires us to first describe the Buddhist chaitya for which the Karle hill is famous.

The Karle *chaitya* is known for the extraordinary feat of excavation that it represents. It was carved from the top of the hill down into the black rock. Its proportions, structure and detailed carvings have been the subject of commentary from the late eighteenth century onwards. The famous grand hall is distinguished by thirty-seven carved octagonal pillars, at the far end of which stands the *stupa* beneath a magnificent carved teak ceiling. At the entrance to the *chaitya* stands a lion pillar on the left (as one enters the cave). Above the great hall are the *vihāras* – the rooms that housed the Buddhist and Jain monks and nuns who lived here in the past. Today, the *chaitya* is deteriorating: tourists climb all over the structure; litter is strewn everywhere; coins are thrown at the now seriously chipped *stupa* at the end of the hall; grass grows from many of the rocks; the temple's exterior has been stripped of vegetation making it more prone to water seepage;[20] and lovers have engraved their names on every spare rock surface.

According to Fergusson (1876, 121), the original structure of the Karle *chaitya* included a second free-standing lion pillar on the right-hand side of the temple entrance, which had 'either fallen or been taken down to make way for the little temple that now occupies its place'. Archaeological Survey of India officials have confirmed that a second pillar did exist at this spot (Interviews, New Delhi, 19 July 2012). The 'little temple' to which Fergusson referred is what is today called the Ekveera Devi Mandir, a small square brick structure covered in blue and pink cloth (Plate 11.1). The bricks seem to be a later addition, for the Ekveera shrine appears to be joined to the rock face and can be approached on three sides only. Although an archaeological excavation is needed to reveal the true physical connection between the Ekveera Devi temple and the Buddhist Karle *chaitya*, early European accounts of the Karle hill complex, examined in the following section, show that the name Ekveera was linked to the site no later than 1809 and that Buddhist control of the site was relinquished to Jains and Hindus in the nineteenth century.

The European discovery of the Ekveera Devi Mandir

As we are not aware of any Indian documentary sources about the historical or cultural evolution of the Karle hill as a sacred site, we have turned to European accounts.[21]

The first European to publish a description of the Karle hill complex was Maria Graham who visited the site on 17 December 1809. She reported that the Karle *chaitya* was often called Ekveera and speaks of a

20 Despite the seepage of water, the Archaeological Survey of India has decided not to resurface the exterior roof of the Karle *chaitya* because similar 'restorations' in other parts of India have shown that the power of the monsoon rains is so great that the waters that cascade onto the Western Ghats might form other more destructive runoffs.

21 We hope that in the future Indian scholars will seek to resolve some of the puzzles we have pointed to in this chapter by looking into the archives of the Peshwas.

dingy village at the bottom of the hill on which the Karle *chaitya* is situated – that 'hamlet' was also called Ekveera: 'it is almost in ruins, and its tank and pagoda are in a state of melancholy decay. It is named Ekveera, and the cave is often called by the same name' (Graham 1812, 68).

These two statements suggest that the religious cult surrounding Ekveera Devi was already established, for why else would the name Ekveera appear? However, we know nothing about the religious rituals conducted at the site, for Graham did not report on these. But she did write that the Karle cave was strikingly different from the temple of Elephanta which she had visited earlier. In contrast to the Brāhminical temple of Elephanta (Michell, 1999), some 13 kms from the port of Mumbai, the Karle cave was 'dedicated to the religion of the Jines [Jains], a sect whose antiquity is believed by some to be greater than that of the Brāhminical faith, from which their tenets are essentially different' (Graham 1812, 65). The site was also inhabited by Jain priests, their wives and children (Graham 1812, 68). At the time she wrote her journal, the relationship between Jainism, Buddhism and Hinduism had not been established; throughout the nineteenth century debate raged about the historical and cultural connections between the three (Schubring 2000, Chapter 1; Brekke 2002, 132-134).[22] Given these uncertainties, Graham's recognition of the unique nature of the Karle *chaitya* demonstrates her acute powers of observation,[23] although she did not recognise the Karle *chaitya* as Buddhist. Nor did she see the uniqueness and separate status of the more modest structure located to the right of the entrance to the Karle cave, namely the Ekveera Devi Mandir. In her report, the name Ekveera crops up but she was unaware that there were two main religious sites in the Karle hill complex: the Buddhist rock cave of Karle and the Ekveera Devi temple.

The next European to report on the Karle hill complex was Fergusson. In 1835 he gave an unflattering description of a 'mean temple' that 'disfigured' the entrance to the Karle cave, which he described as a 'splendid excavation'. From his account, the Buddhist *chaitya* and the *mandir* in

22 The German scholar Hermann Georg Jacobi (1850-1937), who had access to the unique Jain library of the Oswal Jain temple in Jaisalmer, finally resolved the debate (Johnson 1993, 196). Jainism, it turned out, was much older than both Buddhism and Mahavira, the alleged 'founder' of Jainism.

23 She may well have read new work by Major C Mackenzie, Dr F. Buchanan and H.T. Colebrooke on Jainism in *Asiatick Researches* 9 (1807), published only two years before Graham reached Bombay.

front of it, namely the Ekveera Devi temple, had been in the hands of orthodox Hindus:

> Buddha having gone out of fashion, the Hindoos of the more orthodox creed have disfigured the entrance of this splendid excavation, by erecting *a mean temple in honour of Mahadeva* [authors' emphasis] in the front ... other devices have been resorted to, in order to obliterate the principal features of Buddhism (Fergusson 1835, 48).

The 'disfigurement' he described in 1835 continued to anger him. Ten years later he noted that the walls of the Karle *chaitya* were blackened by the smoke from cooking fires lit by resident Shaivites: 'the cave is dedicated to Shiva, the Daghoba performing the part of a gigantic Lingam, which it must be confessed it resembles a good deal' (Fergusson 1845, 29).

Fergusson made it clear in 1845 that he thought the Karle cave to be Buddhist in nature and probably 2,000 years old (Fergusson, 1845, 31), although the dates of construction remained uncertain. During that visit, he was keen to draw the complex but a 'great crowd at the fair and the noise and confusion' prevented him from doing so. Instead he made notes and corrections to a drawing by Salt (see Figure 11.3) which he had carried with him (Fergusson 1845, xii).[24] In the 1880 publication, *The Cave Temples of India,* Fergusson wrote that the base of the second lion pillar, which had either fallen down or been removed, was 'covered by the modern Siva temple' (Fergusson and Burgess 1880, 239).

If we assume that Fergusson's information is correct, then at some time between Maria Graham's visit in 1809 and his first visit in 1835, more than twenty years later, control of the Karle sacred hill had shifted from Jain to Hindu priests. Unlike Graham, Fergusson distinguished between the Karle Buddhist *chaitya* and the Ekveera Devi temple that stood at its entrance. His statements about the Ekveera Devi Mandir suggest that he believed it to be a relatively new addition to the complex, rather than part of the original Karle Buddhist structure. He specifically implied that Hindu control was the result of the policies of the Peshwa state, which had emerged in western India in the early eighteenth century with the decline of the Mughal empire. Fergusson also commented on the popularity of the Karle hill as a sacred pilgrimage site, although he tells us nothing about the pilgrims.

24 These notes accompanied Plate X (Fergusson 1845, 27).

Our understanding of the nature of these two shrines – the Buddhist Karle *chaitya* and the Ekveera Devi Mandir – is improved by the drawings that accompanied the descriptions of the Karle hill site provided by Graham and Fergusson. Already at the age of 24, Maria Graham was a talented artist and a keen observer, as her later fame as a botanist was to demonstrate.[25] The signature in the bottom left-hand corner of James Sargant Storer's engraving of her drawing of the entrance to the Karle *chaitya* (Figure 11.2) reads: 'M.G. del.'[26]

By contrast, Fergusson's drawing, published first in 1876 and again in 1899 (Figure 11.4) was based on an earlier sketch by Henry Salt in 1804. Fergusson said that he had 'corrected' Salt's work. Salt's sketch was preceded by a drawing of the Karle site nine years earlier by John Johnson, a member of the Bombay Engineers who was undertaking a survey of the Nashik-Pune area in the mid-1790s. In his sketchbook there is a watercolour drawing of the entrance to the Karle *chaitya* showing the Ekveera Devi temple on the right (J. Johnson 1795). Its presumed date of execution, 1795, makes this the first image of the Karle site created by a European. It is not known whether Fergusson knew of Johnson's sketch. If he did, he may have chosen to base his own drawing on Salt's in deliberate preference to Johnson's lifeless and not especially attractive watercolour (Salt 1804).

What all four illustrations have in common is that they depict the Ekveera Devi Mandir standing on the right-hand side of the entrance to the Karle Buddhist *chaitya*, in exactly the same spot it occupies today. The shrine to Ekveera has not changed its basic structure in the last 221 years: for example, the four steps which lead to the platform on which the Ekveera Devi temple sits appear in all the illustrations discussed above and in our recent photograph (Plate 11.2).

In summary, since 1795 the Ekveera Devi temple has been depicted in images as standing at the entrance to the Buddhist Karle *chaitya* by Johnson, Salt, Graham and Fergusson. Both Graham and Fergusson provide us with more information about the site, but only Fergusson was aware that it was controlled by a different religious group from the one that built the Karle *chaitya*.

25 Betty Hagglund (2011, 47-48) has recently described Graham as a competent orientalist and botanist.

26 'M.G.' stands for Maria Graham and 'del' for the Latin *delineavit* ('she/he drew it'). 'Del' commonly appears on engravings to identify the artist of the original work. Fourteen other engravings in her *Journal of a Residence in India* are signed similarly.

Figure 11.2: 'Entrance to the Great Cave of Carli'. Just below the image on the left is Graham's attribution and on the right the engraver's name, James Storer (Graham 1812, 65).

When we met the experts at the Archaeological Survey of India in June 2012, they were not aware of the reports of these English observers. In reply to our questions about the origins of the Ekveera temple, they suggested that it was probably a structure that post-dated a central government notice dated 26 May 1909, because that notice makes no mention of Ekveera or any temple with that name. The notice placed the Karle hill complex under the protection of the Indian government's Archaeological Survey of India, an arrangement that continued after Independence in 1947. Our conclusion is that the Indian government must have included the Ekveera temple in its definition of the Karle Buddhist

Figure 11.3: 'View of Cave at Karli (from a Drawing by Mr Salt, corrected by the Author' (Fergusson 1876, 118). The image also appears with the caption 'Façade of Chaitya Cave at Karle, from a sketch by J.F.' in Fergusson and Burgess (1880, 236).

chaitya and that the officials may have been unaware of the separate and unique status of the Ekveera temple.[27] However, the internal structure of the Ekveera shrine perhaps justifies the Archaeological Survey of India's classification, because there is some evidence to support the idea that the Ekveera shrine may have been physically connected to the Karle cave for a very long time, even though it may have been carved out at a later date. Today, the main image inside the Ekveera Devi Mandir is of the goddess Ekveera, which the local *pujari* say is a natural stone formation (*swayambhu*) that is part of the rock face from which the Karle temple has been formed. As a result, visitors can only walk around three sides of the central icon. The image is smeared with *shendur* (red lead paint), as are other autochthonous images of Hindu gods and goddesses, over which an exquisite silver mask of the face of the goddess has been placed. Another mask, the less popular golden one, is hardly ever used, for it makes the image look angry rather than benign.[28]

27 It could also be that the Archaeological Survey of India does not want to attract attention to the complexity of the Karle hill, because, in recent years, it has become the site of a tussle over the conflicting claims of neo-Buddhist dalits, Kolis and Hindus relating to access to various parts of the hill.

28 The silver mask was made about forty-five years ago by a silversmith called Gotre. It shows the goddess as a benevolent and smiling deity. Recently, in 2011, *Koli* leader Anant Tare and Shivasena founder Balasaheb Thackeray commissioned a gold mask from the well-known goldsmith Sanjay Vedak, who has also made all the jewellery for *Siddhivinayak*, the famous *Ganesh* shrine at

In front of Ekveera is a small gold coloured statue of Ganesh. Standing to her right is a four foot high image of the goddess Jogeshwari. The Brāhman pujari in charge of the rituals at the temple told us that the carving of Jogeshwari was part of the wall of the Karle cave (Interview at Ekveera temple, 2012), but this is disputed by the Archaeological Survey of India (ASI) officials who insisted that she is a free standing statue that was installed relatively recently (Interview, Archaeological Survey of India Maharashtra Division, 26 June 2012, Bombay). According to the ASI officials, Jogeshwari is the family deity of the current managers of the Ekveera Devi temple. The priest's version reminds us that there are many interest groups keen to demonstrate that the Ekveera Devi Mandir is an ancient structure, a claim that they hope will legitimise their right to a place on the sacred hill of Karle.

Our conclusion from the available evidence is that, at some time between the construction of the Karle Buddhist *chaitya* in the second century BCE and the Indian government notification of 1909, the Son Kolis of Mumbai appropriated the part of the Karle sacred hill that we today describe as the Ekveera Devi temple. They probably did so with a sense of entitlement, as the worship of Koli mother goddesses long predates the evolution of Buddhism in India. The Son Kolis have also appropriated the use of the *stupa* inside the main hall of the Karle Buddhist cave by circumambulations, to make up for their inability to walk around the Ekveera Devi image. Dhere, however, provides a deeper explanation for the relationship of the Son Kolis with the *stupa*. He disagrees with Kosambi who thought of the *stupa* as a phallic symbol, largely because he looked at it from outside. Instead, Dhere (1978) focuses on the internal nature of the *stupa*, which he likens to a *dagoba* (womb). This interpretation certainly links the *stupa* more closely with the mother goddess worship of the Son Kolis. Up to the early 1990s, the Kolis also performed sacrifices in front of the *stupa*, a practice that was stopped when gates were placed at the entrance to the *stupa* sanctum.

However, the process of appropriation goes two ways, because the neo-Buddhist dalits who worship in the Karle Buddhist *chaitya* also visit the Ekveera Devi temple to pay their respects to Koli's clan goddess.[29]

Prabhadevi and the mask of the goddess *Mahalaxmi* at Kolhapur.

29 The Buddhist Karle *chaitya* may have fallen into disuse with the decline of Buddhist worship in western India from about 1500 onwards, but since the great untouchable leader Dr Ambedkar led thousands of dalits into Buddhism during the first great conversion of 1956, neo-Buddhists have started to reclaim the Karle cave site.

When we asked them why they come to the Ekveera shrine, they typically replied 'Ekveera is the mother of Buddha'. These words are not accidental, for the oral traditions of India acknowledge the age-old importance of mother goddesses in India, predating Buddhism. Other communities also worship on the Karle hill but that story is the subject of another paper that we are writing. For the moment we are focused on the presence of thousands of Son Kolis who have come to dominate the sacred site known as the Karle hill.

Son Kolis' appropriation of Karle hill

The appropriation of the sacred Karle hill site by the Son Kolis of Mumbai has gone beyond the appropriation of the Buddhist *chaitya* and the Ekveera Devi temple next to it. The Son Kolis have also claimed extensive parts of the rest of the hill, as Figure 11.4 shows.

Above the Ekveera temple and to the right, there is a cave that now contains a very large wooden chest that holds the clothes and other objects used to venerate the goddess Ekveera. This cave is probably one of the original sixteen that date from Buddhist times.

The local *pujaris* claim that the chest must be at least as old as the cave because it would have been impossible to carry anything as big as it into a cave with such a narrow opening. Another source, however, revealed that the chest was recently constructed inside the cave to its extremely large dimensions to ensure that it cannot be easily removed and that its components were smuggled into the area, in defiance of the status of the Karle hill complex as a protected area under the control of the Archaeological Survey of India.

There are many other caves to the right and left of the Karle *chaitya*, as Maria Graham and Fergusson noted. To the right of the cave containing the large wooden chest, there is an extensive, horizontal crevice that has also become a site for Koli worship. The gouge in the rock is said to represent Shitalamata, the Hindu smallpox goddess. She is frequently depicted in close relationships with other Koli goddesses and reminds us of a time when smallpox was common and had no cure or prevention. Below this point there is another cave at ground level containing a shivalinga and a wall carving of a Buddhist figure. This cave is located about ten metres to the right of the Ekveera temple and has been the subject of a dispute between the Kolis and the *dalits*. This forced the Archaeological Survey of India to install a gate that prevents easy entry to the cave.

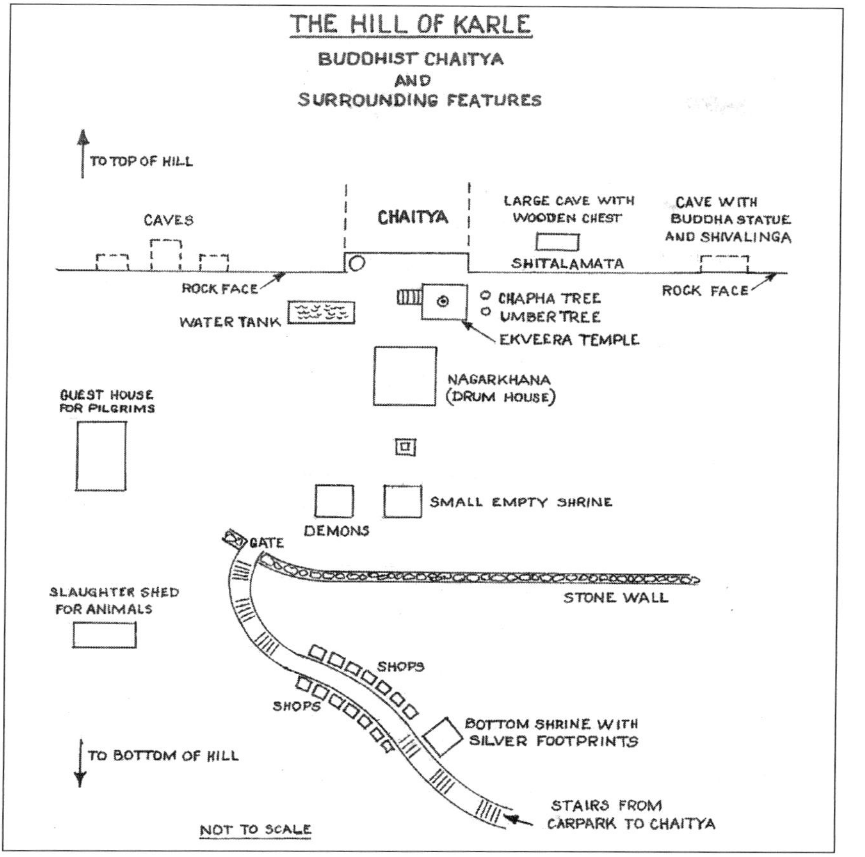

Figure 11.4: The Karle hill, showing the features that now define Koli ritual worship.

The guard at the site is often a Muslim, as this is thought to be more effective in preventing Hindus, Kolis or dalits from entering the cave without authorisation.

Like all the other Koli goddesses, Ekveera Devi is a water goddess so, to the left of her shrine, there is an enormous water tank from which pilgrims can drink (Plate 11.1). The entire hill used to be covered with reservoirs, as Maria Graham reported in the first decade of the nineteenth century: 'The cave of Carli … is situated near the top of a wooded mountain, commanding one of the finest prospects in the world; its reservoirs cut, like itself, out of the living rock, overflow with the purest water' (Graham 1812, 64-65). The tank that visitors see today was built recently, but the springs that feed it are very old and help explain the selection of this particular site as a suitable location for the Karle Buddhist *chaitya* and the Ekveera Devi temple. According to Kosambi, the Pune area in general has a surviving water-goddess cult that has existed for thousands of years. At the entrance to the *chaitya* the words 'Mamala-hara' and 'Mamale' appear in an inscription from the time of Pulumayi II, the Satavahana king who ruled towards the end of the Satavahana dynasty in the first and second centuries CE (Kosambi 1994, 86). Kosambi linked the worship of mother goddesses to the water spirits (*asaras*). These water spirits continue to form an important part of Son Koli worship in Mumbai, where the malevolent *sat* (seven) *asaras* were transformed into the benign village goddesses of the Son Kolis.

Ekveera has other typical Koli traits; she is, for example, not a vegetarian goddess. The Kolis continue to sacrifice animals to her and also offer alcohol. Neither sacrifice nor alcohol is permitted inside the Ekveera Devi temple, so the rituals are conducted outside by a special caste of non-Brāhmin Gurav temple priests, all of whom have the surname Deshmukh and come from the village of Maherghar. The animals are slaughtered at the bottom of the Karle hill after the offerings have been shown to the demons (*daityas*) whose image is located in front of the Ekveera shrine. Today, many of the shops leading to the Ekveera Devi temple sell chicken, goats and sheep to pilgrims for the purposes of sacrifice. Close to the demons there is the large two-storey structure allegedly built by the Peshwas (1674-1818)[30] where Ekveera's ritual drums are kept (Figure 11.5).[31] Ekveera also has a brother, called Bhairavanath, and in this she is similar to other Koli goddesses. The Bhairavanath temple is in the village of Maherghar, which is on a hill opposite the Ekveera Devi Mandir some six kilometres away.

In summary, Figure 11.4 and related evidence show that the Son Kolis of Mumbai have appropriated the caves surrounding the Karle Buddhist *chaitya* and the land on which the water tank, *nagarkhana* (drum house), the demons and slaughter area are situated. In addition to this, they have built a large guesthouse to the left of the temple complex for pilgrims. An exception to this appropriation is a small shrine at the foot of the hill where a Maratha family has installed the silver footprints of Ekveera Devi. Pilgrims first pray at this shrine before commencing their ascent of the hill.

30 The Peshwas and the Maratha Confederacy were formally absorbed into British India in 1818.

31 If we were able to verify the role of the Peshwas in building this structure it would support other claims suggesting that it was the patronage of the Peshwas that ensured the dominance of Hindu priests at this shrine at some time after Maria Graham's visit.

Figure 11.5: The *nagarkhana* dwarfs the Ekveera Devi temple standing behind it and is very large in comparison with the entrance into the Karle Buddhist *chaitya*. (Photo: Jayant Bhalchandra Bapat).

We noted earlier in this chapter another exception when explaining why dalits are also now appropriating parts of the Karle hill: they are visiting the Ekveera Devi temple; they are contesting the use of the Karle Buddhist *chaitya* by Kolis and others; and they are fighting to gain control of some of the caves behind the Karle temple. Other castes also visit the sacred Karle hill, such as Chandraseniya Kayastha Prabhus (CKPs), Guravs, Brāhmins, Sonars, and Kunbis, and their association with the site is a topic investigated by us in another paper. The presence of some of these castes goes back a long time. For example, the care of the Karle caves was shared by Brāhmins and Guravs (a non-Brāhmin priestly caste) in the nineteenth century and before. The Brāhmins waited on the Goddess and the Gurav cleaned the premises (Government Central Press 1885), at a time when there was no official distinction between the Buddhist *chaitya* and the Ekveera Devi temple. Today, the protection of the entire hill is in the hands of the Archaeology Survey of India, but daily administration devolves to the Kolis in the matter of the Ekveera Devi Mandir. The management of the other structures on the hill is contested. Despite these complexities, the overwhelming evidence today is that the Son Kolis have established a dominating presence on the sacred Karle hill.

Conclusion: hypothesis about the appropriation process

In this chapter we have documented the extent to which the Son Kolis of Mumbai have appropriated the sacred Karle hill near Lonavla, including the Buddhist *chaitya,* and the culture of *bhakti* pilgrimage as a way of devoting themselves to Ekveera Devi. We have argued that this process of appropriation is uniquely different from anything in our previous accounts of how the Son Kolis have absorbed, modified and adopted the religious beliefs and practices of other communities that form part of the cultural complexity of Mumbai and India more generally. Ekveera Devi worship has shifted the primary sacred site of the Son Kolis beyond Mumbai and the institution of pilgrimage to the Ekveera Devi mandir has been added to their worshipping rituals. In this way, the veneration of Ekveera Devi contributes to the interconnectedness of the many sub-tribal Koli groups and also what would otherwise remain an artificial bureaucratic creation, namely the state of Maharashtra (Feldhaus, 2003).

What we do *not* know is how and when the Son Kolis came to regard Ekveera as their clan goddess. Moreover, Ekveera Devi is not the monopoly of the Son Kolis, even though they have been her most active devotees; she is also the clan goddess of other Koli groups, including the Mahadev Kolis. We end our analysis with a hypothesis about the manner in which Ekveera Devi and the Son Kolis became involved with each other and how the Son Kolis have moved beyond cultural appropriation into appropriating the benefits of the reservation policies that the Mahadev Kolis had been entitled to since 1950.

There are two aspects to our speculation. First, we suggest that Ekveera Devi was initially the main goddess of the Mahadev Kolis, who are primarily a hill tribe who populated the hilly regions to the north of Pune (Ghurye 1957). The Ekveera Devi temple at the entrance to the Karle Buddhist *chaitya* is at the centre of the part of Maharashtra in which Mahadev Koli kingdoms and rebellions were based for more than 600 years, between 1300 and the 1950s (Hardiman 1995) – that is, the districts of Dhule, Nasik, Ahmednagar, to the north of Lonavla, and Satara and Solapur, to the south (Figure 11.6). Lonavla, the closest town to the Karle *chaitya* and Ekveera Devi temple, is the central point of this diverse region. The founding of the Mahadev Koli Nayak state of Jawhar in 1300 (Hardiman 1995, 96) is especially interesting as it coincided with the rise of the *bhakti* movement. This suggests that from the beginning of the *bhakti* phenomenon, there was probably a close relationship between the Kolis and devotional worship; we noted earlier in this chapter that Raghu Bhangare, one of the great Koli rebel leaders, adopted the garb of a *bhakti* pilgrim in the 1840s, which constituted a claim to political legitimacy by both the rebels and the Koli king that the British could not equal.

In contrast to the upland Mahadev Kolis, the Son Kolis have never been a major hill tribe. They were predominantly fisherfolk inhabiting the islands of Bombay and the western coast of India from the Konkan up to Pakistan. But, given the many dams, rivers and inland water resources in the Western Ghats, no doubt some Son Kolis lived in the hills as fisherfolk. We say this because the historical connection between the seas surrounding Bombay and the mainland rivers was very strong before it was broken by the siltation of the rivers. Nevertheless, by and large, the Son Kolis were not ideally placed to worship Ekveera until fairly recently when better road and rail transport allowed thousands of Son Kolis from Mumbai to undertake the pilgrimage to the Karle hill. In particular, Son Koli access to the Ekveera Devi site has been greatly improved since Anant Tare, a Koli and the Shiv Sena's leader in Thane district, became President of the Ekveera Temple Trust.[32]

Another explanation provided to us by one Koli elder in the Dharavi *koliwada* is that the Son Kolis are descended from those Mahadev Kolis who decided to come down from the hills into the islands of Mumbai. They acquired the name *Son* (meaning 'gold') Koli because their women accumulated much gold which they wore in the form of jewellery. This origin myth links with contemporary claims that the *Son* Kolis are really, and always have been, Mahadev Kolis (outlined below) (Interview with Koli politician, Dharavi, 20 January 2012).

The notion that Ekveera Devi began as a Mahadev Koli goddess is supported by evidence about the location of other Ekveera Devi temples in central India, for example, at Amrawati and Chandrapur. Master (1939, 1012) has suggested that the Mahadev Kolis originated from the Nizam's territory which included Amrawati and Chandrapur, and that they migrated westwards. This raises the possibility that the Ekveera temples in Amrawati and Chandrapur were built and patronised by the Mahadev

32 Shiv Sena politicians in Mumbai's Koli villages are the subject of a forthcoming paper by the authors.

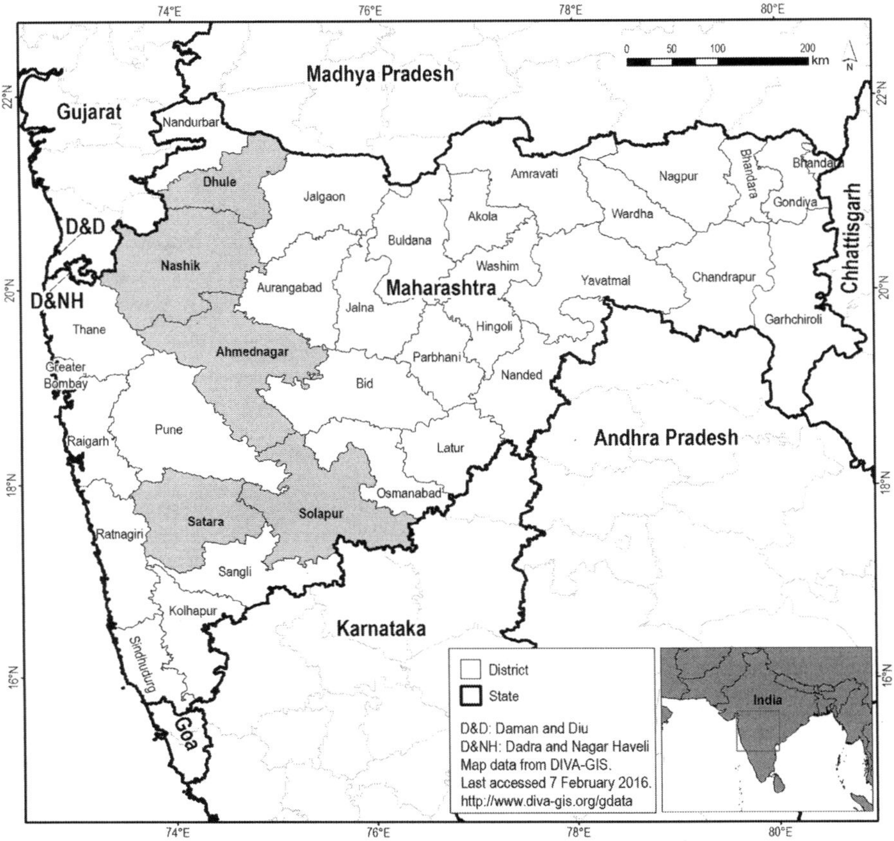

Figure 11.6: Diagram of Maharashtra showing all districts. Those marked in light grey are where the rebellions occurred (Prepared by Dr Uri Gilad, 7 February 2016).

Kolis before they migrated into the western parts of Maharashtra.[33] As they moved into western India, they appropriated and built other temples for their worship of Ekveera, including the structure that came to be called the Ekveera Devi temple at the entrance to the Karle Buddhist *chaitya*. At a much later date, the worship of Ekveera Devi was then taken over by the Son Kolis from Mumbai. In other words, perhaps the Son Kolis of Mumbai have been involved in a double appropriation: first by displacing the Mahadev Kolis as the main worshippers of Ekveera and second by appropriating the sacred hill of the Karle cave complex in the manner we have described in the chapter.

33 Today, the worshippers and pilgrims at Amrawati and Chandrapur come from many different social groups. The exact nature of their participation in worshipping Ekveera is the subject of another paper by us.

Our second observation is that the Son Kolis have not only appropriated the worship of Ekveera Devi but also, more generally, have blended themselves into the Mahadev Koli sub-tribe. The end result of this process of affiliation has been a blurring between the Son Kolis and the Mahadev Kolis and the emergence of a generic Koli tribal clan that minimises inter-group differences. The devotion of the Son Kolis to goddess Ekveera took them into the hills of the Western Ghats as pilgrims. The Mahadev Kolis moved in the opposite direction by migrating into Mumbai city in search of work. The search for urban employment in the rising metropolis of Mumbai was only one index of the rapid socio-economic decline of the Mahadev Kolis. By 1911, the glory days of the Mahadev Koli Nayak Kingdom of Jawhar had ended; in that year the British classified the Mahadev Kolis as 'criminal tribes', a title that described their many long rebellions against colonial rule. However, by the time of the Indian Census of 1931, the Mahadev Kolis had been reclassified as a severely disadvantaged community and were included in a list of 'Scheduled Tribes'. This list was eventually attached to the Indian Constitution of 1950, thus entitling the Mahadev Kolis to the benefits of affirmative action or reservation policies after Independence.[34]

By contrast, the Son Kolis were regarded by the British as rich and influential. This early British perception meant that the Son Kolis became the *de facto* 'rulers' of Bombay, partly because of the gold that they had allegedly hoarded. Even though the economic fortune of the Son Kolis quickly declined to the extent that they became the 'coolies' that built Bombay, giving the tribal name (Koli) to the new British colonial profession of portage ('coolie'), myths about their wealth lingered. The myth of Koli wealth is perhaps the reason that the Son Kolis of Bombay were not classified as Scheduled Tribes in the 1931 Census or in the Indian Constitution of 1950. As a result, the Son Kolis have not been able to access the special programs designed to promote the wellbeing of India's Scheduled Tribes.[35]

Thanks to reservation, the economic prospects of the Mahadev Kolis relative to the Son Kolis were reversed, with the result that thousands of

34 The Mahadev or Mahadeo Kolis were named in Part IX of the Indian Constitution (1950) as one of the three Koli groups deserving reservation or affirmative action (Lok Sabha Petitions Committee 2003, 2; Ranade 2008). These three remain in the Indian Constitution to this day as no. 28 (Koli Dhor, Tokre Koli, Kolcha, Kogha), no. 29 (Koli Mahadeo, Donger Koli) and no. 30 (Koli Malhar).

35 For analysis of the history and implementation of reservation or compensatory discrimination policies, see Mendelsohn and Vicziany (1998, chapters 4 and 5).

Son Kolis began to claim they were Mahadev Kolis or Mahadeos. As the traditional employment opportunities for the Son Kolis in modern Mumbai continued to fall, they were increasingly keen to be seen as disadvantaged Scheduled Tribes. Consequently, during our research on the Son Kolis, it has become increasingly difficult for us to distinguish between Son Kolis and Mahadev Kolis because the Son Kolis now perceive the name 'Son' as something that disqualifies them from the benefits of reservation. While many Son Kolis now claim to be Mahadev Kolis, a small group of politically active Son Kolis are demanding that all Koli sub-tribes be made eligible for reservation. In summary, the cultural appropriation of the Son Kolis has now moved into a new phase of political-cum-economic appropriation in which the Son Kolis are blending their identity with the Mahadev Kolis.

Appendix: Koli interviewees and the village deities they worship

No. of interviewees	Deity/Dieties worshipped	Interviewees' place of residence
Kolis who said that their village deity was the traditional village Devi		
2	Maru aai (Mari Aai) (Village Mother Goddess)	Khar Danda/ Khar
3	Saat Baya (7 Asaras*) and Vetal Dev	Koliwada Trombay/ Sion
1	Khadadevi (Village Mother Goddess)	Colaba
2	Hingaladevi (Mother Goddess)	Versova
3	Gavdevi (Village Mother Goddess)	Vitava, Thane / Navi Mumbai / Navghar Mulund
1	Patadevi (Village Mother Goddess)	Malad
1	Thal, Alibag (Village Mother Goddess)	Colaba
13/27 (48%)		
Kolis who said that their village deity was not a traditional village Devi		
1	Bhairee	Bandra
2	Ekveera (Clan Mother Goddess)	Virar
2	Ganapati (Shiva)	Bandra / Ghansoli
1	Tulja Bahvānī (Shiva)	Bhandup
1	Khandoba (Shiva)	Colaba
1	Bapdev (Shiva)	Sewree Koliwada
1	Hanuman (Vishnu)	Mahul
9/27 (33%)		
Kolis who said that they did not have a village deity		
5	None	Panvel / Bhandup / Belapur, Diwale / Kalyan / Colaba
5/27 (19%)		

Source: Interviews at the Ekveera Devi Mandir, Karle Hill, September 2009, over three days.

* The term *asara* is distinctive, and, although it may have originated from the Sanskrit word *apsaras* (celestial damsel), *asaras* are typically malevolent, which has never been true of *apsarases*.

Acknowledgments

We are grateful to Andrea Di Castro, Ian Mabbett, Jim Masselos and Vivien Seyler for their comments on earlier drafts of this chapter and to Ifti Arman Rashid for his work as our research assistant.

Bibliography

ABC News. 2011. 'Indian guru Sai Baba dies'. 25 April. http://www.abc.net.au/news/2011-04-24/indian-guru-sai-baba-dies/2604852 (accessed 8 April 2016).

Bapat, Jayant, Bhalchandra. 2010. 'The Kolis of Mumbai: the vanishing people'. Paper presented to the *13th International Conference on Maharashtra: Culture and Society*', Bratislava, Slovak Republic, 17-19 June.

Brekke, Torkel. 2002. *Makers of Modern Indian Religion in the Late Nineteenth Century.* New York: Oxford University Press.

Buchanan, F. 1807. 'Particulars of the Jains Extracted from a Journal by Doctor F Buchanan during travels in Canara'. *Asiatick Researches* (Calcutta) 9: 279-286.

Colebrooke, H.T. 1807. 'Observations on the sect of Jains'. *Asiatick Researches* (Calcutta) 9: 287-322.

Dhere, Ramchandra Chintaman. 1978. *Lajjagauri*. Pune: Shri Vidya Prakashan (In Marathi).

Dhere, Ramchandra Chintaman. 2011. *The Rise of a Folk God: Vitthal of Pandharpur,* translated by Anne Feldhaus. New York: Oxford University Press. (Originally published in Marathi in 1984 as *sri Vitthal, eka mahasamanvaya.*)

Eck, Diana. 1998. *Darśan: Seeing the Divine Image in India.* NewYork: Columbia University Press.

Feldhaus, Anne. 2011. 'Preface'. In R.C. Dhere. *The Rise of a Folk God: Vitthal of Pandharpur.* New York: Oxford University Press.

Feldhaus, Anne. 2003. Connected Places: Region, Pilgrimage, and Geographical Imagination in India. New York: Palgrave Macmillan.

Fergusson, James. 1835. 'Cave-temples of India.' *The Asiatic Journal and Monthly Register for British and Foreign India, China and Australasia, new series,* Vol. 18: 41-48.

Fergusson, James. 1845. *Illustrations of the Rock-Cut Temples of India: Text to Accompany the Folio Volume of Plates.* London: John Weale.

Fergusson, James. 1876 (1899 impression). *History of Indian and Eastern Architecture.* London: John Murray.

Fergusson, James and James Burgess. 1880 (1969 reprint). *The cave temples of India.* Delhi: Oriental Books Reprint Corporation.

Ghurye, G.S. 1957. *The Mahadev Kolis.* Bombay: Popular Prakashan.

Government Central Press. 1885. 'The great Vahargaon or Karle rock temple lies within the limits of Vahargaon village'. Poona, 1885.

Graham, Maria. 1812 (2000 reprint). *Journal of a Residence in India*. New Delhi/Madras: Asian Educational Services.

Hagglund, Betty. 2011. 'The botanical writings of Maria Graham'. *Journal of Literature and Science* 4 (1): 44-58.

Hardiman, David. 1995. 'Community, patriarchy, honour: Raghu Bhanagre's revolt'. *Journal of Peasant Studies* 23 (1): 88-130.

Johnson, Donald Clay. 1993. 'Western discovery of Jain temple libraries'. *Libraries & Culture* 28 (2): 189-203.

Johnson. John. 1795. 'The Karle Caves, Karli', f. 7 from a sketchbook dated c. 1795-1801 held in the British Library http://www.bl.uk/onlinegallery/onlineex/apac/other/019wdz000001055u00007000.html (accessed 8 April 2016).
Khandoba.org. 'About Khandoba'. http://khandoba.org/about_khandoba.html (accessed 8 April 2016).
Kosambi, D.D. 2009. 'Dhenukākata'. In *The Oxford India Kosambi: Combined Methods in Indology and Other Writings*, edited by B. Chattopadhyaya, 450-475. New Delhi: Oxford University Press. (Originally published in *Journal of the Bombay Branch of the Royal Asiatic Society* 30 (1955): 50-71).
Kosambi, D.D. 1994. *Myth and Reality: Studies in the Formation of Indian Culture,* Bombay: Popular Prakashan.
Lok Sabha Committee on Petitions. 2003. 'Chapter 1: Petition Requests for Inclusion of Koli Caste in the List of Scheduled Tribes of Maharashtra'. *Twenty Sixth Report, Thirteenth Lok Sabha*, Lok Sabha Secretariat, 23 April.
Mackenzie, C. 1807. 'Account of the Jains, collected from a priest of this sect at Mudgeri, translated by Cavelly Boria, Bráhmen'. *Asiatick Researches* (Calcutta) 9: 244-278.
Master, Alfred. 1939. 'Koḷī or Dhārāḷo, etc'. *Bulletin of the School of Oriental Studies, University of London* 9 (4): 1009-1013.
Mate, Madhukar Shripad. 1962. *Temples and Legends of Maharashtra*. Bombay: Bharatiya Vidya Bhavan.
Mendelsohn, Oliver, and Marika Vicziany. 1998. *The Untouchables: Subordination, Poverty and the State in Modern India.* Cambridge: Cambridge University Press.
Michell, George. 1999. 'The Architecture of Elephanta: An Interpretation', in Doniger O'Flaherty, Wendy; George Michell; Carmell Berkson. *Elephanta: The Cave of Shiva.* Delhi: Motilal Banarsidass Publishers.
Nagaraju, S. 1981. *Buddhist Architecture of Western India (c.250 B.C – c. A.D. 300).* Delhi: Agam Kala Prakashan.
Ranade, Sanjay. 2008. 'The Kolis of Mumbai at crossroads: religion, business and urbanisation in cosmopolitan Bombay today'. In *Is this the Asian Century? Proceedings of the 17th Biennial Conference of the Asian Studies Association of Australia,* edited by M. Vicziany and R. Cribb. http://artsonline.monash.edu.au/mai/files/2012/07/sanjayranade.pdf (accessed 8 April 2016).
Ranade, Sanjay. 2009. 'Livelihood and religion in Mumbai: a study of the Kolis of Dharavi'. Unpublished manuscript.
Rigopoulos, Antonio. 1993. *The Life and Teachings of Sai Baba of Shirdi*. New York: State University of New York Press.
Salt, Henry. 1804. 'Exterior of Rock Temple, Karle', wash drawing held in the British Library. http://www.bl.uk/onlinegallery/onlineex/apac/other/019wdz000001307u00000000.html (accessed 10 April 2016).
Schubring, Walther. 2000. *The Doctrine of the Jainas: Described after the Old Sources*, 2nd rev ed. New Delhi: Motilal Banarsidass. (Translated from the German *Die Lehre der Jainas*, originally published in Berlin, 1935.)
Snodgrass, Adrian. 1985. *The Symbolism of the Stupa.* Ithaca NY: Cornell University.
Sontheimer, Günther-Dietz. 1986. 'Rudra and Khandoba: continuity in folk religion'. In *Religion and Society in Maharashtra*, edited by M. Israel and N.K. Wagle, 1-31. Toronto: Centre for South Asian Studies.
Sontheimer, Günther-Dietz. 1989. *Pastoral Deities in Western India*, translated by Anne Feldhaus. Delhi: Oxford University Press.
Sontheimer, Günther-Dietz. 1997. *King of Hunters, Warriors and Shepherds: Essays on Khandoba*, edited by A. Feldhaus, A. Malik and H. Brückner. Delhi: Indira Gandhi National Centre for the Arts.

Stanley, John M. 1977. 'Special time, special power: the fluidity of power in a popular Hindu festival'. *The Journal of Asian Studies* 37 (1): 27-43.

Vicziany, Marika, Jayant Bhalchandra Bapat, and Sanjay Ranade. 2013. 'Muslim saints and Hindu fundamentalism: co-existence amongst the tribal Koli of Mumbai'. In *Rethinking India: perceptions from Australia*, edited by L. Brennan and Auriol Weigold, 198-221. New Delhi: Readyworthy.

Vicziany, Marika, and Jayant Bhalchandra Bapat. 2009. 'Mumbadevi and the other Mother Goddesses in Mumbai, India'. *Modern Asian Studies* 43 (2): 511-541.

Vicziany, Marika, and Jayant Bhalchandra Bapat. 2008. 'The Khadadevi temple of modern Mumbai'. In *The Iconic Female: Goddesses of India, Nepal and Tibet*, edited by J.B. Bapat and I.W. Mabbett, 189-207. Melbourne: Monash Asia Institute.

Youngblood, Michael D. 2003. 'The Varkaris'. *Critical Asian Studies* 35 (2): 287-300.

Interviews cited

Archaeological Survey of India, Maharashtra office, Bombay, 26 June 2012.
Archaeological Survey of India, National Headquarters, New Delhi, 19 July 2012.
Twenty-seven Koli pilgrims at Lonavla, Maharashtra, September 2009.
Ekveera temple *pujari*, Ekveera Devi Mandir, Lonavla, 2012.
Koli gym instructor, Worli, Mumbai, 27 January 2008.
Koli mother, Worli, Mumbai, 21 January 2008.
Koli old lady, Worli, Mumbai, 21 January 2008.
Koli politician, Worli, Mumbai, 2010-2013.
Koli politician, Dharavi, Mumbai, 20 January 2012.
Koli professional migrant, Sydney, 2 May 2013.

Chapter 12

Modern Appropriations of Devī

Martin Hříbek

I

Appropriation has been one of the favourite strategies in Indian religious traditions for establishing the emerging, hitherto alien and unacceptable, or outright novel ideas, cults, and practices as a continuity of a tradition rather than a disjuncture from it. That strategy has served not just the theological and spiritual, but often worldly political ends too. In medieval India sectarian movements competing for following and patronage did not posit themselves in mutually exclusive terms but were happy to accommodate, appropriate and hierarchically subsume other schools of thought, while at the same time they claimed for themselves the most efficient and ultimate path to the supreme knowledge (Stietencron 2007, 50-89). Kunal Chakrabarti in his extensive study of *Upapurāṇas* from Bengal (Chakrabarti 2001) shows how the Brāhminical appropriation of local cults, in particular of goddesses, resulted through what he terms the 'Puranic process' in a regional tradition. The *Purāṇas,* in his view, served as a medium of 'propagation of brahmanical ideals of social reconstruction and sectarian interests, a medium for the absorption of local cults and associated practices, and a vehicle for popular instruction on norms governing everyday existence' (Chakrabarti 2001, 52).

The *Purāṇas* thus 'performed the delicate task of operating simultaneously at several levels, widening their scope to accommodate local elements as much as possible and involving as many people as permissible without compromising their principal objective of establishing the Brāhminical social order' (*Ibid.*). This appropriation was enacted through 'negotiation of meanings' between the 'great' (pan-Indian), and 'little' (local, Bengali in this case) traditions (Chakrabarti 2001, 317) in between the eighth and the thirteenth centuries.

In the colonial and postcolonial periods of Indian history there has been much diffuse but equally powerful and striking process of 'negotiation of meanings' under way to harness the goddess cult in constructions of competing visions of Indian modernity. I shall call such transformations of the goddess cult 'modern appropriations of Devī'. The ultimate template for modern appropriations of Devī emerged in the form of Mother India, or Bhāratmātā, as perhaps the most all-encompassing unifying symbol for the future nation. In the following pages I will explore the continuities of the modern creative process exemplified by the late nineteenth-century 'Bhāratmātā' and early twenty-first-century 'Svaccha Nārāyaṇī' with the original conception of Devī.

II

The modern *avatāras* of Devī are based upon the basic tenets of goddess worship revealed in the canonical Puranic text *Devī-Māhātmya*, a part of the *Mārkaṇḍeyapurāṇa*.[1] The *Devī-Māhātmya* postulates an omnipresent and omnipotent female energy or *śakti* as the source of the whole creation. The Ādi-śakti, or primordial *śakti*, gives rise to all other forms of goddesses and animates the gods. All those forms are in turn considered to be one aspect or one quality of the all-encompassing transcendental notion of *śakti*.

The introduction to the *Devī-Māhātmya* begins with the story of existential suffering afflicting king Suratha and the trader Samādhi. These two meet in the forest hermitage of the sage Medhas who initiates them into the principles of Goddess worship. The Devī appears to them in the trinity of forms: Mahākālī, a ten-faced goddess whom Brāhmā extolled

1 The *Mārkaṇḍeyapurāṇa* dates back to the first half of the first millennium CE. Out of this vast text, chapters 81-93 form the *Devī-Māhātmya*, or 'Greatness of the Goddess'. *Devī-Māhātmya* is also known as *Śrī Durgāsaptaśatī* (700 verses on Durgā) or *Caṇḍīpāṭha* (Recital on Caṇḍī). According to Winternitz (2003, Vol. I, 540), *Devī-Māhātmya* is a self-contained whole and a later interpolation to the *Mārkaṇḍeyapurāṇa* and could have existed before the seventh century CE. It represents the oldest systematic treatise on goddess worship in the Indian tradition. For an analysis of this seminal text, see Coburn (1984) and Stietencron (2005, 115-172). As the primary text I used a Bengali edition of *Devī-Māhātmya* (*Śrī Śrī Caṇḍī*) by Jagadīśvarānanda (1999), which contains the original Sanskrit and Bengali translation with notes and commentaries.

in order to destroy the demons Madhu and Kaitabha; Mahālakṣmī, a goddess with eighteen hands who is the slayer of the demon Mahiṣāsura; and Mahāsarasvatī, an eight-handed goddess who vanquished Śumbha and other demons. The three forms represent three basic qualities of reality postulated by Samkhya philosophy: darkness or inertia (*tamas*); passion (*rajas*); and purity (*sattva*) respectively. The threefold representation is significant for her latter modern interpretations as well.

The dialectics of ultimate oneness beyond the phenomenal world combined with gendered perception of reality thus create a possibility for a female figure to signify a unity at an abstract level. But at the same time *Devī* appropriates the agency of male gods. The work states that Mahālakṣmī as Mahiṣāsuramardinī, the slayer of the buffalo demon, was created out of a combined radiant glow emanating from foreheads of male gods angry at their defeat by the demon. Before she set forth into fierce battle with the demon, each god gave her one of his weapons. In another seminal text, the *Saundaryalaharī*, attributed to the Ādi-Śankarācārya, the Goddess appropriates the attributes of Śiva (Bake 1955). Her origin in the glow emanating from the male gods and her ability to issue other goddesses of different qualities and to absorb them again underline the dividual nature of her forms, which in turn allows the modern *avatāra*s to be perceived as a continuation of the mythic struggle or an episode thereof. Indeed, the replacement of traditional weapons in the hands of Durgā with another set of objects is one of the favourite ways to refashion the Durgā image for modern purposes.

The first compelling expression of the modern goddess of the nation appeared in the novel *Ānandamaṭh* (The Sacred Brotherhood, 1882)[2] by Bankimchandra Chattopadhyay, an author dubbed the father of the Indian novel. Bankimchandra's historical novels were influenced by those of Sir Walter Scott and his non-fictional writings by the rationalism and humanism of Auguste Comte and the utilitarianism of John Stuart Mill, among others. In his treatise on religion (*Dharmatattva*) he deems that not only gods, kings, upper castes, elders, teachers, husbands etc. but also the state and society should be the object of devotion (*bhakti*). In the same work Bankimchandra asserts that 'Auguste Comte has recommended the worship of the Goddess of Humanity' (Guha 1997, 53). In *Dharmatattva*

2 A translation of the novel with extensive introduction and critical apparatus by Julius Lipner was published in 2005 under the title *Ānandamaṭh, or The Sacred Brotherhood (Chatterji 2005).* Zbavitel (1976) translated the title as *The Monastery of the Anandas*; it has also been translated as *The Abbey of Bliss* and *The Abode of Bliss.*

Bankimchandra neither rejects non-Hindu religions nor sees them as mutually incompatible but, rather, attempts to appropriate them into the *vaiṣṇava dharma* which he considers to be 'the essence of religion' in general: 'The Christian and Brahmo religions are a part of this *vaiṣṇava* religion. Whether I call god, or I call *allah*, I address Viṣṇu, the lord of the universe' (quoted in Kaviraj 1995, 141).

Bankimchandra was appalled by the inactivity of his fellow citizens in the face of foreign domination and, long before Foucault and Said, held that the colonial interpretation of history based on Muslim sources and the British portrayal of Indians in it was to be partly responsible for this passivity: 'Bengal must have her own history. Otherwise there is no hope for Bengal. Who is to write it? You have to write it. All of us have to write it', he exclaimed on the pages of the *Baṅgadarśan* (Mirror of Bengal)[3] in 1880 (quoted in Guha 1997, 153). According to Sudipta Kaviraj (1995, 109), who wrote an extensive essay on Bankimchandra's tryst with history, he wanted Indians to 'assert the right to narratives of the self', to a history which 'shows a world in the making, in its contingency, in its open probabilistic form'. The call for indigenous interpretation of history was closely related to the call for nation formation (*jātipratiṣṭhā*) and to the emphasis on the strength of arms (*bāhubal*). Writing the Hindu history of Bengal and India is presented as restoring the past glory of forefathers. By this equation Bankimchandra sought that 'sentiments, obligations and notions related to the natural family would be transferred increasingly to a larger, ideal family, constructed by political culture as the nation' (Guha 1997, 203). It is indeed a matter of debate as to the extent to which the imagery devised by Bankimchandra for the Nation is inclusive of Muslims or exclusively Hindu.[4]

Bankimchandra was not the first author to imagine the personified territory of India as a goddess and Indians as her children. Sumanta Banerjee traces her popularity to the lyrics of patriotic songs that were sung in the praise of Motherland at Hindu Fairs since their institution in Calcutta by leading Bengali intellectuals in 1867. There were also several theatre plays with Mother India as a character. In both, 'the common theme was based on a trinity of ideas: (i) that Mother India had fallen into bad times;

3 *Baṅgadarśan* was an influential monthly magazine founded by Bankimchandra in 1872. In that journal he published most of his political articles and novels.

4 This issue has been recently taken up by Lipner (2005 and 2008) who struggles to defend Bankimchandra against authors who accuse him of sowing the seed of hatred between Hindus and Muslims.

(ii) that her children were lying deep in slumber, indifferent to her sufferings; and (iii) that this was a call to awaken them' (Banerjee 2002, 198).

Bankimchandra put forward his vision of Bhāratmātā originally in the collection of satirical essays named *Kamalākānta*.[5] One of the essays, *'Āmār Durgotsab'* (My Durgāpūjā Festival), expresses Kamalakanta's visions after having opium on the first day of festivities:

> Being alone makes me very much afraid – so lonely – motherless – Mother! Mother! – I shout. In this vast ocean of time I have arrived in search of mother? Where is Mother! Where is my Mother? Where is Mother Bengal? ... Then I recognised, this is my Mother, my Motherland – this is Mother Mrinmayi – Mother within the clay image – bedecked with countless gems, currently residing in the depository of Time ... Come to us, Mother, come into our homes – six crore of us,[6] your children, shall worship your lotus feet, bow before you, folding our twelve crore arms ... Arise, Mother, Golden Bengal! Arise, Mother! We shall be your worthy children, we shall tread the right path – we shall bring you honour ... Come, let us raise aloft Mother's image with our twelve crore arms, and, carrying her upon our six crore heads, let us bring her home ... Come brothers, let us find and carry Mother back, then our pūjā will be festive like never before (Chatterji 1992, 104-107).

Bankimchandra clearly remains true to the 'trinity of ideas' as identified by Banerjee. Mother is lost, 'residing in the depository of Time', and has to be invoked so that she comes back. Kamalakanta's vision, however, reveals other important contexts. First, the children are only inhabitants of Bengal, not the whole of India. It reflects initial uncertainty among the patriots about the delimitation of the community they imagined. Secondly, by placing this vision into the period of Durgāpūjā and by a reference to the clay idol, the author equates unequivocally the mother of the nation with the Hindu goddess Durgā. Thirdly, the idea of bringing the glory of the Mother/Nation back is consistent with general belief that

5 The title of the book is a name of an Indian opium eater who in his delirious trances questions current social reality. This collection, inspired by Thomas de Quincey's *'Confessions of an English Opium-Eater'*, was originally published in 1875; a rewritten edition appeared in 1885 (see Zbavitel 1976, 242).

6 Sixty million of the then current population of historical Bengal. (One crore = ten million.)

Durgā for the time of the annual *pūjā* descends from the abode of her husband to the houses of her worshippers who treat her as a married-off daughter returning home. This belief reflects the actual custom of married women visiting their parental house during Durgāpūjā. The equation thus brings together three images: the image of one's own mother; the image of the territory of Bengal; and the image of Durgā, the goddess worshipped emotionally by Bengali Hindus. Kaviraj (1995, 136) terms the Devī of *Kamalākānta* 'a Durkheimian goddess, a sacred name of the collective self', noting that 'her seeing these dreams and making her children see them are the same'.

In 1875, the same year that *Kamalākānta* was published, Bankimchandra composed a patriotic song '*Vande Mātaram*' (Hail to the Mother), which later became a battle cry of freedom fighters. Its first eight lines were eventually accepted as the national song of India.[7] Here the equation of mother, land and Durgā is expressed in a much more elaborate and compelling way. '*Vande Mātaram*' is a prayer to the Mother(land) and most of the lines are formed of Sanskrit compounds that qualify her nature. The territory of Motherland is never clearly delimited but a reference to seventy million voices and twice seventy million hands suggests that it was not a different conception from that of '*Āmār Durgotsab*'. The first lines describe the Mother as a beautiful country abundant in greenery, crops etc. The next set of qualifiers emphasise her prowess as a divine force and identify her with Hindu virtues, like knowledge (*vidyā*) or righteousness (*dharma*). Eventually, she is equated with Durgā by stating that 'your images we set up as idols in all temples' and 'you are Durgā wielding ten arms'.[8] This song gained immense popularity a few years later after its composition when Bankimchandra wove its lines as a sort of leitmotif into the novel *Ānandamaṭh*.

The story of the novel begins with a crude description of famine-stricken Bengal. An impoverished landlord, Mahendra Singh, his wife and a little daughter are set to leave their village, already deserted by all other residents. They hope to escape sure death by starvation in a city. After being kidnapped and rescued they end up in a forest ashram of an order of militant holy men who call themselves the Children. The

7 The first lines of '*Vande Mātaram*' appear in '*Āmār Durgotsab*'; see Banerjee (2002, 199).

8 Quotations in the text are the author's translations. For a transcription of '*Vande Mātaram*' and an artistic translation by Sri Aurobindo, see Bandyopadhyay (1986, 336-338); for a less artistic but more accurate translation, see Lipner (2008, 31-32).

Children worship Mother India as their only deity by singing '*Vande Mātaram*' and had renounced all other worldly commitments except service to her. Satyānanda, the leader of Children, guides Mahendra through the ashram and introduces him into the cult. The ashram houses an image of Mother India sitting on the lap of Viṣṇu and worshipped by all other important deities (significantly, her iconography is not elaborated upon) and three other well-described images of the goddess: one representing her glorious past as bountiful Jagaddhātrī; the second her destitute present in the form of terrifying naked Kālī; and the third is a vision of the Mother to become once she is freed by her Children from foreign oppression. This third image is of Durgā in the same form as she is worshipped every year in Bengal. The initial reference to Viṣṇu subscribes the order within the category of *Vaiṣṇavism,* even though its adherents practise goddess worship, which is consistent with the extended notion of *vaiṣṇava dharma*. Moreover, their ashram is actually formed by the ruins of an ancient Buddhist monastery. One of the messages that Bankimchandra wanted to instil to his readers was that in order to achieve broader unity, they had to transcend sectarian divisions.

Mahendra is attracted to join the Children but cannot overcome his attachment to his wife and child. His wife does not want to be an obstacle in his fulfilling of patriotic duties and prefers to poison their little daughter as well as herself as a supreme sacrifice to the Motherland. Mahendra then joins the Children and a heroic epic of their struggle begins and streams towards the final victory over British troops in the name of the Mother.

The story ends with an unexpected dénouement. Satyānanda is worried about the looming menace of the British in Calcutta and realises the impossibility of installation of a Hindu kingdom. A mysterious sage appears and explains to him that his mission is over and that the Children should disband and go back to the plough. Their mission is accomplished because, by fighting the British, who are primarily interested in business and not in administration, they forced them to take over the reins of Bengal from the hands of Muslims. The sage further elaborates that the King of England is a friendly king and that, in order to realise internal, spiritual knowledge, external knowledge has to be promoted first. Since the British are experts in external knowledge, their rule will serve the cause of future installation of Hindu rule.

Bankimchandra immortalised a hitherto only vaguely defined concept of Mother India by creating a modern myth of her worship. *Ānandamaṭh* was as instrumental in establishing the cult of Bhāratmātā as *Devī-Māhātmya* was for that of Durgā. In both, there is a saintly character who initiates a novice, with whom the reader or listener identifies, into the cult. In both, the goddess is revealed in three images which together constitute her whole representation. While in the *Devī-Māhātmya* these are the qualities of reality, in the *Ānandamaṭh* the division is diachronic. Human heroes of both stories are destitute and homeless, and in the initiation process they realise the true reason for their pitiful condition and the means to overcome it. Both are struggling with their individual attachments and, in order to achieve higher goals, they have to discipline them. Both texts abound in vivid descriptions of battles between the forces of good and evil. Yet while the *Devī-Māhātmya* provides a rationale for goddess worship, *Ānandamaṭh* provides a unifying symbol in the form of a goddess for political action.

The narrative of *Ānandamaṭh* is full of refashioned religious symbolism: the idea of goddess as a mother to her worshippers; the idea of asceticism as a disciplinary practice leading to supernatural powers as well as attainment of spiritual upliftment; the prototypical portrayal of characters as embodied representations of different *dharma*; and, finally, the description of the setting. Deep impervious jungle protects the monastery, which has a temple in its centre. From there a tunnel leads to the shrine that houses the image of the Mother of the nation worshipped by avant-garde Children. Pointing to this 'concentric symbolism of enfoldment', Lipner (2005, 52) compares it to 'some powerful device being compressed and primed', ready to release its explosive force. By identifying Bhāratmātā with Durgā in '*Vande Mātaram*' as an image of India, Bankimchandra literally reinvented Durgā according to the needs of late nineteenth-century modernity in the same manner as literary and art forms or social customs were being refashioned during the Bengal Renaissance.

The novel was received with great acclaim, and translations into other Indian languages as well as English soon appeared. That Bankimchandra influenced large audiences and that the discourse he generated became quickly naturalised is attested by newspaper comments and discussions on Durgāpūjā at the end of the nineteenth and beginning of the twentieth centuries. Thus a contributor to *New India* wrote on 4 November 1901:

> To what little profit do they read Chandi [the *Devī-Māhātmya*] who think that there can be anything like an aggregation of the

> divine powers latent in us, powerful to vanquish the evils of the day, by the way in which Shakti is worshipped now in Bengal! Will not this rather perpetuate the reign and oppression of the asuras? (Tattvabhushan 1901).

This comment, with its implicit nationalistic undertones, on the uselessness of the traditional invocation of Durgā in the face of contemporary struggles not only presumes that readers know the story but clearly works on the discourse generated by *Ānandamaṭh*.

Once the concept of Bhāratmātā was firmly established, it lent itself to opposing visual representations. Generally, two modes of representation can be distinguished. One emphasised benign qualities of Mother India, her carefulness, love for her children, compassion, beauty (the traditional virtues of women), the material and spiritual benefits that she will bring, and the oppression she has to withstand under colonial domination. The other explored the potential of a goddess image to inspire violent resistance. Geeti Sen (2002, 34) differentiates between the two agendas when she notes that the former glorifies 'young men sacrificing their lives to the Mother' while the latter promotes 'sacrifice by the men and also the women of India'.

The radicals who promoted the boycott of all British institutions and the recourse to armed struggle adopted '*Vande Mātaram*' as their battle cry and propagated an image of Mother India as the naked goddess Kālī embellished by a necklace of human skulls and a skirt of severed human arms. Other posters of radical content show a woman-like figure of Mother India accepting with gratitude the gift of a martyred freedom fighter's head from his own hands. These colour prints were disseminated by explicitly anti-British presses as well those who were making them just for commercial gain (Pinney 2004, 106). Despite the British attempts at censorship of vernacular textual production as well as seditious visual representations or elements thereof, in such instruments as the Vernacular Press Act of 1910, the religious space of political creativity kept on escaping attempts at regulation. As Pinney (1999, 220) puts it 'Every denial was simultaneously a reinscription of representational potency'.

Later posters, from around the time when India won its independence in 1947, show the first Prime Minister Jawaharlal Nehru receiving the blessings of Mother India. There is a sacred pot, incense, oil lamp and other ritual objects in front of her, as is proper during the *pūjā*. There are also plates with heads of martyred revolutionaries. During actual *pūjā*s to goddesses who require blood offerings, the head of a goat or a buffalo is chopped off and placed on a tray in front of the goddess. Once again a political message is expressed by representational changes in religious symbolism. Another common motif fuses the image of the goddess with the outline of India's territory.[9]

Besides posters, the annual celebrations of Durgāpūjā and Kālīpūjā themselves became a medium for dissemination of nationalist ideas.[10] From the beginning of the twentieth century, celebrations went public, with sporting clubs and similar associations organising festivities in open spaces for spectators who were not limited by affiliation to a family, locality, community or caste, with newspaper announcements like: 'We extend our cordial invitation to our Patrons, Well-wishers, Donors as also the general public irrespective of Caste and Creed to join the function' (*Liberty* 1931a). The emphasis on public access and inclusiveness shows not only that Durgā emerged in her modern incarnation of Bhāratmātā, but also that her annual worship became to some extent a modern institution.

Leading patriots were often among organisers, and competitions in gymnastics or even martial arts used to be part of the social programme. Other activities included hoisting the national flag, fairs of local industries, ostentatious use of locally made (swadeshi) clothes, and putting up posters showing leaders of the Independence movement. A 1930 account from the town of Nabadwip describes how the campaign in support of indigenous products was symbolically enacted on clay statues representing the goddess:

---

9 Of a number of recent studies dealing with the politics of representation of Bhāratmātā, those by Sumathi Ramaswamy (2002; 2008a; 2008b and 2010) deserve most attention in the context of the present discussion, namely her method of analysis along two axes: the sacred–anthropomorphic and the scientific–geographic. See also McKean (1998), Brosius (2005), Uberoi (2002), Neumayer and Schelberger (2008), Freitag (2014).

10 An overview of historical and contemporary representations of Durgā as evidenced in the Durgāpūjā festival in Calcutta has been presented by Pratish Bandopadhayay in this volume. The colonial and postcolonial transformations of Durgāpūjā are more extensively chronicled by Dutta (2003) and analysed, together with annual Kālīpūjā and Jagaddhātrīpūjā festivals, by McDermott (2011). Politicisation of religious festivals was not, however, limited to Bengal. Bal Gangadhar Tilak, one of the leaders of the nationalist movement in Maharashtra, experimented as early as 1893 with the annual festival of Gaṇeśa (see Kaur 2002, 69-96). He considered the religious festival to be a 'powerful engine for imparting instructions to the masses' and his experiment 'marks the emergence of a new performative space in which the visual, dramaturgical, and the processional, start to work together creating new forms of allegorical political discourse' (Pinney 1999, 214).

> The time-honoured custom has been to adorn the images with what is called Dak Shaj [tinsel ornaments] which is an out and out foreign imported stuff of captivating glitter. The recent Congress movement has been, however, so effective an eye-opener for the ordinary people that the charm of foreign stuff had no attraction for them and they almost automatically clad their God-Mother in Khadder [handwoven coarse cotton] and adorned her with decorations made of earth, cotton and cork. ... The colour paint was also of pure indigenous stuff requisitioned from established Indian firms. Economically, again, the cost of decorations has been much lower than in previous years. There was only one instance of an image where Dak Shaj was used but the users had to stick to police help for fear of molestation and immersed the figure in the nearest tank without attempting to join the general procession (*Liberty* 1930).[11]

At times the traditional image of Durgā was altogether replaced by that of Bhāratmātā as the following report testifies.

> The worship of the deity of 'Bharatmata' was celebrated last week under the auspices of the Delua Congress Committee in the Serajganj sub-division. The image was designed according to the description of the Mother in Bankim Chandra's immortal 'Bandemataram' song. Arrangements have been made for offering 'anjali' [offering a flower between one's palms while pronouncing *mantras*] to Her by all sections of the Hindus irrespective of caste and creed and 'Daridra Narayans' [dalits] were sumptuously fed (*Liberty* 1931b).

With India gaining independence, the call of *Ānandamaṭh* has been achieved. The benign mode of representation of Bhāratmātā of the future was replaced by representations fusing Mother India with the postcolonial state, as in the 1957 film *Mother India* or in the personality cult of Indira Gandhi. The violence-inspiring imagery of Bhāratmātā has been adopted by the Hindu right who promote a militant interpretation of India as a mother goddess who has been molested by Muslims (Power and

11 Interestingly, the *swadeshi* nationalist ideology did not cease to inspire social movements, even in postcolonial India. It was re-enacted, for example, in the context of the anti-consumption movement against the Coca-Cola company (Varman and Belk 2009, 686-700).

Bacchetta 2002). Political, cultural and social organisations of the Hindu right worship her as a supreme deity and present her 'as a chaste mother, victimised (by Muslims)' who 'needs the protection of their 'virile sons' (Bacchetta 2004, 27; Kovacs, 2004). Clearly, for them the fight is not yet over.

III

Bhāratmātā is not the only case of a modern appropriation of Devī that goes beyond creative experimentation with an existing cult such as that of Durgā in Bengal. There are other goddesses who descended to earth having been invoked for discernibly modern agendas. In Tamilnadu a parallel to Bhāratmātā evolved in the form of Tamiḻttāy, or Mother Tamil, a goddess personifying the Tamil language and, by extension, the territory and polity. Borrowing from both Sarasvatī and Bhāratmātā in her visual representations, Mother Tamil has been portrayed interchangeably as an ally of Mother India as well as a vehicle of distinct Tamil nationalism to challenge the existence of a unitary Indian state (Ramaswamy 2008b).

And there are goddesses who took their incarnation for more specific causes. In the Menasikyathana Halli village in Karnataka a local high-school teacher started the worship of Mother AIDS, or AIDS-*ammā*, on World AIDS Day in 1997 to raise awareness about the disease. He was prompted to this unusual move after he learnt about a couple with AIDS who had died of starvation after being completely ostracised by the villagers. Although the shrine he established was named 'Temple of Science' and was in practice as much an information centre as a place of worship, he creatively worked with the tradition of disease-related goddesses, such as the goddess of smallpox Māriyamman (Foulston and Abbott 2009, 223).

Another case of a cause-specific *avatar* of Devī is Svaccha Nārāyaṇī, invoked to life by Madhu Kishwar, an academician, activist, and founder of the Delhi-based organisation Manushi, with the aspiration to make her into a pan-Indian goddess. In a series of articles and online presentations, Kishwar tells a harrowing story of Manushi's struggle to empower street vendors against extortionist mafias, corrupt police and politicians, and unsympathetic residents (Kishwar 2001, 2005, 2009, 2012a, 2012b; Schwabenland 2012). This case deserves particular attention in the context of discussion on modern appropriations of Devī, as Svaccha Nārāyaṇī is a direct heir of and departure from Bhāratmātā.

She descended to help street vendors who are an indispensable element of the urban economy all over India. They provide a wide range of easily accessible goods and services for large sections of Indian population. Yet their business is largely unregulated and survives in a semi-legal grey zone. In many places hawkers occupy pavements and roadsides in busy urban areas, effectively blocking the traffic and adding to waste disposed of openly in the streets. They are regularly subjected to eviction drives, confiscation of property and physical abuse by the authorities and face the ire of many upper-class citizens who would like their cities to resemble any Western modern city. At the same time, their semi-legal status makes them extremely vulnerable to extortion rackets, loan sharks and organised crime, in general, as well as to abuse of power by the authorities.

From 2001 to 2008 Manushi was running a pilot project in Delhi's Sewa Nagar Market to test a policy that would allow street vendors to operate under a legal framework, pay reasonable fees instead of bribes and extortion money to the municipal corporation, limit the vending space to designated areas, and ensure environmentally-friendly operation of the market. Despite some high-level political support and a green light for the project from Delhi's municipal corporation, the market area was eventually taken over by local adversaries of the project in a struggle that involved the filing of a large number of criminal cases, blackmail, and physical violence against the vendors and Manushi representatives including Kishwar. The project, however, did initiate changes in law and policy and is alive in other areas of Delhi.

It is the 'emergency descent' of a new deity, Svaccha Nārāyaṇī (Manushi Swachha Narayani), whose 'temple had become an emotional centre point for the project' (Kishwar 2012b), that makes it interesting in terms of the present discussion. This deity, referred to variously in Kishwar's texts as 'goddess of cleanliness', 'goddess of self-discipline', 'secular goddess', and 'goddess of good governance and citizenship rights', was designed for the vendors to 'internalize the importance of cleanliness' and 'imbibe it as a necessary discipline' (Kishwar 2012a). She believed that internalised discipline was essential for the success of the project and that more conventional ways of dealing with the problem, such as hiring extra sweepers, would not be effective to keep the market area clean. That discipline was also directed at the stigma of untouchability which affects those who deal with dirt and unclean substances in general. When I interviewed Kishwar in August 2006 she further elaborated on this point:

> You cannot be a right citizen if you can't be self-governing. ... Accept certain discipline so that you do not cause inconvenience to other citizens. And don't do it just because you are afraid of the Police. But do it because you are a responsible citizen. ... I just had the feeling that we must bring in and invoke it as a sacred duty. The moment you bring in not religion but sacredness people then will slowly accept it as a part of their *saṃskāra* – your internal values, values that you have internalised. ... Those values which are imposed on you because of common pressure or because you will be fined are easily violated.

But the social goals of the broom worship were far from limited to waste management. Kishwar wanted to 'drive home the message that cleaning one's physical environment is as sacred a duty of every citizen as cleansing our system of governance of corruption and abuse of power' (Kishwar 2012a). The worship of the broom as a deity began in August 2001 and became a regular ritual at meetings of Manushi and the vendors. In December that year, when the vendors were to take an oath to a collective discipline,[12] some suggested the inclusion of Gaṇeśa and Lakṣmī in the broom worship on that special day. Kishwar further insisted on including Sarasvatī to 'bestow on pilot project members the foresight and wisdom to build their inner organizational strength through self-regulation' and Durgā 'in order to get the requisite strength and power to combat the forces of evil that engulf the lives and livelihoods of street hawkers' (Kishwar 2012a). The broom, worshipped together with the trinity of Lakṣmī, Sarasvatī and Durgā, slowly developed into a single distinct deity which absorbed the qualities of all the three goddesses. While Manushi originally intended to install the goddess into a new temple planned as a part of the pilot project infrastructure, they eventually decided at a crisis point in March 2005 to call upon her as an 'emergency *avatar*' to 'battle the modern day demons – corrupt officials, lawless police and political mafias' (Kishwar 2012a). The interview with Kishwar in August 2006 gives a picture of how the goddess came into being:

12 Although Kishwar's account shows that the *discipline* was larger, and even a spiritual concept, here the main focus was on the Line of Discipline (*sanyam rekha*) which would demarcate the market area and beyond which the vendors had to take an oath not to extend their goods.

> ... the message that was given is that what we are doing requires the powers of these three divinities. ... The poor, the vendors are often involved in much of internal quarrelling and do not act wisely very often. So that is why invoking the goddess of wisdom Sarasvatī. Lakṣmī because this is the giver of livelihood and we do not have to feel guilty towards the livelihood, we want livelihood to multiply without indignity, so that is why Lakṣmī. And Durgā because we are dealing with demons: the police, the ministerial employees – another demoniac force, the political mafia – another demoniac force. And if you are dealing with demons who are quite capable of slashing you, destroying you, even to mobilise inner resources among street vendors, you have to make them feel and believe that the greater forces of history and givers of justice are on their side and not with the demoniac powers. And Durgā is the slayer of demons. I just wanted to make sure that the message was not too violent. Because I believe the best of thoughts, the best of movements can be spoiled by the use of violence. For cleaning the government of corruption, for keeping the environment clean, cleaning our own minds of bad stupid habits and thoughts, internal rivalries, undermining each other, you need all these things in order to build a beginning of an organisation.

The very image of Svaccha Nārāyaṇī reflects its origin as 'a creative amalgam of the traditional female trinity – Durgā, Lakṣmī and Sarasvatī – with many new attributes and powers required to meet contemporary challenges' (Kishwar 2012a). She stands on a lotus (like Lakṣmī) and is ten-armed as is Durgā worshipped in Bengal. The lotus, an ancient Indian symbol of spiritual upliftment from the mud of ignorance to the realisation of the supreme truth, here signifies the progress of a social movement 'enabling people to move out of squalor and poverty' (Kishwar 2012a). The original statue also had the white dress of Sarasvatī, but a later clay Bengali style image has a red sari. The powers and attributes needed in contemporary struggles are indexed in the image by a set of objects which replace the traditional weapons of Durgā. A broom, the original object of worship, turns into an attribute of the goddess to symbolise cleanliness in the physical as well as moral sense. Moreover, it further carries the message of strength of those who unite for a common purpose.[13] A clock

13 Similarly to the *fascio* of late-nineteenth-century Italian revolutionaries.

serves as an index of changing times and the need for change; a coin stands for dignified livelihood; a weighing balance represents social justice and honesty; a video camera implies accountability and transparency of government; an earthen lamp suggests dispelling darkness; a calculator or account book implies financial accountability and honesty; a pen represents the wisdom and learning of Sarasvatī; a conch shell – a traditional element – stands both for purity and as a clarion call for self-organisation; and a stalk of barley symbolises multiplication of wealth as well as the multiplication of the project's success.

Kishwar also explicitly acknowledges the modern genealogy of Svaccha Nārāyaṇī by referring to her as '*our* Mother India' (Kishwar 2012a (present author's emphasis)). The deictic emphasis in the possessive '*our*' is indeed a conscious departure. In Kishwar's perception the men who invoked Bhāratmātā presented her throughout the freedom movement as a powerless, helpless creature pleading to her sons to liberate her – as a powerless goddess who cannot liberate herself on her own.[14]

The start of Svaccha Nārāyaṇī worship brought a period of calm for Manushi as local residents and even some fierce opponents of the project sought to offer her their prayers. As Kishwar (2012a) puts it, besides becoming a link with local residents, 'she struck a measure of fear in the hearts of our tormentors'. For about a year Manushi managed to continue developing the infrastructure for the pilot project, including building a small marble temple. The adversaries, however, did not give up and adapted to the strategy. Before Svaccha Nārāyaṇī could be moved into the new temple they installed an idol of Hanumān in the precincts and put up a signboard on a newly constructed toilet block which read 'Ancient Hanumān Temple'. According to Kishwar, they also unsuccessfully tried to instigate a local *imam* to bar Muslims from worship at the temple and complained to state authorities that worship of the broom 'hurts Hindu sentiments' and defiles upper-castes, as does the worship of an 'imaginary' goddess (Kishwar 2012b). The conflict intensified, and after numerous ugly physical confrontations Manushi had to abandon it and focus on overall policy and law reforms and on projects in other localities. The worship of Svaccha Nārāyaṇī continues as part of those projects.

14 Cf. the discussion of the word *āmār* (my) in Bankimchandra's '*Āmār Durgotsab*' by Sudipta Kaviraj (1995, 136).

IV

The modern appropriations of Devī discussed in this chapter are part of a larger complex of ideas and practices whereby Indian modernity is in the making. Annual festivals of Hindu deities have been particularly fertile ground for merging narratives and images from within and outside of the Hindu tradition and reinterpreting them via iconographical modifications of the central image (see Hříbek 2002). Technologies for the cheap reproduction of images introduced in the late nineteenth century and the advent of private TV channels and the Internet in the late twentieth century brought two dramatic waves of change to the representation of deities. Besides the festivals, there are practices such as fasting and public display of asceticism in general as a means of harnessing mass agency for political goals, (re)construction of public space as a sacred space, and religious justification of ecological movements, such as the Save Ganga Movement.

Vrinda Dalmiya, in her reflection on merging Indian spiritual concepts with ecofeminism in the work of Vandana Shiva, observes that 'we regularly find secular organisations engaging in the political theatre of invoking religious rituals to mobilize popular sentiments for environmental agendas' (Dalmiya 2014, 167), but at the same time she warns against potential 'Hindu appropriation of spiritual-environmentalist rhetoric' (180). This argument can well be generalised to all constructions of Indian modernity rooted in Hindu ritual practice. Bankimchandra's point of departure was a Hindu universalism in the concept of *vaiṣṇava dharma* as the essence of all religions and the image of India as a Hindu goddess. Universalist ideologies tend to justify hegemony, and, in the hands of Veer Savarkar and his followers, the worship of Mother India becomes mandatory for every Indian, who has to be a Hindu first and only then can he be anything else, for example, a Muslim.

While Bankimchandra's Bhāratmātā links the worship of Durgā with an imagined national community, its past and its future in a veiled critique of the colonial state, Kishwar's Svaccha Nārāyaṇī presents a reimagination of that community and a critique of the postcolonial state. Her narrative emphasises the unity of street vendors and the inability of their adversaries to divide them along communal lines. To underline this further her articles showcase a Muslim vendor who 'came to act by common consensus as the chief priest of the Goddess' (Kishwar 2012b). Much as Kishwar wants Svaccha Nārāyaṇī to be a pan-Indian goddess, one can imagine there might be limits to extrapolating such a consensus. The efficacy of goddess worship in secular politics is also based on a specific understanding of 'Indic civilisation' where religious and secular are not in opposition and goddesses in various forms have always descended to people. In the words of Madhu Kishwar:

> In the Indic civilisation there is no sharp divide between the religious and the secular. ... We also have a long tradition of the divine coming down to help mortals, of Gods and Goddesses taking avatars in newer and newer forms all the time. It is not as if there is a fixed number of deities and you cannot negotiate with it anymore. ... We don't say that I conceived this, we don't say I invented, that's others who are using the word – how did you invent a Goddess, how did you create a Goddess? Goddess is an avatar. ... So also throughout history and mythology, which are mixed together in such an interesting colourful way, people do it all the time. ... So the point is that the Goddesses have always come to lend support to human beings in their daily struggles (Interview, August 2006).

Both Bhāratmātā and Svaccha Nārāyaṇī are descendants of the Devī worship tradition expounded in the *Devī-Māhātmya*. In all three narratives the goddess is a dividual entity and appears in a trinity of forms. They all work with the dynamics of the internal and the external. Both the Bhāratmātā and the Svaccha Nārāyaṇī narratives seek to transform the external through the cultivation of the internal. To all, a notion of particular discipline on the part of the devotee is central; and here, perhaps, is the key to the nature of modernity envisaged for India in the images of Bhāratmātā and Svaccha Nārāyaṇī.

The functionality of modern states is based on various kinds of 'discipline' in the Foucaultian sense. By discipline Foucault understood specifically new methods of coercion developed in the beginning of European modernity that used classification and mechanical organisation of individuals to effectuate dissociation of body from its power:

> In organising 'cells', 'places' and 'ranks', the disciplines create complex spaces that are at once architectural, functional and hierarchical. It is spaces that provide fixed positions and permit circulation; they carve out individual segments and establish operational links; they mark places and indicate values; they

> guarantee the obedience of individuals, but also a better economy of time and gesture (Foucault 1995, 140).

Foucault refuses to include pre-modern phenomena, such as asceticism or monastic discipline, into his concept in order to make the paradigm shift brought by modernity stand out. The modern appropriations of Devī, however, cross over such a division with ease and derive discipline for the Indian nation and state from the sources of Indian, mostly Hindu, tradition.

Bibliography

Bacchetta, Paola. 2004. *Gender in the Hindu Nation. RSS Women as ideologues.* New Delhi: Women Unlimited.

Bake, A.A. 1955. 'The appropriation of Śiva's attributes by Devî'. *Bulletin of the School of Oriental and African Studies, University of London* 14 (3): 519-525.

Bandyopadhyay, Asit. 1986. *History of Modern Bengali Literature.* Calcutta: Modern Book Agency.

Banerjee, Sumanta. 2002. *Logic in a Popular Form: Essays on Popular Religion in Bengal.* Calcutta: Seagull.

Brosius, Christiane. 2005. *Empowering Visions: the Politics of Representation in Hindu Nationalism.* London: Anthem.

Chakrabarti, Kunal. 2001. *Religious Processes: The Purāṇas and the Making of a Regional Tradition.* New Delhi: Oxford University Press.

Chatterji, Bankimchandra. 1992. *Kamalakanta: A Collection of Satirical Essays and Reflections*, translated by M.R. Chatterjee. Calcutta: Rupa.

Chatterji, Bankimchandra. 2005. *Ānandamaṭh, or The Sacred Brotherhood*, translated with an introduction and critical apparatus by Julius J. Lipner. New York: Oxford University Press.

Coburn, Thomas B. 1984. *Devī-Māhātmya: the Crystallization of the Goddess Tradition.* Delhi: Motilal Banarasidass.

Dalmiya, Vrinda. 2014. '"Epistemic multiculturalism" and objectivity: rethinking Vandana Shiva's ecospirituality'. In *Asian and Feminist Philosophies in Dialogue Liberating Traditions*, edited by A. Butnor and J McWeeny, 167-184. New York: Columbia University Press.

Dutta, Abhijit. 2003. *Mother Durga: an Icon of Community & Culture.* Calcutta: Readers Service.

Foucault, Michel. 1995. *Discipline & Punish: the Birth of the Prison.* New York: Random House.

Foulston, Lynn, and Stuart Abbott. 2009. *Hindu Goddesses: Beliefs and Practices.* Brighton: Sussex Academic Press.

Freitag, Sandria B. 2014. 'The visual turn: approaching South Asia across the disciplines', *South Asia* 37 (3): 398-409.

Guha, Ranajit. 1997. *Dominance without Hegemony: History and Power in Colonial India.* Cambridge Mass: Harvard University Press.

Hříbek, Martin. 2002. 'Smoking the demon out: Pathways and intersections of two contemporary rituals'. *Cargo* 2002 (1-2): 81-93.

Jagadīśvarānanda, Svāmī. 1999 [1940]. *Śrī Śrī Caṇḍī.* Kālīkātā: Udbodhan Kāryālay.

Kaur, Raminder. 2002. 'Martial imagery in Western India: the changing face of Ganapati since the 1890s'. *South Asia* 25 (1): 69-96.

Kaviraj, Sudipta. 1995. *The Unhappy Consciousness: Bankimchandra Chattopadhyay and the Formation of Nationalist Discourse in India*. Delhi: Oxford University Press.

Kishwar, Madhu Purnima. 2001. 'Jhadu Pooja at Sewa Nagar: Manushi's campaign for cleansing governance'. *Manushi* 127: 3-11.

Kishwar, Madhu Purnima. 2005. 'Emergency *avatâr* of a secular goddess! Manushi Swachha Narayani descends to protect street vendors'. *Manushi* 147: 4-15.

Kishwar, Madhu Purnima. 2009. 'The Descent and Defiling of the Broom Wielding Goddess of Good Governance: Need to Affirm the Sacredness of Human Rights' 9 September. http://www.slideshare.net/ManushiIndia/the-descent-and-defiling-of-the-broom-wielding-goddess-of-good-governance (accessed 12 April 2016).

Kishwar, Madhu Purnima. 2012a. 'The making and unmaking of a model market for street vendors. Part I: *Avatār* of goddess of good governance and citizenship rights', Manushi, 29 February. http://www.manushi.in/articles.php?articleId=1586 (accessed 12 April 2016).

Kishwar, Madhu Purnima. 2012b. 'The making and unmaking of a model market for street vendors. Part II: Criminal mafias take over Sewa Nagar pilot project', Manushi, 29 February. http://manushi.in/articles.php?articleId=1587 (accessed 12 April 2016).

Kovacs, Anja. 2004. 'You don't understand, we are at war! Refashioning Durga in the service of Hindu nationalism', *Contemporary South Asia* 13(4): 373–388.

Liberty. 1930. 'Rosh-Purnima festival at Nabadwip. Triumph of the Swadeshi'. *Liberty*, 11278 1930.

Liberty. 1931a. Baghbazar Sarbajanin Durgotsav Committee (advertisement). *Liberty*, 8 November 1931.

Liberty. 1931b 'Bharatmata Image: New Deity Worship at Pabna Village'. *Liberty*, 10 November 1931.

Lipner, Julius. 2005. 'Introduction'. In Chatterji, Bankimcandra, *Ānandamaṭh, or The Sacred Brotherhood, translated with an introduction and critical apparatus by Julius J. Lipner*. New York: Oxford University Press.

Lipner, Julius. 2008. 'Icon and mother: an inquiry into India's national song'. *Journal of Hindu Studies* 1 (1-2): 26-48.

McDermott, Rachel Fell. 2011. *Revelry, Rivalry and Longing for the Goddesses of Bengal: the Fortunes of Hindu Festivals*. New York: Columbia University Press.

McKean, Lise. 1998. 'Mother India and her militant matriots'. In *Devi: Goddesses of India*, edited by J.S. Halley and D.M. Wulff, 250-280. Delhi: Motilal Banarsidass.

Neumayer, Erwin, and Christine Schelberger. 2008. *Bharat Mata: India's Freedom Movement In Popular Art*. New Delhi: Oxford University Press.

Pinney, Christopher. 1999. 'Indian magical realism'. In *Subaltern Studies X*, edited by G. Bhadra, G. Prakash and S.J. Tharu, 201-233. Delhi: Oxford University Press.

Pinney, Christopher. 2004. *Photos of the Gods: the Printed Image and Political Struggle in India*. London: Oxford University Press.

Power, Margaret, and P. Bacchetta. 2002. *Right-Wing Women: from Conservatives to Extremists Around the World*. London: Routledge.

Ramaswamy, Sumathi. 2002. 'Visualising India's geo-body: globes, maps, bodyscapes'. *Contributions to Indian Sociology* new series 36 (1-2): 151-189.

Ramaswamy, Sumathi. 2008a. 'Maps, mother/goddesses, and martyrdom in modern India'. *Journal of Asian Studies* 67 (3): 819-853.

Ramaswamy, Sumathi. 2008b. *When a Language Becomes a Mother/Goddess: An Image Essay on Tamil* (South Asian Visual Culture Series, No. 1). Heidelberg: Tasveer Ghar.

Ramaswamy, Sumathi. 2010. *The Goddess and the Nation: Mapping Mother India*. Durham NC: Duke University Press.

Schwabenland, C. 2012. 'Swachh Narayani: the creation of a goddess as an organisational intervention'. In *Against the Grain: Advances in Postcolonial Organisation Studies*, edited by A. Prasad, 73-94. Copenhagen: Liber/ Copenhagen Business School Press.

Sen, Geeti. 2002. *Feminine Fables: Imaging the Indian Woman in Painting, Photography and Cinema*. Ahmedabad: Mapin.

Stietencron, Heinrich von. 2005. *Hindu Myth, Hindu History, Religion, Art, and Politics*, Delhi: Permanent Black.

Stietencron, Heinrich von. 2007. 'Religious configurations in medieval India and the modern concept of Hinduism'. In *The Oxford India Hinduism Reader*, edited by V. Dalmia and H. von Stietencron, 50-89. New Delhi: Oxford University Press.

Tattvabhushan, Pandit Sitanath. 1901. 'Durga, Vedic and Puranic'. *New India (For God, Humanity and the Fatherland)* 4 November 1901.

Uberoi, Patricia. 2002. 'Unity in diversity? Dilemmas of nationhood in Indian calendar art'. *Contributions to Indian Sociology new series* 36 (1-2): 191-232.

Varman, Rohit, and Russell W. Belk. 2009. 'Nationalism and ideology in an anticonsumption movement'. *Journal of Consumer Research* 36 (4): 686-700.

Winternitz, Maurice. 2003 [1981]. *History of Indian Literature* (3 vols). Delhi: Motilal Banarsidass.

Zbavitel, Dušan. 1976. *Bengali Literature (History of Indian Literature, vol. 9)*. Wiesbaden: Otto Harrassowitz.

About the Editors and Contributors

Editors

Jayant Bhalchandra Bapat

Jayant Bapat holds doctorates in Organic Chemistry and Indology and is an adjunct research fellow at the Monash Asia Institute. His research interests include Hinduism, Goddess cults, the Fisher community of Mumbai, and Jainism, and he has published widely in these areas. He is co-editor of *The Iconic Female: Goddesses of India, Nepal and Tibet* (Monash University Press, 2008) with Ian Mabbett, and *The Indian Diaspora: Hindus and Sikhs in Australia* (DK Printworld, 2015). For his work in education and for the Indian community, Jayant was awarded the Order of Australia Medal (OAM) in 2011.

Ian Mabbett

Ian Mabbett is an adjunct research fellow at Monash University, where he has taught Asian history since 1965. He has also conducted teaching and research in Singapore, Princeton and Nagoya. His main research interests are in ancient Indian history, Buddhist philosophy and history, and the comparative study of Asian religions. He is co-editor of *The Iconic Female: Goddesses of India, Nepal and Tibet* (Monash University Press, 2008) with Jayant Bapat. Ian is also the co-author of *The Sociology of Indian Buddhism,* with Greg Bailey (2003) and editor of *Prācyaprajñāpradīpa* (2012), a volume that felicitates Professor Samaresh Bandyopadhyay.

Contributors

Angelo Andrea Di Castro

Angelo Andrea Di Castro has conducted archaeological investigations in Italy, Nepal and China. He is a specialist in the archaeology of South and Central Asia, in particular Gandhara and the Himalayan regions of

India. Andrea has lectured in archaeology at Monash University. His current research projects include the Silk Road oasis of Kashgar, the connection between religion and archaeology, and the history of cultural exchange between India, China and the Western world.

David Templeman

David is an adjunct research fellow at the Monash Asia Institute. He has worked for many years on the writings of 17th-century Tibetan prelate Tāranātha, especially his autobiography. David's most recent works have been *A Historical Dictionary of Tibet* (Scarecrow Press, 2012), with John Powers, and *Asian Horizons: Giuseppe Tucci's Buddhist, Indian, Himalayan and Central Asian Studies* (Monash University Publishing, 2015), with Andrea Di Castro.

Greg Bailey

Greg, formerly a reader in Sanskrit, is an Honorary Research Fellow in the Program in Asian Studies, La Trobe University, Melbourne. He has published translations and studies of the *Gaṇeśa Purāṇa*, Bhartṛhari's *Śatakatrayam* and books on the god Brahmā and early Buddhism. Greg has also published many articles on Sanskrit literature.

John Dupuche

The Reverend Dr John Dupuche is a senior lecturer at MCD University of Divinity and Honorary Fellow at Australian Catholic University. His doctoral studies are in the field of Kashmir Shaivism. He is the author of *Abhinavagupta: The Kula Ritual as Elaborated in Chapter 29 of the Tantrāloka* (Motilal Banarsidass Publishing, 2003), *Jesus, the Mantra of God* (David Lovell Publishing, 2005), and *Towards a Christian Tantra* (David Lovell Publishing, 2009).

Martin Hříbek

Martin Hříbek is assistant professor in Bengali and Indian Studies at the Institute of South and Central Asia, Faculty of Arts, Charles University in Prague. Trained in both ethnology and modern Indology, he works on contemporary goddess worship in India, nature symbolism in Bengali literature, and Czech representations of the Orient.

Madhavi Narsalay

Madhavi Narsalay is an assistant professor and Head of the Department of Sanskrit, University of Mumbai. She specialises in the areas of Veda and Religious studies. She has twenty-five publications to her credit, including a book titled *Epics and Mahāpurāṇas on the Vedic Sacrifice* (Aryan Books International, 2015).

Peter Friedlander

Peter Friedlander is a senior lecturer in Hindi-Urdu at the Australian National University. He did his PhD at London on the poet-saint Ravidas and has taught at La Trobe University in Melbourne and the National University of Singapore. He was honoured for his contributions to Hindi at the Vishva Hindi Sammelan in 2012 and was the invited keynote speaker at World Hindi day in Mauritius in 2016. Recent publications include book chapters on Hinduism, Buddhism and politics in the second edition of the *Routledge Handbook of Religion and Politics* (2016), journal articles on Kabir (*Oral Tradition* 29 (2) October 2015), Hindi detective fiction (*Situations* 8 (2) 2015) and a book with Harry Aveling on the poet-saint Charandas (Prestige, 2014).

Pratish Bandopadhayay

Pratish Bandopadhayay is a Hindu priest from Bengal and has an academic interest in the social and historical context of the practice of Durgā Pūjā in Bengal. In his previous career, he was a principal research scientist with CSIRO (Melbourne, Australia), where he worked for over thirty years.

Marika Vicziany

Marika Vicziany is Professor Emerita and Director of the National Centre for South Asian Studies in the Faculty of Arts, Monash University. For over forty years she has published on India, particularly on long-term economic development, international trade/investment, poverty and religious/ethnic minorities. Among her recent publications is *The European Union and India: Rhetoric or Meaningful Partnership?* (Edward Elgar, 2015), with Pascale Winand and Poonam Datar.

Index

In bold are chapters focused on the index entry.
Parentheses contain (less common) alternative spellings, clarifications, and translations.

Abhiniṣkramaṇa (Buddha's Great Departure) 27
Achaemenid (Empire) 19, 34–36, 48
Achilles 28
Ādi-Śankarācārya 83
Aelian (Claudius Aelianus, c.175–235 CE) 48
Afghanistan 25–26, 34, 43, 50, 213, 221
Agathocleia (Agathocles) 37–38, 41, 47
Agri 225
Ahatmilku (queen of Ugarit, 13th cent. BCE) 32–33
Ahimsak Gurav *see* Gurav
Ai Khanum 48–49
Allah 231, 260; *see also* Muslim
Alvar (Vaiṣṇava holy man) 98
Amalthea 31, 42
Amarakośa 99
Ambādevī 83
Ambā-Durgā 39
Ambedkar, Dr B. R. 139, 227, 243
Ambejogāī 19, 199
Āmrapura 183, 191
Amrawati 249–250
Amyntas 42
Anāhitā 27, 35–36, 42–44, 46, 48
Ānandamaṭh 164, 259, 262–265, 267
Andhaka 57, 61, 64–65, 69–70, 191
Andragoras 36–37
aniconism 135, 202, 207
Añjali mudrā 27
Aphrodite Anaitis 35
appropriation **1–23** (Chapter 1)
  bottom-up (social climbing) 4–6, 11, 13, 16
  definition of 6
  external top-down 4, 6, **25**, **30**, **34**, **36–37**, **44–46**, **48-50** (Chapter 2), **160–177** (Chapter 8); *see also* symbols
  integration (as alternative to) 5, **56–64** (Chapter 3), 74–76, 152
  internal top-down 3, 14–16, **73–76**, **78**,**88**, **98** (Chapter 4), **179–180**, **182**, **194**, **204**, **207–208** (Chapter 9), **225–255** (Chapter 11)
  metropolitan-provincial 17, 19, **25–54** (Chapter 2)
  re-appropriation 2, 22, **145–146**, **157** (Chapter 7)
  recent examples of 23, **226–227**, **233**, **243–244**, **246**, **248**, **250**, **252** (Chapter 11), **257–258**, **268**, **273** (Chapter 12)
  simultaneous upward and downward 5, 17–18, **102**, **104**, **119**, **123–124** (Chapter 5)
  subversive **126–129**, **140** (Chapter 6)
Ārādhī (Ārādhinī) 206
Arajā 20, 64–65, 69–71, 74–75
Archaeological Survey of India 236–237, 241–244
Ardoksho (Ardokþo) 19, 28–29, 36, 42–46
Artemis 31, 201
Arthaśāstra 9
Asaras 246, 253 (Table)
Ashurbanipal 33
Ashursharrat 33
Aši (Iranian goddess of fortune) 35
assimilation 58, 61–63, 180; *see also* cultural process
Astarte 31
Augsburg, Diet of 3
Augustus 41
authority
  Brāhminical 2, 5, 8–9, 134, 151
  British authorities 166, 233

family 75
Indian authorities 269, 272
through religious materials 180
temple 206
avatāra 23, 62–63, 99, 129, 165, 174, 258–259
Avesta 35, 43
Azes 38, 42, 223
Bactria 26–27, 31, 33–37, 40, 42, 49–50
Bakimchandra *see* Chattopadhyay
Baluchistan 34, 50
Banerjee, Mamata 21, 169–172, 175
Bapat, Jayant Bhalchandra 1, 14, 16, 19–20, 78, 87, 99, 149, 152, 202, 204, 209, 225, 232, 247
Barber, Benjamin 10–11, 235
Baroyāri 164
battlements *see* symbols
begging (jogavā) 193
Berossus 35
Béyül 214
Bhagat 134
Bhairava 187, 190, 194–195, 204
Bhairavanath 246
Bhairavī 187–188
Bhakti 20–21, 62, 133, 140, 226–234, 248–249, 259
movement 140, 227–229, 249; *see also* pilgrimage
Bhandari 225
Bhangare, *see also* Koli rebellion
Raghu 233, 249
Rama 233
bharaṇe 235
Bhāratmātā (Bhāratamātā) *see* Mother India
Bhavani 87, 234
Bhavik Gurav 80
Bhīmādevī 44–45
Bibi Nani 50
Boḍaṇa 197, 200–201
Bordave 85
Brāhmin *see* appropriation *and* Sanskritisation
Brekke, Torkel 238
Briggs, George W. 131–132, 135, 190
British
and Durga Puja in Bengal 21 *see also* appropriation
and resistance 23, 233, 249, 251, 263, 265 *see* also Mother India *and* Koli
rule 135, 246
Buddha 27, 43, 136, 157, 171, 215, 224, 226, 239, 244
Buddhism **211, 213–215, 217–219, 222–224** (Chapter 10)
buffalo demon 194, 201 *see also* Mahiṣāsura *and* demon
Buktara 27
bull 39–40, 42, 222, 236
Burgess, James 239, 242
Cakra 55, 108–109, 117, 130, 148, 187–188, 203
Calcutta *see* Kolkata
Camār 20, 127, 132, 135; *see also* Chamar
cave temples 20, 44, 46, 97, 183, **226, 236, 238–239, 241–247, 250** (Chapter 11)
chaitya 16, 86, 149, 226–227, 230, 233, 236–240, 242–248, 250
Chamar (Camār) 20–21, 127, 131–137, 139–140
Chandraprabha (temple) 82–83, 85
Chandrapur 249–250
Chandraseniya Kayastha Prabhus (CKP) 230, 247
Chattopadhyay
Bankimchandra 23, 164–165, 259–264, 272–273
Jogeshchandra 166
Chinnamastā 22, 143–145, 147–153, 157
Chinnamuṇḍā 143–145, 148
Chinvat bridge 221–222
Chitral 221
Chötin Norbu Doshal 214
Citpāvana(s) 182, 202
Citrāṅgadā 20, 64–66, 68–69, 71–73, 75
CKP *see* Chandraseniya Kayastha Prabhus
clan deity (kuladaivata) 179, 186, 192, 194–195, 198, 205–207, 209, 234
clan goddess (kulasvāminī) 180, 197, 203, 205

Clemens of Alexandria 35
Clive, Robert 162
Colebrooke, H. T. 238
Communist Party of India (Marxist) (CPI(M)) 168–169, 171–172
contestation 5, 18, 21, 126–127, 129, 133–135, 137, 139–140
coolie 251
Copland, Ian 9, 12
cornucopia *see* symbols
cradle songs (joguḷa) *see* Jogulamba
criminal tribes 251; *see* Mahadev Kolis
cūḍākarman 235
cultural process 17, 59, 62; *see also* appropriation *and* assimilation
Cybele 31, 33, 48–49
dagoba 243
Ḍākinīs 154, 219
Dakṣa sacrifice 192
dalit 21, 137, 228, 230, 242–245, 247, 267; *see also* untouchable
Daṇḍa 64–66, 69, 71, 73, 75, 183
darshan 133, 229
Dattatreya 234
Demeter 42
Demetrios I 39
demon(s) 157, 184, 191 214, 218, 240, 243, 246
  Dantāsura 185, 191, 206
  modern-day 270–271
  see Andhaka, Mahiṣāsura
Deshmukh 246
Devak 79
Devīmāhātmya (Devī-Māhātmya) 11, 14, 57, 61, 63, 184, 206, 258, 264, 274
Devī tīrtha 46
Dharavi 230, 249
Dhere, Ramchandra Chintaman 15, 64–65, 193–195, 230–231, 234, 243, 263
Digambara Yakṣa Sarvahna 86
dominance 2, 17, 113–114, 246
Drala (outrider attendant) 222–223
Drupasaya (duṣprasahya) 39–40
Dumont, Louis 3
Durgā (durga)
  Durgā-Saptaśatī 93, 258
  Durgā Yogeśvarī / Durgādevī 194, 196–197, 202–205, 207
  Durgāpūjā in Bengal 21, **160–176** (Chapter 8), 261–262, 264, 266
  in formerly Jain temples 14, 19, 78, 80, 83, 93, 96, 100
  as little mother 184, 258–259, 261–268, 270–271, 273
  local goddess appropriation/ assimilation 4, 14, 61, 234
  as mother (India) 2, 184, **261–264, 266** (Chapter 12)
  on numismatic and sculptural representations 36, 39–40, 46–50
  in *Vāmana Purāṇa* 63
  sacrifice 152
  trinity (as part of, with Laksmi and Saraswati) 23
East India Company 163; *see also* British
Eaton, Richard 14
Eck, Diana 22, 85, 128, 144, 147–150, 157, 182, 214, 218–219, 229, 261, 265
Ekveera Devī Mandir 226, 230, 232, 236–240, 242–243, 246–248, 253 (Table)
Ekveera 16, 20, 149, 225–227, 230–251, 253 (Table)
Elam 33–34, 48, 212
elephant *see* symbols
Ellora 191
embedded myths 64, 70–71, 73, 75
enlightenment 110, 136, 144, 147–149, 151–152, 155, 226, 228
Enthoven, R.E. 78–80
epigraph 183, 208
Eucratides I 38
family records (kulavṛttāntas) 203
fecundity goddess 27
Feldhaus, Anne 206, 230, 248
Fergusson, James 237–240, 242, 244
five m's (pañcamakāra) 192
  in contrast to three m's 117
flames *see* symbols
fortune 21, 26–27, 29, 31, 35–36, 42, 48, 50, 86, 167, 201, 251
Gandhāra 26–28, 31, 33–34, 36, 40, 42–43, 45–46, 48–50
Gandhi, Indira 175, 267

Gandhi, Mahatma (as sannyasi) 233
Gandhi, Sonia 7, 21, 175
Ganesh 166, 183, 203, 231, 242–243
Gaṅgā (Ganges) 4, 20–21, 89, **126**, **127**, **130–140** (Chapter 6), 266, 273
Ganga dynasty 98
Gangeshwar temple 89
gārhāne karaṇe 86
Gāvarhātī 89
Gegs 218; *see also* demon
Gentoo 163
geography 11, 22, 199, **215**
Ghadi pujari *see* pujari
Ghurye, G.S. 248
globalisation 4, 9, 11–12
goddess/fertility cults (early, local Indian) 14, 57, 61, 176, 184, 200, 206, 246, 264
Gomateshwara 97
Gondhaḷa 87
gosavi 233
Graham, Maria 237, 239–240, 244–246
Grāmadevatā 19, 180
Great departure *see* Abhiniṣkramaṇa
Greco-Bactrian 26–27, 36–37; *see also* Bactrian
Guhagar 194, 196, 202–204, 207
Gungtang 217
Gupta (Empire/period) 19, 25, 33, 36, 43–44, 62, 130
Gurav (low-rank temple priests) **78–100** (on the subject of Jain Guravs)
  Ahimsak (vegetarian) 84
  group division (Bhavik, Kadu Lingayat, Śiva) 80
  pujārī 204; *see also* pujari
  Son Koli 246–247; *see also* Son Koli
Hadda 43, 55
Hagglund, Betty 240
Halbfass, William 10
Hardiman, David 128, 233, 248
Hārītī 28–30, 44–46
Hattusha/Boğazköy 32
Heesterman, J.C. 152
Hellenistic 25, 33–34, 36, 41–42, 49; *see also* Greco-Bactrian, Indo-Greek
Hepat 32
Hesychius 40
Hidden land 22–23, 211–216, 219, 221, 224
hierarchy 2–3, 17, 21, 79–80, 100, 128, 179–180, 200, 202, 207–208, 227–228; *see also* varna
Hindu Kush 221
Hinglaj 50
Hippostratos 38
Hittite 32–33
horn of plenty *see* symbols
Hume, Cynthia Ann 11, 14
Huviṣka 27, 29, 43–44, 48
identification 4–5, 29, 37, 60, 74, **108**, **121**, **124**, 186, 194–195, 208
Inanna 34
Inappropriate, the, appropriation of **102–103**, **117**, **124**, 140, 211
Indian Constitution 251
Indian freedom movement 164, 166
Indo-Greek 26–27, 36–38, 47
Indo-Parthian 42
Indo-Scythian 29, 36, 41–43, 46
initiation
  of disciples **22**, **113–115**, **118**, **124** (Chapter 5)
  of mythical heroes 264
inscription 183
integration *see* appropriation *and* cultural process
intercourse
  as *maithuna,* part of the five 'm' 143, 192
  as way to bliss **106**, **108**, **117**, **esp. 119–121**
Ishtar 34–35
Islam *see* Muslim
Jain 14, 19, 78–89, 91–100, 146, 149, 236–239; *see also* Kokaṇastha Brāhmins
  Baba 100
  Brāhmaṇa 83, 100, 149
  Goddess 14, 19, 78, 81, 91–92, 94, 97, 100; *see also* Durga
  Gurav 78–82, 93, 95–96, 98–100
  Munjeshwar 86
  Pashan 86, 89, 96, 99–100
  Tīrthaṃkar 14, 19, 78, 82–85, 89, 91–97, 100, 149

Jainācā Khāmb (Jainacha khamb) 93
Jāti 18, 56, 260
Jatra 90
javal (rite) 235
Jejuri 194, 230–231
Jogeshwari (Jogeśvarī) 202, 243
Jogulamba 193
Johnson, Donald Clay (scholar) 238
Johnson, John (engineer) 240
Jomo Yangri Chugmo 23, 149, 214, 216–222, 224
Justin (Roman emperor) 37
Jyotirliṅga 196
Kadak 231
Kadu Gurav *see* Gurav
Kāli 186
Kalsuli 83–85, 96, 100, 149
Kamalākānta 261–262
Kangsanarayan 160–161
Kaniṣka 29, 44, 47–48 *see also* Nanā
Kaniṣka I 44
Kapilavastu 27–28, 43
Kapiśa 38
Karle 16, 20, 149, 226–227, 230, 233, 236–250, 253 (Table)
- chaitya 227, 230, 236–240, 243–244, 248
- hill 20, 227, 233, 236–242, 244–249, 253 (Table)

Kartri 142–143, 149
Kasar (maker of bangles) 91–92
Kashmir 22, 39, 44–46, 49, 102–104, 106, 121, 124, 168, 188
- Śaivism 22

Kashmir Smast 44–46
Kauṭilya (author of Arthasastra) 9
Kayastha prabhus 230, 247
Khadadevi 230
khāmb *see* Jainācā Khāmb
Khandoba 231, 235
Kharepatan 82–83, 85
Kharoṣṭhī 40
Khecarī mudra 187–188
Khvareno (Xvarənah, Xvarənō) 29
Kinsley, David 149, 152, 186, 188
Kisan pawar 206, 209
Kishwar, Madhu 23, 268, 274
Kokaṇastha 2, 3, 4, 6, 14, 16, 17, 19, 20, 22, 24, 25, 27, 28, 29, 180–182, 184, 192, 194–195, 197–198, 200, 202–203, 205–207
- brāhmins 19, 92, 181–182, 184–186, 192, 194–198, 202–207, 227

Koli 16, 20, 225–236, 242–253 (Table)
- Mahadev 20, 226, 248–252
- rebellion 248, 250–251
- Research Project (Monash University) 232
- Son 16, 20, 225–228, 231–234, 236, 243–244, 246–252

Koliwada 225, 249
Kolkata 160, 162–165, 167–173, 260, 263, 266
Konkan 19, 81–83, 85, 88–89, 91, 95–96, 180–182, 189, 194, 196–198, 200, 202–204, 207, 249
Kosambi, D.D. 58, 236, 243, 246
Krishna (Kṛṣṇa) 15, 120, 128, 162, 184, 232
Kṛṣṇācārya 219
Kshatriya 230
Kubaba 33
Kudal 82–83, 89, 91
Kunakeshvara (Kunakeshwar, Kuṇakeśvara) 89
Kunbis 247
Kunga drölchog 219
Kunte (religious couple) 81, 83, 85, 195, 203–204
Kuṣāṇa 25–29, 33–34, 36, 39–40, 43–45, 47–48, 50, 55
Kuṣāṇo-sasanian 27, 42
Kuśīnagara 27
ladder of degree 2–3, 9
Lajjāgaurī 45, 152, 193, 202
Lakṣmī (Lakshmi) 23, 26, 36, 38, 40, 43–44, 46, 61, 93, 160, 185, 191, 197, 201, 203, 259, 270–271; *see also* Durgā *and* Pārvatī
lamp *see* symbols
Langtang 212
Liṅga 45, 84–85, 99–100, 185, 196
Lingayat Gurav 80
Lingayatism 80–81
little mother 184; *see also* Durgā
Lok Sabha Petitions Committee 251
Lonavla 226, 232, 235, 248

lotus *see* symbols
Machene 41
Mackenzie, C. 238
Madh Island 230
Madhu 259
Mahabharata 228
Mahadev 20, 138, 226, 233, 239, 248–252
  Kolis *see* Koli
Mahalaxmi 243
Maharashtra 19–20, 78, 81–83, 85, 87, 89, 91–92, 96–99, 173, 180–182, 184–185, 189, 193–196, 200–203, 205, 226, 228, 230–231, 234, 243, 248, 250, 266
Māhātmya(s) 179, 184, 186, 189, 191, 192, 206, 207
Mahavira 238
Maherghar 246
Maheśvara 44, 46, 67, 120, 124
  śiva 44, 46
Māheśvarī 45
Mahiṣāsura (Mahishasura) 50, 62–63, 160, 168, 172–174, 194, 197, 201–202, 234–235, 206, 259; *see also* demon.
  mardinī 50, 62–63, 160, 174, 197, 202, 259; *see also* Durgā
Mali 57, 61, 213, 217, 220, 222, 228
Maṇḍaṇa Miśrā 99
Mandir 226, 230, 232, 236–240, 242–243, 246–248, 253 (Table)
Mandu 23, 136–137, 212
Mangaon 81, 91–94, 100
Mangyül 216
Manushi 268–270, 272
Manusmṛti 3, 70
Mao (Mah) 43
Maratha 19, 182, 189, 202–203, 234, 246
Master 11, 154, 183, 187, 216, 249
Māṭ 48
Mate, Madhukar Shripad 231, 235
Mathura 40, 48, 86
Maues 41
Menander 41
Mendelsohn, Oliver 227, 251
Menmo 217; *see also* demon
Mesopotamia 33–34, 50
Mhasobā (Mhaskobā) 189, 190
Michell, George 238
moon/lunar crescent *see* symbols
Moon God 231
mother goddess
  appropriation to/from virgin deities 182, 184–186, 188, 190
  Devī as 23
  Durga as 2, 21
  Ganges as 20, 126, 130
  integration into Puranic narrative **56**, **58**, **60** (Chapter 3)
  as Jogāī **192–194**, **197**, **199–202**, **206**, **208** (Chapter 9)
  Koli versions 16, **231**, **233–234**, **243–244**, **246** (Chapter 11)
  Phrygian 33
Mother India (Bhāratmātā) 21, 23, 164–165, 167, 172, 258, 260–261, 263–268, 272–274; *see also* British *and* Durga
Mukundarāja 189–190
Mumbadevi 225, 230
Mumbai 16, 20–21, 89, 168, 172–173, 188, 225–233, 235–236, 238, 243–244, 246, 248–252
mural crown *see* symbols
murti 233
Mus, Paul 6, 17, 146–147, 151, 155
Musa 41
Muslim
  external top-down appropriation 4–5, 225; *see also* appropriation
  hostility with Hindus 164, 260, 263
  Islam 5, 186, 221
  and Mother India 267–268, 272–273
  rule 19, 135, 189
  saints 225
  sources 260
  Sufi 138, 153
  tolerance 231–232, 245, 260
nagaradevatā (nāgaradevatā) 27, 50
Nagaraju, S. 236
Nagarkhana 246–247
namokara (mantra) 97
Nanā (Nano, Nanaia) 19, 33–36, 46–50

Nāṇe Ghāṭa (Nane Ghat) 97
Narendra Modi 174
Nātha 189–190, 193, 207
navas 231
Nayak Kingdom of Jawhar 251
Nayanmar 98
Nehru, Jawaharlal 126, 265
Népémakö *see* Padma-bkod
Ngagchang Shakya Zangpo 216
Nineveh 33
Nizam (ruler of Hyderabad) 203, 205, 249
non-dualism 99, **102–106**, **113**, **117**, **121–122**, **124** (Chapter 5)
Nyanang 216
Nyen (Tibetan bringers of sickness) 217
Nyingmapa 216
Oanindo (Kushana winged goddess) 43
Ommo (Umā) 44
Orientalism 10
Osmanabad 234
Oti 235; *see also* bharaṇe
Padma-bkod 213
Padmasambhava 149, 213, 215, 219
pādukā (paduka) 93–94, 229
pairika 23, 219–222
Paitava 43
Pakistan 26, 44, 55, 175, 221, 249
Pal, Ramesh Chandra 167
Palmotang 217
pañcamakāra *see* five m's
Pañcika 29
Pandals 160, 165, 167–168, 172
Pandharpur 203, 229–233
Panjikant 44
Pantaleon 37
Paraśurāma 181, 193, 195, 197
Parinirvāṇa 27
Parthia 36, 41–42, 55
Pārvatī (Parvati) 20, 48, 57, 64–65, 70, 185–186, 191, 195, 198, 201, 234; *see also* Lakshmi
Pausanias 31
Pematsal 211, 214, 216
Penthesilea 28
People of India Series 79
peri *see* pairika
personal deity 136–137, 234
Peshwas (Peśvās) 184, 192, 202–205, 207–208, 237, 246
Peucolaos 38, 40
Pharro 29–30; *see also* Khvareno *and* Royal Glory
Phraataces 41–42
Phraates IV 41–42
pilgrimage
  away from metropolitan centres 20, **226**, **228–236**, **239**, **245–246**, **248–251** (Chapter 11)
  as devolved institution 11
  to metropolitan centres 6
  part of appropriation 60, 179, 207
  Vindhyavāsinī 14–15
Pocock 16
Poliadic goddesses 27, 31, 33, 36, 50
Pollock, Sheldon 9
Polos 27, 31
Poseidon 39
possession 6, 14, 16, 32, 91, 129, 139, 231
Pothī Prem Ambodh 133, 135, 137
power
  political 8–9 19, 33, 50
  religious 8–9, 180
Prabhadevi 243
procrastinated marriage 196–197
public space(s) 127, 129, 133–135, 139; *see also* sacred space(s)
pujari (pujārī) 11
  Ekveera 242–244
  Ghadi 87–88
  Gurav 204
  in Mangaon/Konkan 83, 85–88, 93–94, 96, 100
Pune 81, 97, 133, 226, 231, 240, 246, 248
Purāṇas
  Bhaviṣya(-ottara) 185
  classical 16
  Devībhāgavata and Kālikāpurāṇa 190
  Markaṇḍeya 258 (and Harivaṁśa 184)
  Skanda 194, 205
  and status of goddess Ambejogāī 199

Upa 257
Vāmanapurāṇa and integration of goddesses/women 20, **56**, **58–60**, **62**, **74–75**; *see also* integration
Puruṣa 151, 156–157
Puṣkalavatī (Peukelaitis) 38–40, 50
Rabatak 47–48
Rajghat 139
Ramayana 228
Ranade, Sanjay 16, 20, 149, 193, 225, 232, 251
Ravidās 5, 20–21, 126–127, 129, 132–140
Rāmāyaṇa 137–138
rebellion *see* Koli *and* British
religious power *see* power
Renuka (Reṇukā) 186, 193–195, 200
reservation 20, 248, 251–252
Rigopoulos, Antonio 232
Rigzin Chogden Gonpo 216
Rigzin Nyida Longsel 213
Ringstones 46
Rooster 196
Royal Glory 29; *see also* Khvareno *and* Pharro
sacred space(s) 119, 127, 134–135; *see also* public space(s)
sacrifice 22, 28, 45, 65, 109–110, 115–116, 147, 150–152, 154–157, 161–162, 166, 172, 174, 189–192, 206, 231, 243, 246, 263, 265
sādhus 11
Sahlins, Marshall 12
Sahri Bahlol (archaeological site, Pakistan) 45
Sahyādrikhaṇḍa (Puranic text) 195, 202
Sai Baba (Shirdi Sai Baba) 232
Said, Edward 10
saints 98, 133, 222, 225, 228–229, 231
Śaivites 39–40, 45–46, 48, 50, 68, 84, 98
Śaka (Śāka) 26, 40
Śāktas 46, 50, 191–192, 201, 208
Śaktipīṭha 179, 191–193, 205, 208
Śāligrāma 135, 137
Salt, Henry 239–240, 242
samadhi 229
Samartha, Swami 234
sampradaya 232
Sanātana Dharma 99
Sandhipūjā 161–162
Śaṅkardigvijaya 97
Sanskrit
alphabetic symbolism 106, 112
conventions in this book xi
monopoly and control of 227–228
Puranas 56–58, 60–61, 73, 75
Sanskritisation 199
conceptualisation of **3–6**, **13–14**, **16**, **18**
outside Indian subcontinent 127–128
Santeri temple 91
Santosh Mitro 168–169
sannyasi (mendicant) *see* Gandhi, Mahatma
Sapadbizes 47
Sārvajanīna 164–165, 170
Sasanian period (3rd–7th cent's) 27, 35–36, 41–42, 44
Satavahana (dynasty and king) 246
scheduled tribes 80, 226, 251–252; *see also* Indian Constitution
Schubring, Walther 238
Seer Goverdhanpur 138–139
sex *see* intercourse
Shamans 91
Shastri, Ramesh 160–161
Shendur 242
Shirdi (home of Sai Baba) 232
Shitalamata 244
Shiv Sena 20, 249
Shiva *see* Śiva
Shivaji 234
shivalinga 244
shoulders *see* symbols
Shravanabelagola 97
Shridharaswami 97, 99
Siddha 11, 113, 131, 134, 153–155, 188–189, 194, 219
Śiva (Shiva)
divine relatives and devotees 20, 57, 62, 64–67, 69–70, 72, 74, 129–130, 152, 170, 179, 185, 187, 190–192, 196, 198, 201
in general temples 44, 46, 183, 239, 244

Gurav (group) 80–81
līlāmṛta 97, 99
meaning within Trika system 22, 103, 105–113, 115–116, 120–122
in Sanskritisation examples 14, 39–40, 230–231, 234, 259
sūtra 103
worship in formerly Jain areas 83–87, 89–90, 94–100
slaughter 246
Snodgrass, Adrian 226
Sobhabazar Rajbari 162–163
social climbing *see* appropriation
Sogdian(a) 34, 44
Son Koli *see* Koli
Sonars 247
Sontheimer, Gunther-Dietz 83, 194, 204, 231
Śrāvastī 43
Śrī 43, 46, 48, 66–68, 74, 104, 113, 154, 185, 206, 258
-lakṣmī 26, 36
staff *see* symbols
Stanley, John M. 231
Storer, James Sargant 240–241
Stupa 157, 226, 236–237, 243
subordination 2
subversion 2, 5, 6, 17
Sufi *see* Muslim
Sun God 231
Susa 34, 42, 128
Svaccha Nārāyaṇī 23, 258, 268–269, 271–274
Swat 23, 27–28, 44, 46, 55, 92–93, 99
symbols
battlements 26, 35
crescent 46–47
cornucopia 19, 26–29, 31, 42–46
elephant 26, 38, 238
flames 29–30, 189, 217
lamp 41, 84–85, 119, 161, 193, 205, 265, 272
lotus 38–41, 43–44, 50, 161, 187, 195, 211, 213, 261, 271
mural crowns 19, 26–28, 30–33, 35–38, 41–42, 44
palm (tree) 26, 38, 41, 217
shoulders (bearing other symbols) 28–30
staff 26, 41–42, 149, 166, 183
thunderbolt 183
towers 26, 28, 33, 35
trident 9, 39–40, 45, 48, 64, 191
triśūla 39
wheel 41, 108–109
wreath 26, 41–43, 217
syncretism (of cults of deities) 25, 36, 46, 49, 226–227
tantra 12, 22, 70, 102–103, 105, 112, 114, 122–123, 143, 152, 187–188, 190, 192, 194, 200–202, 204, 206–207
Tapa sardār (archeological site) 50, 55
Tare, Anant 242, 249
Taxila 41
temple *see* authority, cave, mandir, Chandraprabha, Gangeshwar, Kunakeshwara, Santeri, Vaiṣṇavite
terrorism (Mumbai attacks) 21, 172–173
Thackeray, Balasaheb 242
Theotropou 41
Tillia tepe 25
Tīrthaṃkar *see* Jain
Tribal shrine 208
trident *see* symbols
Trinamul Congress Party (TMC) 168–170, 172
Tripurasunardī 198
Troilus and Cressida 3
Trojan cycle 28
Tsen 214, 217
Tuljapur 234
tutelary couple 27–29, 43
Tyche 19, 26–27, 31, 36–38, 40–42, 46, 50
Ugarit 32
Umā *see* Ommo
untouchable 3, 20, 127, 133, 135, 138, 227, 229, 243; *see also* dalit
Uruk 34, 62–63
Vāc 46, 112
vāhana (vehicle) 48, 130
Vaijanātha/Vaidyanātha 196–198, 202
Vaishnavite (Vaiṣṇavite) 149, 233
Temple 78
Vajravairocanī / Vajravarṇanī (Yoginīs) 142–143
Vajrayāna 50

Vajrayoginī 142–143, 148–149, 154
Vāmanapurāṇa *see* purāṇa
Van Kooij, Karel 144
Varanasi 138–139
varṇa
  hierarchy 3, 56, 73
  theory 3
Vedak, Sanjay 242
Veeragul (Veerkallu) 83
vegetarianism 80, 84, 93, 205, 246
Verardi, G. 48, 50, 55, 98
vertical dimension (of social influence) 2, 18; *see also* appropriation
Vetāla 85, 87–89
Vicziany, Marika 16, 20, 225, 227, 232, 251
victory
  goddess of 43, 148, 166, 201, 234, 263
  symbols of 38, 41
village deities/religion 10, 80, 180, 234, 253 (Table)
Vindhyachal 14–15
Vindhyavāsinī 6, 11, 14
Virgin goddess (kumārī) 185, 187–189, 195–197, 199–201
Viśvakarman 65–69, 71–75
Vithoba 230–231
Viṭṭhalādevī 83
Vivekananda, Swami Narendranath Datta 12, 128
Vivekasindhu 180
Vyāḍeśvara/Vāḍeśvara 196, 203, 205
Wakhan 221
Warkari 233; *see also* pilgrim *and* bhakti
water
  goddess 245–246
  spirits (asaras) 225, 246
Western ghats 226, 236–237, 249, 251
wheel *see* symbols
Wima Kadphises (Scythian ruler) 39
women, independence of 70–71
Worli 230, 235
wreath *see* symbols
Xuan Zang 44
Yakṣa 14, 85–86, 89, 93–94, 96, 146
  Maṇibhadra 86
Yakṣiṇī (Devī) 19, 40, 47, 91–94, 96, 100
Yazılıkaya 32
Yogāsana posture 86
Yogeśvarī 180, 183–185, 188, 191, 193–199, 201, 204–205, 207–208
yogi (yogī) 108, 114, 115, 119–120, 122–123, 138, 142–143, 148–149, 154, 183–193, 195, 198, 202, 205, 216
Yoginī 183–191, 195, 202, 205
Yolmo 23, 149, 211–217, 219–221, 224
  Gangra 23, 211–214, 216–217, 219
Youngblood, Michael D. 232
Yuezhi 40
Zoroastrianism 220–221